Implementing Enterprise Risk Management

Founded in 1807, John Wiley & Sons is the oldest independent publishing company in the United States. With offices in North America, Europe, Australia and Asia, Wiley is globally committed to developing and marketing print and electronic products and services for our customers' professional and personal knowledge and understanding.

The Wiley Finance series contains books written specifically for finance and investment professionals as well as sophisticated individual investors and their financial advisors. Book topics range from portfolio management to e-commerce, risk management, financial engineering, valuation and financial instrument analysis, as well as much more.

For a list of available titles, visit our Web site at www.WileyFinance.com.

Implementing Enterprise Risk Management

From Methods to Applications

JAMES LAM

WILEY

Published by John Wiley & Sons, Inc., Hoboken, New Jersey.

Published simultaneously in Canada.

For general information on our other products and services or for technical support, please contact our Customer Care Department within the United States at (800) 762-2974, outside the United States at (317) 572-3993 or fax (317) 572-4002.

Wiley publishes in a variety of print and electronic formats and by print-on-demand. Some material included with standard print versions of this book may not be included in e-books or in print-on-demand. If this book refers to media such as a CD or DVD that is not included in the version you purchased, you may download this material at http://booksupport.wiley.com. For more information about Wiley products, visit www.wiley.com.

Library of Congress Cataloging-in-Publication Data is Available:

ISBN 9780471745198 (Hardcover)
ISBN 9781118221563 (ePDF)
ISBN 9781118235362 (ePub)

Cover Image: © canadastock/Shutterstock
Cover Design: Wiley

Printed in the United States of America

SKY10074568_050724

For my father, and best friend, Kwan Lun Lam

Contents

PART THREE

Governance Structure and Policies

Preface

Confucius said: "I hear and I forget. I see and I remember. I do and I understand."

Indeed, the value of knowledge is not in its acquisition but in its application. I am grateful that I have had opportunities to apply risk management in a wide range of roles throughout my 30-year career in risk management. As a consultant, I've worked with clients with different requirements based on their size, complexity, and industry. As a risk manager, I've implemented enterprise risk management (ERM) programs while overcoming data, technical, and cultural challenges. As a founder of a technology start-up, I've worked with customers to leverage advanced analytics to improve their risk quantification and reporting. In the past four years, as a board member and risk committee chair, I've worked with my board colleagues to provide independent risk oversight while respecting the operating role of management.

These experiences have taught me that knowledge of ERM best practices is insufficient. Value can be created only if these practices are integrated into the decision-making processes of an organization. The purpose of this book is to help my fellow risk practitioners to bridge the gap between knowledge and practical applications.

In my first book, *Enterprise Risk Management—From Incentives to Controls* (Wiley, 1st edition 2003, 2nd edition 2014), the focus was on the *what* questions related to ERM:

- What is enterprise risk management?
- What are the key components of an ERM framework?
- What are best practices and useful case studies?
- What are the functional requirements for credit, market, and operational risks?
- What are the industry requirements for financial institutions, energy firms, and non-financial corporations?

In this companion book, the focus is on the *how* questions:

- How to implement an ERM program?
- How to overcome common implementation issues and cultural barriers?

- How to leverage ERM in all three lines of defense: business and operational units, risk and compliance, and the board and internal audit?
- How to develop and implement specific ERM processes and tools?
- How to enhance business decisions and create value with ERM?

The publication of my first ERM book was one of the most gratifying professional experiences of my career. The book has been translated into Chinese, Japanese, Korean, and Indonesian. It has been adopted by leading professional associations and university programs around the world. On Amazon.com, it has ranked #1 best-selling among 25,000 risk management titles. In a 2007 survey of ERM practitioners in the United States and Canada conducted by the Conference Board of Canada, the book was ranked among the top-10 in ERM books and research papers. In addition, the book has brought me countless consulting and speaking opportunities internationally.

In my travels, risk professionals most often request practical approaches and case studies, as well as best-practice templates and examples that can assist them in their ERM programs. Based on this feedback, I have structured this book to focus on effective implementation of ERM.

OVERVIEW OF THE BOOK

This book is organized into seven parts. Part One provides the overall context for the current state and future vision of ERM:

- Chapter 1 introduces the notion that *risk is a bell curve*. It also lays out the fundamental concepts and definitions for enterprise risk management. We also discuss the business case for, and current state of, the practice of ERM.
- Chapter 2 reviews the key trends and developments in ERM since the 2008 financial crisis, including lessons learned and major changes since that time.
- In Chapter 3, a new performance-based continuous model for ERM is introduced. This new model is more fitting for global risks that are changing at an ever faster speed (e.g. cybersecurity, emerging technologies). As part of this discussion, seven specific attributes for this new ERM model are provided.
- In addition to the board and management, other stakeholders such as regulators, institutional investors, and rating agencies are increasingly focused on ERM. Chapter 4 discusses their requirements and expectations.

ERM is a multi-year effort that requires significant attention and resources. As such, Part Two focuses on ERM program implementation:

- Chapter 5 lays out the scope and objectives of an ERM project, including the need to set a clear vision, obtain buy-in, and develop a roadmap. This chapter also provides an ERM Maturity Model and an illustrative 24-month implementation plan.
- One of the key success factors in ERM is addressing change management and risk culture. Chapter 6 describes risk culture success factors and the cognitive biases and behavior obstacles that risk professionals must overcome.
- Given the wide range and complexity of risks, having a structured and organizing ERM framework is essential. Chapter 7 provides an overview of several published frameworks and an ERM framework that I've developed to support performance-based continuous ERM.

The next four parts provide deep dives into the key components of the ERM framework. Part Three focuses on risk governance and policies:

- Chapter 8 discusses two versions of the "three lines of defense" model—the conventional model and a modified model that I've developed to reflect better the role of the board.
- Chapter 9 goes further into the important role of the board in ERM, including regulatory requirements and expectations, current board practices, and three key levers for effective risk oversight.
- Chapter 10 describes my first-hand experience as an independent director and risk committee chair at E*TRADE Financial. This case study discusses our turnaround journey, the implementation of ERM best practices, and the tangible benefits that we've realized to date.
- As expected, the rise of the chief risk officer (CRO) is correlated to the adoption of ERM. Chapter 11 discusses the evolution in the role of the CRO, including key responsibilities, required skills, and desired attributes. The chapter also provides professional profiles of six prominent current or former CROs.
- Chapter 12 focuses on one of the most important risk policies: risk appetite statement. This chapter provides practical steps and key requirements for developing an effective risk appetite statement.

Risk analytics provide useful input to business and risk leaders. Risk assessment and quantification is the focus of Part Four:

- Chapter 13 discusses the implementation requirements, common pitfalls, and practical solutions for developing a risk-control self-assessment process.

- What gets measured gets managed, so it is not enough only to identify and assess risks. Chapter 14 provides a high-level review of risk quantification models, including those designed to measure market risk, credit risk, and operational risk.

ERM can create significant value only if it supports management strategies, decisions, and actions. Part Five focuses on risk management strategies that will optimize an organization's risk profile:

- The integration of strategy and ERM, also known as strategic risk management, is covered in Chapter 15. The chapter outlines the processes and tools to measure and manage strategic risk, including M&A analysis and risk-based pricing. Case studies and examples of strategic risk models are also provided.
- Chapter 16 goes further into risk-based performance management and discusses other strategies to add value through ERM, such as capital management and risk transfer.

Board members and business leaders need good metrics, reports, and feedback loops to monitor risks and ERM effectiveness. Part Six focuses on risk monitoring and reporting:

- Chapter 17 discusses the integration of key performance and risk indicators, including the sources and characteristics of effective metrics.
- Once these metrics are developed, they must be delivered to the right people, at the right time, and in the right way. Chapter 18 provides the key questions, best-practice standards, and implementation requirements of ERM dashboard reporting.
- Once an ERM program is up and running, how do we know if it is working effectively? Chapter 19 answers this critical question by establishing a quantifiable performance objective and feedback loop for the overall ERM program. An example of a feedback loop based on earnings-at-risk analysis is also discussed.

Chapter 20 in Part Seven provides additional ERM templates and outlines to help readers accelerate their ERM initiatives.

Throughout this book, specific step-by-step implementation guidance, examples, and outlines are provided to support risk practitioners in implementing ERM. They are highlighted below:

- Example of a reputational risk policy (Chapter 4, Appendix A)
- ERM Maturity Model and benchmarks (Chapter 5, Appendix A)

- Practical 24-month plan for ERM program implementation (Chapter 5, Appendix B)
- 10-step process for developing a risk appetite statement, including examples of risk metrics and tolerance levels (Chapter 12)
- Implementation of the RCSA process, including common pitfalls and best practices (Chapter 13)
- Example of a strategic risk assessment (Chapter 20)
- Structure and outline of a CRO report to the risk committee (Chapter 20)
- Example of a cybersecurity risk appetite statement and metrics (Chapter 20)
- Example of a model risk policy (Chapter 20)
- Example of a risk escalation policy (Chapter 20)

SUGGESTED CHAPTERS BY AUDIENCE

Given its focus on ERM implementation, this book does not necessarily need to be read in its entirety or in sequence. Readers should select the relevant chapters based on the implementation phase and ERM maturity at their organizations. In general, I would suggest the following chapters by the seniority of the reader:

- Board members and senior corporate executives should read Chapters 1, 3, 6, 9, 10, 12, 15, and 19.
- Mid- to senior-level risk professionals, up to a CRO, should read the above chapters plus Chapters 4, 5, 7, 8, 11, and 16.
- Students and junior-level risk professionals should read the entire book.

Acknowledgments

I would like to thank the Enterprise Risk Management team at Workiva for contributing to this book through excellent research and editorial support. In particular, I would like to thank Joe Boeser, Melissa Chen, Adam Gianforte, Garrett Lam, Jay Miller, Diva Sharma, Rachel Stern, and Zach Wiser. I want to especially thank Mark Ganem and Neil O'Hara for their outstanding editorial support. This book was the result of a collaborative team effort and it was truly my pleasure to work with such a great team.

I would also like to extend my appreciation to Paymon Aliabadi, Matt Feldman, Susan Hooker, Merri Beth Lavagnino, Bob Mark, and Jim Vinci for sharing their stories and experiences as chief risk officers across different industry sectors. Their experiences in ERM implementation provide useful and practical insights. They also offer good advice to risk professionals who aspire to become a CRO. Their compelling stories are featured in Chapter 11. I am confident that risk professionals, regardless of where they are in their careers, will be inspired by their stories and benefit from their advice. I know I have.

Finally, I would like to thank Bill Fallon and Judy Howarth from John Wiley & Sons for their patience and assistance throughout the book production process.

Implementing Enterprise Risk Management

ERM in Context

Fundamental Concepts and Current State

INTRODUCTION

In October 1517, Ferdinand Magellan requested an investment of 8,751,125 silver maravedis from Charles I, King of Spain. His goal: to discover a westerly route to Asia, thereby permitting circumnavigation of the globe. The undertaking was extremely risky. As it turned out, only about 8 percent of the crew and just one of his four ships completed the voyage around the world. Magellan himself would die in the Philippines without reaching home.

What would motivate someone to undertake this kind of risk? After all, Magellan stood to gain only if he succeeded. But those long-term rewards, both tangible and intangible, were substantial: not only a percentage of the expedition's revenues, but also a 10-year monopoly of the discovered route, and numerous benefits extending from discovered lands and future voyages. What's more, he'd earn great favor with a future Holy Roman Emperor, not to mention fame and the personal satisfaction of exploration and discovery.

But I doubt that even all of these upsides put together would have convinced Magellan to embark on the voyage if he knew that it would cost him his life. As risky as the journey was, most risks that could arise likely appeared manageable. Magellan already had a great deal of naval experience and had previously traveled to the East Indies. He raised sufficient funding and availed himself of the best geographic information of the day.[1]

All in all, Magellan's preparations led him to the reasonable expectation that he would survive the journey to live in fame and luxury. In other words, by limiting his downside risk, Magellan increased the likelihood that he would reap considerable rewards and concluded that the rewards were worth the risk.

3

Whether taking out a loan or driving a car, we all evaluate risk in a similar way: by weighing the potential upsides and trying to limit the downsides. Like Magellan, anyone evaluating risk today is taking stock of what could happen if things don't go as planned. Risk measures the implications of those potential outcomes. In our daily lives, risk can cause deviation from our expected outcome and keep us from accomplishing our goals. Risk can also create upside potential. We will use a similar definition to define risk in business.

The purpose of this book is to provide the processes and tools to help companies optimize their risk profiles, but first we must have the necessary vocabulary for discussing risk itself. Then we can begin to construct a working model of an enterprise risk management (ERM) program, which we will flesh out over the course of this book. This chapter will cover the fundamental concepts and summarize ERM's history and current state of the art.

But first, some definitions.

WHAT IS RISK?

Risk can mean different things to different people. The word evokes elements of chance, uncertainty, threat, danger, and hazard. These connotations include the possibility of loss, injury, or some other negative event. Given those negative consequences, it would be natural to assume that one should simply minimize risks or avoid them altogether. In fact, risk managers have applied this negative definition for many years. Risk was simply a barrier to business objectives, and the object of risk management was to limit it. For this reason, risk models were designed to quantify expected loss, unexpected loss, and worst-case scenarios.

In a business context, however, risk has an upside as well as a downside. Without risk there would be no opportunity for return. A proper definition of risk, then, should recognize both its cause (a variable or uncertain factor) and its effect (positive and negative deviation from an expected outcome). Taken thus, I define risk as follows:

> *Risk is a variable that can cause deviation from an expected outcome, and as such may affect the achievement of business objectives and the performance of the overall organization.*

To understand this definition more fully, we need to clarify seven key fundamental concepts. It is important not to confuse any of these with risk itself, but to understand how they influence a company's overall risk profile:

1. Exposure
2. Volatility

3. Probability
4. Severity
5. Time Horizon
6. Correlation
7. Capital

Exposure

Risk exposure is the maximum amount of economic damage resulting from an event. This damage can take the form of financial and/or reputational loss. All other factors being equal, the risk associated with that event will increase as the exposure increases. For example, a lender is exposed to the risk that a borrower will default. The more it lends to that borrower, the more exposed it is and the riskier its position is with respect to that borrower. Exposure measurement is a hard science for some risks—those which result in direct financial loss such as credit and market risk—but is more qualitative for others, such as operational and compliance risk. No matter how it is measured, exposure is an evaluation of the worst–case scenario. Magellan's exposure consisted of the entire equity invested by King Charles I, his own life, and the lives of his crew.

Volatility

Volatility is a measure of uncertainty, the variability in potential outcomes. More specifically, volatility is the magnitude of the upside or downside of the risk taken. It serves as a good proxy for risk in many applications, particularly those dependent on market factors such as options pricing. In other applications it is an important driver of the overall risk in terms of potential loss or gain. Generally, the greater the volatility, the greater the risk. For example, the number of loans that turn bad is proportionately higher, on average, in the credit card business than in commercial real estate. Nonetheless, real estate lending is widely considered to be riskier, because the loss rate is much more volatile. Lenders can estimate potential losses in the credit card business (and prepare for them) with greater certainty than they can in commercial real estate. Like exposure, volatility has a specific, quantifiable meaning in some applications. In market risk, for example, it is synonymous with the standard deviation of returns and can be estimated in a number of ways. The general concept of uncertain outcomes is useful in considering other types of risk as well: A spike in energy prices might increase a company's input prices, for example, or an increase in the turnover rate of computer programmers might negatively affect a company's technology initiatives.

Probability

The more likely an event—in other words, the greater its probability—the greater the risk it presents. Events such as interest rate movements or credit card defaults are so likely that companies need to plan for them as a matter of course. Mitigation strategies should be an integral part of the business's ongoing operations. Take the case of a modern data center. Among potential risks are cyberattack and fire, with the probability of the latter considerably lower than that of the former. Yet should the data center catch fire, the results would be devastating. Imagine that the company maintains backup data as part of its cybersecurity program. Simply housing that data in a separate, geographically remote facility would address both risks at a cost only incrementally greater than addressing just one. As a result, the company can prepare for the highly unlikely but potentially ruinous event of fire.

Severity

Whereas exposure is defined in terms of the worst that could *possibly* happen, severity, by contrast, is the amount of damage that is *likely* to be suffered. The greater the severity, the greater the risk. Severity is the partner to probability: If we know how likely an event is to happen, and how much we are likely to suffer as a consequence, we have a pretty good idea of the risk we are running. Severity is used to describe a specific turn of events, whereas exposure is a constant which governs an entire risk scenario. Severity is often a function of other risk factors, such as volatility in market risk. For example, consider a $100 equity position. The exposure is $100, since the stock price could theoretically drop all the way to zero and the whole investment could be lost. In reality, however, it is not likely to fall that far, so the severity is less than $100. The more volatile the stock, the more likely it is to fall a long way—so the severity is greater and the position riskier. In terms of a credit risk example, the probability of default is driven by the creditworthiness of the borrower, whereas loss severity (i.e., loss in the event of default) is driven by collateral, if any, as well as the order of debt payment.

Time Horizon

Time horizon refers to the duration of risk exposure or how long it would take to reverse the effects of a decision or event. The longer an exposure's duration, the greater its risk. For example, extending a one-year loan is less risky than extending a 10-year loan to the same borrower. By the same token, highly liquid instruments such as U.S. Treasury bonds are generally less risky than lightly traded securities such as unlisted equity, structured derivatives, or real estate. This is because investors can shed their positions in liquid vehicles quickly should the need arise while illiquid investments would take longer to sell, thus increasing time horizon—and risk. When it comes to operational risk, time horizon often depends on a company's level of preparation. A fire that burns a computer center to the ground will leave a company exposed until backup facilities come online, so the risk is greater for organizations that do not have well-established and tested procedures in place. Monitoring, preparation, and rapid response are key. With cybersecurity, preventing all attacks is an unrealistic expectation, but malware detection ("dwell time") and risk mitigation ("response time") are critical drivers of potential damage. Problems arise when companies do not recognize that a risk event has occurred, thus lengthening the time horizon associated with that risk, or if they have not developed a proper risk mitigation strategy.

Correlation

Correlation refers to how risks in a business are related to one another. If two risks behave similarly—that is, they increase for the same reasons or by the same amount—they are considered highly correlated. The greater the correlation, the greater the risk. Correlation is a key concept in risk diversification. Highly correlated risk exposures increase the level of risk concentrations within a business. Examples include loans to a particular industry, investments in the same asset class, or operations within the same building. Risk diversification in a business is inversely related to the level of correlations within that business. Financial risks can be diversified through risk limits and portfolio allocation targets, which cap risk concentrations. Operational risk can be diversified through separation of business units or through the use of redundant systems. A key objective in operational risk management is to reduce "single points of failure," or SPOFs.

A word of caution, however: Seasoned risk professionals recognize that price correlations approach one during times of crisis. For example, during the 2008 financial crisis, all global asset prices (e.g., real estate, equities, bonds, and commodities) fell in concert, with the exception of U.S. Treasuries. For this reason, companies should stress-test their correlation assumptions, as diversification benefits may evaporate just when they are most needed.

Capital

Companies hold capital for two primary reasons: The first is to meet cash requirements such as investments and expenses, and the second is to cover unexpected losses arising from risk exposures. The level of capital that management wants to set aside for these two purposes is often called *economic capital.* The overall level of economic capital required by a company will depend on the credit rating it wants. A credit rating is an estimate of how likely a company is to fail. It is less likely to fail if it has more capital to absorb any unexpected loss. The more creditworthy it wants to be, the more capital it will have to hold against a given level of risk. The allocation of economic capital to business units has two important business benefits: It links risk and return and it allows the profitability of all business units to be compared on a consistent risk-adjusted basis. As a result, business activities that contribute to, or detract from, shareholder value can be identified easily so management has a powerful and objective tool to allocate economic capital to its most efficient uses.

In addition to economic capital, risk managers should consider human capital (management talent, experience, and track record) and liquidity reserves relative to a company's risk profile. The combination of economic capital, human capital, and liquidity reserves represents the "risk capacity" of the company.

WHAT DOES RISK LOOK LIKE?

The above concepts interact to determine the specific risk levels and enterprise risk profile of an organization. For individual risks—such as credit, market, and operational—the risk levels are greater the higher the exposures, probabilities, severities, and time horizons of the specific positions. At the portfolio level, the risk profile will be greater the higher the concentrations and correlations *within* that portfolio of risks. At the overall level, the correlations *across* risk portfolios (e.g., credit risk, market risk, operational risk, etc.), and the organization's risk capacity, will determine the enterprise risk profile.

Risk Is a Bell Curve

A simple visualization effectively synthesizes these ideas: a bell curve. The notion that *risk is a bell curve* is a key idea that I will discuss throughout the book. When using bell curves to represent risk in a given context, each point on the curve represents a different possible outcome. The horizontal axis provides the range of outcomes, and the vertical axis provides the probabilities associated with those outcomes. As such, the bell curve is a vector of probabilities and outcomes, and collectively these probabilities and outcomes represent the aggregate risk profile. Figure 1.1 provides an illustration of a bell curve.

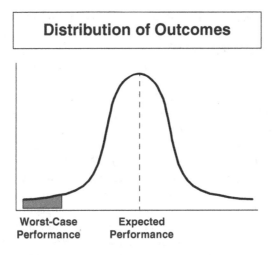

FIGURE 1.1 Risk as a Bell Curve

It is important to consider the following points when conceptualizing and quantifying risk as a bell curve:

- **Risk comes in different shapes and sizes.** Some risks—such as interest rate risk or market risk—tend to be symmetrical.[2] These risks are normally distributed where there is equal probability of gains or losses of similar sizes. Other risks—such as credit risk or operational risk—are asymmetrical with more downside than upside. If a loan pays off, the lender gains a few percentage of interest income, but if it defaults, the lender can lose the entire principal. If a core IT operation is running smoothly, it is business as usual, but a failure can cause significant business disruption. Risks can also be asymmetrical with more upside than downside, such as an investment in a new drug or a disruptive technology. Such investments can produce unlimited upside but the downside is limited to the amount of the investment.
- **Risk should be measured relative to business objectives.** The risk metric used should be based on the context of the specific business objective and desired performance. For example, at the enterprise level the risk metrics can be earnings, value, and cash flows to quantify earnings-at-risk (EaR), capital-at-risk (economic capital or CaR), and cash flow-at-risk (CFaR), respectively. Such performance-based models can support the organization in managing corporate-wide objectives related to earnings performance, capital adequacy, and liquidity risk. At the individual

business or risk level, the risk metric used should be linked to the specific business objective, such as sales performance, IT resilience, and talent management.

- *The bell curve provides the downside, but also the mean and upside.* Risk managers tend to focus mainly on downside risk. For example, EaR, economic capital, and CFaR models usually quantify the downside outcome at a 95–99% confidence level. However, a proper definition of risk must include all eventualities. The bell curve provides the full spectrum of risk, including the mean (i.e., expected outcome) as well as the downside and upside scenarios. By adopting a more expansive consideration of potential outcomes, risk managers can make more informed risk-based business decisions. The same variables that can produce unexpected loss can also produce unexpected gain. Downside risk analysis can inform capital management, hedging, insurance, and contingency planning decisions. Analyses of expected value can support financial planning, pricing, and budgeting decisions while upside risk analysis can shape strategic planning and investment decisions.

- *The objective of management is to optimize the shape of the bell curve.* It has often been said that value maximization is the objective of management. To accomplish this objective, management must maximize the risk-adjusted return of the company. In other words, it must optimize the shape of the bell curve. For example, management should establish risk appetite statements and risk transfer strategies to control downside tail risks. Pricing strategies should fully incorporate the cost of production and delivery, as well expected loss and economic capital cost. Strategic planning and implementation should increase expected earnings and intrinsic value (moving the mean of the bell curve to the right). This objective extends to a non-profit organization, but return is driven by its organizational mandate.

By conceptualizing—and ideally, quantifying—any risk as a bell curve, companies can manage them most effectively. This applies even to intangible risks that are difficult to quantify. Let's use reputational risk as an example. The mean of the bell curve represents the current reputational value of the organization. Reputational risks would include the key variables and drivers for the organization in meeting the expectations of its main stakeholders: customers, employees, regulators, equity holders, debt holders, business partners, and the general public. As with other risks, these variables and drivers can be measured and managed to enhance the organization's reputation, including downside and upside risk management.

ENTERPRISE RISK MANAGEMENT (ERM)

The concepts I've described so far form the foundation for risk analysis, but understanding risk is just a preliminary step toward managing it. We are now ready to lay the groundwork for implementing enterprise risk management (ERM). Specifically, we will discuss:

- A definition of ERM
- Early development of risk management
- The development of ERM in the 1990s

This brief overview of ERM will show how the events of the past half-century have shaped ERM's current critical role in business strategy.

What Is Enterprise Risk Management?

A proper definition of ERM should describe what it is, how it works, its main objective, and its main components. With these criteria in mind, I will define ERM as follows:

> *ERM is an integrated and continuous process for managing enterprise-wide risks—including strategic, financial, operational, compliance, and reputational risks—in order to minimize unexpected performance variance and maximize intrinsic firm value. This process empowers the board and management to make more informed risk/return decisions by addressing fundamental requirements with respect to governance and policy (including risk appetite), risk analytics, risk management, and monitoring and reporting.*

Let's briefly expand on this definition. First, ERM is a management process based on an integrated and continuous approach, including understanding the interdependencies across risks and implementing integrated strategies. Second, the goal of ERM is to minimize unexpected performance variance (defensive applications) and to maximize intrinsic firm value (offensive applications). As discussed, risk management is not about minimizing or avoiding risks, but optimizing risk/return trade-offs (the bell curve). Third, an ERM program supports better decisions at the board and management levels. Board decisions may include establishing risk appetite, capital and dividend policy, as well as making strategic investments.

Management decisions may include capital and resource allocation, customer and product management, pricing, and risk transfer. Finally, the key components of ERM include governance and policy (including risk appetite), risk analytics, risk management, and monitoring and reporting. These four components provide a balanced and integrated framework for ERM.

Early Development of Risk Management

Protecting ourselves against risk is a natural practice that goes back well before Magellan. In fact, one could argue that risk management has existed as long as human history. As long as attacks from animals, people, or businesses have been a threat, we have constructed safeguards and defenses. As long as buildings have faced floods and fires, risk management has included structural design and materials used, or, in modern times, transferring that risk to an insurer. As long as money has been lent, lenders have diversified among borrowers and discriminated between high- and low-risk loans. Despite the intuitive nature of risk management—or perhaps because of it—it did not become part of formal business practice until the second half of the last century.

It wasn't until 1963 that the first discussion on risk appeared in an attempt to codify and improve such practices. In their *Risk Management and the Business Enterprise,* authors Robert Mehr and Bob Hedges posited a more inclusive risk-management practice that went beyond the status quo of merely insuring against risk. They proposed a five-step process reminiscent of the scientific method: Identify loss exposures, measure those exposures, evaluate possible responses, choose one, and monitor the results. They also described three general approaches to handling risks: risk assumption, risk transfer, and risk reduction. At this early stage, risk management emphasized hazard risk management. Financial risk entered the scene later. These traditional theories focused on what are called "pure" risks, such as natural disasters, which result either in a loss or no change at all, but never an improvement. Modern ERM practice now encompasses speculative risk, which involves either loss or gain. Stock market investment is a classic example of speculative risk.

The lack of attention to financial risk in early risk management programs reflected the comparative stability of global markets at the time. This began to change in the following decade. In 1971, the United States abandoned the gold standard, and in 1972, many developed countries withdrew from the 1944 Bretton Woods agreement, which had kept most foreign exchange rates within narrow bands since World War II. This brought an unprecedented volatility to global exchange rates. The Seventies also brought soaring oil prices due to the decision by the Organization of Petroleum Exporting Countries (OPEC) to decrease global supply after the 1973 Yom Kippur

War. Like the proverbial butterfly's wings, this had multiple effects around the globe. Rising oil prices drove up inflation, which caused the U.S. Federal Reserve to raise interest rates to historical levels, a response that fueled volatility not only in the United States but worldwide as well. These economic changes created a need for financial risk management that companies had not experienced before.

The Seventies and early Eighties saw the introduction of new financial risk-management tools, particularly derivatives such financial futures, options, and swaps. These new tools allowed companies to manage volatile interest rates and foreign exchange rates and were effective when used properly. But some firms suffered severe losses from ill-conceived derivatives trades. In 1993, the German corporation Metallgesellschaft barely avoided bankruptcy after a $1.3 billion loss due to oil futures contracts. The next year, Procter & Gamble lost $157 million due to an injudicious swap. In the Nineties, devastating losses due to operational risk were all too common, often for lack of standard controls such as management supervision, segregation of duties, or basic checks and balances. In 1995 Barings Bank was driven bankrupt after a loss of $1.3 billion due to unauthorized derivatives trades. Only months later, Daiwa Bank was forced to end all U.S. operations in the aftermath of a $1.1 billion scandal surrounding unauthorized derivatives trading. Early risk managers operating under traditional practices simply overlooked operational risk, leaving it to the relevant business units.[3]

THE CASE FOR ERM

Despite the high-profile losses, the 1990s saw important steps forward in ERM. Risk quantification became more sophisticated with the advent of value-at-risk models (VaR). Before VaR, the primary risk measure was probable maximum loss, which is similar to the potential loss and can be expressed in the question, "What's the worst that could (reasonably) happen?" By contrast, a VaR metric predicts, to a specific level of confidence, potential losses over various time intervals. Early versions of modern ERM appeared around this time as companies developed more sophisticated risk quantification methods for market risk and credit risk, as well as initial operational risk management programs. In the mid-1990s, companies began appointing chief risk officers (CROs) to establish a C-suite executive who could integrate the various risk management functions under a single organization. Steady progress continued until the 2008 financial crisis, which revealed numerous shortcomings in risk management models and reminded businesses of the need for improvement.

Organizations continue to discover the value of ERM and work to implement their own customized programs. Let us look at three perspectives:

- The current demand for ERM
- The current state of ERM
- What ERM can look like and what it can do

The Current Demand for ERM

We work in a business climate rife with volatility and risk. A recent survey by the Association for Financial Professionals (AFP) found that 59 percent of financial professionals consider their firms to be subject to more earnings uncertainty now than five years previously. Only 12 percent believe they are operating with more certainty today.[4] A similar majority said it is more difficult to forecast risk than it was five years ago and foresaw it getting even more difficult three years hence. Risks considered to have the greatest impact on earnings were (in order of decreasing frequency): customer satisfaction and retention, regulatory risk, GDP growth, political risk, energy price volatility, labor and HR issues, and natural disasters.

So what are firms doing to prepare for these risks? By their own admission, less than they would like. Only 43 percent of respondents to the AFP study felt their ability to forecast crucial variables was relatively strong while the rest needed improvement; 10 percent even considered their capabilities weak to nonexistent. Companies recognize a growing need for changes in risk management processes. Organizations are hiring risk professionals, investing in IT systems, automating financial processes, and placing a greater focus on risk awareness and culture. Many have beefed up executive review of business strategy and assumptions (63 percent) while others have increased risk analysis and forecasting as well as reports to management.

The individual ultimately responsible for managing this growing risk is frequently the CFO, named by 38 percent of the firms surveyed. Another 28 percent named the CEO or COO; 14 percent operated under a risk committee, 11 percent named the treasurer, and only 9 percent had a chief risk officer (CRO) as the primary overseer of risk management. It is important to note that these results were based on a cross-industry survey.

Old Methods Won't Work

Today, companies recognize the need for better risk management, but amplifying old methods or tweaking existing structures to deal with increased risk carries dangers. Just one example: the highly interdependent risks that organizations frequently face. Figure 1.2 provides an illustration of risk interdependency in the form of a Venn diagram.

Key interdependencies exist between financial and business risk, business and operational risk, and operational and financial risk. Furthermore, each major risk category comprises subcategories. For example, financial risk, as demonstrated in the figure, can be broken down into market risk, credit risk, and liquidity risk. These financial risks in turn have their own interdependencies.

Let's examine loan documentation as a practical example of a key interdependency between operational risk and financial risk (in particular credit risk). As a business process, loan documentation quality is considered an operational risk. If a loan is performing (i.e., the borrower is making timely interest and loan payments), the quality of that specific loan document has no real economic impact. But if the loan is in default, the documentation quality can have a significant impact on loss severity because it affects collateral and bankruptcy rights. Loss analyses conducted by James Lam & Associates at lending institutions revealed that up to one-third of "credit losses" were associated with operational risks.

According to the AFP survey above, about 12 percent of firms still use a siloed, decentralized structure. But in a complex, interlocking system of company-wide risks, this strategy is clearly insufficient. Some risks may remain poorly understood or even ignored. Gaps and redundancies may go unnoticed and unaddressed. And aggregate risk exposures across the organization could pose hidden threats. For example, if business units use different methodologies and systems to track counterparty risk, then it is difficult to quantify the aggregate exposure for a single counterparty. While the individual exposures at each business unit might be acceptable, the total counterparty exposure for the organization may exceed tolerance levels.

On the other hand, an overly centralized system of risk management can fail to integrate the relevant risk information into the decision-making processes of an organization. A full 28 percent of organizations have a centralized risk management system, which can lead to ineffectual top-down management of risk-related decisions. Most organizations (60 percent) operate under a structure with centralized processes but decentralized implementation. In this arrangement, the risk monitoring, reporting, and systems are centralized, but the implementation of risk management strategies is in the hands of each business unit.[5]

In a volatile economic climate, the most successful companies establish comprehensive, fully integrated risk management processes at each level of decision-making. ERM provides integrated analyses, strategies, and reporting with respect to an organization's key risks, which address their interdependencies and aggregate exposures. In addition, an integrated ERM

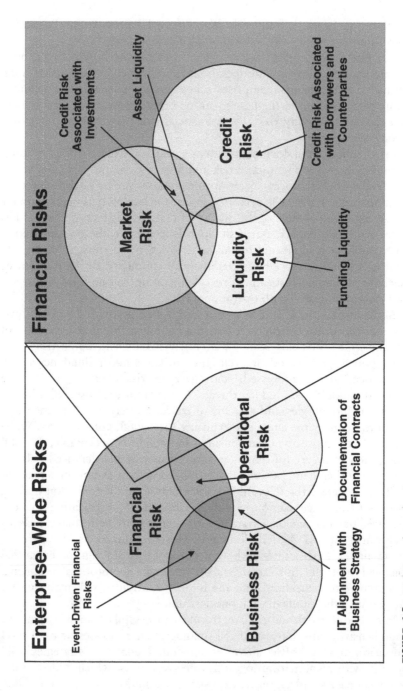

FIGURE 1.2 Risk Interdependencies

framework supports the alignment of oversight functions such as risk, audit, and compliance, which rationalizes risk assessment, risk mitigation, and reporting activities. It also considers how macroeconomic factors, such as interest rates, energy prices, economic growth, inflation, and unemployment rate, can impact the organization's risk/return profile. This interweaving of ERM into an organization adds strength throughout, whereas merely applying a superstructure from the top down may leave weaknesses unaddressed.

Integration Adds Value

The value that integration adds is visible in many areas of business and life, including fitness and sports. Over the past few decades, many disciplines have experienced greater effectiveness through integration. Take the example of cross-training in fitness. By integrating cardiovascular workouts with strength training, flexibility, and endurance, athletes can prevent and rehabilitate injuries as well as enhance strength and power. Similarly, the integration of various fighting styles into mixed martial arts (MMA) has added value to centuries-old practices and beliefs. Whereas martial artists once argued about which style was superior, the emergence of MMA has changed their attitude. Mixed martial artists combine karate, kung fu, jujitsu, tae kwon do, wrestling, and multiple other fighting styles, allowing them to adapt to any situation. This gives them a significant advantage over a fighter trained in a single style.

So too, integration of ERM into business strategy leads to more informed and effective decisions. In fact, I believe the integration of strategy and risk is the next frontier in ERM, as it allows a company's board and management to understand and challenge the underlying assumptions and risks associated with their business strategy. Expanding technological capabilities have put this within the grasp of most companies. System integration allows for enterprise-level data management, robust business and data analytics, straight-through transaction processing, and more effective reporting and information sharing.

According to a 2013 Deloitte study, 81 percent of the executives surveyed now have an explicit focus on managing strategic risks, in contrast to the traditional focus on financial, operational, and regulatory ones.[6] The study suggests a reason, too: Strategic risks represented approximately 36 percent of the root causes when publicly traded companies suffered significant market value declines over the past 10 years. This was followed by external risks (36 percent), financial risks (17 percent), and operational risk (approximately 10 percent).[7]

WHERE ERM IS NOW

The numbers show that corporations around the world are recognizing risk management as a priority and moving toward integrated ERM. The 2013 Deloitte Global Risk Management survey indicated that 83 percent of all global financial institutions have an ERM program or are in the process of implementing one, up from 59 percent in 2010.

As a management framework, ERM has been more widely adopted than other management frameworks (e.g., reengineering, balanced scorecard, total quality management). Organizations with established ERM programs have realized and reported significant benefits. For example, 85 percent of financial institutions that had ERM programs in place reported that the total value derived from their programs exceeded costs.[8] Three quarters of today's executives feel that their ERM programs provide significant value compared with merely half in 2008.

As ERM adoption has increased over the past several years, the CRO has grown in stature. The 2013 Deloitte Global Risk Management survey indicated that 89 percent of global financial institutions had a CRO or equivalent position. Moreover, 80 percent of the institutions said their CRO reports directly to the CEO and had a formal reporting relationship with their board, up from about 53 percent in 2010.

Outside the financial sector, it's a different story, however. A 2012 paper produced by McKinsey & Company[9] pointed out that, unlike financial institutions, most corporates still do not have a CRO, leaving the de facto role of risk manager to the CFO. Furthermore, the goals for ERM improvement vary between the two sectors. Financial institutions are keen to improve their risk culture, IT, and data infrastructure while corporates focus on improving risk-related decisions and processes. Still, the frequency and heft of the CRO is growing throughout all sectors.

Board involvement in ERM has increased as well, particularly since the global financial crisis. Several surveys indicate that risk management has replaced accounting issues as the top concern for corporate boards. Approximately 80 percent of boards now review risk policies and risk appetite statements.[10]

Although ERM has made significant progress over the past decade, much remains to be done. In a sense, the global financial crisis was the ultimate risk management "stress test." Many organizations failed, and even those with established ERM programs reported mixed results. Today, organizations appear to understand the need for change. Deloitte's 2013 survey reported that 94 percent of organizations have changed their approach to strategic risk management over the previous three years. Companies cite cultural issues and integrating data across the organization as the two biggest stumbling blocks to improvement.[11]

WHERE ERM IS HEADED

With ERM's role increasing within organizations and across industries, the roles of the board and upper management have to adapt. Certainly, the CRO bears the brunt of this change, but the CEO, CFO, and board of directors all find that ERM is taking a more prominent position in their priorities. Here's how these parties will increasingly work together as ERM becomes embedded in corporate culture.

The CRO carries the central responsibility of ensuring that each gear in the ERM process is meshed and moving properly. He or she develops the risk appetite statement (RAS) in collaboration with the CEO and the CFO to ensure that it complies with regulations, current markets, and the organization's business strategy and objectives. The CRO monitors the risk climate, ensures compliance with regulations, sees that the firm operates within its risk appetite, and keeps the CEO and the board of directors well informed through established reporting processes.[12]

The CEO in turn sets "the tone from the top" in words and actions. He or she sets the appropriate business and risk management objectives, holds organizational leaders accountable for their decisions and actions, and ensures that a strong risk culture is in place. The CFO is responsible for incorporating the RAS into financial decision making, including investment, funding, and hedging strategies. If risk exposures exceed the RAS, the CFO, along with the CRO, must take mitigating action and bring it to the attention of the CEO and board.

Finally, the board of directors provides risk governance, independent oversight, and credible challenge. It reviews the RAS for compatibility with the organization's goals, approves it, and holds senior management accountable for its implementation. The board monitors the business plans against the RAS to check if they are aligned. The board also provides oversight of key business, regulatory, and reputational risk issues, as well as monitors the organization's ERM effectiveness and risk culture.

As we've seen, ERM is providing value for a large number of corporations despite its current challenges. But it is my view that we're really just beginning to see how much value ERM can offer. In less than a decade, risk management has risen to the top of corporate agendas for senior management and the board across all industry sectors. What form are these efforts taking? This question will be the focus of the next chapter, in which we'll take a deeper look at the economic, financial, and cultural drivers that are changing the face of enterprise risk management.

NOTES

1. Findlay, James. "Marvellous Countries and Lands," Bienes Center, 2002.
2. Certain factors such as the prepayment option in mortgage loans and securities can create negative convexity, or a disadvantaged, asymmetrical interest rate risk profile for the mortgage lender or investor. For example, when rates rise and mortgage prepayment speeds decrease, the longer duration will produce a greater value loss. Conversely, when rates drop and mortgage prepayment speeds increase, the shorter duration will produce a smaller value gain.
3. D'Arcy, Stephen P. and Brogan, John C. "Enterprise risk management," *Journal of Risk Management of Korea*, 12, 2001. http://www.casact.org/.
4. Wittenberg, Alex. *2013 AFP Risk Survey*, Association for Financial Professionals, 2013.
5. Wittenberg, Alex. *2013 AFP Risk Survey*.
6. Global Risk Management Survey, Eighth Edition: "Setting a Higher Bar," Deloitte Touche Tohmatsu Limited, 2013.
7. Kambil, Ajit. "The Value Killers Revisited: A Risk Management Study," Deloitte LLP, 2014.
8. Global Risk Management Survey, Seventh Edition: "Navigating in a Changed World," Deloitte Touche Tohmatsu Limited, 2011.
9. Pergler, Martin. *Enterprise Risk Management*, McKinsey &Company, 2012.
10. GRM Survey, Eighth Edition, Deloitte.
11. *Exploring Strategic Risk: A Global Survey*, Deloitte Touche Tohmatsu Limited, 2013.
12. "Principles for an Effective Risk Appetite Framework," Financial Stability Board, 2013.

CHAPTER 2

Key Trends and Developments

INTRODUCTION

The world of risk management fundamentally changed in late 2007 with the onset of the global financial crisis. Longstanding financial institutions such as Lehman Brothers and Washington Mutual were left to fail, while many other banks and non-banks received bailouts from nervous national governments around the world. It was clear that excessive debt and fatally compounded risks were the primary drivers of the crisis. What's more, a relatively strong global economy had disguised the fact that many institutions were betting on unsustainable levels of growth in pursuit of greater market share and increased profitability. In this chapter, we'll review the lessons learned from the financial crisis and other corporate disasters, and how the practice of enterprise risk management has fundamentally changed.

LESSONS LEARNED FROM THE FINANCIAL CRISIS

The economic landscape that emerged following the Great Recession was vastly different from what existed prior to the 2007–2008 period. Regulators demanded that banking institutions increase capital and liquidity reserves, enhance transparency, curb risk appetite, and tighten controls. This had positive as well as negative effects. On the positive side, the regulations provided a basis for forward-looking analysis such as stress testing and scenario modeling. On the downside, however, many companies failed to take these hard-won lessons to heart, focusing exclusively on meeting regulatory requirements without considering ERM in a broader, more strategic context. In addition, many firms effectively overreacted to the economic hardship that followed the crisis. Rather than becoming risk-smart, they became risk-averse. Without risk, of course, there can be no reward, so these companies stumbled on without much of a strategic outlook beyond mere survival.

In all, seven fundamental trends emerged after the financial crisis that together have shaped the practice of risk management for the past decade:

1. Much stricter compliance requirements
2. Increased board-level risk oversight
3. Greater risk management independence
4. Focus on enterprise-wide risk management
5. Improved board and management reporting
6. Creation of objective feedback loops
7. Better incentive compensation systems

Below, we'll take a look at each of these in greater detail.

Much Stricter Compliance Requirements

For better or worse, compliance quickly became a primary driver of risk management. The formalization of heightened regulatory scrutiny in the financial services industry fundamentally increased the scope and responsibility of the risk management function. The same held true in other sectors as well. The insurance industry, for example, implemented the Own Risk and Solvency Assessment (ORSA) in order to determine the ongoing solvency needs of insurance institutions with regard to their specific risk profiles.

Compliance with laws and regulations is an important objective in any risk management program, but we must remember that it is a necessary but insufficient condition for success. Regulations are blunt instruments designed to establish minimum standards for an entire industry, but they don't always represent best practices. For example, banking regulators established Basel II, and more recently Basel III, to link regulatory capital requirements with a bank's risk profile. However, leading banks have developed more sophisticated economic capital models that better represent the risk-return economics of their businesses. Moreover, new regulations often overreact to past problems. The Sarbanes-Oxley Act (SOX), for example, was enacted in the aftermath of accounting frauds at large corporations such as Enron and WorldCom. While accounting controls are important, they are only a subset of operational risk management techniques, and operational risk is itself a subset of enterprise-wide risks. In fact, one can argue that the emphasis on accounting controls in the post-SOX period has been misguided, given that risk is mainly driven by future events, whereas accounting statements reflect past performance. In order to be effective, a risk management program must be forward-looking and driven by the organization's business objectives and risk profile, not by regulatory requirements.[1]

Increased Board-Level Risk Oversight

These new laws and regulations also shaped risk governance and oversight at the board level. Section 165 of the Dodd-Frank Wall Street Reform and Consumer Protection Act specifies that "FRB (Federal Reserve Bank) must require each publicly traded bank holding company with $10 billion or more in total consolidated assets... to establish a risk committee [of the board]... Risk committee must... include at least 1 risk management expert having experience in identifying, assessing, and managing risk exposures of large, complex firms."[2]

According to PwC's 2014 corporate directors survey, boards are becoming increasingly uncertain that they have a solid grasp on their company's risk appetite, with 51% saying they understand it "very well" in 2014, down from 62% in 2012.[3] It seems that boards are beginning to recognize that it's not enough to be the "audience" with respect to risk reporting and updates, but they must become active "participants" in providing credible challenges and setting policies and standards. In the past, boards approved risk policies, reviewed risk reports, and viewed PowerPoint presentations designed mainly to assure them risks were well managed. In order to provide effective oversight, however, boards must be active participants in the risk management process. They must debate risk-tolerance levels, challenge management on critical business and financial strategies, and hold management accountable for the risk–return performance of past decisions. To strengthen their oversight, boards should consider establishing a separate risk committee, especially at risk-intensive companies (e.g., banking, insurance, energy). At a minimum, each board and its standing committees must ensure that risk management is allocated sufficient time and attention. Boards should also consider adding risk experts to their ranks.

Greater Risk Management Independence

During the excesses of the pre-crisis environment, where was risk management? Why didn't we hear about chief risk officers going directly to the board, or quitting out of protest given what was going on under their watch? I believe a central issue was the continued lack of true independence of risk management, which companies are only now beginning to address seriously. Since the trading losses suffered by Barings and Kidder, Peabody in the mid-1990s, companies have worked to ensure that the risk management function was independent relative to trading, investment, and other treasury functions. However, companies are finally going further to ensure that risk management remains independent relative to corporate and business-unit management as well. This is similar to the independence that internal audit enjoys, though to a lesser extent because risk management should function both as a business partner and risk overseer. One organizational solution has been to establish a dotted-line reporting relationship between the chief risk officer (and chief compliance officer) and the board or board risk committee. Under extreme circumstances (e.g., CEO/CFO fraud, major reputational or regulatory issues, excessive risk taking), that independent dotted-line reporting relationship can ensure that the chief risk officer can go directly to the board without concern about his or her job security or compensation. Ultimately, risk management must have an independent voice to be effective. A direct communication channel to the board is one way to provide that.

Focus on Enterprise-Wide Risk Management

A key lesson from the latest financial crisis as well as those preceding it is that major risk events are usually the consequence not of one risk, but of a confluence of many interrelated ones. Historically, companies managed risk within silos, with each organizational division handling its own, but, in 2008, it became glaringly obvious that this approach could lead to catastrophic failure. Even as the crisis was unfolding, the *Wall Street Journal* reported that the risk model used by AIG to manage its credit derivatives business only considered credit-default risk, but not the mark-to-market or liquidity risks associated with the business.[4] Companies should implement ERM programs to analyze multi-risk scenarios that may have significant financial impact. For banks, that means integrating analyses of business, credit, market, liquidity, and operational risks. Insurance companies must also assess the correlations between investment, liability, interest-rate, and reinsurance risks. All companies must manage strategic risks and the critical interdependencies across their key risks on an organization-wide basis.

In the United States, the Federal Reserve implemented a series of formal stress-testing requirements for banks to quantify their vulnerability to various risk scenarios. The Fed's Comprehensive Capital Analysis and Review (CCAR) assessment provides independent review of the capital plans for banks and bank holding companies with assets in excess of $50 billion. Additionally, the adoption of Dodd-Frank mandated that all banks with greater than $10 billion in assets must conduct stress testing on an annual basis. The Office of the Comptroller of the Currency (OCC) published final rules in 2014 to meet the stress-testing requirement. Known as DFAST (Dodd-Frank Act Stress Test), the rules require all banking institutions with between $10 billion and $50 billion in assets to conduct and report results of formal stress testing exercises.

Improved Board and Management Reporting

It would be difficult if not impossible to implement ERM while companies continue to measure and report risks in silos. There is a general sense of dissatisfaction among board members and senior executives with respect to the timeliness, quality, and usefulness of risk reports. About a third of respondents to a 2016 *Corporate Board Member* survey felt information flow between their board and management could be improved through a higher frequency of updates (36%), more concise reporting (31%), or more time to review materials prior to a meeting (34%).[5] Many companies still analyze and report on individual risks separately. These reports tend to be either too qualitative (risk assessments and heat maps) or too quantitative (financial and risk metrics). Risk reports can also focus too much on past trends and current risk exposures. In order to establish more effective reporting, companies should develop forward-looking, role-based dashboard reports. The risk team should customize these reports to support the decisions of their target audience, whether the board, executive management, or line and operations management. Dashboard reports should integrate qualitative and quantitative data, internal risk exposures and external drivers, and key performance and risk indicators. Moreover, risk analyses should be reported in the context of business objectives and risk appetite.

Creation of Objective Feedback Loops

How do we know if risk management is working effectively? This is perhaps one of the most important questions facing boards, executives, regulators, and risk managers today. The most common practice is to evaluate the effectiveness of risk management based on the achievement of key milestones or the lack of significant risk incidents and losses. However, qualitative milestones or negative proves should no longer be sufficient. I made this point when I was interviewed by the *Wall Street Journal* on the rise of chief risk officers in the aftermath of the financial crisis. In the article,[6] I emphasized the need for an objective feedback loop for risk management, and was quoted as saying, "AIG and Bear Stearns were doing fine until they weren't." My point was made in jest but boards and management should not rely on the absence of a bad situation as evidence that effective risk management is in place.

Organizations need to establish performance feedback loops for risk management that are based on defined objectives, desired outcomes, and data-driven evidence. Other corporate and business functions have such measures and feedback loops. For example, business development has sales metrics, customer service has customer satisfaction scores, HR has turnover rates, and so on.

While various types of feedback loops can benefit an ERM program at every level, one that should be considered by all for-profit companies incorporates ex-ante analysis of earnings at risk followed by ex-post analysis of earnings attribution. Over time, the combination of these two analyses would provide a powerful performance measurement and feedback loop. (I offer a complete description of this feedback loop in Chapter 20.) This would help the board and management ensure that risk management is effective in minimizing unexpected earnings volatility—a key goal of enterprise risk management. Finally, I believe this type of analysis should be provided alongside the earnings guidance of publicly traded companies. Relative to the current laundry-list and qualitative approach to risk disclosure, earnings-at-risk and earnings-attribution analyses can provide much higher levels of risk transparency to investors.

Better Incentive Compensation Plans

The design of executive incentive compensation systems is one of the most powerful levers for effective risk management, yet companies have so far paid insufficient attention to how incentive compensation systems influence risk-return decisions. For example, if executive compensation is driven by revenue or earnings growth, then corporate and business executives might be motivated to take on excessive risks in order to produce higher levels of revenue and earnings. If executive compensation is driven by stock price performance via stock options, decision-makers might also be motivated to take on excessive risks to increase short-term stock price appreciation. Unethical executives might even be tempted to manipulate accounting rules.

Traditional executive compensation systems do not provide the appropriate framework for risk management because they motivate excessive risk taking. Moreover, the corporate structure creates potential conflicts between management and investors. In essence, executives are betting with "other people's money": Heads they win, tails investors lose. To better align the interests of management and investors, long-term, risk-adjusted financial performance must drive incentive compensation systems. Boards and management must consider not only *what* business performance was produced, but also *how*. Companies can achieve this by incorporating risk management performance into their incentive compensation systems; establishing long-term risk-adjusted profitability measurement; and using vesting schedules consistent with the duration of risk exposures and/or clawback provisions.

THE WHEEL OF MISFORTUNE REVISITED

In my previous ERM books I introduced the Wheel of Misfortune, which illustrates that risk management disasters can come in many different forms and can strike any company within any industry. Beyond purely financial losses, the mismanagement of risks can result in damage to the reputation of the companies, or a setback for the careers of individual executives. The Wheel of Misfortune is the response I use to those managers and executives who aren't swayed by the potential pain of ineffective risk management. These doubters will often express the sentiment that "it couldn't happen here" or "if it isn't broke, don't fix it." In these cases, it is worth reminding the skeptics that history has repeatedly demonstrated how bad things can and do happen to good companies.

When my first ERM book was published in 2003, the direst illustration of how negative events can quickly escalate was the cumulative losses suffered by U.S. thrifts in the mid-1980s. These losses not only bankrupted individual companies, but also threatened the entire industry. There were other examples as well. Important spokes of the Wheel included accounting fraud, trading losses, and misrepresented revenue.

Now, however, risks are even more diverse and unpredictable. They can start anywhere in the world and quickly ripple across the global economy, affecting industries that on the surface had little in common with those at the epicenter of crisis. Figure 2.1 represents the new Wheel of Misfortune.

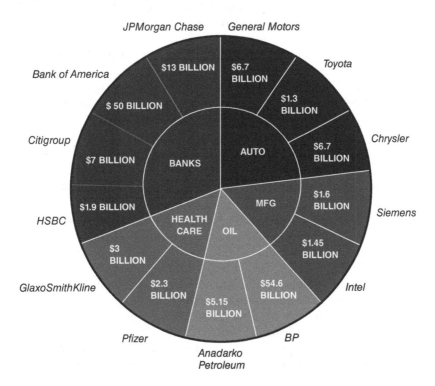

FIGURE 2.1 Wheel of Misfortune

A close examination of these disasters underlines the importance of risk management, including how the nature, velocity, and impact of risks have evolved. Here's a brief, woeful look at the some major corporate disasters, many of which are shown in the new Wheel of Misfortune. Take note that those caught up in the Wheel represent some of the world's best-known and most highly regarded brands.

Operational Risk involves any event that disrupts normal business operations. Losses resulting from operational risk may stem from inadequate or failed processes, people, systems, or external events. It includes employee errors, fraud, or criminal activities, as well as the failure of information, manufacturing or other systems:

- In 2012, UK-based drug maker **GlaxoSmithKline** paid a $3 billion fine for illegally marketing the depression drug Paxil. The company was found to have deceived and bribed doctors into prescribing the drug for children, with whom it has been shown to increase the likelihood of suicide.[7]
- **Pfizer**, the world's largest drug company, reached a $2.3 billion settlement with U.S. federal prosecutors in 2009 for promoting the painkiller Bextra for unapproved uses that endangered patients' lives.[8]
- In 2014, auto manufacturer **Toyota**, often lauded for its Toyota Production System intended to reduce error and waste, agreed to pay $1.3 billion to avoid prosecution for covering up severe safety problems with "unintended acceleration" and continuing to make cars with parts the FBI said the company "knew were deadly."[9]

Bribery and Corruption are risks that any company working with governmental agencies around the world may face. The risks are multifold: costs associated with "shakedowns" of corrupt officials, loss of reputation, and, of course, the financial consequences of prosecution.

- German manufacturer **Siemens** paid fines and other penalties totaling $1.6 billion in the United States and Germany after pleading guilty to violations of the U.S. Foreign Corrupt Practices Act (FCPA) in 2008. The company admitted that bribery had become a common way win government contracts around the globe.[10]
- **Alstom**, a French power and transportation company, paid a $772 million fine in 2015 for FCPA charges related to a widespread corruption scheme involving at least $75 million in secret bribes paid to government officials in numerous countries; falsifying its books and records; and failing to implement adequate internal controls.[11]

Antitrust regulations in most countries aim to foster open competition and prevent market-share leaders from artificially manipulating price, supply, and other factors. What constitutes anticompetitive behavior is in the eye of the beholder, varying from country to country and court to court. As a result, some companies may face costly litigation for what they feel are legitimate business practices. Others, however, clearly intended fraudulent activity.

- After years of litigation, **Visa** and **MasterCard** reached a $7.25 billion settlement in 2013 for a class-action lawsuit claiming that the companies conspired to force merchants to pay excessive fees and follow onerous rules for accepting their credit cards. The settlement was recently thrown out by a federal appeals court as "unfair to retailers."[12]
- In 2014, chip-maker **Intel** paid a $1.45 billion fine in Europe for unfair and damaging practices against its rival AMD. This was in addition to a $1.25 billion settlement with the United States in 2009.[13]
- Taiwan-based **AU Optronics** paid $500 million in the United States for participating in a conspiracy to fix prices on LCD panels. Two of the company's senior executives were sentenced to three years in prison and fined $200,000. The Justice Department claimed that AU Optronics was part of a price-fixing cartel involving every major manufacturer of standard-sized LCD panels, including LG and Samsung.[14]

Mortgage Underwriting

- **Bank of America** paid a cumulative total of $50bn in U.S. government settlements between 2009 and 2014, when it coughed up a record $16.65 billion to resolve allegations it misled investors in its mortgage-backed securities.[15] In similar cases, **JPMorgan Chase** paid $13 billion,[16] and **Citigroup** $7 billion.[17]

Foreclosure Practices

- In 2012, the U.S. Federal government and state attorneys general reached a $25 billion agreement with the nation's five largest mortgage servicers: **Bank of America, JPMorgan Chase, Wells Fargo, Citigroup and Ally Financial.** Violations included the use of "robo-signed" affidavits in foreclosure proceedings, deceptive practices in the offering of loan modifications, failures to offer alternatives before foreclosing on federally insured mortgages, and filing improper documentation in federal bankruptcy court.[18]
- The following year, 13 mortgage servicers, including **Bank of America, Wells Fargo,** and **JP Morgan Chase,** paid $9.3 billion to settle similar charges.[19]

Department of Justice Prosecutions are risks that any U.S. company faces not just for intentionally fraudulent behavior, but also as a result of unintended negligence.

- **Anadarko Petroleum** paid a record $5.15 billion in 2014 to settle a DoJ prosecution over toxic waste at about 4,000 locations over decades caused by a company it had acquired in 2006.[20]
- In 2012, **BP** paid $4.525 billion and pled guilty to 11 counts of manslaughter, two misdemeanors, and a felony count of lying to Congress and agreed to four years of government monitoring of its safety practices and ethics over the 2010 Deepwater Horizon spill. In 2015, the company paid an additional $18.7 billion in fines.[21]

SEC Actions: Though it has been criticized for not coming down hard enough on financial institutions whose risky behavior triggered the 2008 meltdown, the SEC is still a force to be reckoned with, pursuing violations of disclosure and other regulations.

- In 2010 **Goldman, Sachs & Co.** paid $550 million and agreed to reform its business practices to settle SEC charges that the firm misled investors in a subprime-mortgage product just as the U.S. housing market was starting to collapse.[22]
- In 2012 **BP** paid a $525 million penalty to the SEC for securities fraud stemming from the Deepwater Horizon spill. The SEC charged the company with misleading investors by significantly understating the oil flow rate in multiple reports filed with the commission.[23]

Trading Losses: Organizations trading in the financial (and energy) markets can suffer large losses due to unauthorized activities or trades executed beyond reasonable limits.

- In January 2008, the French bank **Société Générale** lost approximately $7 billion due to fraudulent transactions created by a trader with the company.[24]
- In the infamous "London Whale" incident, a team of **JPMorgan Chase** traders bet on derivatives in 2012 that ultimately cost the bank $6.2 billion. Moreover, JPMorgan Chase later paid about $920 million in fines to U.S. and U.K. regulators for engaging in "unsafe and unsound practices."[25]

Anti–Money Laundering has become a hot-button issue for governments with the growth of terrorism and illicit drug trade. Financial institutions that turn a blind eye to suspicious behavior (or actively solicit it) face heavy fines and tremendous reputational damage.

- In 2013, **HSBC**, Europe's largest bank, paid $1.9 billion in an agreement with the United States to resolve charges it enabled Latin American drug cartels to launder billions of dollars. HSBC was accused of failing to monitor more than $670 billion in wire transfers and more than $9.4 billion in purchases of U.S. currency from its Mexico subsidiary. The bank was also accused of violating U.S. economic sanctions against Iran, Libya, Sudan, Burma, and Cuba.[26]
- In 2014, France's largest bank, **BNP Paribas,** pleaded guilty to concealing billions of dollars in transactions for clients in Sudan, Iran, and Cuba in violation of U.S. sanctions and agreed to pay $8.9 billion in fines. Prosecutors say BNP, France's largest bank, went to elaborate lengths to disguise illicit transactions with sanctioned countries.[27]

Market Manipulation on a global scale seems like the stuff of James Bond movies or wild conspiracy theories. But at least two major cases show that large financial institutions are exposed to significant financial and reputational damage by the actions of their employees.

- In 2012, Swiss banking giant **UBS** agreed to pay U.S., U.K., and Swiss regulators $1.5 billion for its role in a conspiracy by multiple banks to manipulate the LIBOR rate that banks charge each other for short-term loans. The banks were falsely inflating or deflating their rates so as to profit from trades, or to give the impression that they were more creditworthy than they were.[28]
- In 2015, five global banks including **Citigroup** were fined $5.7 billion for fixing benchmark foreign exchange rates by colluding in online chat rooms to make transactions minutes before rates were set. When it comes to crime, Citibank has a lot to learn about risk vs. reward: The bank suffered about $2.5 billion in fines for illegal activity that netted a mere $1 million.[29]

Tax Evasion, typically via financial privacy-friendly havens such as Switzerland, the Cayman Islands, Bermuda, Panama, and Luxembourg (among many others), can lead to reputational damage even when legal. But pressure from governments across the globe has led some jurisdictions to name names, so to speak, resulting in fines and other penalties.

- In 2009, in a deal to avoid its criminal prosecution, **UBS** agreed to pay $780 million in fines, penalties, and restitution to the U.S. government and provide names of suspected U.S. tax cheats. UBS had an estimated 19,000 U.S. customers with undisclosed Swiss accounts.[30]

- In 2014, another Swiss bank, **Credit Suisse,** pled guilty and paid $2.6 billion to settle U.S. tax evasion charges in addition to the $196 million penalty it paid the SEC earlier that year. A Senate subcommittee report detailed malpractices by the bank's employees to earn more business from U.S. citizens looking to hide income and assets.[31]
- In 2016, the Panama Papers data leak of 11.5 million files from the database of the world's fourth biggest offshore law firm, **Mossack Fonseca,** revealed the secretive offshore tax-avoidance schemes of thousands of individuals, ensnaring 12 national leaders, including Vladimir Putin and David Cameron, in embarrassing scandal.[32]

Government Bailouts: During the 2008 financial crisis the U.S. federal government took the controversial decision to bail out some of the country's largest financial institutions and manufacturers amid fear that their failure could lead to an even more catastrophic economic meltdown. The bailouts, while they may have saved many companies from extinction, came at the price of greater public and government scrutiny (or outright control), reputational damage, and costly financial terms, not to mention additional regulation and the threat, as yet unrealized, of breaking up institutions deemed "too big to fail."

- In 2008 **AIG's** $85 billion bailout package left the U.S. government with a 79.9% equity stake in the insurer. The two-year loan carried an interest rate of Libor plus 8.5 percentage points.[33]
- Later that same year, **General Motors** and **Chrysler** received a total of $13.4 billion in federal loans. As a result of the bailouts, GM emerged from bankruptcy as a new company majority owned by the U.S. Treasury, and Chrysler emerged owned primarily by the United Auto Workers union and Italian automaker Fiat.[34,35]

Sustainability: As public concern continues to focus on environmental and social issues, many companies are making sustainability a top priority. Environmental disasters such as oil spills, chemical releases, or nuclear accidents can cause horrendous damage, nearly limitless liability, and destroyed reputations. But even lesser missteps along the path to sustainability can raise accusations of "greenwashing" and call unwelcome attention to environmental practices and records.

- **BP's** Deepwater Horizon oil spill of 2010, was the largest marine oil spill in history, causing untold environmental damage and dire economic effects across the Gulf Coast states. The disaster made BP CEO Tony Hayward a source of global derision and had the additional economic consequence of a moratorium on offshore drilling that left an estimated 8,000–12,000 temporarily unemployed. By the following year, Hayward lost his job and the company had lost almost a quarter of its market value.[36] As of 2015, BP estimated the disaster cost the company $54.6 billion.[37]

- **Wal-Mart** built the promise of "everyday low prices" into the largest retailer in the world. But fulfilling that promise means squeezing profit out of every transaction throughout the supply chain and labor market. How long, critics wonder, can this business model sustain itself?[38] As Michelle Chen argued in a 2015 article in *The Nation*, "Every pricetag in Walmart's food inventory—which accounts for a quarter of the nation's grocery bill—is the product of agricultural subsidies, financialized commodities exchanges, and hyperinflated marketing."[39] Similarly, a report by Americans for Tax Fairness concluded that Walmart's low-wage workers cost U.S. taxpayers an estimated $6.2 billion in public assistance, including food stamps, Medicaid, and subsidized housing.[40] Walmart's success at addressing the economic and social costs of these practices around the world has been mixed. In 2005 the company set out bold environmental goals including making 100 percent of its energy supply renewable and create zero waste, which have not met initial timelines. The retailer's own guidelines for ethical and sustainable sourcing, which pledged that outlets and suppliers "must fully comply with all applicable national and/or local laws and regulations ... related to labor, immigration, health and safety, and the environment," while admirable, have drawn unwelcome attention to its own labor practices.[41]

Cybersecurity:

- In 2013, **Target** said at least 40 million credit cards were compromised by the breach during the holiday shopping season, and the attack might have resulted in the theft of personal information, such as email addresses and telephone numbers, from as many as 110 million people. According to Target, the breach cost the company $252 million by the end of 2014,[42] with some estimates rising as high as $1 billion when all is said and done.[43] Gregg Steinhafel, Target's CEO at the time, was forced to resign following the data breach.[44] This was a watershed moment—Target became the first Fortune 100 company to oust its CEO due to a cybersecurity breach.

- Following the **Target** event, **Sony America's** CEO and the **United States Office of Personnel Management** director were also fired for cyber-breaches.

The large losses above clearly demonstrate the financial and reputational consequences when companies do not manage their risks effectively. As I often say in speaking engagements: Over time there is only one alternative to risk management, and that is crisis management, and crisis management is much more costly, time consuming, and embarrassing.

GLOBAL ADOPTION

In the aftermath of the global financial crisis, ERM has emerged as a critical issue for organizations across different industry sectors. Recent surveys have indicated that managing risk has become the top agenda item for corporate directors and executives as well as the heads of numerous governmental entities.[45]

Key Drivers

What are the key drivers for ERM? Let's examine five current trends that underpin the global adoption of ERM practices.

Financial and Corporate Disasters The global financial crisis of 2008 represented a dramatic and painful wake-up call with respect the consequences of ineffective risk management. At the 2009 World Economic Forum, it was reported that at its peak the global financial crisis destroyed 40–45% of world wealth.[46] The crisis resulted in several of the biggest U.S. corporate bankruptcies in history, including Lehman Brothers, Washington Mutual, and General Motors. Many firms had to be bailed out by the U.S. government to avoid bankruptcy, and few businesses were left unscathed. One key lesson learned is that major disasters are often caused by a confluence of risk events, and that organizations need to manage risks and their interdependencies on a comprehensive and integrated basis. With this lesson in mind, organizations have reexamined their ERM processes to identify key areas of improvement. These include:

- Board risk governance, oversight, and reporting
- Risk policies with explicit risk tolerance levels
- Integration of ERM into business processes
- Risk analytics and dashboards, with a focus on liquidity, counterparty, and systemic risks

- Assurance and feedback loops on risk management effectiveness
- Risk culture, including change management processes
- Alignment of executive compensation and risk management objectives

We will discuss these and other challenges in greater detail in the rest of the book.

Regulatory Requirements In response to the corporate disasters, regulators have established more stringent governance and risk standards, as well as new examination, regulatory capital, and disclosure requirements. The developments include:

- In December 2009, the SEC established new rules that require disclosures in proxy and information statements about the board governance structure and the board's role in risk oversight, as well as the relationship between compensation policies and risk management.
- In July 2010, Dodd-Frank was signed into law. The Act requires a board risk committee be established by all public bank holding companies (and public non-bank financial institutions supervised by the Federal Reserve) with over $10 billion in assets. The board risk committee is responsible for ERM oversight and practices, and its members must include "at least one risk management expert having experience in identifying, assessing, and managing risk exposures of large, complex firms."
- In September 2010, the Basel Committee on Banking Supervision announced a new global regulatory framework for bank capital adequacy. Basel III calls for higher capital requirements, including leverage limits and capital buffers; greater risk coverage including counterparty risk and model risk; and establishing a minimum liquidity coverage ratio.

The consequences of these and other regulatory requirements go beyond publicly traded companies and financial institutions. As seen in the global impact of Sarbanes-Oxley, these requirements will have far-reaching influence on regulatory standards and risk management practices.

Industry Initiatives Beyond regulatory requirements, a number of industry initiatives have established clear governance and risk standards around the world. The Treadway Report (United States, 1993) produced the COSO framework of internal control while the Turnbull Report (United Kingdom, 1999) and the Dey Report (Canada, 1994) developed similar guidelines. It is noteworthy that the Turnbull and Dey reports were supported by the stock exchanges in London and Toronto, respectively. Moreover, the Toronto Stock Exchange requires listed companies to report on their enterprise risk management programs annually. COSO published *Enterprise Risk Management: Integrated Framework* (2004) and plans to release an updated ERM framework in 2017. The International Organization for Standardization published ISO 31000:2009 Risk Management (2009). The National Association of Corporate Directors published *Risk Governance: Balancing Risk and Reward* (2009). These industry initiatives have gained significant attention from corporate directors and executives. Collectively, they provide a significant body of work on the key principles, standards, and guidelines for ERM.

Rating Agencies and Investors   Other key stakeholders have espoused the merits of ERM. In 2008, Standard and Poor's (S&P) started to incorporate ERM assessments into its corporate rating processes. While less formalized than S&P, the other rating agencies (Moody's, Fitch, A.M. Best) are also increasing their focus on risk management capabilities as part of their rating processes. Similarly, equity analysts and institutional investors are paying more attention to ERM. These trends clearly show that debt and stock analysts recognize the important role that ERM plays in a firm's creditworthiness and valuation. Given the lack of risk transparency during the global financial crisis, it is likely that rating agencies, stock analysts, and institutional investors will demand more timely and detailed disclosures on a firm's major risk exposures and ERM practices.

Corporate Programs   Ultimately, firms will not continue to invest in ERM unless they see potential value. In this regard, corporations have reported significant benefits from their risk management programs, including stock price improvement, debt rating upgrades, early warning of risks, loss reduction, and regulatory capital relief. In addition to anecdotal evidence and published reports, a growing body of empirical studies have associated superior financial performance and stock valuation with better corporate governance and ERM practices. Organizations with advanced ERM see their programs as a competitive advantage that helps them mitigate complex risks and achieve business objectives.

The financial crisis and subsequent recession created hardship that for some companies became an exercise in survival. For many, risk management became risk avoidance in response to grim market conditions. As companies focused on survival and viability, they placed little emphasis on forward-looking risk management initiatives.

Between an unprecedented regulatory burden and reactive risk aversion, ERM programs appeared to offer little more than additional expense, yielding little in the way of business value beyond mere compliance. Is there a way for companies and their shareholders to realize a return on their risk management investments? The answer, as we'll see in Chapter 3, is a resounding "yes."

NOTES

1. Lam, James. "What Is Wrong with Risk Management? The Reasons Why Risk Management Should Take a Front Seat in Today's Corporate Decision Making," Association for Financial Professionals, 2009.
2. Dodd-Frank Wall Street Reform and Consumer Protection Act (H.R. 4173 (111th)), 2010.
3. "Trends Shaping Governance and the Board of the Future: PwC's 2014 Annual Corporate Directors Survey," PwC, 2014.
4. Mollenkamp, Carrick, Serena Ng, Liam Pleven, and Randall Smith. "Behind AIG's Fall, Risk Models Failed to Pass Real-World Test," *Wall Street Journal*, October 31, 2008.
5. Nolen, Melanie. "Half Empty: What Directors Think," *Corporate Board Member*, 2016.
6. Davy, Peter. "Cinderella Moment," *Wall Street Journal*, October 5, 2010.
7. "GlaxoSmithKline to pay $3bn in US Drug Fraud Scandal," BBC, July 2, 2012. Retrieved from http://www.bbc.com/news/world-us-canada-18673220.
8. Harris, Gardiner. "Pfizer Pays $2.3 Billion to Settle Marketing Case," *New York Times*, September 2, 2009. Retrieved from http://www.nytimes.com/2009/09/03/business/03health.html.
9. Cowan, Jane. "Toyota to Pay $1.3 Billion for Deadly Defect Cover-Up," Australian Broadcasting Corporation, March 19, 2014. Retrieved from http://www.abc.net.au/news/2014-03-20/toyota-pays-1-3-billion-for-defect-cover-up-statements/5332894.
10. Lichtblau, Eric and Dougherty, Carter. "Siemens to Pay $1.34 Billion in Fines," *New York Times*, December 15, 2008. Retrieved from http://www.nytimes.com/2008/12/16/business/worldbusiness/16siemens.html.
11. U.S. Department of Justice. "Alstom Sentenced to Pay $772 Million Criminal Fine to Resolve Foreign Bribery Charges," Press release, November 13, 2015. Retrieved from https://www.justice.gov/opa/pr/alstom-sentenced-pay-772-million-criminal-fine-resolve-foreign-bribery-charges.
12. Stempel, Jonathan. "Visa, MasterCard $7.25 Billion Settlement with Retailers Is Thrown Out," Reuters, June 30, 2016. Retrieved from http://www.reuters.com/article/us-visa-mastercard-settlement-idUSKCN0ZG21E.
13. Lohr, Steve and Kanter, James. "A.M.D.-Intel Settlement Won't End Their Woes," *New York Times*, November 12, 2009. Retrieved from http://www.nytimes.com/2009/11/13/technology/companies/13chip.html.
14. Hurley, Lawrence. "UPDATE 1—U.S. Top Court Rejects AU Optronics over $500 Million Price-Fixing Fine," Reuters, June 15, 2015. Retrieved from http://www.reuters.com/article/usa-court-pricefixing-idUSL1N0Z10QC 20150615.

15. Protess, Ben and Corkery, Michael. "Bank of America Offers U.S. Biggest Settlement in History Over Toxic Mortgage Loans," *New York Times*, August 6, 2014. Retrieved from http://dealbook.nytimes.com/2014/08/06/bank-of-america-nears-17-billion-settlement-over-mortgages/.

16. Barrett, Devlin and Fitzpatrick, Dan. "J.P. Morgan, U.S. Settle for $13 Billion," *Wall Street Journal*, November 19, 2013. Retrieved from http://www.wsj.com/articles/SB10001424052702304439804579207701974094982.

17. U.S. Department of Justice. "Justice Department, Federal and State Partners Secure Record $7 Billion Global Settlement with Citigroup for Misleading Investors about Securities Containing Toxic Mortgages," Press release, July 14, 2014. Retrieved from https://www.justice.gov/opa/pr/justice-department-federal-and-state-partners-secure-record-7-billion-global-settlement.

18. U.S. Department of Justice. "Federal Government and State Attorneys General Reach $25 Billion Agreement with Five Largest Mortgage Servicers to Address Mortgage Loan Servicing and Foreclosure Abuses," Press release, February 9, 2012. Retrieved from https://www.justice.gov/opa/pr/federal-government-and-state-attorneys-general-reach-25-billion-agreement-five-largest.

19. U.S. Board of Governors of the Federal Reserve System and Office of the Comptroller of the Currency. "Amendments to Consent Orders Memorialize $9.3 Billion Foreclosure Agreement," Press release, February 28, 2013. Retrieved from http://www.occ.gov/news-issuances/news-releases/2013/nr-ia-2013-35.html.

20. U.S. Department of Justice. "Historic $5.15 Billion Environmental and Tort Settlement with Anadarko Petroleum Corp. Goes into Effect," Press release, January 23, 2015. Retrieved from https://www.justice.gov/opa/pr/historic-515-billion-environmental-and-tort-settlement-anadarko-petroleum-corp-goes-effect-0.

21. Gilbert, Daniel and Kent, Sarah. "BP Agrees to Pay $18.7 Billion to Settle Deepwater Horizon Oil Spill Claims," *Wall Street Journal*, July 2, 2015. Retrieved from http://www.wsj.com/articles/bp-agrees-to-pay-18-7-billion-to-settle-deepwater-horizon-oil-spill-claims-1435842739.

22. U.S. Securities and Exchange Commission. "Goldman Sachs to Pay Record $550 Million to Settle SEC Charges Related to Subprime Mortgage CDO," Press release, July 15, 2010. Retrieved from https://www.sec.gov/news/press/2010/2010-123.htm.

23. U.S. Securities and Exchange Commission. "BP to Pay $525 Million Penalty to Settle SEC Charges of Securities Fraud During Deepwater Horizon Oil Spill," Press release, November 15, 2012. Retrieved from https://www.sec.gov/News/PressRelease/Detail/PressRelease/1365171485962.

24. Clark, Nicola and Jolly, David. "Société Générale loses $7 billion in Trading fraud," *New York Times*, January 24, 2008. Retrieved from http://www.nytimes.com/2008/01/24/business/worldbusiness/24iht-socgen.5.9486501.html.

25. Kopecki, Dawn. "JPMorgan Pays $920 Million to Settle London Whale Probes," Bloomberg, September 20, 2013. Retrieved from http://www.bloomberg.com/news/articles/2013-09-19/jpmorgan-chase-agrees-to-pay-920-million-for-london-whale-loss.

26. Smythe, Christie. "HSBC Judge Approves $1.9B Drug-Money Laundering Accord," Bloomberg, July 3, 2013. Retrieved from http://www.bloomberg.com/news/articles/2013-07-02/hsbc-judge-approves-1-9b-drug-money-laundering-accord.

27. Douglas, Danielle. "France's BNP Paribas to Pay $8.9 billion to U.S. for Sanctions Violations," *Washington Post*, June 30, 2014. Retrieved from https://www.washingtonpost.com/business/economy/frances-bnp-paribas-to-pay-89-billion-to-us-for-money-laundering/2014/06/30/6d99d174-fc76-11e3-b1f4-8e77c632c07b_story.html.

28. Memmott, Mark, "UBS to Pay $1.5 Billion for 'Routine and Widespread' Rate Rigging," NPR, December 19, 2012. Retrieved from http://www.npr.org/sections/thetwo-way/2012/12/19/167604390/ubs-to-pay-1-5-billion-for-routine-and-widespread-rate-rigging.

29. Freifeld, Karen, "Five Global Banks to Pay $5.7 Billion in Fines over Rate Rigging," Reuters, May 20, 2015. Retrieved from http://www.reuters.com/article/us-banks-forex-settlementa-usa-idUSKBN0O51PY20150520.

30. Barrett, William P. and Novack, Janet. "UBS Agrees to Pay $780 Million," *Forbes*, February 18, 2009. Retrieved from http://www.forbes.com/2009/02/18/ubs-fraud-offshore-personal-finance_ubs.html.

31. "Credit Suisse Pleads Guilty, Pays $2.6 Billion to Settle U.S. Tax Evasion Charges," *Forbes*, May 20, 2014. Retrieved from http://www.forbes.com/sites/greatspeculations/2014/05/20/credit-suisse-pleads-guilty-pays-2-6-billion-to-settle-u-s-tax-evasion-charges/#52398f3512d5.

32. Harding, Luke. "What Are the Panama Papers? A Guide to History's Biggest Data Leak," *The Guardian*, April 5, 2016. Retrieved from https://www.theguardian.com/news/2016/apr/03/what-you-need-to-know-about-the-panama-papers.

33. Karnitschnig, Matthew, Deborah Solomon et al. "U.S. to Take Over AIG in $85 Billion Bailout; Central Banks Inject Cash as Credit Dries Up," *Wall Street Journal*, September 16, 2008. Retrieved from http://www.wsj.com/articles/SB122156561931242905.

34. Whoriskey, Peter. "GM Emerges from Bankruptcy After Landmark Government Bailout," *Washington Post*, July 10, 2009. Retrieved from http://www.washingtonpost.com/wp-dyn/content/article/2009/07/10/AR2009071001473.html.

35. de la Merced, Michael and Maynard, Micheline. "Fiat Deal with Chrysler Seals Swift 42-Day Overhaul," *New York Times*, June 10, 2009. Retrieved from http://www.nytimes.com/2009/06/11/business/global/11chrysler.html?_r=0.

36. Pallardy, Richard. "Deepwater Horizon Oil Spill of 2010," *Encyclopedia Britannica*, n.a. Retrieved from http://www.britannica.com/event/Deepwater-Horizon-oil-spill-of-2010.

37. Clements, Lana. "BP Racks up £2.7BILLION Loss after Further Gulf of Mexico payouts," Daily Express, July 28, 2015. Retrieved from http://www.express.co.uk/finance/city/594418/BP-racks-up-2-7BILLION-loss-after-further-Gulf-of-Mexico-payouts37.

38. Holt, Steve. "Walmart's Sustainability Promises: Myth vs. Reality," *Civil Eats*, June 5, 2015. Retrived from http://civileats.com/2015/06/05/walmarts-sustainability-promises-myth-vs-reality/.

39. Chen, Michelle. "Here Are All the Reasons Walmart's Business Is Not Sustainable," *The Nation*, June 5, 2015. Retrieved from http://www.thenation.com/article/here-are-all-reasons-walmarts-business-not-sustainable/.

40. O'Connor, Clare. "Report: Walmart Workers Cost Taxpayers $6.2 Billion in Public Assistance," *Forbes*, April 15, 2014. Retrieved from http://www.forbes.com/sites/clareoconnor/2014/04/15/report-walmart-workers-cost-taxpayers-6-2-billion-in-public-assistance/#6e012d967cd8.

41. Chen, Michelle. "Walmart's Business Is Not Sustainable."

42. McGinty, Kevin. "Target Data Breach Price Tag: $252 Million and Counting," Mintz Levin, February 26, 2015. Retrieved from https://www.privacyandsecuritymatters.com/2015/02/target-data-breach-price-tag-252-million-and-counting/.

43. Seals, Tara. "Target Breach Costs Could Total $1Bn," *Infosecurity*, February 28, 2015. Retrieved from http://www.infosecurity-magazine.com/news/target-breach-costs-could-total-1bn/.

44. O'Conner, Clare. "Target CRO Gregg Steinhafel Resigns in Data Breach Fallout," *Forbes*, May 5 2014. Retrieved from http://www.forbes.com/sites/clareoconnor/2014/05/05/target-ceo-gregg-steinhafel-resigns-in-wake-of-data-breach-fallout/#500c3f076e61.

45. 2014 Annual Corporate Directors Survey, PwC.

46. Conway, Edmund. "WEF 2009: Global Crisis 'Has Destroyed 40pc of World Wealth,'" *The Telegraph*, January 28, 2009. Retrieved from http://www.telegraph.co.uk/finance/financetopics/davos/4374492/WEF-2009-Global-crisis-has-destroyed-40pc-of-world-wealth.html.

CHAPTER 3

Performance-Based Continuous ERM

INTRODUCTION

From its beginnings in the early 1990s to its current incarnation, enterprise risk management (ERM) has undergone a dramatic transformation. Over time, ERM has evolved in response to a number of large-scale macroeconomic events as well as the business and regulatory changes those events precipitated. In so doing, ERM has adjusted its core focus and expanded the scope of risks it covers.

This continuing evolution can be organized into three major phases to reflect the changing landscape of enterprise risks in the past, present, and foreseeable future. Figure 3.1 provides a summary of the two major phases between the early 1990s and the present, as well as the next phase looking forward to the next 5–10 years.

Phase One: Financial and Operational Risk

Financial institutions began developing ERM programs in the early 1990s to address financial concerns such as aggregate market risk and credit risk. In 1993, the Group of 30's (G30) "Derivatives: Practice and Principles" addressed risk areas such as credit, market, operations and systems, accounting, and disclosures for derivatives dealers and end users.[1] Financial risks continue to be focal points of ERM functions, especially within the banking and financial-services industry.

Unfortunately for a number of derivatives end users—including Orange County, Procter & Gamble, and Gibson Greetings—the risk management practices recommended by the G30 Report didn't arrive on time to prevent significant losses in 1994. At about that period, risk professionals began addressing operational risk, which grew to prominence thanks to the trading scandals (e.g. Barings, Kidder, and Daiwa) that rocked the marketplace

State of ERM	Major Events and Risks	Key Developments
Phase One Early 1990s to mid-2000s	▪ Derivatives losses (1994): Orange County, Procter & Gamble, Gibson Greetings ▪ Rogue traders (1994–1995): Barings, Kidder, Daiwa ▪ Accounting fraud (2000/2001): Enron, WorldCom, Tyco	▪ Group of 30 Report ▪ Sarbanes-Oxley ➤ VaR models ➤ Real-time market risk management ➤ Operational risk management
Phase Two Mid-2000s to present	▪ Global financial crisis (2008): Lehman, Bear Sterns, AIG ▪ Recent events: oil price drop; China slowdown, negative interest rates; cyberattacks	▪ Dodd-Frank ▪ Basel II; ORSA ➤ Stress-testing ➤ Scenario analysis ➤ Strategic risk management
Phase Three The next 5–10 years	▪ Cybersecurity ▪ "Internet of Everything" ▪ Climate change ▪ Geopolitical risks ▪ Global terrorism	▪ Basel III ▪ Cybersecurity Disclosure Act ➤ Continuous ERM ➤ Collaborative reporting ➤ Evidence-based assurance

FIGURE 3.1 The Past, Present, and Future of ERM

in the mid-1990s. These incidents highlighted the importance of applying risk management techniques to ongoing operational processes, and ensuring that protocols, policies, and procedures align with the organization's risk appetite. During this period, the role of chief risk officer (CRO) began to take shape as the executive leader for ERM. A rash of accounting fraud cases in the early 2000s, headlined by the dramatic failures of Enron and WorldCom, led many companies to adopt operational controls specifically aimed at fraud prevention and detection.

Regulators, too, got into the fold. The Sarbanes-Oxley (SOX) Act of 2002 mandated increased oversight with a set of detective and preventative controls to ensure integrity in the financial reporting processes for publicly listed companies.[2] A few years later, Basel II sought to provide a framework within which financial institutions could manage their financial and operational risks.[3] The framework established minimum capital requirements, supervisory and regulatory review standards, and marketplace transparency guidelines. Although these regulations addressed unexpected losses resulting from certain financial and operational risks, their limitations would become all too clear.

Phase Two: Compliance-Driven Approach

The global financial crisis of 2008 fundamentally changed the world of risk management. The bankruptcy or near-death experience of large banks and the freefall in asset prices around the world left many to ponder the effectiveness of risk management at even the most sophisticated companies.

Regulators demanded that banking institutions take further strides to protect themselves against excessive risk. In the United States, the adoption of Dodd-Frank required banks to conduct stress testing on an annual basis.[4] These stress-testing requirements were designed to quantify and address vulnerability to various risk scenarios. The Federal Reserve established stress-testing rules, known as CCAR, for banks with assets of at least $50 billion while the OCC established similar rules for banks holding $10–$50 billion in assets known as DFAST. Such laws and regulations resulted in massive investments in risk, compliance, and audit functions. They also shaped risk governance and oversight at the board level.

Beyond the banking industry, companies have learned critical lessons about systemic risks and the shortcomings of their own risk management programs. As a result, the scope and responsibility of risk-oversight functions have increased significantly in all industry sectors. That positive outcome has been tempered, in my view, by two unfortunate if entirely understandable trends: a primary focus on regulatory compliance, and risk aversion. As a result, forward-looking, strategic risk management initiatives have not been given sufficient attention.

PHASE THREE: CREATING SHAREHOLDER VALUE

Today, the global economy may have climbed out of the depths of recession, but companies face increasing uncertainty in a wide array of new and emerging risks. Recent headlines have focused our attention on Federal Reserve interest-rate policy; an economic slowdown in China; declining oil prices; Middle East instability; "Brexit"; international and domestic terrorism; and cybersecurity. The ever-evolving globalization of competitive markets exposes many organizations to a new breed of risks, many of which they neither had planned for nor could have even anticipated.

In its *Global Risks Report 2016*,[5] the World Economic Forum identified five global risks with the greatest potential impact:

1. Failure of climate change mitigation and adaptation
2. Weapons of mass destruction
3. Water crises
4. Large-scale involuntary migration
5. Severe energy price shock

Globalization is the common driver among these five risks. No industry, geography, or business model is immune to them. These global risks are also similar in a way that underlies their significance: They are all systemic in nature. If any of these risks—much less a confluence of them—comes to fruition, the downstream impact on business would be catastrophic. In order to respond to these risks tomorrow, institutions must understand their interrelationships and potential impacts today.

Addressing these major risks reactively is not a viable solution. Their potential scope and severity are so great that doing so could mean economic destruction. Instead, risk management should become proactive, not simply minimizing negative risk but also maximizing opportunity. To do so, ERM must be a continuous process, constantly monitoring and assessing risk in a forward-looking way that provides companies with a path toward opportunity.

For these reasons, ERM is entering a third phase in its development focused on continuous monitoring, business-decision support, and maximization of shareholder value. Let's examine in great detail what the future of ERM may hold.

PERFORMANCE-BASED CONTINUOUS ERM

We now live and work in a new world that is more volatile and uncertain than ever. The speed of change and the velocity of risk have increased significantly. In addition to the uncertain business environment caused by globalization, companies must also deal with shifting consumer preferences, emerging technologies, demographic and workforce changes, climate-change impacts, and natural-resource constraints.

ERM programs must adapt: A monthly or quarterly process is no longer sufficient. Just as risks and opportunities are changing constantly, ERM programs should monitor and respond on a continuous basis. This is no pipe dream; it has a precedent in market risk management. During the 1990s, trading firms operating in global financial and commodity markets successfully transitioned from daily to real-time risk management.

In addition to becoming a continuous process, ERM must support key business decisions and add shareholder value. In addition, companies must measure the effectiveness of their ERM programs with objective performance metrics and closed feedback loops.

There are seven key attributes of evidenced-based continuous ERM:

1. ERM is a **continuous** management process that provides early-warning indicators for business leaders.
2. **Strategic** risk management receives the highest priority.
3. **Dynamic** risk appetite drives risk policies to balance business objectives and prudent risk taking.

4. Risk **optimization** is the primary objective of ERM. Companies achieve this by influencing the shape of their risk/return bell curve.
5. ERM is **embedded** into business decisions at all three lines of defense, supported by integrated risk assessment and analytics.
6. A collaborative **dashboard** reporting system delivers ongoing risk and performance monitoring.
7. Performance **feedback loops** assure ERM effectiveness and support continuous improvement.

Let's look at each of these in greater detail.

Attribute #1: ERM Is a Continuous Process

ERM is moving from a periodic monthly or quarterly process to a continuous one. This is essential to align the cadence of ERM with the velocity of risk. As a continuous process, ERM can provide business leaders with timely information and predictive analytics on their sensitivity to key business drivers, including:

Macroeconomic environment: In an interconnected world, regional, national, and global economic trends can impact the financial performance of any company. A continuous ERM process monitors leading economic indicators for interest rates, energy prices, manufacturing activities, economic growth, business investment, and capital flows. Management can compare these new economic data sets with the assumptions used in the business plan to support timely decisions regarding spending and capital investments.

Business processes and operations: On a daily basis, changes in the business and operating environment can have a significant impact on a company's risk profile. For example, management must respond immediately if there is a supply chain disruption. It may need to take mitigation actions if a key investment falls below expectations or a risk exposure exceeds appetite. Conversely, the company may want to increase risk if the market presents attractive risk-adjusted return opportunities.

Employee support and oversight: Employees represent the lifeblood of any organization. A continuous ERM process supports front-line employees in their day-to-day work, including decisions on risk acceptance or avoidance, product pricing, risk-transfer strategies, and risk escalation and communication protocols. Employee behavior can also have a material impact on a company's operational and reputational risk. Continuous ERM supports management oversight with respect to employee performance and feedback, compliance with policies and regulations, workplace safety, and risk-mitigation strategies.

Customer service: in order for an individual customer to be profitable, his or her lifetime value must exceed the cost of acquisition. It stands to reason, then, that even small improvements in customer retention can have a large impact on a company's profitability. In fact, a classic study by Bain & Co. indicated that reducing customer defections by 5% boosts profits 25% to 85%.[6] Given the importance of customer service and retention, business managers should continuously monitor customer service levels, customer complaints and time to resolution, and customer-retention metrics against risk tolerance levels.

Counterparties and business partners: Companies increasingly rely on third parties to support their business and financial operations, including suppliers and vendors, business and outsourcing partners, and financial counterparties. The performance and creditworthiness of these third parties can have an immediate and long-term effect on a company's business model. A continuous ERM process monitors vendor performance against service-level agreements, counterparty stock prices and credit spreads, and problem-resolution rates.

Environmental and social impacts: Long-term sustainability, relative to environmental standards and social expectations, has become a top corporate priority. This includes how a company impacts its environment as well as how the environment impacts the company. The former requires a continuous monitoring of environment and social performance indicators, daily press coverage, and social-media posts. The latter requires monitoring extreme weather patterns, natural-resource constraints, and business contingency readiness.

IT infrastructure and cybersecurity: Companies rely increasingly on their IT infrastructures. With the advent of cloud computing, big data, predictive analytics, and the Internet of Things (IOT), IT performance and cybersecurity requirements have become a top concern for most organizations. A continuous ERM process monitors IT availability and performance as well as cybersecurity metrics such as patch management, incident rate, and time to detection and recovery.

Attribute #2: Strategic Risk Management

Strategy and risk are two sides of the same coin. Strategic planning and ERM should be integrated to support the development, implementation, and performance monitoring of corporate and business-unit strategies.

Companies ignore strategic risks at their peril. Independent studies of the largest public companies have shown time and again that strategic risks account for approximately 60 percent of major declines in market capitalization, followed by operational risks (about 30 percent) and financial risks (about 10 percent).[7] Yet, in practice, many ERM programs downplay strategic risks or ignore them entirely.

Strategic risk can arise throughout the strategy development and implementation processes. The integration of strategy and ERM, or strategic risk management, can add long-term shareholder value in a number of important ways. Strategic risk management helps companies make more informed decisions when they:

- Choose between alternative corporate strategies—e.g., organic growth, acquisition, stock buyback—based on their impact on enterprise intrinsic value.[8]
- Ensure that corporate strategies are well-aligned with the company's core mission and values, business-unit strategies, and operating budgets.
- Assess the strategic and resultant risks from the implementation of corporate strategies, including the utilization of risk appetite and risk capacity.[9]
- Support the implementation of corporate strategies to achieve key organizational objectives.
- Monitor the actual performance of corporate strategies against management assumptions and expectations, and make timely adjustments as appropriate.

To support strategic risk management decisions, the company's performance management system must integrate key performance indicators (KPIs) and key risk indicators (KRIs). An integrated performance and risk monitoring process would include the following steps:

1. Define the business strategy through a set of measurable strategic objectives.
2. Establish KPIs and targets based on expected performance for those strategic objectives.
3. Identify strategic risks that can drive variability in actual performance, for better or worse, through risk assessments.
4. Establish KRIs and risk tolerance levels for those critical risks.
5. Provide integrated reporting and monitoring in support of strategic risk management.

Unfortunately, many companies perform these actions in two distinct silos. As part of strategic planning they perform steps 1 and 2 and report the results to the executive committee and full board. Separately, as part of risk management they perform steps 3 and 4 and report the results to the risk and audit committees. In order to effectively manage strategic risks, these steps must be fully integrated.

Attribute #3: Dynamic Risk Appetite

An integral part of continuous ERM is the development of key risk metrics, exposure limits, and governance and oversight processes to ensure enterprise-wide risks are within acceptable and manageable levels. A best-practice approach to addressing these requirements is to implement a formal risk appetite statement (RAS). Corporate directors who are ultimately responsible for overseeing their companies' risk management indicated that this practice is not fully developed. According to a National Association of Corporate Directors (NACD) survey, only 26 percent of companies have a defined risk appetite statement.[10]

An RAS is a board-approved policy that defines the types and aggregate levels of risk that an organization is willing to accept in pursuit of business objectives. In determining the appropriate risk appetite, an organization should also consider its risk capacity (also known as risk-bearing capacity), which represents a company's overall ability to manage the risk and absorb potential losses. Companies can measure risk capacity in terms of liquidity and capital reserves, as well as management capabilities and track record in managing the specific risks.

A dynamic RAS would include the following components:

1. Qualitative statements and guidelines, as well as quantitative metrics and risk tolerance levels for all key risks.
2. A cascading structure of risk tolerance levels with drill-down capability from the board (Level 1) to executive management (Level 2) to business units (Level 3).
3. Continuously updated RAS dashboard reports, including commentaries and expert analysis.
4. Risk-mitigation strategies and exception reporting in the event risk exposures are above tolerance levels.
5. Dynamic adjustments to tolerance levels to reflect risk-return opportunities. For example, if the market provides attractive return opportunities and the company has excess risk capacity, the risk tolerances may be increased accordingly.

The following example breaks down a strategic RAS into its three primary components:

- **Qualitative statement:** "To ensure strategic alignment, we will limit business activities that are not consistent with our overall strategy and core competencies."

- **Metric:** Non-core investment capital ÷ total capital.
- **Risk tolerance level:** "Non-core capital ratio will not exceed 10 percent."

Attribute #4: Risk Optimization

The risk bell curve is a graphical depiction of risk with respect to probabilities and outcomes, including expected value (the mean of the bell curve) as well as the potential upside and potential downside (the tails). The objective of ERM is to assess, quantify, and optimize the shape of the bell curve for all of the key risks on an ongoing basis.

Although all key risks take the form of a bell curve, not all bell curves are alike. Figure 3.2 shows how the bell curve can be used to capture various risks.

For example, credit risk has more downside risk (potential loss of principal) versus upside gain (interest income). Market risk (including interest rate risk) follows an essentially symmetrical curve, as market prices (and interest rates) have an equal chance of moving favorably or unfavorably. On the other side of the spectrum, operational risk has a limited upside but a lot of potential downside. After all, not having any IT, compliance, or legal issues simply means business as usual. But a major negative event, such as a cybersecurity breach, IT downtime, or regulatory issue, can have tremendous consequences.

Credit Risk
   Earnings volatility due to variation in credit losses

Market Risk
   Earnings volatility due to market price movements

Operational Risk
   Earnings volatility due to people, process, technology, or one-off events

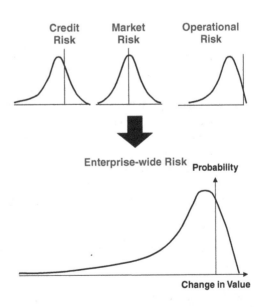

FIGURE 3.2 Bell Curve Shapes

If managed well, strategic risk (not shown) is unique in that its downside can be limited while its upside can be unlimited. For example, the maximum loss of a new investment is 100 percent of the investment, but a new business venture can produce multiples of the investment. An asymmetrical bell curve with significant upside risk can describe any new product or business opportunity, whether that opportunity is part of a corporation's growth strategy or a venture capital firm's new investment.

Consider a decision tree that maps the probabilities and consequences of different decision paths.[11] This map not only provides a better picture of the risks and rewards involved, but also helps identify trigger points for action if the initiative lags behind expectations. Taken this way, the optimum strategic risk profile resembles a call option: limited downside exposure with unlimited upside potential. A company can also limit downside risk by "failing faster." The sooner a company recognizes an initiative is in trouble, the sooner it can take corrective action—such as getting the initiative back on track, deploying risk mitigation strategies, or shutting it down.

Minimizing downside risk and increasing the upside is the objective of "real option theory." A real option is the right, but not the obligation, to undertake a business investment or change any aspect of that investment at various points in time, given updated information. The beneficial asymmetry between the right and the obligation to invest under these conditions is what generates the option's value.

Venture capital (VC) firms take advantage of this asymmetry as part of their business model. According to research by Shikhar Ghosh, a senior lecturer at Harvard Business School, about 75 percent of venture-backed investments in the United States do not return investors' capital, 20 percent achieve subpar returns, and only 5 percent achieve or exceed the projected return on investment.[12] To maintain an ideal risk profile, VCs carefully stagger funding rounds in order to reap outsized returns on the 5 percent of firms that are successful while exiting or minimizing their investments in the other 95 percent. This risk/return profile is why VC firms are always concerned about the size of the market. They don't hit often but when they do they need to hit it big!

Pharmaceutical companies take a similar portfolio approach. They invest in drug development internally or acquire promising patents or entire drug companies. They can then continue to make limited, iterative investments in successful ventures and bow out of those that fail to achieve expected performance levels.

However, the enterprise-wide risk profile shown in Figure 3.2 is more indicative of a bank, for which the upside is limited to net interest income (about 2–3% of average assets) plus fee income while the downside can include large loan losses. This is also known as "fat-tail" risk. The ideal risk profile would be skewed to the right, which is more indicative of venture capital and pharmaceutical firms, which have more upside than downside. Regardless of the industry, companies must make the appropriate business decisions to optimize the shape of their risk bell curves.

Attribute #5: ERM-Based Decision Support

In order to add value, companies must integrate the continuous ERM process into their strategic, financial, and operational decisions. Generally speaking, organizations have the following options available to them in response to risk:

Risk acceptance or avoidance: The organization can decide to increase or decrease a specific risk exposure through its core business, mergers and acquisitions (M&A), or financial transactions. This includes new product development, market expansion, acquisitions and divestitures, capital budgeting, and investment and financing activities.

Risk mitigation: An organization can establish risk-control processes and strategies in order to manage a specific risk within a defined tolerance. This includes constructing a risk appetite statement with explicit risk tolerance levels, corporate risk policies, risk measurement and monitoring systems, and risk-control strategies and contingency plans.

Risk-based pricing: All firms take risks in order to be in business, but there is only one point at which they receive compensation for the risks that they take. That is in the pricing of their products and/or services. A product's price must always incorporate its share of the cost of risk. Similarly, companies should fully account for the cost of risk to measure the risk-adjusted profitability of business units.

Risk transfer: An organization can decide to implement risk-transfer strategies through the insurance or capital markets if risk exposures are excessive and/or if the cost of risk transfer is lower than the cost of risk retention. Risk-transfer strategies include hedging; corporate insurance and captive insurance strategies; and securitization programs.

Resource allocation: An organization can allocate human and financial resources to business activities that produce the highest risk-adjusted returns in order to maximize firm value. This includes rationalizing the allocation of staff resources, economic capital, and financial budgets based on projected risk-adjusted performance.

While it is important to understand the general categories of choice an organization can make as discussed above, in practice, each business or risk decision falls to a specific committee, function, or individual. These decision makers can be members of the board, corporate management, or business and functional units. Here is a summary of key risk management decisions based on the "three lines of defense" model:

- **Business units and support functions** represent the first line of defense. The first line is ultimately accountable for measuring and managing the risks inherent in their own businesses and operations. Since they must assume some level of risk to achieve their business objectives, the goal is to take intelligent risks. Key business and risk management decisions include accepting or avoiding risks in day-to-day business activities and operations; including the cost of risk in product pricing; managing customer relationships; and implementing risk-mitigation strategies and contingency plans in response to risk events.
- **Corporate management,** supported by the ERM and compliance functions, represents the second line of defense. Management is responsible for establishing and implementing risk and compliance programs, including risk policies and standards, appetite and tolerances, and reporting processes for the board and management. The second line of defense is accountable for ongoing risk monitoring and oversight. This level's key business and risk management decisions include allocating financial and human capital resources to business activities that produce the highest risk-adjusted profitability; implementing organic and/or acquisition-based growth strategies; and devising risk-transfer strategies to reduce excessive or uneconomic risk exposures.
- **The board of directors**, with the support of internal audit, represents the third line of defense. The board is responsible for establishing the company's risk governance structure and oversight processes; reviewing, challenging, and approving risk policies; and overseeing strategy execution, risk management, and executive compensation programs. The third line of defense is also accountable for the periodic review to assure risk management effectiveness. Key business and risk management decisions include establishing the statement of risk appetite and risk-tolerance levels; reviewing and approving management recommendations with respect to capital structure, dividend policy, and target debt ratings; and reviewing and approving strategic risk management decisions, including major investments and M&A transactions.

Attribute #6: Collaborative Dashboard Reporting

One of the key objectives of continuous ERM is to promote risk transparency with enhanced reporting. The old adage "what gets measured gets managed" certainly holds true in risk management, and business leaders appear to be getting the message. In a 2011 Deloitte study of approximately 1,500 executives across various industries, 86 percent identified "risk information reporting" as a high or moderate priority, making it the most highly prioritized of 13 risk initiative options.[13] What's more, this priority was followed closely by "risk data quality and management" (76 percent) and "operational risk measurement system" (69 percent). Clearly, management understands that establishing a robust risk measurement and reporting system is critical to ERM success.

The ideal way to achieve this objective is with a real-time collaborative dashboard reporting system. This system would produce role-based reports designed to support the decision-making requirements of each recipient. When designing a role-based dashboard report, it is useful to determine the key questions each recipient needs to address. For example, the ERM dashboard for the board and senior management may address the following five basic questions:

1. **Are any of our business objectives at risk?** As discussed, a company's RAS defines risks according their effects on primary business objectives. The ERM dashboard should similarly organize risk information (e.g., quantitative metrics, qualitative risk assessments, early warning indicators) within the context of key strategic and business objectives. For each objective, the dashboard report might show green, yellow, or red indicators to signal that its achievement is on-track, threatened, or off-track, respectively. For objectives with yellow or red indicators, the board and management should be able to drill down to underlying analyses and data.
2. **Are we in compliance with policies, regulations, and laws?** The ERM dashboard should indicate at a glance the company's compliance status in regard to key policies, regulations, and laws. Again, traffic-light signals would highlight whether the company is in full compliance (green), approaching violation (yellow), or in violation (red). Drill-down capabilities would support further analysis with respect to more detailed legal analyses, compliance metrics, and regulatory reports.
3. **What risk incidents have been escalated?** The ERM dashboard should be able to escalate critical risk incidents to the appropriate board members, executives, or managers in real time. This capability would require

a system to capture incidents throughout the company that meet a defined threshold (e.g., customer or reputational impact, financial exposure, etc.). Moreover, the ERM dashboard needs an embedded algorithm that prioritizes risk incidents and escalates them to the proper individuals. The most critical incidents should prompt alerts via email, text, or other system for immediate response.

4. **What key performance indicators (KPIs), key risk indicators (KRIs), or early warning indicators require attention?** A key goal of an ERM dashboard is to highlight potential problems before they become critical. For that reason, the dashboard should include early warning indicators that help foreshadow such issues. A well-designed ERM dashboard would provide KPIs and KRIs that are most relevant to the decision-making needs of each user, whether at the board, management, or business-unit level. To provide context, each metric should include performance thresholds and/or risk tolerance levels to provide benchmarks for evaluation.

5. **What risk assessments must we review?** Risk assessment is an ongoing process, with top-down risk assessments, bottom-up risk-control self-assessments (RCSAs), regulatory examinations, and audit reports taking place on a regular basis. Given that these assessments include mainly qualitative information, the dashboard need only provide a summary of key findings and analyses. Each such summary should indicate whether it meets board and management expectations (green), is near those expectations (yellow), or falls short (red). When more detailed review is necessary, the actual risk assessments and reports would be available via linked files.

In addition to the above components of dashboard reporting, new features are surfacing that are becoming part of the emerging reporting standards. An established dashboard system should incorporate the following elements for streamlined reporting:

Single-source publishing: Software that publishes the same data in multiple places at once across a platform effectively eliminates duplicate content and version-control issues. Single-source publishing not only makes reporting more accurate, it also increases efficiency and frees up time for making important business decisions instead of managing data. The same technology can also produce dynamic charts that respond to data as it changes.

Collaborative real-time editing: Advanced software platforms, often cloud-based, permit multiple users to work on a single document at the same time, with changes displayed in real time. Such functionality permits each user to have the latest data as soon as it is available. This technology is becoming increasingly powerful and simpler to deploy across the organization, making it essential to support continuous ERM reporting.

Data visualization: Many dashboard applications now have the ability to create graphs or presentations seamlessly with underlying data, making it far more impactful and actionable. Consider the impact and clarity of a pie chart or bar graph compared to a dense table of numbers. Whether the user is a chief risk officer or an IT manager, being able to clearly visualize risk data can dramatically improve risk monitoring and decision-making.

Interactive data displays: The best data presentation is dynamic, allowing users to see summaries but giving them the ability to drill down into the underlying details. The next step in interactivity, however, will allow users to have a "conversation" with the data, by asking human-readable questions of the database and receiving answers pertinent to business objectives. While this is still a mostly experimental feature of dashboards, the advances in artificial intelligence should make such features available in the coming years.

Attribute #7: ERM Performance Feedback Loops

Performance feedback loops support self-correction and continuous improvement by adjusting a process according to the variances between actual and desired performance. As a foundational component of the scientific method, the feedback loop has long been an essential tool used to support advances in many fields, including economics, engineering, and medicine. More recently, the innovative use of feedback loops has been reported in the hedge fund industry[14] and the effective altruism movement.[15] It would be difficult to evaluate and improve any process efficiently without a performance feedback loop. Risk management is no exception.

In order to establish a performance feedback loop for ERM, companies must first define its objective in measurable terms. I believe that the primary objective of ERM is to minimize unexpected earnings variance. See Chapter 19 for a full discussion on feedback loops and an example that illustrates the use of earnings volatility analysis as the basis of a performance feedback loop to do exactly that.

Perhaps the best way to illustrate how these seven attributes work together in a corporate environment is with a story. The following account is fictional, but the situations I describe are ones that real-life companies are likely to face.

CASE STUDY: LEGACY TECHNOLOGY

Elizabeth Heath is the CRO of Legacy Technology, a large, well-established tech company. Recently, Legacy determined that the best way to extend its reach into emerging cloud technologies would be to acquire a company with the capabilities and markets it sought. Legacy found such a company in Galactic Cloud Magic, whose product line and expertise made it well positioned to meet Legacy's strategic needs. Thanks to the backing of her CEO and board, Elizabeth was an integral member of the team that vetted acquisition candidates and ultimately negotiated a deal with Galactic. As we'll see, the process ran into some unexpected issues that might well have torpedoed the deal, but Elizabeth and her team were able to apply all seven attributes of evidence-based continuous ERM to find a solution. Here's how:

Managing Strategic Risk (Attribute #2)

As part of an integrated strategic-planning and ERM process, Elizabeth and her team were fully engaged in the M&A analysis and due-diligence process. After thoroughly reviewing Galactic's risk profile, they calculated a cost of risk of $10 per share based on the severity and likelihood of numerous risks. They also determined the level of economic capital Legacy would have to maintain in order to safely absorb these risks post-merger. As a result, the risk team concluded that a properly priced acquisition of Galactic would optimize Legacy's risk profile and add value for its shareholders. The acquisition team, seeking a RAROC of about 12%, agreed on an offer of $100 per share, which Galactic accepted.

The deal was set to close in a couple of weeks when Elizabeth received an early morning call from Legacy's CEO. He just learned that Galactic had suffered a massive cyberattack overnight that may have exposed private customer data. The CEO called together the acquisition team to review their options.

The COO and CIO both argued that Legacy should call off the deal: Galactic's reputation was likely to be irreparably damaged by the breach, and the company was facing multiple potential lawsuits from its customers. Elizabeth argued, however, that it was premature to pull the plug, and urged the group to wait for more information.

A Robust and Continuous Process (Attribute #1)

As it turns out, Galactic was well prepared for a potential breach. As soon as the attack was detected, the system went into automatic lockdown and customers were informed, as well as required to change their login information with double authentication. A previously created "SWAT team" of technicians, attorneys, security experts, and communications experts was called into action to determine root causes and solutions, assess the damage, minimize impact, and report progress to all stakeholders. Elizabeth's team was equally prepared. They tapped into Galactic's team to receive continuous updates on the situation. They then used this information, as well as governmental data and analyses of similar attacks, to analyze the event's potential strategic, financial, and reputational impact on the acquisition.

Relevant Data, Informed Decisions (Attribute #4)

As information became available, the risk team updated its assessment and models based on the new risks related to the cyberattack. They also updated their original heat map to indicate a higher level of risk due to the dramatically increased likelihood of consequences such as lawsuits and reputation damage. Finally, they revised their calculation of the cost of risk in the acquisition, which increased from $10 to $25. As a result of this analysis, Elizabeth and her team proposed incorporating this increased cost into a reduced acquisition offer, from $100 to $85.

Mitigating Risk to Create Opportunity (Attribute #5).

Executives at Galactic balked at the lower acquisition price, and it looked as though the deal was all but dead. But Elizabeth had an idea. She reached out to Legacy's corporate insurance provider to obtain a quote on a risk-transfer strategy that would cover losses resulting from the cyberattack above a certain level. It was a buyer's market in cyberinsurance, so the premium was economical. In other words, the cost of risk transfer was lower than the cost of risk retention. The overall reduction in risk cost allowed Legacy to raise its offer to $90. At the same time, it lowered projected earnings from the acquisition somewhat. This transaction optimized the risk profile for the company given the new risks, risk-transfer costs, and business requirements. Overall, it meant that Legacy was able to offer a price acceptable to Galactic while still achieving its desired return on investment.

Engaging the Three Lines of Defense (Attribute #6)

Throughout the process, Elizabeth and her team took care to inform and engage the three lines of defense: operating units, management, and the board.

The first line of defense, which consists of the company's business and operating units, as well as its support functions, gathered ongoing data. In particular, the IT function kept the board and management apprised of the situation as it unfolded. IT provided the risk and deal teams with expert interpretation of the information coming in from Galactic, analyzing it against known scenarios to project likely outcomes.

The CRO and ERM function, along with corporate management, provided the second line of defense. This group was tasked with reevaluating the risk level of the situation as it developed. Elizabeth's team updated assessment and qualification models to recalculate the cost of risk, and formulated the risk transfer strategy. Other members of the management team evaluated these results and offered additional input to fine-tune the ERM team's conclusions. The CEO maintained communication with Galactic, worked with the deal team to build consensus around a revised proposal, and obtained approvals from the board.

Finally, the third line of defense—the board—conducted calls and meetings on an as-needed basis to monitor the situation, challenge management's risk assessment, and approve the risk transfer strategy and new acquisition price.

Although it was a coordinated effort, Elizabeth and her risk team were instrumental in saving the day. The deal, once thought to be dead in the water, was consummated just a month behind schedule.

Reevaluating Risk Appetite (Attribute #3)

After a short celebration, the CRO and risk team went back to work to tackle the post-merger integration risks. These risks included continued fall-out from the cyberattack (lawsuits, technology updates), performance of the risk-transfer strategy, and integration of management teams, customers, and technology platforms. They also added new metrics and risk-tolerance levels to Legacy's risk appetite statement to reflect these changes.

Supporting Ongoing Collaboration (Attribute #7)

The successful acquisition paid Elizabeth an additional benefit. Her contribution won over a number of her peers in the C-suite and beyond who had questioned the value of Legacy's continuous ERM program. These former doubters were impressed that the program could escalate and address a new threat on a timely basis. And they were swayed by Elizabeth's ability to quantify and illustrate pre- and post-merger risk profiles, which led to informed decisions about the cost of risk, risk-transfer strategy, and updated acquisition price and expected return.

What's more, they, along with other internal stakeholders, were engaged in the process as it unfolded on the customized risk dashboards that the ERM team had created for them. Even after the deal was signed, these dashboards continued to assist the integration team, senior management, and the board in monitoring and oversight.

For Legacy, ERM was a game-changer. What's more, Elizabeth put to rest the common misperception that ERM's role is to put the brakes on a company's ambitions. Far from impeding a strategically important deal, risk management actually provided a path forward.

The global economy and business world have evolved significantly over the past three decades, and so has the practice of ERM. As companies face great financial and reputational damage from derivatives losses, unauthorized trading, accounting fraud, global recession, and cybersecurity threats, the scope and focus of ERM has expanded to include strategic risk, financial risk, operational risk, regulatory-compliance risk, reputational risk, and cybersecurity risk.

Given the increase in macroeconomic and business uncertainties, regulatory standards, and risk velocity, ERM must continue to evolve. In the following chapters, we'll turn our attention to ERM at the organizational level, starting with the many stakeholders whose requirements must be addressed.

NOTES

1. The G30 report on the derivatives market provided foundation for risk management frameworks and areas of focus. *Derivatives: Practices and Principles*, Group of Thirty, 1993.
2. Sarbanes-Oxley increases oversight of publicly registered companies and the methods and processes used in their public financial reporting and disclosure mechanisms through formalization of control structure and the appointment of an independent oversight body over public accounting firms, the Public Company Accounting Oversight Board (PCAOB). *Sarbanes-Oxley Act of 2002*, Pub.L. 107–204, 116 Stat. 745, enacted July 30, 2002.
3. Basel provides recommendations on banking law and regulations. The Basel II Accord sought to address capital needs and reserves necessary to guard against an institution's financial and operational risk. The Office of the Comptroller of the Currency implemented as a final rule the advanced approaches of Basel II on November 1, 2007.
4. Section 165(i)(2) of the Dodd-Frank Wall Street Reform and Consumer Protection Act introduced the stress testing regulatory requirement. The *Dodd–Frank Wall Street Reform and Consumer Protection Act* (Pub.L. 111–203, H.R. 4173).
5. Global Risk Report 2016, 11th edition, The World Economic Forum, 2016.
6. Reichheld, Frederick and Sasser, Earl. "Zero Defections: Quality Comes to Services," *Harvard Business Review*, 1990.
7. Lam, James. *Enterprise Risk Management: From Incentives to Controls*, 2nd edition, Wiley, 2014, pp. 434–436.

8. A strategy will add to enterprise intrinsic value if the risk-adjusted return on capital (RAROC) is higher than the company's cost of equity (Ke). See *Strategic Risk Management: The Next Frontier for ERM*, Workiva, 2015.

9. Lam, James. *Implementing an Effective Risk Appetite*, IMA® (Institute of Management Accountants) Statement on Management Accounting, August 2015.

10. *Public Company Governance Survey*, National Association of Corporate Directors, 2013–2014.

11. The classic decision tree is a similar construct to a bell curve, except that it is displayed sideways and used to support decision-making at critical junctures.

12. Gage, Deborah. "The Venture Capital Secret: 3 Out of 4 Start-ups Fail," *Wall Street Journal*, September 20, 2012.

13. Global Risk Management Survey, 7th edition: "Navigating in a Changed World," Deloitte, February 2011, p. 42.

14. Bridgewater is one of the largest and most successful hedge funds in the world. The founder, Ray Dalio, argues for the use of a performance feedback loop to monitor and shape organizational effectiveness. See Dalio, Ray, "Principle #66, *Principles*, www.bwater.com, 2011.

15. Effective altruism is a new, evidence-based approach to charitable giving. The cofounder, William MacAskill, advocates the use of objective feedback loops to determine the effectiveness of altruistic pursues. See MacAskill, William, *Doing Good Better*, Gotham Books, 2015.

CHAPTER 4

Stakeholder Requirements

INTRODUCTION

Who are the stakeholders of a company? How do we incorporate stakeholder value management into risk management? What steps should we take to implement it?

Any group or individual that supports and influences the survival and success of the company can be considered a stakeholder. A company's interactions with its key stakeholders shape its reputation, and the monitoring and management of stakeholders' feedback and opinions is a key element of reputational risk management. This chapter will first discuss the key stakeholder groups and their primary requirements. These stakeholder groups include:

- Customers
- Employees
- Regulators
- Communities and environmental groups
- Stock exchanges and rating agencies
- Business partners
- Institutional investors
- Proxy advisory firms
- Activist investors

The risk management function should understand their expectations, monitor their perception of the company, and provide risk transparency to them. For example, regulators need assurance that the company complies with laws, regulations, and internal policies. Stock analysts and rating agencies want to know how the company manages risk in its business and financial activities. Investors need financial and risk data to make informed decisions.

Management must provide greater transparency into the company's risk profile as the informational needs of key stakeholders continue to grow. Boards need summary information that highlights key risks and trends. Stock analysts, more concerned about return on equity capital, seek risk-adjusted profitability metrics to compare with their own benchmarks and models. Rating agencies want to know about capital plans and underlying exposures, particularly in regard to debt service and concentrated risks. And communities and environmental groups need to be satisfied that the company is operating in a way that is socially and environmentally responsible.

In this chapter, we'll discuss how to leverage stakeholder relationships within an effective ERM program and offer strategies to address stakeholder needs. We'll also review case studies illustrating successful stakeholder management and offer a four-step process to engage stakeholders and earn their support.

STAKEHOLDERS DEFINED

When people think of stakeholders, they most likely have in mind whoever holds the company's equity and perhaps its debt. However, a stakeholder can be any individual or group that supports and influences the success of a company. Stakeholders can be internal (employees, board members) and external (customers, suppliers, creditors, analysts, interest groups, regulators, and local communities).

Taking the time to manage stakeholders offers numerous rewards. First of all, it creates value by maximizing shared benefits: Addressing customer and other stakeholder interests can and should improve corporate performance. Engaging stakeholders also reduces the risk of being targeted by groups such as activist investors, environmentalists, consumer protection organizations, and others. Finally, managing these relationships helps manage reputational risk. By addressing issues communities and interest groups raise with the firm, companies can prevent damage to their brand and image, avoiding lost sales, unhappy customers, legal expenses, and other negative consequences. Let's take a closer look at each type of stakeholder and discuss how to identify and address their needs.

Customers

Customers are the most important external stakeholders for any company. Without them, the business would not exist. Meeting customer needs is a strategic imperative and one of the primary objectives for a business.

The relationship between a company and its customers should be mutually beneficial. Customers are also critical when it comes to managing reputational risk.[1]

Strong customer relationships don't just drive current sales. They also lay the foundation for future growth via loyalty, evangelism, and even innovation. One of the traits that has been attributed to Steve Jobs, the late founder and CEO of Apple, is that he knew what customers wanted before they did. Yet despite evidence that increasing customer retention rates even marginally can dramatically improve profitability, just 32% of executives say retaining existing customers is a priority.[2]

Know the Customer Everyone within a business should know who the company's primary customers are. Companies that know their customers and act strategically on that knowledge can improve customer satisfaction and retention. This includes what they need, want, require, expect, and intend. Customers may fall into one or more of these categories:

- **Client:** The customer of a professional service provider
- **Purchaser:** The customer of a supplier that places the order and authorizes the payment
- **Beneficiary:** The customer of a charity
- **Consumer:** The customer of a retailer
- **End-user:** The person who ultimately uses the goods or services that are purchased, perhaps by someone else

Customer insight isn't limited to *who* they are, but also *where* they are, *how* best to reach them, and *what* they need. In addition to traditional market research, companies can listen to the voice of the customer through service and support requests, social media, and data mining. Amazon.com is a familiar example. With each order, the retailer can draw from a vast repository of data to recommend other products that may interest a customer—even on his or her first visit to the site. Of course, this type of data mining has its own risks. If companies use data improperly or fail to secure it, they run the risk of losses, lawsuits, and negative publicity.

Customer Acquisition Good customer management does not mean that a company should attempt to obtain all possible customers in an effort to maximize revenues. Rather, they need to identify and retain the *right* customers—those who will help increase overall profitability, and not necessarily total revenues.

Consider a supermarket chain—a volume business if ever there was one. Gaining new customers and increasing market share would seem to be all-important. However, not every customer is equally profitable. Some may be attracted by discounts, cherry-picking purchases to take advantage of deals. Others are willing to pay a premium for high-quality products. Rather than offering steep discounts, then, a supermarket may do well to introduce high-margin luxury items, thereby encouraging profitable customers and leaving the others to competitors.

Customer Retention As important as it is for a business to attract new customers, it is even more crucial that it keeps them. Many studies have confirmed the value of customer retention. Acquiring a new customer costs far more than retaining an existing one.[3] Existing customers tend to buy more, are less price-sensitive, and bring in more new customers than recently acquired customers do. In some industries, reducing customer turnover by as little as 5 percent can increase profitability by more than 50 percent.[4]

Customer retention is one result of effective customer relationship management, or, to put it another way, of customer satisfaction. Not only does a company lose the business of dissatisfied customers, but it may also lose the business of the potential and existing customers that the dissatisfied customers warn off. Therefore, customer loyalty and satisfaction, not just acquisition, are vital parts of the relationship.

Unfortunately, customer satisfaction does not always correlate with customer loyalty: A customer may be satisfied but still leave. Consider the U.S. automotive market. While consumers regularly report satisfaction levels for their current auto of about 80 percent, that high figure does not translate into strong loyalty. Even customer-loyalty leaders such Toyota, Ford, and BMW only see repurchase rates ranging from 30 to 40 percent. The lesson? Loyalty requires more than delivering products people like. Companies need a deeper understanding of their customers' ongoing needs and learn how to meet them on a continuous basis.

Handling Crisis With the rise of social media and instant news updates, managing reputational risk has become an irreplaceable skill among businesses. One seemingly minor slip-up can have major repercussions that can destroy a company's reputation. No one likes to think about worst-case scenarios, but having a contingency plan *before* any crisis arises is an important step in managing your company's reputation.

A sound crisis strategy involves not just customer-facing employees and managers, but the board and senior management as well. Preparing them for an eventual incident escalation can save valuable time if and when a crisis occurs. To develop a broad response plan, begin by creating several "what-if" scenarios and discuss a plan of action to address each. Incorporate these into reputational risk training. Think of it as stress testing for your company's reputation. Appropriate responses may include locking down virtual or physical infrastructure, deploying quick-response teams to address issues, alerting law enforcement and/or emergency services, isolating responsible individuals within the organization, keeping the public informed, and finally, accepting responsibility.

We can learn a great deal from the ways in which other companies handled crisis. A classic example—still relevant today—is how Johnson & Johnson managed the Tylenol crisis in 1982. When J&J first learned that an unknown person added a deadly amount of cyanide to some of their leading product, they responded by immediately recalling all their product from the shelves. J&J took full responsibility, even though they knew it was not their fault, and made public announcements through various media outlets warning users of potential danger. Then, over a number of years, they slowly reintroduced the product to the market with new safety features.[5] Compare this to the callow response of then-BP chairman Tony Hayward to his company's Deepwater Horizon disaster in 2010 that killed 11 workers. Whatever good he may have done, he will always be remembered as the guy who publicly complained, "I'd like my life back."

The keys to crisis management are twofold: Make contingency plans in advance, and never compound the problem by trying to cover it up or deny responsibility. If a crisis occurs, the company must act quickly, be honest, and keep customers and the general public informed. Today, it is no longer realistic to believe that the truth will never come out or that financial damage can be postponed indefinitely. Attempting to cover up a debacle may result in greater reputational damage to the company than openly admitting any mistakes that have been made. The company's response should focus on its long-term good rather than on minimizing immediate losses.

While crisis strategy is a primary driver in mitigating reputational risk, it is not the only one. Reputational risk management has become a key component of ERM and developing a reputational risk policy is an emerging practice. Appendix A provides an example of a reputational risk policy.

Employees

Many companies pay lip service to the value of their employees, but few demonstrate a clear understanding of their workforce's true worth. A company seeking to extract the maximum value from its employees must carefully manage both upside and downside risks throughout the duration of an employee's tenure with the firm, beginning with recruiting and ending with the employee's retirement, termination, or resignation. "Extracting value," by the way, doesn't mean working them as hard as possible and limiting benefits. Rather, the most productive employees are those who feel valued, and who recognize their job as an investment. As a result, they bring heightened passion, productivity, and focus to the table, helping the company become more successful. A good example is Tony Hsieh, founder and CEO of Zappos, who made "delivering happiness" a core strategy to empower employees and delight customers. This focus helped drive sales to top $1 billion. Zappos was acquired by Amazon for more than $1.2 billion in 2009.

Beyond traditional full-time employees, companies today must manage a growing number of "free agents"—individuals who see themselves less as employees and more as hired guns. These include independent contractors, temporary employees, and even full-time employees who don't feel beholden to any one employer. These individuals are having an increasing impact on today's working world. According to a 2015 study by temp agency Kelly Services, almost one-third of all workers identify as free agents.[6]

Companies operating in unionized industries face additional risks: strikes, wage contracts, and pension liability. Large-scale union strikes, while less common now than in the past, remain disruptive and costly. The recent strike of nearly 40,000 Verizon workers cost investors 5 to 7 cents per share according to CFO Fran Shammo,[7] or up to $285 million.

As Peter Drucker has said: "Companies have to attract people, hold people, recognize and reward people, motivate people, and serve and satisfy people."[8] Effective employee management not only saves unnecessary cost due to turnover, but also generates value for the company and its shareholders. Let's have a look at best practices for internal corporate governance as well as ways to keep employees engaged with the firm at every interaction: selection, retention, and development.

Employee Selection   The first HR challenge companies face is hiring the right employees. The risk involved in hiring the wrong employees can be tremendous. In an extreme case, such as that of a rogue trader, one hiring mistake can bring down an entire company. For many years, companies such as Fidelity Investments and Disney have instituted background checks as part of their pre-employment screening process. Today it has become standard practice for even small to midsize firms.

Many companies would benefit from putting more resources and emphasis into recruiting. As the job market has become more competitive, companies have had to take more time and effort in hiring the right employees, who spend less and less time at any given company. While compensation is often cited as the top incentive for candidates to choose one employer over another, many recruiters see money as simply "table stakes" rather than a true differentiator. Instead, they focus on tangible and intangible benefits that relate to employee retention, such as a positive corporate culture and opportunities for professional development.

Employee Retention If hiring the right employees is important, keeping them is crucial. Employee turnover is costly; not only might valuable people, skills, and information be lost, but they may be transferred to competitors. Then, of course, there is the cost of recruiting and training new employees. According to one study, this lies somewhere between 1 and 2.5 times the salary of the open position; the more sophisticated the position, the higher the cost.[9]

One significant but all-too-often overlooked method of employee retention is developing a welcoming company culture. A survey by U.K.-based B2B marketplace Approved Index found that 42% of respondents have left a job because of a bad boss while nearly a third of them feel their current boss is a bad manager.[10] But bad managers—those who fail to recognize their employees, blame their team for failures, or micromanage—are likely the products of an indifferent or even toxic corporate culture. By contrast, environments in which employees thrive build company loyalty. Elements of a strong culture include openness to new ideas, employee recognition, respectful questioning of authority, professionalism, accountability, camaraderie, and collaboration.

Engagement is the other component to employee retention. According to a 2016 survey by HR software company Quantum Workplace, engaged employees are more productive, more profitable, more customer-focused, and more likely to stay.[11] The top drivers of engagement cited in the study include a belief that company leaders are committed to making the company a great place to work; that they are setting the right course; that they value people as their most important resource; that they will lead the company to future success; and that there is the opportunity for professional growth and career development.

Employee Development Developing a company's talent pool offers value to employees and employers alike. Training and education are investments that pay off with improved employee capabilities. Some firms go beyond specific job-related learning to support a wider range of professional development opportunities. One critical tool is succession planning. In addition to reducing key-man risks, succession planning ensures senior leaders and managers are prepared for the next phase of their careers at the company. This process may include training, job rotations, executive coaching, and formal professional certification and development programs.

Regulators

Regulatory compliance has become increasingly important for firms across most industries, especially after the financial crisis of 2008. With proliferating rules and regulations, maintaining compliance can be extremely challenging. In this section, we will discuss approaches for handling multiple, sometimes overlapping regulations, including several industry-specific requirements.

Many argue that the fear caused by economic turbulence resulted in a wave of overzealous regulation that smothers rather than protects, heavily burdening U.S. companies that are used to a more laissez-faire approach. Others argue that the lack of effective regulatory enforcement is what allowed the financial crisis to happen in the first place. Among the most highly regulated industries are financial services, pharmaceutical companies, healthcare companies, and energy firms (particularly those that deal in nuclear energy).

The new regulatory requirements have mainly focused on risk management practices, executive compensation programs, capital requirements, and disclosure rules. Consider the 2010 updated SEC disclosure requirement, which mandates that companies disclose the role of the board with regard to risk management in their proxy and annual statements. This new requirement is an attempt to enhance transparency into the governance and risk management practices of publicly traded companies. In addition, the SEC requires companies to provide a risk assessment of their compensation programs.

Dodd-Frank, also enacted in 2010, was designed to target the root causes of the financial crisis: lack of transparency, excessive risk-taking, and the too-big-to-fail conundrum. While its objectives are commendable, the document itself is an unwieldy 848 pages long. *The Economist* wryly quips that the only people who have ever read the document in its entirety are its correspondent in New York and the Chinese government.[12] The bulk and complexity of Dodd-Frank and similar regulations highlight the tendency of lawmakers to address all potential situations. Critics of such rules-based regulations argue that they are costly and ineffective, and suggest that "principles-based" regulations (similar to those in Canada and Europe) are more useful.

Regulators have subjected the banking industry to particular scrutiny. Banks are now required to hold more capital and liquidity reserves, and are also subject to entirely new regulatory bodies such as the Consumer Financial Protection Bureau. Other new requirements for banks include more stringent stress testing and orderly liquidation plans known as "living wills." Based on my work with banks, I would estimate that banks spend approximately 12–15% of their total operating budget on risk, compliance, and audit activities, up from under 5% prior to the financial crisis.

The new regulatory environment has created significant challenges for banks, such as how to allocate economic capital. In the past, economic capital levels calculated by internal models were almost always higher than regulatory capital requirements, but now, we often see the reverse. What are banks to do? Should they continue to allocate economic capital according to business needs, or do they allocate regulatory capital and simply treat the excess as a cost of doing business? Another challenge is how to balance regulatory requirements against sound business practices—since the former does not necessarily lead to the latter. The cost of risk and compliance has reached historical levels, especially at financial institutions. One of the key benefits of ERM is the opportunity to rationalize the costs and processes of risk, compliance, and audit activities.

Let's take a look at some practical ways to meet regulatory requirements:

- **Deploying technology:** Many software applications are now able to automate regulatory compliance, allowing companies to shift people and resources from satisfying regulators to managing the needs of other stakeholders. Many of these applications are cloud-based and offer linking capabilities, which can reduce error and time spent aggregating and transferring data.
- **Staying current.** Companies must also stay up to date on new and upcoming regulations. By keeping ahead of the curve, your organization can more efficiently make a transition to new regulations, even when that means reorganizing processes.
- **Monitoring compliance.** Improving your monitoring process will help keep compliance as streamlined as possible. While this might take some time to assess and address, it is well worth the effort. Updating your applications and your processes can keep your company on track to satisfy regulatory stakeholders.
- **Improving relationships.** Finally, regulators have some leeway in their examination and resolution processes. Companies should communicate the board and management's commitment to a strong risk culture and providing evidence-based assurance that effective risk, compliance, and audit programs are in place. Moreover, open communication channels should be maintained, formally and informally, to develop trust with the regulators.

Communities and Environmental Groups

These stakeholders include individuals or groups interested in social impact and environmental sustainability. They may include governmental entities, such as the Environmental Protection Agency (EPA), local communities, NGOs, or organizations such as Earthjustice or the Environmental Defense Fund. Like regulators, these stakeholders monitor and influence corporate activity for what is considered to be the greater good.

More and more, consumers, governments, and special-interest groups are judging companies on their performance in the areas of environmental sustainability and social responsibility. At the same time, sustainability has worked its way up from feel-good promotional efforts to strategic objective for a simple reason—it's good for business. As customers and other stakeholders demand transparent and effective sustainability efforts, companies are responding by making their plans public and publishing progress reports on a regular basis.

Executive Order 13693   Recently there have been major changes to the federal demands for sustainability. On March 18, 2015, President Barack Obama signed the executive order "Planning for Federal Sustainability in the Next Decade." The order set ambitious sustainability mandates for the federal supply chain and operations. These include reducing greenhouse gas emissions by 40%, making 30% of building electricity supply renewable, and requiring 50% of new passenger vehicles to be zero-emission, all by 2025.[13] This sets a high bar for federal contractors—and their competitors—to ramp up their sustainability efforts.

Creating an Environmental Sustainability Plan   In complying with these and other sustainability requirements, it helps to create a plan to foster environmental sustainability. Here is a roadmap to create a sustainability plan:

1. **Write a vision or mission statement.** Take into consideration key stakeholders' environmental concerns, as well as your own, and leverage them to create a sustainability vision for the company.
2. **Identify priorities.** Perform research inside and outside the organization to identify areas that can have a positive environmental impact. Then outline specific goals and targets based on your results.
3. **Implement goals.** Determine how you will implement the goals above, and set timelines for each.
4. **Create a reporting plan.** Decide what metrics you will use to measure your goals, how you will report on them, and how often.[14]

Having a sustainability plan will help your company both meet the expectations of environmental interest groups and regulatory stakeholders, and also increase transparency in internal operations.

Major multinationals, including GE, L'Oreal, and Unilever, realized early on that sustainability was neither a distraction nor simple public image posturing. Properly executed, sustainability policies promote faster growth and reduce risk, which benefits the company and its stakeholders—including employees, shareholders, regulators, and the communities in which it operates. In fact, sustainability touches every aspect of a company's ability to manage risk and grow its business.

The power of sustainability in driving growth transcends industries and geographic regions. For example:

- According to its 2012 global impact report, GE invested nearly $2 billion in research and development for sustainability innovation. Concurrently, its Ecomagination products generated some $25 billion in revenue.[15]
- Consumer products giant Procter & Gamble surpassed its goal of $50 billion in cumulative sales of Sustainable Innovation Products by $2 billion in 2012.[16]
- German power and healthcare conglomerate Siemens reported in 2013 that revenue from its environmental portfolio equaled 46% of total sales.[17]
- Unilever, the Anglo-Dutch consumer products group, has rooted its entire growth strategy in the principles of sustainability. As a result, between 2008 and 2012 Unilever increased sales by 30%, beating its major competitors.[18]

These companies are growing in no small part because they embrace sustainability and position themselves as good corporate citizens. In fact, companies that downplay or ignore sustainability run a serious risk: Sooner or later, they are likely to encounter avoidable problems with regulators, investors, or non-governmental organizations, or inflict lasting damage to their reputation because of questionable operating practices.

Sustainability practices can represent a learning curve, if a worthwhile one. When PepsiCo came under fire in 2006 for excessive water usage in India, the company launched a program to achieve "positive water balance"—saving more water than it uses through sustainable agriculture initiatives, recycling, and recovery. In its *Corporate Citizenship Report 2010/11*, PepsiCo India reported saving 10.143 million liters of water while using 5.826 million liters in 2010.[19] The critics, who question

PepsiCo's accounting of water usage and savings, have not been completely silenced, but the company now has a global reputation as a leader in water management.

Integrating Sustainability into ERM Investors have come to recognize the value of sustainability as well. In a June 2012 green paper, DB Climate Change Advisors, a Deutsche Bank unit, reported that without exception, academic studies find that companies with high ratings for corporate social responsibility (CSR) and environmental, social, and governance factors (ESG) enjoy a lower cost of capital for debt and equity. High CSR and ESG scores are also strongly correlated to superior corporate financial performance by both accounting and market measures.[20]

To enjoy these advantages, however, companies must do more than make empty gestures. When sustainability first emerged as a management concern in the early 1990s (about the same time as ERM) it was a far cry from what was to come. Early policy statements did well to address environmental stewardship but fell short of establishing measurable targets and success metrics.

A modern sustainability policy is both broader in scope yet more focused—incorporating quantifiable objectives and target dates for employee health and safety, environmental impact, corporate governance, shareholder relations, and community outreach.

Sports apparel giant Nike has developed a new method for making running shoes that cuts waste by about 80% compared to traditional methods. Additionally, they developed a new waterless dyeing process that could reduce its water usage by up to 5%. Initiatives like these illustrate how sustainability can be a win-win proposition that contributes to both a company's success and desirable societal goals.

An emerging trend among sustainability leaders takes the concept one step further—to strive for a net positive impact. For example, BT, the U.K. telecommunications service provider, estimated that in 2013, its total carbon emissions roughly matched the emissions its products and services helped customers avoid. By 2020, BT aims to help customers reduce carbon emissions by at least three times that amount.[21]

Although many companies now recognize how important sustainability is, few have yet to incorporate it in their ERM frameworks. However, as illustrated above, sustainability does involve significant strategic, business, and operational risks, which can be addressed through:

- **Governance and policy:** How should the board and management be organized to provide effective risk governance and oversight? What policies should be established to communicate expectations and risk tolerance levels?

- **Risk assessment and quantification:** How should the company make more informed, risk-based business decisions?
- **Risk management:** What strategies should the company implement to optimize its risk/return profile?
- **Reporting, monitoring, and feedback:** How should board and management reports be structured to provide effective monitoring of risk, including objective feedback loops?

Sustainability leaders recognize a symbiotic relationship between the market for their products and their roles in society at large. In fact, a company today ignores social and environmental impact at its peril. Integrating sustainability into ERM puts companies in control of their destinies, enabling them to be proactive and forestall stakeholder pressures that might otherwise pose a threat to existing operations or future growth. Moreover, companies with strong sustainability track records represent more attractive employment for a workforce (e.g., Millennials) that is growing more concerned about these issues.

Stock Exchanges and Rating Agencies

Beyond government regulators, private organizations such as stock exchanges and rating agencies also impose requirements that companies must meet in order to participate or earn a certain level of accreditation. Each exchange, for example, sets its own standards for listing and trading stock including minimum financial and business standards. The exchanges also set criteria for delisting.

Credit rating agencies such as Standard & Poor's (S&P) and Moody's have become increasingly focused on companies' ERM efforts over the past decade. This makes intuitive sense—a credit rating represents the probability of default or the relationship between capital and risk. ERM provides organizations with enhanced capabilities to protect their capital base from unexpected loss. In fact, a reasonable measure of risk appetite is a company's target credit rating or its market-based proxies (e.g., debt or credit default swap spreads). An effective ERM program also offers some assurance that a rating, once issued, will remain accurate for a reasonable length of time.

In 2005, S&P developed a series of ratings criteria related to ERM practices. Through this evaluation, S&P rates companies as "excellent," "strong," "adequate," "adequate with strong risk controls," "adequate with positive trend," or "weak."[22] S&P begins by examining the risk management culture at the firm. It evaluates the company's governance structure, overall risk tolerance, role and seniority of risk executives, and the caliber of the risk management professionals among other aspects. The goal is to determine as accurately as possible the role risk management plays in the organization's decision-making process.

S&P also evaluates the company's risk control processes to determine how well it identifies, monitors, and manages different types of risk, such as credit, market, and operational. In addition, S&P looks at how resilient a company is to extreme events. Areas of concern include stress-testing frameworks, scenario analysis, early-warning indicators, and event-simulation exercises.

Finally, the agency assesses the organization's methods for calculating strategic asset allocation, product risk and reward, risk-adjusted results, adjustments to dividend payments, and retained risk profile. In addition, S&P considers a firm's approach to risks that are currently immaterial but could have an impact in the future, such as proposed changes in regulation.[23]

At the conclusion of this process, S&P combines each subcategory's rating to calculate an overall score. It's fair to ask how accurate or predictive this analysis really is. To answer that question, S&P examined the stock price performance before and after the 2008 financial crisis of insurance companies that it rated for ERM quality.[24] Overall, companies with superior ratings performed better in both 2008 and 2009. For example, while the average stock price of companies with weak ERM declined by about 60 percent in 2008, firms with excellent ERM saw only half that decline on average. In 2009, the average price stock of excellent ERM firms rebounded by about 10 percent while the average stock price of weak ERM firms continued to decline by a similar margin.

Business Partners

Strategic alliances have become a critical tool for many companies navigating today's fast-moving, networked economy. An alliance can help a company speed up product introductions, obtain access to new markets, share the financial risks of developing a new technology, or profit from economies of scale. In fact, the number of strategic alliances grew by 50 percent in the three years prior to 2012.[25] However, there are abundant risks inherent in such agreements. Consider that 40 to 60 percent of these partnerships ultimately fail to achieve their goals, while 70 percent of joint ventures end in a sale by one of the partners.[26] Failed ventures waste a company's resources, causing it to fall behind competitors or suffer reputational damage. Other perils include loss of intellectual capital, conflicts of interest, and legal disputes over intellectual property rights. In order to avoid these pitfalls companies must manage risk during three critical stages: evaluating an alliance, finding the right partner, and monitoring progress.

Evaluating an Alliance A successful alliance begins with a specific goal to create value. Those born of desperation are more likely to fail. Consider a weaker company joining forces with a stronger one only to be acquired at an unfavorable price. Or two poorly performing companies coming together in the hopes of shoring up their competitive position.

Partnering with another company is typically a shortcut to achieving goals the company might otherwise reach through internal development, acquisition of patents and technologies, or vertical or horizontal integration. But shortcuts can be thorny paths. It's not enough for the goal to be achievable through a strategic alliance. In order to succeed, the alliance must be a better solution than the other options available.

When is that the case? In general, an alliance is suitable when both parties are contributing unique capabilities but internal development is prohibitively expensive or difficult. They may also allow potentially incompatible partners to work together without the risks of a full-blown merger.

Poorly organized or implemented partnerships can put intellectual capital at risk. Alliance partners may be competitors in one area who join forces for an initiative in another. On the one hand, mistrust could make necessary data sharing difficult. On the other, one or both partners may lose control of proprietary information. Before entering any alliance, then, a company should assess the risk involved in sharing information with their prospective partner. That will vary depending on the nature of the intellectual capital, the capabilities of the alliance partner, and the nature of the alliance itself.[27]

The automotive industry provides a familiar use case. An auto manufacturer must determine how best to obtain each of the 15,000-odd parts needed to assemble a car: Should it build them? Buy them on the open market? Or should it acquire the manufacturer? In many cases, none of these solutions are practical or financially viable. An alliance, however, allows the car and parts manufacturer to share information where advantageous and establish a reliable stream of transactions while leaving the management of individual processes to the teams that understand them best.

Finding the Right Partner Choosing an inappropriate alliance partner is a fast route to failure. Since an alliance partner must be compatible in a large number of ways (cultural fit, competitive position, legal status), it is crucial that those involved in the selection process screen potential partners on each of these dimensions. All members of the decision-making team need to agree on what the goals of the alliance are in order to make a coherent decision.

The first step is to establish criteria for evaluating potential partners. This ensures that important factors are not overlooked, provides support for the eventual decision, and screens out unsuitable candidates. Questions to ask in setting the criteria include:

- Do the two firms have similar interests and goals?
- What are the business and benefits for each firm?
- Do they have complementary resources and skills?
- Is each firm dealing from position of strength, or could one wind up exploiting the other?
- Do they have similar work styles, cultures, and business practices?
- Can they trust one another?

After meeting with each company, members of the selection committee might grade the potential partner on each criterion. The selection discussion should begin with the company that received the highest overall score, but that shouldn't be the only factor. It's likely wiser to go with a universally accepted second choice than a higher scoring one that raises serious reservations with some team members.

Monitoring Progress   Regular status checks are a critical if often overlooked component to a successful partnership. All too often companies give more attention to the selection process than maintenance of the subsequent relationship.

Undoubtedly there will be routine differences of opinion or reorientation of work efforts, but major reassessments are not out of the question. The goals and needs of partners are likely to evolve over the multi-year lifespan of most alliances. While it is important to evaluate the alliance at regular intervals and take corrective steps as soon as possible, participants should not be overzealous. Like any relationship, alliances often go through growing pains, particularly once the honeymoon phase has passed.

What's more, alliance projects often break new territory, meaning that standard financial measures of success may not apply at the outset. Rather than results, early evaluation should focus on the quality of the relationship. Not only is this the best time to correct any misalignments, it also sets the stage for future success.

One critical driver of success is consistency. Partnerships depend on harmonious collaboration and building shared intellectual capital. This delicate ecosystem is easy to disrupt with the loss of key players. High turnover within the alliance team is almost always a recipe for disaster, just as it can be for a company as a whole.

The evaluation, selection, and monitoring requirements discussed above extend beyond business alliances, but should also include all material third-party product and service providers. Given the reliance on business partners and vendors, third-party risk oversight and monitoring have become a critical element of ERM. Programs include risk rating based on business and operational impact, ongoing performance monitoring, annual reviews, risk acceptance and exception reporting, and termination contingency planning.

Institutional Investors

Institutional investors such as pension funds, mutual funds, insurance companies, investment banks, and hedge funds account for half of the trading volume on the New York Stock Exchange and so wield extraordinary influence not only with individual companies but also with entire markets. These giant investors are not timid about exercising their ownership positions to make sure corporate governance meets their standards,[28] while activist investors such as hedge funds may go a step further, wielding their voting rights to make significant changes to the company's structure.[29]

Institutional investors participate in corporate governance with a number of goals in mind. These include enhancing financial performance, proper board oversight, rules on voting and board membership, restrictions on shareholdings or exercise of control, appropriate disclosure, and proper execution of fiduciary responsibilities and published guidelines.[30]

Large institutions typically have entire teams dedicated to corporate governance who direct the investor's proxy voting. BlackRock, a publicly held for-profit asset manager, has a Corporate Governance and Responsible Investment (CGRI) team that acts "as a clearinghouse across BlackRock's investment teams and monitors as well as engages with the companies to help protect shareholders' interests."[31] The CGRI team consists of 20 professionals in offices around the world responsible for developing proxy voting guidelines.[32] Other large investors such as State Street Global Advisors[33] and Fidelity Investments practice proxy voting in similar ways.[34]

Pension funds, such as the California Public Employees' Retirement System (CalPERS), also focus on governance issues. CalPERS maintains a Shareowner/Corporate Engagement Program to intervene in companies that are underperforming in terms of stock price, financials, or corporate governance.

The deep involvement of institutional investors in governance issues makes them an important stakeholder in any company's ERM program. What's more, their interests typically parallel those of the risk management function. They push for strengthened governance policies and processes; they promote adherence to international standards of disclosure and transparency, and they insist that boards exercise their oversight responsibilities toward management—all primary goals of ERM.[35]

Proxy Advisory Firms

Institutional investors often hire large proxy advisory firms to provide them with information and recommendations. Their services include receiving proxy ballots, working with custodian banks, executing votes on their clients' behalf, maintaining vote records, and providing voting reports. Two proxy advisory firms, Institutional Shareholder Services (ISS) and Glass Lewis, dominate the industry. In a 2015 blog post, Tom Quaadman, SVP of the U.S. Chamber of Commerce's Center for Capital Markets Competitiveness, notes that these two firms, with their combined 97% market share, influence 36% of all proxy votes through their clients.[36] Quaadman goes on to decry the lack of transparency and potential conflicts of interest this arrangement can lead to. One firm, he points out, is owned by an institutional investor while another offers advisory services to companies it reviews.

In response to these concerns, the SEC issued guidance on proxy advisory firms in 2014 requiring disclosure of conflicts of interest as well as correlating proxy advice to economic return and the fiduciary duties of their clients. More recently, Congress has introduced legislation that would require proxy advisory firms to register with the SEC and make publicly available information about their advisory practices.[37] Firms would also need to describe any potential or actual conflicts of interest. This includes whether they engage in consulting services and the amount of those revenues, as well as a list of their 20 largest clients and how they prevent such clients from having "undue influence."

Activist Investors

Included among institutional investors are so-called activist investors. Activist investors may include "corporate raiders," hedge funds, venture capital firms, and wealthy individuals. They advocate strongly for significant measures to increase shareholder return, such as board and management changes, stock buybacks, dividend payments, mergers, or outright sale of a company.[38] Activist investors don't hold enough equity to force through such moves, so they must convince other major shareholders—that is, traditional institutional investors—to support them.[39]

For example, the mutual fund company Vanguard sided with activist investor Bill Ackman in a 2012 effort to replace the CEO and board of Canadian Pacific Railway.[40] Vanguard also allied with the hedge fund company Corvex, when it successfully organized a campaign to replace the entire board of Commonwealth REIT in 2014 in response to the company's poor performance and governance record. [41]

The relationships between traditional institutions and activist hedge funds are sometimes even deeper. Institutional investors may hold shares in activist hedge funds. This creates, in a sense, a division of labor in which large institutions use activist investors to promote changes that serve their mutual interest.[42] Recent studies have shown that activist investing outperforms stock indices and other investment strategies. For example, one study showed that in 2013 activist investing was the top-performing hedge fund strategy, producing an average return of 16.6% compared to 9.5% for all other strategies.[43]

MANAGING STAKEHOLDER VALUE WITH ERM

An organization can provide many types of value to a stakeholder. We've already discussed a number of these in the section above. Economic or monetary value may be the most common stakeholder benefit, but other forms of value still play an important role.

Some stakeholders, such as employees and customers, gain *extrinsic* value, which can be economic or non-economic. Employees receive compensation, and may gain career promotion and recognition. Customers receive goods and services, but they also gain informational and customer-experience value. These same stakeholders may also receive *intrinsic* value, which is not provided directly by the company, but arises internally. Examples include job satisfaction or learning transferable skills. Stakeholders may also derive value from people or surroundings as a result of business actions, for example, customer satisfaction, team success, or positive environmental impact.[44]

The Value of ERM to Stakeholders

Not only can stakeholders gain value from the organization, but the reverse is also true, particularly in the case of enterprise risk management. An ERM program that has strong stakeholder support has a far greater chance of success than one lacking it. With stakeholders on board, the value of an ERM program can increase exponentially, provided the risk function makes clear its value proposition to each shareholder group. Consider the ways in which an effective ERM program contributes to stakeholder value:

- **Aligning risk appetite:** ERM prioritizes the development of a risk appetite that aligns strategic objectives across the organization and among stakeholders. It then integrates risk appetite into daily business decisions.
- **Prioritizing strategy:** ERM prioritizes the organization's and stakeholder's strategic objectives by providing timely risk information necessary to their pursuit.

- **Providing early warning indicators:** ERM allows company leaders to identify potential risk events affecting stakeholders in time to respond.
- **Enhancing transparency:** Stakeholders, along with company leadership, can view risk information and integrate it into their decision-making.
- **Identifying opportunities.** Opportunity is a corollary to risk. In managing risk, companies and their stakeholders can take greater advantage of unanticipated opportunities.

These are only a sampling of the benefits of ERM for stakeholders. There are numerous others that can affect stakeholders and the company, adding value to both parties, as we'll see in the next section.[45]

Obtaining Stakeholder Support for ERM

Successful ERM implementation depends on a healthy risk culture and a solid understanding of stakeholder requirements. Gaining and maintaining stakeholder support is critical in sustaining the organizational commitment throughout the implementation period. Here are a few strategies to get stakeholders on board with a new ERM program:

- Identify the key stakeholder groups for your organization, as well as their needs and requirements.
- Seek out influencers within each group to serve as liaisons and advocates for the risk management program.
- Identify any opponents to the program within the company, and engage them in the earliest stages of implementation by asking for input to win their support—or at least neutralize their opposition.
- Keep stakeholders engaged in the ERM program following implementation via strategic communication with consistent messaging throughout the organization.
- Focus ongoing communication on ERM's ability to help the organization achieve its strategic goals.

Obtaining stakeholder support in this way will help implementation proceed smoothly and facilitate a more successful program overall. When stakeholders are engaged, both they and the company benefit.

IMPLEMENTING A STAKEHOLDER MANAGEMENT PROGRAM

In developing and applying stakeholder management models, companies should first take advantage of other related programs (such as CRM and

ERP systems) that can provide valuable information or tools. While the discipline of stakeholder management is relatively new, businesses have always implemented programs to identify, monitor, and improve their business processes. These corporate-wide efforts produce detailed process maps and performance metrics.

As a starting point, the methodologies and results from these initiatives—identify key stakeholders, learn about their needs and expectations, develop positive relationships with stakeholders—can be used to gain a deeper understanding of the general scope and specific issues that the stakeholder management program must address. The development of stakeholder management models should incorporate the following steps:

Step 1: Establish the Objectives and Requirements of Key Stakeholders

The design of stakeholder management models should always start with the end goal(s) in mind: What are the key objectives for the company and its stakeholders? These objectives generally fall into three categories: business performance, financial performance, and compliance. Business performance objectives include product innovation; customer acquisition and retention; and market share. Financial objectives include earnings growth, risk-adjusted profitability, and shareholder value. Compliance objectives should encompass internal risk policies and limits, as well as external regulatory and legal requirements.

Step 2: Identify the Core Processes That Support These Objectives

Most companies view their businesses vertically in terms of operating units, support functions, product lines, or customer segments. However, companies must manage their business processes horizontally to address stakeholder management because many stakeholders interact with the company across multiple verticals. Consider the customer journey. Your customers' first interactions may be with the marketing department, then sales. From there, they may move on to customer service, support, and if satisfied with these interactions, go on to evangelize for the brand. How well is the company meeting stakeholder needs and expectations along that journey? Is it able to anticipate future needs? How consistent is the messaging along the way? Where are the stakeholder's pain points, and how can the company better address them? Where do their interests align with those of the company and other stakeholders? Where do they potentially conflict? By taking this perspective, risk managers can forge a mutually beneficial relationship between company and stakeholder at every point of contact.

Step 3: Define Performance and Risk Metrics, Including Goals and Maps

The company must define clear performance and risk metrics for each of its core processes. For a key software application essential to day-to-day operations, a company might set 100% systems availability as a goal and 99.99% as a minimum acceptable performance (MAP). By the same token, companies can consider stakeholders as risks that influence performance positively and negatively. They therefore require the same type of goals, MAPs, and monitoring processes as any other risk. Let's use the example of ratings agencies. In its risk appetite statement, a company may set a MAP of maintaining an investment-grade rating from the major agencies. It might further stipulate surplus capital and liquidity as a percentage of total requirements to support this goal. In this way, the company can monitor all of its operations against specific benchmarks. Should a process perform below MAP, management can intervene with corrective action. For processes that consistently perform above goal, the board or management may choose to raise the goal and/or MAP to encourage continuous improvement.

Step 4: Implement Organizational and Risk Mitigation Strategies

With a clear understanding of stakeholder objectives and the processes that support them, the company is ready to execute the appropriate stakeholder management strategies. These strategies may include:

- Training programs
- Communication plans
- Process redesigns
- Management restructuring
- Additional project governance
- Investigations and corrective actions
- Risk transfer through insurance programs

Risk mitigation strategies may also include discussion forums to resolve any misunderstandings or conflicts. GE is well known for its "workouts" in which cross-functional teams come together to discuss and resolve operational issues in an open forum. To highlight the importance of this process, senior executives typically attend the last session to receive an in-person report from the team leaders on how they plan to address any outstanding issues.

Step 5: Create Informational Value with Key Stakeholders

As discussed above, the ERM function can provide useful information and risk transparency to key stakeholders, such as:

- **Employees:** risk training, risk-based decision support (e.g., pricing), and continuous compliance monitoring
- **Customers:** risk/return information relative to customer objectives (e.g., portfolio construction in asset management based on investor objectives and risk appetite)
- **Business partners:** performance data relative to service-level agreements
- **Regulators:** risk, audit, and corporate compliance reports that can support regulatory oversight and examination processes
- **Stock exchanges and rating agencies:** corporate performance against corporate governance and listing requirements, as well as forecasted and stressed debt-service capabilities
- **Institutional investors and proxy advisory firms:** risk-adjusted performance, stock performance, and corporate governance information
- **Communities and environmental groups:** social and environmental performance data

As discussed in this chapter, meeting stakeholder expectations and informational needs will result not only in improved stakeholder relationships but also better corporate performance. Risk managers can also gain valuable information on key opportunities and emerging risks from stakeholders. If organized appropriately, stakeholder feedback and information can provide early warning indicators and crowd-sourced risk assessment data. In the next chapter, we'll look at another side of the stakeholder-management coin: managing the ERM development project.

APPENDIX A: REPUTATIONAL RISK POLICY

The following is an example of a reputational risk policy, based on an actual document developed for a large and diversified company.

I. Summary

This Reputational Risk Policy (the "Policy") applies to the management of reputational risk for ABC Corporation ("ABC") and all of its business units, legal entities, and operations (collectively "ABC"). This Policy outlines the processes for the identification, assessment, control, monitoring, and reporting of reputational risk at ABC. The Policy applies to all strategies, products, services, events, and activities that subject ABC to reputational risk. This Policy applies to all directors, officers, employees, and contractors of the Company.

II. Purpose and Scope

The purpose of this Policy is to outline how reputational risk impacts management's strategic decisions, as well as how ABC approaches the assessment of reputational risks inherent in its choice of products and services, business operations, execution and interactions with customers, regulatory agencies, stockholders, employees, and key stakeholders in the course of doing business. Reputational risk is typically the result of an event that impacts the other major risk types that ABC is subject to: strategic/business, financial, operational, and regulatory/compliance risks.

III. Legal / Regulatory

ABC is committed to conducting its activities in accordance with the highest ethical standards and applicable laws and regulations.

The Company also strives to create a safe workplace, protect the environment, and foster a fair and diverse work environment. Accordingly, this Policy should be read in conjunction with the other corporate policies, in particular the Risk Appetite Statement, Code of Conduct, and Delegation of Authority.

IV. Reputational Risk Policy

A strong, cohesive and integrated governance structure for managing corporate communications, including social media initiatives, as well as a cross-departmental escalation and crisis communication plan provides an integrated approach to managing reputational risk.

A. Definition of Reputational Risk Reputational risk is the potential business and economic impact due to negative opinion as viewed by ABC's stakeholders, including customers, employees, shareholders, government, rating agencies, and the general public. Reputational risk is often a second-order impact from other risk events. It is also affected by ABC's response to such events and communication with stakeholders.

Reputational risk emerges as a result of other various risk types as follows:

- **Strategic/Business risk** is the potential business and economic impact arising from adverse business decision, corporate and business strategies, ineffective implementation of such strategies, failure to respond to industry and technological changes, and insufficient business diversification.

- **Financial risk** is the potential business and economic impact resulting from adverse movements in market prices and rates, borrower or counterparty defaults, and inability to meet cash flow requirements in a timely and cost-effective manner.
- **Operational risk** is the potential business and economic impact resulting from human error or malfeasance, failed internal processes or systems, or external events and disasters.
- **Regulatory/Compliance risk** is the potential business and economic impact, such as regulatory sanctions, financial loss, or damage to reputation, resulting from failure to comply with applicable laws and regulations.

In addition, reputational risk can emerge in other ways, including but not limited to:

- Errors in communicating with the investor community or the public at large
- The perception of customers or other external parties, such as stockholders, debt holders, external analysts, rating agencies, regulators, and mass media, based on their experiences dealing with ABC
- The public perception of other constituencies connected with ABC
- Systemic reputational risk failures at the industry level

B. Reputational Risk Metrics, Tolerance Levels, and Reporting A sound reputational risk framework includes a set of metrics and tolerance levels that support the identification, measurement, and management of reputational risks. While reputational risks are largely qualitative, quantitative metrics, such as frequency and numbers of complaints, can provide useful information in anticipating and managing the organization's reputation risk. The following metrics are examples to monitor reputation risks:

- Customer perspective
  - Customer complaints, time to resolution, customer feedback on resolution
  - Customer satisfaction and loyalty indicators
  - Customer service levels
- Employee perspective
  - Employee satisfaction, 360, or risk culture surveys
  - Employee turnover rates by performance rating
  - Diversity metrics vs. goals
- Shareholder perspective

- Stock performance vs. peer group
- Investor ratings
- Corporate governance ratings
- Bond credit spreads vs. similarly rated firms
- Credit default swap (CDS) prices
- General public and media coverage
  - Environmental and social performance indicators
  - Positive vs. negative press weighted by relative importance
  - Surveys of company perceptions and brand values
  - Social media posts
- Regulatory and legal perspective
  - Regulatory examination reports
  - Regulatory issues or violations
  - Legal complaints and settlements

V. Roles and Responsibilities

The roles and responsibilities for the Policy are as follows:

- **Board of directors:** reviewing, challenging, and approving this Policy on at least an annual basis; and providing oversight of the CEO as the owner of the reputational risk of ABC
- **ERM function:** providing oversight and administration of this Policy, including monitoring compliance with this Policy and providing reports to management and the Board
- **Business and operating units (first line of defense):** identifying, assessing, managing reputational risks and reporting those risks to the ERM function
- **Corporate Communications department:** Overseeing and facilitating widely distributed internal and external communications
- **Legal/compliance function:** advising the board and management with respect to potential legal or other liability that could impact the Company's reputation
- **Human resources:** ensuring that employees read, understand, and acknowledge the Policy and related documents, and providing training programs that will inform employees of the value placed on ethical behavior
- **Internal audit:** planning and conducting internal audits of processes that impact reputational risks and providing such audit reports to the Audit Committee

NOTES

1. Toni, Laura. "Managing Reputation Risk: What Is Your Company's Reputation Worth," Deloitte, 2014.
2. "Mastering Revenue Lifecycle Managements: Customer Engagement Leads to Competitive Advantage," *Forbes Insight*, February 2016. Retrieved from http://www.forbes.com/forbesinsights/servicesource/index.html.
3. Frenz, Helena. "Don: Need to Ensure that Customers Are Fully Satisfied," *Business Times*, February 8, 1999.
4. Reichheld, Frederick F. *The Loyalty Effect*, Harvard Business Review Press, 1996, 33–37; Victor L. Hunter, *Business to Business Marketing: Creating a Community of Customers*, NTC Business Books, 2001.
5. Kaplan, Tamara. *The Tylenol Crisis: How Effective Public Relations Saved Johnson & Johnson*, Paul Griffin Communications. Corporate Communications Counsel, 2005.
6. *2015 Global Free Agent Research*, Kelly Services, 2015. Retrieved from http://www.kellyservices.com/Global/Free-Agent.
7. Nayak, Malathi. "Verizon Strike Seen Hitting Second-Quarter Earnings: CFO," Reuters, June 8, 2016. Retrieved from http://www.reuters.com/article/us-verizon-strike-idUSKCN0YU23X.
8. Drucker, Peter F. "The New Society of Organizations," *Harvard Business Review*, September–October 1992, p. 100.
9. "Don't Let the Talent Crunch Hurt Your Company's Chance for Success; Seven Tips to Reduce Employee Attrition," The Free Library, 1999.
10. Higginbottom, Karen. "Bad Bosses at the Heart of Employee Turnover," *Forbes*, September 8, 2015. Retrieved from http://www.forbes.com/sites/karenhigginbottom/2015/09/08/bad-bosses-at-the-heart-of-employee-turnover/#345ab9d64075.
11. Hackbarth, Natalie, Dan Harris and Hilary Wright. *2016 Employee Engagement Trends Among America's Best Places to Work*, Quantum Workplace, 2016.
12. "Over-Regulated America," *The Economist*, Feb. 18, 2012, p. 2.
13. Obama, Barack H. Executive Order 13693: Planning for Federal Sustainability in the Next Decade, March 19, 2015.
14. York, Peter. "The Sustainability Formula: How Nonprofit Organizations Can Thrive in the Emerging Economy," TCC Group, 2009, p. 13.
15. "GE Releases 2012 'Global Impact' Report," CSRwire, 2013. Retrieved from http://www.csrwire.com/press_releases/35851-GE-Releases-2012-Global-Impact-Report.
16. *P&G 2012 Sustainability Overview*, The Procter & Gamble Company, 2013. Retrieved from http://www.pg.com/en_US/downloads/sustainability/reports/PG_2012_Sustainability_Overview.pdf.
17. *Environmental Portfolio Report 2013*, Siemens AG, 2013. Retrieved from http://www.siemens.com/sustainability/pool/de/umweltportfolio/ep_report.pdf.

18. "Unilever Sustainable Living Plan Helping to Drive Growth," Press release, Unilever, 2013. Retrieved from https://www.unilever.com/news/press-releases/2013/13-04-22-Unilever-Sustainable-Living-Plan-helping-to-drive-growth.html?criteria=year%3d2013%26topics%3d408268.

19. *Corporate Citizenship Report 2010/11*, PepsiCo India, 2011. Retrieved from http://www.pepsico.com/Download/India_Sustainability_Report.pdf.

20. *United States Building Energy Efficiency Retrofits: Market Sizing and Financing Models*, DB Climate Change Advisors, March 2012. Retrieved from http://www.rockefellerfoundation.org/uploads/files/791d15ac-90e1-4998-8932-5379bcd654c9-building.pdf.

21. *A Responsible and Sustainable Business Leader: BT Better Future Report 2013*, BT Group plc, 2013. Retrieved from http://www.btplc.com/betterfuture/betterfuturereport/pdf/2013/Better_Future_Report_2013_Full_Report.pdf.

22. Murray, Mark. "Rating Agencies Are Positive on ERM," Willis Towers Watson, September 2013. Retrieved from https://www.towerswatson.com/en-US/Insights/Newsletters/Global/emphasis/2013/rating-agencies-are-positive-on-erm; "North American and Bermudan Insurers Continue to Step Up Their ERM Efforts," Standard & Poor's, May 3, 2011, 3.

23. "Methodology: Assessing Management's Commitment to and Execution of Enterprise Risk Management Processes," Standard & Poor's, December 17, 2009. Retrieved from https://welcome.willis.com/mcoroundtable12/BIOS%202012/CoolStuff/SnP%20Assessment%20Criteria.pdf.

24. "Enterprise Risk Management Continues to Show Its Value for North American and Bermudan Insurers," Standard & Poor's, February 1, 2010, p. 2.

25. Harper, Pamela S., and Harper, D. Scott. "Building Powerful Strategic Alliances: How Companies of All Sizes Can Increase Their ROI," Business Advancement Inc., 2012, p. 3.

26. Ibid.

27. For a more in-depth treatment of these issues, see C. Christopher Baughn, Johannes G. Denekamp, John H. Stevens, and Richard N. Osborn, "Protecting Intellectual Capital in International Alliances," *Journal of World Business* 32, no. 2, 1997, pp. 103–115.

28. Lumpkin, Stephen A. "Governance Of and By Institutional Investors" (presentation, 5th Round Table on Capital Market Reform in Asia), Tokyo, November 19–20, 2003.

29. Rock, Edward B. "Institutional Investors in Corporate Governance," Faculty Scholarship. Paper 1458, 2015. Retrieved from http://scholarship.law.upenn.edu/faculty_scholarship/1458.

30. Lumpkin, "Governance Of and By Institutional Investors," p. 12

31. *2013 Corporate Governance and Responsible Investing Report: Taking the Long View*, BlackRock, 2013, p. 7. Retrieved from http://blackrock.uberflip.com/i/300264.

32. *Proxy Voting Guidelines for US Securities*, BlackRock, 2015. Retrieved from https://www.blackrock.com/corporate/…/blk-responsible-investment-guidelines-us.pdf.

33. *Proxy Voting and Engagement Principles*, State Street Global Advisors, March 2016. Retrieved from https://www.google.com/search?q=Proxy+Voting+Guidelines+for+US+Securities&ie=utf-8&oe=utf-8#.

34. Rock, "Institutional Investors in Corporate Governance," p. 9.

35. Lumpkin, "Governance Of and By Institutional Investors," p. 13.

36. Quaadman, Tom. "Proxy Advisory Firms: A Journey of a Thousand Miles," U.S. Chamber of Commerce, November 16, 2014. Retrieved from https://www.uschamber.com/above-the-fold/proxy-advisory-firms-journey-thousand-miles.

37. Chiu, Ning. "Proposed Legislation on Oversight of Proxy Advisory Firms," DavisPolk, May 2016. Retrieved from http://www.briefinggovernance.com/2016/05/proposed-legislation-on-oversight-of-proxy-advisory-firms/.

38. Rock, "Institutional Investors in Corporate Governance," p. 26.

39. Ibid., p. 27.

40. Ibid., p. 31.

41. Ibid.

42. Ibid., p. 27.

43. Wood, John and Dysart, Theodore. "Assessing the Merits of an Activist Investor's Point of View," Transaction Advisors, June 2015.

44. Argandoña, Antonio. "Stakeholder Theory and Value Creation," University of Navarra—IESE Business School Working Paper no. 922, 2011, p. 1–13. Retrieved from http://doi.org/10.2139/ssrn.1947317.

45. "Articulating the Value of Enterprise Risk Management," *The CRO Agenda*, PwC, November 2014.

Implementing an ERM Program

CHAPTER 5

The ERM Project

INTRODUCTION

Implementing ERM is a time- and resource-intensive undertaking—a multi-year effort that requires foresight, dedication, and patience. Whether the project is the company's first venture into enterprise risk management or the latest iteration toward a more comprehensive and mature program, it will not happen overnight.

The implementation process involves an important balance between "hard" and "soft" efforts. On the hard side, the company must develop the ERM infrastructure: Formalize the policies, governance structures, systems, and processes. On the soft side, the implementation team must obtain buy-in and address change management requirements: Keep key stakeholders at every level supportive, committed, and engaged. Too much focus on the hard elements may create apprehension and pushback, which can lead to difficulty in adopting and integrating the program. If the team is overreliant on the soft elements, the resulting program could lack repeatable processes such as effective governance and adequate reporting. This can result in a lack of accountability and ownership, resulting in a program that is neither sustainable nor effective.

BARRIERS TO CHANGE

While effective ERM can add substantial value to the board and management in improving business performance, natural tensions and conflicts can represent significant barriers to sustained change and enterprise-wide adoption. Let's consider some of the common barriers in order to provide some context to the ERM implementation effort.

Organizational Barriers

Companies often face barriers to the cross-functional collaboration essential to ERM implementation due to organizational structures, mandates, and incentives. Let's recall the key objectives of the three lines of defense:

- **First line of defense:** Business units are focused on generating growth and profits (upside bias).
- **Second line of defense:** Risk and compliance units are focused on risk policies and limits, ongoing monitoring, and compliance with laws and regulations (downside bias).
- **Third line of defense:** The board of directors is focused on independent risk oversight (governance); the internal audit is focused on adequacy of internal controls and the integrity of financial statements (assurance).

These objectives may result in conflicts or "turf wars" between organizational units and functions. In my experience in ERM, I have seen first-hand the following examples of organizational conflicts:

- **First line and second line managers:** The former is concerned with growing the business and generating profits and the latter is concerned with controlling risks.
- **Finance and risk management:** Finance is a well-established corporate function while the risk unit may be the "new kid on the block." They may have different methodologies and perspectives on strategic and investment decisions.
- **Corporate oversight functions:** Control units such as internal audit, risk, compliance, and legal may fight over who has the ultimate risk management mandate.
- **Management and the board:** CEOs and business unit executives like their autonomy but the board's role is to provide effective challenge and independent oversight.

Psychological Barriers

Barriers to collaboration on risk issues can also be caused by cognitive biases, behavioral economics, and other psychological issues. Risks, by their nature, are messy and unpredictable. Managers like to be seen as being in control, which makes risk discussions difficult across an organization and especially with superiors.

Many companies define risk in negative terms (e.g., actual and potential losses, regulatory events or fines, worst-case scenarios). They ignore the upside of risk. This problem is exacerbated since business managers are naturally optimistic about their business prospects and tend to avoid negative conversations.

Risks that are highly improbable but consequential (black swans) and risks with long-term implications are often discounted or ignored.

Analytical and Data Barriers

As discussed in Chapter 1, risk is a bell curve. However, the methodologies used in management and finance often focus on expected value (e.g., NPV, IRR, discounted cash flow analysis, balanced scorecard). These performance metrics ignore the full-spectrum of probabilities and outcomes, or bell curve, which is required to understand a company's risk profile and make informed risk/return decisions. As such, the implementation of risk management tools and models requires significant education and training, as well as alignment with existing management and financial models.

Additionally, the qualitative and quantitative data requirements to support ERM analytics and reporting are substantial. Numerous surveys have indicated that the lack of useful data represents a key barrier to implementation. The use of proxy data can sometimes be a good interim solution. Over time, the ERM team needs to develop a risk data management capability to support the planned analytical and reporting processes.

The impact of these barriers and the appropriate solutions will differ by organization. Regardless, the ERM team should consider these barriers as part of the change management strategy in the implementation plan. The core elements of an effective ERM implementation plan include the establishment of a vision, obtaining buy-in from stakeholders, assessing current capabilities against best practices, and developing an ERM road-map. Let's consider each of these core elements in turn.

ESTABLISH THE VISION

An ERM project cannot succeed without a clear vision that sets the overall direction for the program. This may be expressed in a concisely written vision statement. Formulating and writing this statement forces management to clarify its ERM goals and avoids confusion among staff, who must set up the program's systems and processes.

Research studies have lent credence to the idea that putting goals in black and white leads to a greater likelihood of achieving them. This makes intuitive sense: being able to visualize the goal allows individuals to focus their efforts on achieving it. In our case, the goal is a successful ERM project that adds value to the business.

The key word is *visualize*. A vision is something more than a goal: It is the fully imagined (if yet unrealized) "end state" that may in fact comprise many goals. A vision is critical to successful communication, because it establishes a narrative that stakeholders can share and buy into. As it relates to an ERM project, a successful vision has the following characteristics:

- **It is specific.** The vision serves as the compass for the ERM project in order to guide the actions of the ERM implementation team. The vision should clearly specify how the business will operate with ERM.
- **It is measurable.** An ERM project with measurable time-based milestones, benchmarks, and goals lets management track progress and results. It allows for accountability and continuous improvement.
- **It is realistic.** Don't mistake *vision* for *fantasy*. If the plan includes overly aggressive deadlines or unrealistic goals given the organization's readiness to change and available resources, it is doomed to failure. The vision should also be appropriate for the size and complexity of the organization.

With these criteria in mind, those tasked with creating the ERM program should be able to construct a vision that describes how ERM impacts the business. The vision should include how ERM will affect the board, internal audit, risk and compliance, business units, support functions, and other stakeholders as discussed in the previous chapter. Each company should have its own unique vision. Certainly, all ERM programs must meet basic regulatory requirements and incorporate proven processes and standards found in published frameworks. But simply utilizing a framework "off the shelf" without adapting it to the company's unique needs and culture will not be sustainable in the long run.

When developing the vision, companies should determine who will be responsible for risk oversight and who makes critical risk management decisions. The answers to these questions help identify people who should have input on the shape of the program and the information it provides to various parties. For example:

- What is the company's overall business strategy and risk appetite? The ERM program must capture the appropriate business and risk metrics.
- What analytical inputs do key stakeholders use to make risk management decisions? The ERM program must produce the information key decision makers need.
- How will the company monitor the performance of risk management decisions? There should be feedback loops in place to capture and report on this data.

A strong vision is indispensable to the success of ERM, as my own experience shows. As an example: Some years ago a new CRO reached out to introduce himself after a speaking engagement. In the course of our conversation, I asked about his vision for the new role, what expectations the company had for the CRO, and what they expected of its risk management program. He didn't have clear answers to any of these questions and said they were focused on initial research on ERM practices. About a year later I read in a press release that the company had appointed a new CRO. In short, lack of vision can be terminal.

OBTAIN BUY-IN FROM INTERNAL STAKEHOLDERS

A successful ERM project results in more than a change in policies. It should provide the impetus for a broad shift in the way the company approaches risk. It increases risk awareness and intelligence throughout the organization and offers management and the board a fresh perspective on their strategic priorities and business objectives.

Buy-in is a "soft" but essential aspect of ERM. Many organizations begin the process of formalizing their ERM program at the request or demand of their boards. An increasing number of boards are embracing the concept of ERM and the underlying value it can create. A board's comfort level with various risk management approaches and strategies can be just as informative and telling as the organization's financial performance.

However, while it is widely understood in the risk management domain that ERM generates significant business value, getting the organization as a whole to recognize that may be a formidable task. One way to influence internal groups is to articulate clearly a strong business case for ERM implementation. The idea is to show how ERM will enable a more proactive risk management mindset, improve company performance, move the company forward, and generate a competitive edge.

Shifting the culture of an entire organization is far from easy, yet it is critical for the success of a new ERM program. People resist change, all the more so when the change appears to be unnecessary or even counter to their business goal. The ERM vision is the ideal tool for obtaining buy-in from internal stakeholders, but to communicate it effectively one must make clear to stakeholders the benefits they and the company will realize.

The Board and CEO

A top-down process of change management may be the most expedient, starting with the CEO and the board of directors. Why start at the top?

Because the CEO and the board set the tone for the rest of the company with respect to direction and priorities. Aligning ERM with the organization's strategy is essential to the program's value proposition, and it lends credibility to the initiative from the outset. An involved CEO and board can make the difference between success and failure by making clear the centrality of risk in the company's strategy as well as by holding management accountable for the ERM project's progress.

Management

The board and CEO may help to set the tone from the top but the support from all members of corporate management will determine the ultimate success of ERM implementation. In order to gain this support, the ERM project must demonstrate how ERM can create value in corporate-level decisions, such as strategic planning and execution; new product and business development; M&A analysis and due diligence; capital allocation and management; and risk transfer strategies. By helping corporate executives make more informed risk-based decisions, ERM will be seen not simply as a risk oversight function but also a strategic advantage.

Risk and Audit Functions

Winning over the traditional risk (e.g., credit risk, market risk) and audit functions requires an altogether different approach. These groups can easily see ERM as a territorial threat, so it is crucial to define roles and responsibilities from the outset. In fact, the introduction of a formal ERM program helps clarify such roles: The audit team focuses on monitoring internal and financial controls, while risk managers focus on forward-looking risk assessments, risk quantification, and risk mitigation strategies for known threats and potential risks.

Front-Line Management and Employees

Foremost, we must consider front-line management and employees. As the first line of defense against risk, their everyday actions directly affect how well the company manages and mitigates risk. While corporate policies and controls are powerful tools to shape the behavior of front-line managers and employees, it is not enough—particularly if they've had little input in its formulation. Rather, one should consider a multi-channel communication strategy to increase risk awareness so that employees go beyond simply following policy, to use their intelligence and experience to identify risk, ensure risk information flows up and down the organization, and develop smart solutions to common issues. A comprehensive education program, designed for all management and employees, creates a common terminology for risk, establishes a source of accurate information, and generates understanding of ERM. These elements also work to establish and mature the organization's risk awareness culture.

Achieving the buy-in of so many different stakeholders requires excellent communication and leadership skills. ERM project managers need tact and diplomacy—a high EQ as well as a high IQ. They must anticipate roadblocks and enlist help from senior management to sway parties who might obstruct successful implementation. Key individuals can make or break the success of the project, but once leaders are on board they can set the tone and motivate their direct reports to comply.

In my experience, the critical factor for successful ERM is senior management support and sponsorship. This top-down approach sets the tone for ERM. As such, it requires dedication and clear communication. I experienced this first hand during my first effort at implementing an ERM program. When I was hired in 1993 to be the CRO of GE Capital Markets Services, the division was in the midst of the start-up phase with aggressive growth and profitability targets. In order to ramp up the organization, the company hired a team of traders from a foreign bank, hoping to benefit from their industry contacts and years of experience. As part of GE Capital, with its pristine triple-A credit ratings, the new business needed to establish a comprehensive ERM framework—and quickly.

So I hit the ground running. I spent my first few months with my risk and operations teams focusing on the hard side of risk management—setting up policies and limits, analytical models, and an integrated system and reporting structure. However, I immediately came up against opposition, because the traders had never encountered such a controlled environment in their previous jobs. They didn't take risk management seriously and were entering only 80–90 percent of their trades. Each morning the risk reports were full of errors because they didn't represent the full portfolio of positions. When I went to discuss this issue with the head trader at the time, he rejected my authority and brushed me off. "We know the risk of our portfolio like the back of our hands," he told me dismissively. "We don't really need your system to tell us about our portfolio. Our team is busy building the business and making money. We will enter the trades when we have free time."

Frustrated, I informed the group president that I couldn't do my job without the cooperation of the traders. I have to admit, I was impressed by his response. He shut down all business operations for two days and put all of the employees through a risk management bootcamp at GE's corporate training center in Crotonville, New York. We reviewed all the ERM policies, why they were set in place, and exactly who was accountable for each step of the process. His decision demonstrated that he was determined to set the tone from the top. At the end of the training, he conveyed a clear message: We would run the business in a risk-controlled environment, and if the traders didn't change their behavior, we could and would change the traders.

That was a defining moment in GE Capital's ERM efforts. From that point on, the traders evinced a drastic change in attitude and we had 100 percent compliance with the ERM framework. In fact, the capital markets group was recognized as an example of best practice in risk management within GE Capital, and the company honored me with its Pinnacle award (the highest recognition for GE Capital employees). We went on to capture a 25 percent market share with no policy violations. My experience at GE Capital has taught me just how important it is to balance both the hard and the soft sides of ERM.

ASSESS CURRENT CAPABILITIES AGAINST BEST PRACTICES

Current corporate practices determine the starting point for any ERM implementation. The goal for ERM, whether a new project or a revamp of existing efforts, should always be to bring the most value to the enterprise and to enhance the resilience of the organization.

To extract maximum potential from their ERM projects, companies should look to industry leaders and best practices for inspiration and guidance. Otto von Bismarck once said: "Only a fool learns from his own mistakes. The wise man learns from the mistakes of others." This certainly applies to ERM, which depends upon learning not only from one's own mistakes but from the mistakes (and successes) of others as well.

The appropriate ERM implementation depends on whether the company is setting up a new program or updating an existing one. A new effort will focus on discovering external best practices, customizing them, and adopting them. An update of past ERM projects requires an additional step: identifying the current status of ERM components, determining how those components stack up to best practices, and deciding how to adapt them to fit into future ERM efforts.

When researching best ERM practices, companies will naturally focus on those adopted by leaders in their industry. But there are rewards for looking beyond this scope as well. This is particularly true of sectors that have been slow to adopt ERM, and thus have few best practices to draw from. But even if ERM is well established in the company's industry sector, there can be much to learn elsewhere. Risk incidents can be difficult to predict, yet still cause millions in damages. It is entirely possible that leaders in other industries may have already discovered ways to manage risks other industries haven't yet considered.

Mere mimicry does not suffice, however. Adopting best practices without customizing them to a company's specific circumstances, business goals, and vision is a recipe for failure. No two ERM programs will (or should) ever be the same. Industry leaders can provide invaluable guidance, but companies should not adopt practices blindly. Some best practices may not fit right out of the box and so require adaptation while others may not be relevant at all. A customized ERM program provides the most useful information to aid decision-making.

Another key practice in assessing current capabilities is understanding and accepting the existing level of ERM maturity, then setting goals and milestones to take it to the next level and beyond. There are numerous reputable ERM maturity models in the marketplace. Nearly all large accounting and consulting firms (e.g., McKinsey, Deloitte) have their own. An increasing number of professional associations (e.g., RIMS and the Society of Actuaries) have developed models as well. Any of these would provide a sound foundation for a current-state assessment. However, it can be difficult to identify what specific, actionable steps can be taken to develop the program from the perspective of these various models.

ERM is an evolutionary, dynamic process, encapsulating both defined structure, governance, and process as well as diplomacy, communication, and an understanding of an organization's culture. An ERM maturity model allows any organization to benchmark its current practices against best practices over different stages of development. The following ERM maturity model incorporates each of the seven key attributes of Performance-Based Continuous ERM, as described in Chapter 3. Figure 5.1 summarizes the core components of each attribute at each of the five levels of maturity, as outlined below:

> **Level 1: Crisis-Based:** Responsive and defensive in approach, crisis-based ERM is situational and intended to minimize the business impact of an actual or potential risk event.
>
> **Level 2: Compliance-Based:** This approach focuses on compliance with rules, regulations, and company policies and procedures in order to avoid the regulatory penalties and reputational risks associated with non-compliance.
>
> **Level 3: Control-Based:** A focus on bolstering internal and financial controls allows companies to better manage operational risks.

	Crisis-Based ERM	Compliance-Based ERM	Control-Based ERM	Tolerance-Based ERM	Performance-Based ERM
Frequency	Events	Regulatory Requirements	Annual	Monthly/Quarterly	Continuous
Scope	Tactical Response	Regulatory Defined	Operational	Financial	Strategic
Risk Appetite	Disaster Avoidance	Regulation Based	Internal Control Standards	Risk Limits/Tolerance	Dynamic & Evolutionary
ERM Objective	Minimize Impact of Crisis	Meet Regulatory Requirements	Minimize Organizational Failures	Minimize Financial Loss	Maximize Stakeholder Value
Risk-Based Decisions	Crisis Solution	Compliance Focused; Policies & Procedures	Process & Operational Controls	Risk Transfer Strategies	Strategic & Business Decisions
Monitoring and Reporting	Ad Hoc Reporting	Regulatory Reporting	Audit & Internal Control Assessments	Static Dashboard	Continuous Dynamic Dashboards
Assurance and Effectiveness	Crisis Resolution	Regulatory Ratings/Feedback	Audit and Internal Control Ratings	Policy Limit Conformance	Performance-Driven Feedback Loops

FIGURE 5.1 Performance-Based ERM Maturity Model

Level 4: **Tolerance-Based:** Proactive and deliberate, this approach operates by establishing foundational goals, measurements, and operational limits. It has a heightened focus on quantitative measures of risk, risk appetite, and indicators of potential risk issues.

Level 5: **Performance-Based:** At this level, the company has embedded each of the 7 key attributes of the Performance-Based Continuous ERM Model into the ongoing risk management activities of the organization. The focus is on improving business and risk management performance, including objective feedback loops.

Appendix A provides more detailed information on the ERM Maturity Model.

Integrating Performance Measures and Feedback Loops One key challenge for companies implementing ERM programs is how to measure success. It may be tempting to evaluate ERM effectiveness based on the achievement of development milestones, and the reduction or absence of risk losses and incidents. In the former, ERM teams often track their progress against plans and milestones. However, these input-oriented indicators do not provide objective measurement of whether the policies, processes, and systems put in place are indeed effective. In the latter, companies also track risk losses, regulatory fines, and other metrics that they would like to minimize. As one example, several large asset management firms track the operational loss-to-revenue ratio as a risk management performance metric. As another example, a popular metric of risk management in manufacturing is the "number of days since last accident"—a clear performance measurement of efforts to reduce workplace injuries. Such output-oriented indicators are useful but insufficient on their own. Companies that experienced significant losses and regulatory events, as highlighted in the Wheel of Misfortune in Chapter 2, often enjoyed periods of relative calm and good performance in preceding years.

In addition to milestones and negative events, effective ERM generates many positive results, which may include:

- Incorporating the total cost of risk in product pricing to ensure that risk-taking activities are appropriately rewarded.
- Increasing the speed to market by establishing more efficient business approval processes for new products and business ventures.
- Informing M&A decisions with respect to diversification benefits, impact on debt ratings and enterprise value, and the appropriate price to pay for an acquisition.
- Rationalizing risk transfer decisions (e.g., corporate insurance, hedging) and increase risk coverage and/or reduce risk transfer costs.

One of the most critical objectives of ERM is to reduce unexpected variances in business performance. Business performance can be measured in terms of profitability, enterprise value, and risk-based losses and incidents. Once these performance-based metrics are established, feedback loops can be implemented to effect continuous improvement in the ERM program. A simple feedback loop occurs if, when an organization experiences a risk event, it can see that specific risk was addressed in its risk assessments and audit reports. If that risk was not covered, then the efficacy of those processes should be examined.

I will explore feedback loops more thoroughly in Chapter 20, but for now it is sufficient to understand that embedded feedback loops are an indispensable tool for informing decisions throughout the enterprise, from line employee to the board. The feedback drives ongoing improvement in the ERM program. It can be used to make incremental improvements, to improve business efficiency, or even reshape the program to address risks previously omitted or emerging risk areas. Feedback loops depend on ERM performance metrics. There are two key considerations for each metric of the ERM program. First, how can one derive meaningful analysis from the metric? And then, how does the program adjust in reaction to the movement of this metric? These two questions will need careful consideration, and are key to the success of the feedback loop. However, once these are answered, just like the selection of metrics and many parts of the ERM program, they will need to be revisited to be sure that they are in alignment with current ERM program focus.

DEVELOP A ROADMAP

ERM implementation is a complex process that may take years to complete. Understanding and aggregating risk both horizontally and vertically is by itself a vast undertaking. What's more, many steps are dependent on the completion of others, and must take place in the proper order for greatest efficiency.

A roadmap can illustrate how the project will progress from the drawing board to influencing business decisions. Reaching the end of the roadmap does not signal the end of changes to the ERM program, however—that's where feedback loops come in.

The roadmap for ERM guides the implementation process from the vision and gap analysis to a mature program continuously improved by its feedback loops. Figure 5.2 provides an example of an ERM roadmap. A good roadmap will answer the following questions.

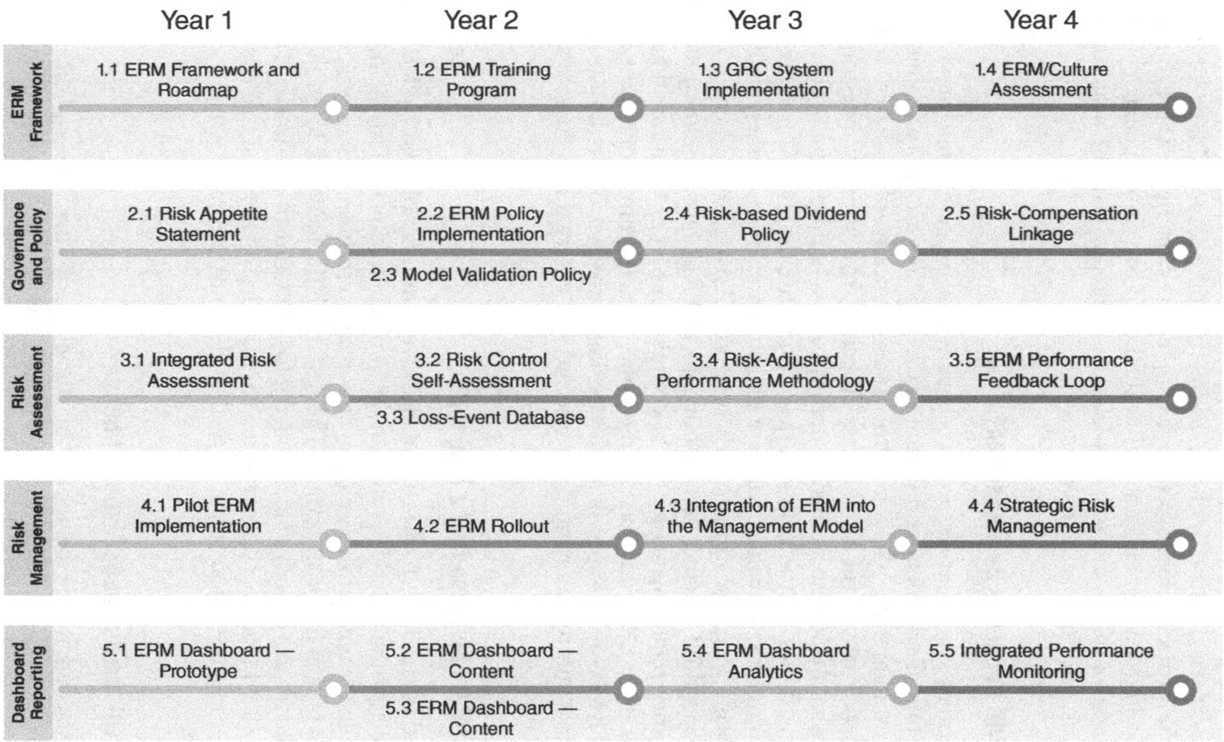

FIGURE 5.2 ERM Roadmap

Who Is Leading the Project?

A complex project such as ERM implementation requires clear roles and responsibilities. Those in charge of steering take responsibility for making sure the project achieves its critical milestones on time. The project also needs a high-level sponsor, either at the board or senior-management level. The sponsor plays an active role in guiding the project, monitoring its progress, and supporting its needs.

How Will Progress Be Measured?

Companies can measure progress against an expected timeframe broken down into checkpoints or milestones. Checkpoints are typically time-based, such as quarterly, while milestones are typically phase-based (i.e., the completion of certain capabilities). Together, checkpoints, milestones, and timeframe shape perceptions about the progress of the project. If checkpoints and milestones are too granular, they exaggerate the enormity of the project and clutter the timeline. Too few checkpoints, on the other hand, make it difficult to gauge the project's progress. A company's specific timeline will depend on whether certain portions of ERM face deadlines, including regulatory requirements for ERM completion or key decisions that would benefit from ERM analysis. At the same time, the timeframe must be realistic: ERM won't happen in a short period in the best of circumstances, and it's important to understand the internal and external influences that affect timeframe.

Who Will Be Involved in the Project?

Beyond the leadership roles outlined above, a number of stakeholders should be directly or indirectly involved in the implementation project. Work groups and pilot teams help to achieve buy-in and establish the approach ERM should take in the organization. They establish the feedback loops that monitor and improve the system during deployment and after maturity. The pilot teams should look for opportunities to gather lessons learned that can inform other implementation steps, as well as demonstrate early wins to enhance buy-in.

How Will the Company Manage Change?

As discussed in the beginning of the chapter, there are significant barriers to the implementation of ERM. How a company handles change can easily make or break an organization-wide endeavor such as ERM.

The implementation team needs to develop and share a thorough agenda to facilitate change management. Critical to the change management process in implementing ERM are the following five requirements:

1. A well-defined conflict-identification and resolution process
2. Integrated consensus-building across the program
3. A communication channel to allow for transparent information flow in the midst of implementation
4. Effective board and management training
5. Incentives redesigned to align to the needs and expectations of the ERM Program

The process must identify and overcome pockets of resistance, so the roadmap should include strategies for gaining buy-in from those parties. The implementation team should also keep in mind the time required to achieve buy-in and other change-related goals when building the roadmap so that it reflects realistic target dates for the checkpoints.

One proven tool for aiding in buy-in and communication is a proof-of-concept plan. Such a plan, while fairly consequential in terms of time and resources, can be invaluable in cases where established best practices don't fit the situation, or the company is not familiar with formal risk management.

What Capabilities Will the Program Require?

The ERM system may also depend on technical products—perhaps a new database—which need to be set up correctly prior to fully implementing ERM. However, companies can accomplish ERM without a technology solution. One approach may be to implement an ERM program manually first to build understanding, and then automate the process. A manual process gives workers and management a better grasp of what the technology solution does—and may enable them to step in to save the day should the technology go offline.

Yet another approach engages and embraces technology as a key component to program development and ERM maturity evolution. By incorporating technology within the ERM program at an early phase, the organization can enhance its use of technology as the ERM program matures. Essentially, technological sophistication grows alongside programmatic sophistication. An added benefit of this approach is that technology may be able to provide additional framework and structure considerations as organizations build out their ERM programs.

APPENDIX A: ERM MATURITY MODEL

Figure 5.1 provided a summary of the ERM Maturity Model for a performance-based continuous ERM program. The following sections offer more detailed benchmarks for the five stages of maturity.

Stage I: Crisis-Based ERM (White Belt)

This is the lowest level of maturity where no formal risk management process is in place. In Stage I the organization is mainly in a reactive mode. Risk mitigation is driven by risk events or crises and the objective of ERM is to minimize their financial and reputational impact.

- **Frequency:** Event-based risk mitigation which only occurs in urgent situations needing immediate attention.
- **Scope:** Limited predefined approach in addressing risk. Focus is largely on a tactical, pointed response.
- **Risk Appetite:** Focus on disaster avoidance rather than definition of risk tolerance and thresholds.
- **ERM Objective:** Minimization of impact of the risk event. Main focus is on loss minimization.
- **Risk-Based Decisions:** Decisions focus on addressing the crisis/risk event at hand.
- **Monitoring and Reporting:** No formal reporting and monitoring with limited ad hoc reporting as necessary.
- **Assurance and Effectiveness:** Effectiveness is measured with the success and cost of the resolution to the crisis.

Stage II: Compliance-Based ERM (Yellow Belt)

In Stage II the organization is building the foundational elements of ERM but the early practices are focused on existing or new regulatory requirements, perhaps in response to regulatory findings and fines. The objective is to achieve full compliance with regulatory standards and address specific weaknesses highlighted by regulatory exams.

- **Frequency:** Based on regulatory deadlines that the organization is under pressure to meet.
- **Scope:** Dependent on regulatory guidance and requirements and the necessary compliance to meet such requirements.
- **Risk Appetite:** Risk appetite and tolerances are based on the severity of regulatory actions and consequences.

- **ERM Objective:** Focus on achieving and maintaining full compliance with regulatory expectations within the specified timeframe.
- **Risk-Based Decisions:** Decisions are centered on meeting the mandated requirements in a cost-effective manner, as well as improving regulatory relationships.
- **Monitoring and Reporting:** Processes are designed to update the board and management on the progress against the resolution plan.
- **Assurance and Effectiveness:** Effectiveness is measured by the resolution of outstanding issues, readiness to meet regulatory requirements going forward, and the rating or feedback received from regulatory bodies.

Stage III: Control-Based ERM (Green Belt)

In Stage III the organization is establishing processes related to risk identification and assessment, internal controls testing, and risk mitigation plans to address control weaknesses. The objective is to increase risk awareness, enhance control effectiveness, and produce qualitative risk reporting.

- **Frequency:** Annual (or quarterly) process based on the cadence of risk assessment, internal audit, and controls testing schedules.
- **Scope:** Enhanced ability to manage and mitigate operational risks through risk assessments and control definition and operation.
- **Risk Appetite:** Internal control inputs and effectiveness outputs drive risk appetite and corresponding tolerances.
- **ERM Objective:** Minimization of operational failures in key business areas through control implementation and monitoring.
- **Risk-Based Decisions:** Focused on specific business and operational processes and the inherent risk present in those processes.
- **Monitoring and Reporting:** Monitoring and reporting-based internal control processes, procedures, and requirements. May include "heat maps" and risk assessment reports.
- **Assurance and Effectiveness:** Effectiveness is measured by audit reviews and corresponding internal control ratings. Feedback is provided by control failures and operational losses.

Stage IV: Tolerance-Based ERM (Brown Belt)

In Stage IV the organization is focused on developing quantitative models and key risk indicators to measure enterprise risks, as well as developing the appropriate risk transfer strategies to reduce tail risk losses. Moreover, a robust risk appetite statement provides definition and quantification of acceptable risks. The objective is to minimize unexpected variance in financial performance.

- **Frequency:** ERM process tends to be more frequent (typically monthly or quarterly), as enterprise risk exposures and tolerance levels are adjusted to new business and market conditions.
- **Scope:** Focus is to manage financial and operational risks based on a more robust metric-based risk management system.
- **Risk Appetite:** A formal risk appetite statement is established and enforced to define the types and levels of risk that the organization is willing to accept.
- **ERM Objective:** Minimization of unexpected variance in financial performance, including metrics such as earnings-at-risk, value-at-risk, and cash flow-at-risk.
- **Risk-Based Decisions:** Focused on risk transfer (insurance, hedging) decisions to manage financial variances within risk appetite levels. Risk-based pricing decisions to account for the cost of risk.
- **Monitoring and Reporting:** Monthly or quarterly reporting based on the risk quantification intervals. Static dashboard reports support board and management monitoring.
- **Assurance and Effectiveness:** Effectiveness is measured by conformance with risk policies and risk appetite statement, as well as the level of unexpected variance in financial performance.

Stage V: Performance-Based ERM (Black Belt)

In Stage V the organization has reached the highest level of ERM maturity. The ERM program exhibits all seven attributes discussed in Chapter 3. The objective is to optimize the risk/return profile of the organization on a continuous basis given the dynamic changes in the business and operating environment.

- **Frequency:** Continuous ERM process that provides early-warning indicators for business leaders with respect to risks and opportunities.
- **Scope:** Key risk focus is on those risks most directly tied to organizational strategy and business performance.
- **Risk Appetite:** Dynamic risk appetite is well defined in risk policies to balance business objectives and prudent risk taking.
- **ERM Objective:** Primary objective is maximizing stakeholder's value through risk/return optimization.
- **Risk-Based Decisions:** Embedded into business decisions at all three lines of defense, supported by real-time risk and data analytics.
- **Monitoring and Reporting:** A collaborative dashboard reporting system delivers ongoing risk and performance monitoring.
- **Assurance and Effectiveness:** Effectiveness is measured by the objective feedback loops tied to real-time data and outcomes.

APPENDIX B: PRACTICAL PLAN FOR ERM PROGRAM IMPLEMENTATION

This section provides an illustrative ERM implementation plan, including the key activities, deliverables, and timeframes for each phase. While each organization must customize its program according to its own maturity and requirements, the following plan should provide some useful benchmarks. This plan is generally appropriate for an organization that is currently in Stage III as discussed in the previous Appendix.

Phase I: ERM Framework Design and Development (6 months)

The key deliverables for Phase I include:

- Overall ERM framework, mission statement, and policy document
- Multi-year ERM roadmap with specific deliverables and milestones
- Risk appetite statement (RAS), including an initial set of risk metrics, risk tolerance levels, and dashboard reports
- Integrated risk identification and assessment methodology, including risk-control self-assessments (RCSAs) and independent assessments from the risk, compliance, and internal audit functions
- Risk quantification methodology that integrates organizational objectives, key performance indicators (KPIs), and key risk indicators (KRIs)
- Initial ERM scorecards and dashboards for workgroup reporting, management reporting, and board reporting
- Evidence-based ERM performance feedback loops designed to address the key question: How do we know if the ERM program is working effectively?

Step 1: Project Scoping, Planning, and Organization (Month 1)

- Establish an initial project plan, including scope and objectives, workgroup representation, deliverables, accountabilities, and target dates.
- Determine the appropriate governance and oversight requirements (e.g., board-level engagement and updates, ERM steering committee updates, workgroup updates, and overall project management).
- Meet with select board members, senior executives, and other internal stakeholders to understand their expectations and requirements.
- Update the project plan and organization as appropriate.

Step 2: ERM Education and Current-State Assessment (Months 2 and 3) The current-state assessment will focus on existing governance, risk, compliance, and audit processes, as well as the company's core strategic, business, and operational decision-making processes.

- Provide educational sessions on ERM to key internal stakeholders, including board members as requested.
- Review the key corporate and functional decision-making processes, measures of success, and performance management processes.
- Assess the current ERM, internal audit, and compliance functions, including risk assessments, risk metrics, information sharing, and reporting processes.
- Perform a deep dive into the current ERM program, including organizational resources, annual plans and goals, and risk analytics and technologies.
- Review board- and management-level governance structure and risk oversight committees, including committee charters, reporting processes, and risk oversight responsibilities.
- Assess the current set of risk management policies, including any RASs and risk tolerance levels.
- Conduct best-practice benchmarking visits to a select number of organizations within and without the company's industry.

Step 3: Future State Assessment (Month 4) The future-state assessment will focus on developing a clear vision for the target state of ERM, including an initial ERM program-implementation roadmap.

- Develop an ERM maturity model based on industry best practices, benchmarking visit findings, and regulatory requirements.
- Establish a strawman vision of ERM, including performance criteria and metrics with respect to the overall ERM program.
- Facilitate visioning sessions with workgroups to establish a consensus ERM vision.
- Review the ERM vision with select board members and executives to obtain their feedback.
- Develop an initial ERM implementation roadmap, including change management plans, resource requirements, and expected cost/benefit.

Step 4: Initial ERM Framework Design and Development (Months 5 and 6) Based on the initial ERM implementation roadmap, develop and implement the foundational components of the ERM program.

- Establish board- and management-level governance structure, risk oversight committees, and roles and responsibilities.
- Develop an ERM framework and policy, including RASs and risk tolerance levels.
- Establish an integrated risk assessment and identification methodology, including RCSAs, and risk, compliance, and internal audit assessments.
- Design role-based ERM dashboard reports that support key business decisions at the board, corporate management, business unit, and workgroup levels.
- Develop an integrated strategy and ERM monitoring process that links strategic objectives, KPIs, risk assessments, and KRIs.
- Determine the appropriate set of risk analytics, technologies, and other ERM tools. These tools may include (a) stochastic models to quantify earnings-at-risk, capital-at-risk, and cash flow-at-risk, (b) ERM systems, and (c) data analytics.
- Evaluate vendor-supplied systems and internal development capabilities, and determine buy-versus-build decisions.
- Develop an ERM toolkit that provides specific guidelines, best practices, templates, and practical examples to support functional areas in their ERM efforts (e.g., risk identification and assessment, RASs and metrics, dashboard reporting, loss/event data tracking).
- Establish an objective evidence-based ERM performance feedback loop.

Phase II: Pilot ERM Implementation, Risk Training and Culture (Months 7 to 12)

The key deliverables in Phase II include: (1) pilot ERM implementation, (2) revised ERM roadmap, (3) additional ERM training, and (4) risk culture assessment.

- Select functional areas for pilot ERM implementation, and secure management buy-in and support.
- Implement the ERM framework at the pilot functional areas. Based on the maturity of ERM at the functional area, these pilots may focus on specific areas of the ERM framework, such as risk appetite and/or dashboard reporting.
- Conduct postmortem reviews of the pilot implementations, and gather lessons learned and key success factors.
- Update the ERM framework and toolkit based on pilot results.
- Update the ERM roadmap and implementation plans, including change management and resource requirements.

- Provide additional ERM training sessions to various internal groups.
- Assess risk culture via a periodic risk survey to provide ongoing monitoring and assessment.

Phase III: System-wide ERM Implementation (Months 13 to 24)

Based on the results of the pilot implementations and revised ERM roadmap, focus should shift to support the system-wide ERM implementation. Key Phase III tasks include the following:

- Address the ERM program's key challenges and opportunities. This approach should leverage existing strengths while adding best practices, resulting in a comprehensive ERM program that includes process design and supporting technology.
- Rationalize the company's governance structure, including board- and management-level committees, to clearly define roles and responsibilities across the enterprise.
- Implement risk assessment processes that integrate top-down and bottom-up assessments, resulting in (a) prioritization of enterprise-level risks, (b) explicit linkage to system-wide and functional area objectives, and (c) reduced complexity and enhanced visibility in board- and management-level risk reporting.
- Develop ERM policies and RASs that clearly measure the board's and management's risk tolerance levels for all major risks.
- Integrate ERM into the decision-making processes at the board, executive-management, and functional levels. These decisions may include optimizing the strategic risk profile (board), allocating human and financial resources effectively (executive management), mitigating business and operational risks at a tactical level (functional area), and transferring risks through the insurance and/or capital markets (corporate and shared services).
- Enhance risk analytics, information sharing, and dashboard reporting through the implementation of new analytical tools and advanced technologies. The analytical and technology platform should support the business decisions discussed above, as well as provide effective board- and management-level reporting.
- Define clear performance criteria and metrics with respect to the overall ERM program. This will include objective feedback loops and consideration of integrating risk management performance into executive compensation programs.

CHAPTER 6

Risk Culture

INTRODUCTION

Think about it: Stepping into a car is probably the riskiest thing most of us do on a daily basis. Because of the inherent risks involved in auto transportation, policymakers have implemented numerous systems and controls to reduce the instance of accidents and mitigate their severity. Rules about what to do at stop signs and intersections permit drivers to cross safely each other's path; tools such as speedometers and fuel gauges facilitate compliance with those rules and promote intelligent decision-making; and safety devices including seatbelts and airbags reduce the severity of accidents. And yet every day, thousands of drivers fail to comply with these rules, often at the cost of their lives and the lives of others. Some run red lights or exceed the speed limit. Others drink and drive or text behind the wheel. Many don't wear seatbelts. Clearly governance structures and policies are of little use if drivers ignore or devalue them. Drivers must internalize the proper values and attitudes to make these policies successful. As a society, we need a sound driving culture.

Just as policymakers cannot maximize motor vehicle safety merely by enacting rules and regulations, corporations cannot optimize risk management simply by establishing oversight committees, audit processes, and risk reports. These processes and systems, which comprise what I call the "hard" side of risk management, become useless without the soft side: all the factors that influence individual decision-making and behavior. Together, these factors form the organization's *risk culture*. In a sound risk culture, everyone not only knows and understands the policies, but also shares the values behind them. Employees and managers alike are aware of risk and adjust their behavior accordingly. Together, the hard and soft sides of risk management determine the risk profile of a business. While the hard side involves *enablers*, which establish the capacity for sound risk practice, the soft side includes *drivers*, which impel the actual execution of sound risk practice. The dynamic nature of risk underscores the importance of developing a good risk culture. Since every risk is unique—and since risks are ever changing—having a policy on the hard side for every risk situation is no more feasible than having a rule for every situation that one encounters while driving.

By "culture," I am referring to a set of repeated, observable patterns of a group's behavior. It is shaped by a broad spectrum of forces: leadership, shared values and beliefs, habit, and incentives, both positive and negative. Culture in turn drives human behavior, hence its value to risk management. In a typical risk culture, people will do the right thing when told what to do. In a poor one, people may actually do the *wrong* things even when rules are laid down. But when a powerful risk culture has taken root, *people are likely to do the right things even when they are not told what to do.* By embedding risk awareness and accountability into a positive corporate culture, managers needn't spend a lot of time brainstorming policies for every last risk situation, but can instead allocate their resources elsewhere.

As you can see, I believe strongly that the soft side of risk management is at least as important as the hard side. Yet it was only following the recent financial crisis that firms have begun seriously addressing issues of culture. I can't say that comes as a surprise. Risk culture has long been a vague concept that practitioners and academics alike have failed to define with sufficient clarity. The chief reason for this failure is that employee sentiment is considered to be all but un-measurable—or at least difficult to measure accurately compared to hard numbers such value at risk or risk-adjusted return on capital.

In addition to policies, an organization must find other ways to foster a strong risk culture. Management should encourage intelligent risk taking, even if it results in failure, while showing zero tolerance for unauthorized and unethical behavior. Leadership is a key driver: The "tone from the top" is crucial to establishing honesty and integrity as paramount values. Trustworthy leaders, ongoing training, and clear communication all reinforce risk culture.[1]

In this chapter, we will attempt to correct this oversight by establishing a framework for individual decision-making and develop a toolbox for managing a business's risk culture. First, we will identify the key steps that each individual must take when making risk-related decisions. Next, we will see why human nature (as described by psychology and behavioral economics) and conventional business structures present imposing obstacles to each step. We'll also highlight the common deficits that managers wishing to improve a company's risk culture should address. Finally, we will take a look at best practices for measuring and managing these factors and consequently improving a business's risk culture.

RISK CULTURE SUCCESS FACTORS

Trying to repair a problem you don't fully understand is a fool's errand, and improving risk culture is no exception. Before we can develop strategies toward establishing a sound risk culture, we need to understand what goes into creating one in the first place. The circumstances surrounding each risk decision are unique, and erroneous practices can arise at many levels, ranging from a single rogue trader motivated by a higher bonus to a group of individuals using unsound business practices that have been accepted (or even encouraged) by management. Some risks unfold over the course of an hour while others take place over months or years. Despite the many differences, there are several common themes that emerge in the process of neutralizing or mitigating risks at the level of individuals and business units. We can distill these into eight key steps:

1. Hire the right people.
2. Set the tone from the top.
3. Make good risk culture easy and accessible.
4. Use an appropriate yardstick.
5. Understand the information.
6. Communicate the problem.
7. Act on it.
8. Assess the risk culture regularly.

We'll look at each of these steps in turn and identify the inherent obstacles that companies face while executing them.

Having discussed the importance of risk culture, we will now turn to how to create a strong risk culture. I noted earlier that the soft side of risk management seems difficult to hone because it resists quantification and objective measurement. Here we would benefit to remember the words of the philosopher Aristotle: "It is the mark of an educated man to look for precision in each class of things just so far as the nature of the subject admits." Aristotle meant that different fields, and even sub-disciplines within each field, require varying degrees of exactitude; we expect more atomic-level precision from a physicist than a biologist, and more cellular-level precision from a biologist than a psychologist. The same applies to risk management: The hard side deals with policies, systems, and limits—similar to science. The soft side deals with people, their values and principles—similar to art. Therefore, while we should still expect some quantitative measures when shaping risk culture, we can justifiably turn to qualitative measures and success stories from case studies as well.

There are useful parallels between sound corporate risk culture and sound driving culture in our society. In fact, we can learn a great deal about the art of molding a good risk culture by examining the process of creating a good driving culture.

Step 1: Hire the Right People

No one can legally sit behind the wheel of a car for the first time and jump onto the highway. The first measure toward establishing a good driving culture consists of setting up numerous barriers to entry: Age restrictions control for maturity and experiential aptitude, driver's education and paper examinations control for theoretical knowledge, and the road test controls for practical competency. The first way to prevent unsound driving is screening out unprepared drivers from ever getting behind the wheel in the first place. This will succeed only if the "hiring process" for approving new drivers aligns with the values and qualities that comprise a good driving culture.

Businesses can learn from this example. The employees of a company are fundamental to its risk culture being effective. The first step to establishing good risk culture is to limit whom the company hires. Studies have shown over 50% resumes contain inaccuracies.[2] Basic controls include employment and background checks. As a recent example, a simple background check would have saved Yahoo's board the trouble of ousting Scott Thompson, the company's fourth CEO in five years, because he falsely claimed a computer science degree.[3] But this is not enough—a growing number of companies also conduct behavioral and honesty testing to screen employees.[4]

A basic strategy for minimizing risky behavior is to prevent questionable job candidates from ever becoming employees. Since the specific values, attitudes, and beliefs of a company's business units define its risk culture, it would do well to screen potential hires for desirable attitudes, such as honesty and integrity. I've found that emphasizing the importance of references (and even asking candidates what they believe their references will say about them) strongly incentivizes the candidate to be honest about their work history.

Questions evaluating competency in core areas have become the standard in hiring practices. For a company aiming to open the door only to sound risk practitioners, why not include risk awareness as a target competency? Interview questions might include:

- In your last job, did you ever face a tradeoff between profitability and risk? How did you handle the issue?
- Describe the last time one of your superiors put forth an idea that you strongly believed was incompatible with the company's strategic objectives. How did you respond?

■ In your previous job, were you ever aware of a risk that wasn't being adequately addressed? How did you deal with it?

When a company refuses to hire a top performer who does not mesh with its risk appetite, it has succeeded in the first step toward developing a sound risk culture. As a bonus, screening for risk-culture fit will likely reduce employee turnover, meaning that the lengthy and costly process of hiring will consume fewer resources.

Step 2: Set the Tone from the Top

If you are a parent, I'm sure you try especially hard to display good driving behavior when your kids are in the car. You probably also become particularly frustrated when you see a police officer park illegally or make an illegal turn. What merits these actions and reactions? They come from our realization that the actions of senior figures and those in authority become the standard for acceptable behavior. Since the attitudes and values of these higher-ups often trickle down and influence others, they set precedents and therefore ought to be considered carefully.

In risk management, even more than other corporate initiatives, the involvement of senior management (and of the CEO in particular) is critical to success. Why is this? As we reviewed earlier, many aspects of risk management run counter to human nature. While people are eager to talk about their successes, they are generally much less enthusiastic about discussing actual or potential losses, particularly those related to their businesses. Overcoming this reluctance requires applied authority and power. The CEO must therefore be fully supportive of the risk-management process, and set the tone not only through words, but through actions as well. He or she must first communicate that risk management is a top priority for the company in presentations, meetings, town halls, and other settings. More importantly, the CEO must demonstrate commitment through actions, by exemplifying and embodying the values they espouse. Does the CEO actively participate in risk management meetings? Has the company allocated an appropriate budget to support the program? Are senior risk executives involved in major corporate decisions? What happens when a top producer violates risk-management policies? How the CEO and senior management respond to these questions will speak volumes about their true commitment to the risk management process.

Those at the top of the corporate ladder have a responsibility to embrace an open culture that gives people the freedom to voice concerns when they arise. If authority figures welcome critical opinions from those in lower positions and give them the proper consideration, they send a message that ideas will be judged on their own merit, no matter the source.

An effective practice to set the tone from the top is to articulate the key principles for strong risk management. As an example, when I was the Chief Risk Officer for Fidelity Investments, I established the following principles:

1. Business Units Drive the Car

   Business units are fully responsible and accountable for managing risk, with support from risk professionals providing tools and strategies for effective risk management.

2. Equip the Car with Instruments

   We must strive to increase the transparency of risk through measurement and reporting, and communicate exposures through escalation procedures.

3. Fast Cars Need Good Brakes

   We should set boundaries to avoid undesirable risk or behavior, as well as limits to manage our risk concentration.

4. Get to the Finish Line without Crashing

   We need to balance our business and control requirements, because risk management is a necessary but insufficient requirement for success. In order to be successful, businesses must strive for growth and profitability.

5. We Win or Lose as a Team

   Given that we must manage risks on an integrated basis—across different risks, processes, business units, and countries—risk management is everyone's job.

As another example, JP Morgan Chase, which is widely regarded as a best-practice organization in risk management, has set forth the following principles:

1. Defined risk governance
2. Independent oversight
3. Continual evaluation of risk appetite, managed through risk limits
4. Portfolio diversification
5. Risk assessment and measurement, including Value-at Risk analysis and portfolio stress testing
6. Performance measurement (shareholder value added) that allocates risk-adjusted capital to business units and charges a cost against that capital.

Some people may say that risk management is analogous to the brakes in a car—getting in the way of growth or speed. However, the fastest cars have the best brakes. Good brakes give the driver the confidence they need to go faster—safely.

Step 3: Make Good Risk Culture Easy and Accessible

Driving a car doesn't require detailed knowledge of the internal combustion engine. The third lesson that driving culture teaches us, then, is that easy driving is good driving. Two important ways of making driving easier are investing in human capital, and investing in driving infrastructure. The first way that the government can make driving easier and safer is by investing in human capital: namely, the knowledge of the drivers. Driver education courses, lessons, and public service campaigns about seatbelts and texting behind the wheel all serve to create competencies and habits that make safe driving easy.

Establishing a sound risk culture among business units is no different. Remember the story in the previous chapter about the president of GE Capital shutting down business for two days of risk training? The commitment to risk management he demonstrated was just the first step in improving the company's risk culture. The training he instituted provided core competencies that traders lacked. A major obstacle toward sound risk practice is the lack of risk knowledge and awareness. For CEOs wishing to improve their company's risk culture, workshops and training programs are a necessary first step. Between these training programs, executives should make sure to communicate the importance of risk management and risk culture throughout the organization.

The second way driving can be made easier is by investing in the right infrastructure. Imagine what the accident rate would be if cars lacked speedometers or freeways lacked speed limits, or if those tools were inconvenient to access? Auto designers have given careful thought to creating dashboards that communicate critical data at a glance to reduce this risk. All of these tools make driving easier by integrating information and allowing for well-informed decisions.

The value of integration applies equally in a business setting. By establishing an infrastructure that increases the flow of risk information among business units, management can ensure that decision makers have all the information they need. When risk exposures are correlated and move dependently relative to each other, their severity increases. How are business units supposed to respond appropriately when they lack the proper infrastructure to understand all the risks involved?

A study of retirement savings habits clearly illustrated the value of making the best choice the easiest one. In the study, experimenters measured 401(k) participation rates among employees and manipulated the ways in which employees could enroll.[5] When the 401(k) was presented with opt-in enrollment, only 40% of the employees joined. However, when enrollment was made easier with a simple checkbox, 50% enrolled. And when employees were forced to decide whether to enroll or not, enrollment climbed to 70%. We can interpret the last two cases as instances where (among other factors) the opportunity cost of a certain behavior is reduced, and we find that decreasing the opportunity cost of desirable behavior increases its likelihood. Increasing risk information integration, then, is akin to decreasing the opportunity cost of sharing important risk indicators.

Step 4: Use the Right Yardstick

Car owners face very high costs—from the cost of the car itself, any loans taken out for the car, gas, maintenance, and so on. Insurance premiums are generally some of the highest costs a car owner faces. As car owners become better drivers, they are rewarded. The insurance company measures a variety of behaviors to track and reward drivers. The fewer accidents and speeding tickets one has, the lower one's insurance premium will be. Making good driving appealing increases the likelihood that we'll practice it. The negative incentives are strong as well. Policymakers use negative incentives to encourage desired behavior: They set numerous rules and enforce them with penalties to suit the infraction, such as fines, points, suspension, and even jail time. Similarly, CEOs and board members should incentivize good risk management both positively (by spelling out the rewards of sound risk practice) and negatively (with strict policies against unauthorized and unethical behavior).

The measures a company uses (or fails to use) to track and compensate individual and group performance comprise a key driver of behavior. Most companies establish performance goals in terms of sales, revenue, and profitability, reinforcing the desired behavior with incentive compensation. But increasingly, management experts are recognizing that performance measurement should not be limited to these parameters alone, and have devised frameworks that take into account broader considerations. One such framework is the Balanced Scorecard, which augments financial measures with metrics pertaining to customer satisfaction, operational efficiency, and organizational learning. In the same way, if management wants to gain a proper risk/return perspective, it must incorporate risk measures into the processes that generate management reports and track performance. (We'll examine risk frameworks in greater detail in the following chapter.)

The most important tool at a CEO's disposal is compensation. It has often been said that people don't do what you *want* them to do; they do what you *pay* them to do. And, as we discussed earlier, a compensation scheme that overemphasizes profitability can set a company up for risk hazard far beyond its appetite. In order to prevent this, key risk metrics must factor into performance evaluations to reward employees not for the highest returns per se, but for the highest *risk-adjusted* returns.

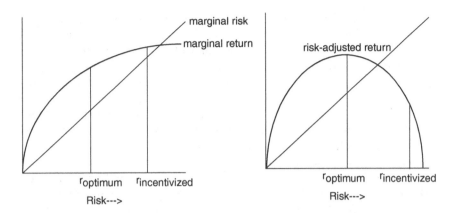

FIGURE 6.1 Risk Hazard

Figure 6.1 shows two different perspectives on revenue-based incentives. In the graph to the left, note that as risk increases, so does marginal return, though along an ever-flattening curve. Many companies evaluate and reward employees based on sales or revenue results alone, without considering risk exposures or losses. Now take a look at the graph to the right, which reveals *risk-adjusted return.* As you can see, at a certain point, risk-adjusted return peaks as risk increases before descending precipitously. As a result, this company is incentivizing its employees to expose it to increasingly higher levels of risk that may ultimately surpass its risk appetite. Such a company has opened itself to *risk hazard,* in which there is a fundamental misalignment between performance measures and compensation incentives of a company and the optimal level of risk it should take on.

The presence of *risk hazard* among companies is rampant. One need look no further than the 2008 financial crisis to see the adverse consequences that result from a focus on sales and earnings targets at the expense of risk. Too often, companies attempt to influence a single consequence of certain decisions (e.g., increased revenue) rather than the justification for those decisions (e.g., taking risk into consideration). They set aggressive earnings growth targets in the range of 15 to 20 percent per year. But are these targets realistic when the general economy is growing at 3 to 4 percent? What kind of pressures do they put on business units? How will people behave if aggressive sales and earnings goals, all tied to compensation, do not account for appropriate risk measures and controls?

Rules and exhortations are useless unless they are backed with fair and consistent enforcement, which not only corrects individual behavior, but also deters others from committing the same transgression. Drivers (or traders or accountants) are unlikely to follow the rules if they see others flout them with impunity. What message does it send to employees when management looks away as a rogue trader takes excessive risks simply because she's on a winning streak? Or when a business unit operates within risk policies without recognition or reward? In my practice, I've often found that management fails to distinguish between useful and reactive criticism. Consider two traders within a bank: One produces a gain but failed to adhere to risk policy. The other produces a loss but stayed within established tolerance levels. Management's response to these disparate results speaks volumes about the risk culture.

Effective risk management is about insight and foresight on current and *future* risks. Unfortunately, many companies struggle to anticipate emerging risks. Apart from our tendency to think in the short term based upon recent experience, we're all too busy focusing on the business at hand to give much thought to the future. But risk anticipation and modeling are essential components to crisis aversion. Consider Sarbanes-Oxley: While the regulations adequately responded to the recession of the early 2000 and the fraud and accounting scandals of companies like Enron and WorldCom, it failed to anticipate a key factor in the later economic meltdown—subprime lending.

Another difficulty in identifying risks stems from the fact that we tend to use *heuristic* strategies—shortcuts that facilitate decision-making at the cost of accuracy—when dealing with risk information. By contrast, proper risk management demands *algorithmic* strategies: well-defined steps that are more likely accurate. When identifying risks, many people succumb to availability bias, in which we judge things that we remember more easily as occurring more frequently or being more important than they actually are. For example, people often believe that flying has become riskier after news of a plane crash, when in reality the risk has not changed. Because we recall anecdotes with ease, they skew our perception of risks.[6]

Step 5: Understand the Information

Even for companies that collect the right data, a serious obstacle remains: understanding what that data actually means. We must be able to get from point A to point B without allowing our biases to lead us astray. Risk management demands objective analysis of probabilities and their implications. In this section, we turn to the shortcomings of human psychology that make quantitative understanding so difficult.

Something That Appears Certain May Be Highly Unlikely Take the oft-conflated terms *frequency* and *probability*. *Frequency* describes the number of times something happens while *probability* describes the likelihood that something will happen in the future. Generally speaking, people are better judges of frequency than they are of probability. We need to address this problem, also known as *frequency bias*, since a proper understanding of probability is essential to risk management. To appreciate this bias, consider this example: Imagine that you go into the doctor's office to be tested for a rare disease that affects only 0.001% of the U.S. population. You are told that the equipment used to detect the disease is quite accurate. If you have the disease, the test results will be positive 100% of the time. Meanwhile, the *specificity* of the test is 99.9%, which means if you do not have the disease, the tests results will show positive just 0.1% of the time.

The test results come back positive. Should you be worried? Most people give a quick yes, arguing along these lines: "If I have the disease, the results will always be positive. My results are positive, so I probably have the disease." The problem with this reasoning is that there is an enormous difference between the chance of testing positive, given that you have the disease, and the chance of having the disease, given that you test positive. In the situation presented, if you test positive, the probability that you have the disease is only 0.1%.[7] In the case of business management where a large portion of planning is contingent on likely scenarios, there is a lot of planning based around the expected, but not necessarily the unexpected or full range of possible outcomes. Risk management should be careful to properly analyze events past and present, taking frequency bias into account, and create multiple contingency plans; otherwise it is likely they will fail.

Something That Feels Highly Unlikely Could Be a Sure Thing Consider two scenarios. In the first, you're in a room with 29 other people. What are the odds that two of you share a birthday? You might reason that with 365 days in the year, any given person has a 1/365 (0.2%) chance of sharing another's birthday, so among 30 people, it is unlikely that two individuals share a birthday. In the second, you are given the name of every person in Michigan (roughly 10 million), and asked to randomly pick 10,000 names. What is the chance that at least one person gets picked twice? You reason that for each pick, a person has a 1/10,000,000 chance of being selected. For the person who was picked first, he has about a 1/1,000 chance of being picked again in one of the 9,999 future picks, so the odds of someone being picked twice are quite slim.

Both of those conclusions are incorrect. The chance of at least two people in a room of 30 sharing a birthday is greater than 70%. The chance of at least one person in Michigan being picked twice? Over 99%. You can find a full mathematic explanation elsewhere. The key point I want to make here is that the original reasoning above neglected the interconnectivity of the individuals in each situation. This is a common shortcoming of human perception, and it holds many consequences for standard risk practice. When risks are interdependent or *correlated*, their consequences are multiplied. In business terms, correlated risks introduce greater earnings volatility. If management fails to recognize the interconnectivity of the company's risks, it may exceed its risk appetite due to the wrong interpretation of the right data.

Other Problems with Understanding Data   The previous two examples highlight our inability to grasp the actual probabilities inherent in risk situations. But humans also have a tendency to inject entirely extraneous information into certain decisions based on preconceived notions. We will glance at the ones most pertinent to risk management now:

Framing effect: The same information, presented in different ways, can significantly alter how people perceive a situation. If people hear that a medical treatment offers a 95% chance of survival, they will be more amenable to it than if they learn that there is a 5% chance of death. Perhaps the most common instance of framing in the business setting is the sunk-cost fallacy, in which people make present decisions based on previous investments. For example, imagine that a manager has invested $100 in a machine that he values at $120. A negligent employee damages it during installation, rendering it useless. If the manager were to refrain from buying a new machine, reasoning that it would be an effective $200 payment for a $120 machine, he would be acting irrationally since the $100 previous investment is a "sunk cost," that is, unrecoverable under any situation.

Conjunction fallacy: Where do more murders occur each year: Michigan or Detroit? Since Detroit is in Michigan, it is logically impossible for Detroit to have more murders. Yet when a large sample of college students were asked to estimate the number of murders in either the city or the state, the median estimate of Detroit murders was twice as high! In another study, 89% of participants thought that it was more likely that a woman was a bank teller *and* active in a feminist movement than just a bank teller alone. In both cases, people based their estimates of probability on impressions and stereotypes, erroneously concluding that the conjunction of two events is more likely than either alone.

Anchor effect: Do you think that a porcupine has more or less than 5,000 quills? Guess how many. You probably guessed somewhere around 5,000, because of our tendency to anchor our actions around previous information. This effect even takes place when the information is entirely unrelated; people with higher Social Security numbers, after writing them down, tend to give higher estimates for the number of doctors in New York.

Step 6: Communicate the Problem

Once a business unit adequately evaluates a risk and establishes a response, it must relay this information to risk management and integrate it into its practices and decision making in a meaningful way. Often, this means discussing loss and other unpleasant topics, which few businesspeople enjoy doing. After all, those who go into business tend to be optimistic and ambitious, highly focused on success and what they are doing right. Successful people get promoted so it becomes a virtuous circle. But a large portion of ERM deals with what has gone wrong, what is going wrong, and what could go wrong. As a result, I often see risk managers characterized unfairly within their organization as Dr. Nos and naysayers. To use a complaint often lobbed at the Fed, risk managers seem to "take away the punchbowl just as the party gets going."

Of course, nobody wants to be a party-pooper. And if management is pleased to see what appear to be positive results from an initiative, individuals have little incentive to speak up when they have concerns about a looming risk. This attitude can infect an entire organization. How often have we read about financial institutions that turned a blind eye to the trader delivering 20% returns annually year after year—in a market that was growing much more slowly? Such miraculous results should merit skepticism at the very least, but more often than not, these seemingly invincible individuals are instead given a pass when it comes to established oversight and controls.

In a healthy risk culture, people are comfortable identifying risks and discussing mistakes. They're prepared to pull projects and reject ideas when the risks involved exceed a company's appetite. They don't simply roll over just because management is enthusiastic about results, nor do they assume that an individual's or business unit's past success guarantees positive results in the future. Sure, they might pull the punchbowl just as the party's getting started, but maybe it's because the partygoers have to get behind the wheel later in the evening.

Step 7: Act on it

Suppose a business unit has the right incentives to consider risks and properly understands the bell curve. It objectively examines the problem at hand and, appreciating its severity, communicates the problem to the pertinent actors. Surely then it would act appropriately? Not necessarily. The growing field of behavioral economics has spurred a departure from our classical assumption of man as *Homo oeconomico* by exposing major flaws in our ability to make fully rational decisions. In particular, the phenomena of *hyperbolic discounting* and *risk aversion* present major obstacles to sound risk practice in an otherwise strong culture, and we will consider each in turn.

Hyperbolic Discounting and Delayed Gratification There is nothing inconsistent about valuing something in the present more than something better in the future. For example, it would be rational to take a $100 payment today versus a $110 payment in a week if you could invest that $100 and, in a week's time, earn a return greater than 10%. However, it is inconsistent to change preferences depending on how far into the future the dilemma is presented. That is, we tend to give greater weight to immediate rewards, whether rationally or not. A funny example of this comes from gym memberships: Many people sign up for memberships as a cheaper alternative to paying for each visit, but end up going so little that they effectively increase their cost per visit. To see how this works numerically, imagine that exercising costs 80 points today (you exert effort and spend money), but results in a 100-point benefit tomorrow. (You feel better and improve your health.) Let's say that your bias toward the present means that you give full weight to events today, but just 75% to things that happen tomorrow. When we sign up for gym memberships, we are imagining the costs and benefits in the future, so we calculate $.75(100 - 80) = 15$ net points, and conclude that it is best to enroll. But on any given day, we feel the full weight of the dumbbells and less so the delayed benefits. On those days, we calculate: $-80 + .75(100) = -5$ net points, and procrastinate.

The implications for risk management should be clear. Even if we rationally calculate that creating value in the future would be objectively better (whether more profitable or less risky), we might wish to realize the profit immediately due to our biases. Moreover, we might rationally understand that investing in some future technology would be better for the company, but decide not to.

Prospect Theory According to a rational model of human behavior, people should make decisions with the highest expected utility. However, research conducted by Daniel Kahneman and Amos Tversky in the late 1970s shows that people act inconsistently with this model by exhibiting risk-prone behavior with respect to potential losses and risk-adverse behavior with respect to potential gains.[8] For example, when people must choose between a guaranteed $250 gain versus a 25% chance of a $1,000 gain (and a 75% chance of a $0 gain), they tend to choose the former. Yet when they choose between a guaranteed $250 loss versus a 25% chance of losing $1,000 (and a 75% chance of losing nothing), they tend to choose the latter. This directly interferes with a sound risk practice by cutting off the right tail of the bell curve (potential positive results) while fattening the left-hand, negative tail. This is a reflection of the problem we encountered with typical incentive structures. While many compensation incentives push business units to exceed a company's risk appetite, yielding a lower than optimum risk-adjusted return, our psychological preference for realizing gains immediately may prevent us from taking the appropriate amount of risk. The result, again, is lower than optimum risk-adjusted return.

Step 8: Assess the Risk Culture

Safe driving isn't just about teaching the right skills and hoping drivers will apply them properly. Policymakers must also take time to track driving trends so they may better respond to changing behaviors and implement appropriate measures. Take, for example, the issue of texting behind the wheel—a problem that didn't even exist until relatively recently, but which has emerged as a particularly deadly trend. Policymakers in nearly every state responded by banning the practice, while insurers and other organizations produce PSAs to warn drivers of the danger. Likewise, companies should track and record both internal and external trends and respond to the data with their own measures. One of the easiest ways to do so is to create a schematic of key risk culture categories—each with its own metric—and benchmark the results.

Few policymakers could have predicted in the 1990s that texting while driving would grow to become a serious, widespread issue. But continued research and trend analysis led to a quick response that has likely saved untold lives. In the same way, being open to and prepared for change in your company, your industry, and the economy at large will ensure that you face fresh challenges effectively well into the future. For this reason, a company must monitor progress to refine the behavioral change initiatives set forth by management. Consider an internal survey that asks the following questions:

- *Leadership.* Do the board, executive, and line management set the appropriate "tone from the top" with respect to risk management?
- *Accountability.* Do employees understand and accept their risk management roles and responsibilities? Are there consequences if they don't?
- *Challenge.* Does the company have a strong feedback culture in terms of raising issues and challenging existing practices? Do leaders encourage such views and challenges?
- *Transparency.* Is there a clear process to communicate and escalate risks? Do we use the right metrics and incentives to support risk-related decisions?
- *Value-added.* Is there an appropriate balance between business and risk requirements? Does risk management add value to the business?

The results of these surveys can help companies understand risk drivers as well as the effectiveness of their risk-management processes. As the data accumulate year after year, they measure the evolution of risk culture and promote swifter response to the changing needs of the business.

BEST PRACTICE: RISK ESCALATION

An effective risk-escalation process is a vital component of enterprise risk management. The objective of this process is not to undermine accountability for risk mitigation at the front lines, but to ensure that greater potential risks receive the swift, broad responses they may require. Proper escalation also enhances transparency and aids in data collection.

Risk escalation should never be left to chance. Rather, companies must set clear policies and processes in place to carry it out. Such policies exist in our everyday life as well as in business environments. Consider the "If You See Something, Say Something" campaign in the United States. The Department of Homeland Security has set a clear risk-escalation policy: If you see something appears suspicious, you should say something.[9] This initiative gives clear instructions—call Homeland Security and describe the following things:

- Who or what you saw
- When you saw it
- Where it occurred
- Why it's suspicious

Similarly, businesses must set clear policies to deal with risk. Corporate disasters, such as the BP oil spill of 2010, began as lesser, often preventable problems.[10] See Chapter 20 for a best-practice benchmark outline and illustrative content for a risk-escalation policy.

CONCLUSION

The dynamic and multiform nature of risk means that making rules is simply not enough to keep it in check. Instead, it is imperative that your company create a strong risk culture so that people know what to do in most situations even if they do not have specific instructions. By contrast, a poor or inconsistent risk culture could easily lead to ignoring the rules even when they're explicit. What's worse, many companies talk the risk culture talk, but when it comes down to brass tacks—that is, incentivizing behavior via compensation, rewards, and correction, they focus on results and ignore risk altogether.

Creating a positive risk culture is not as nebulous a process as many assume. Rather, it is a systematic endeavor that begins with a framework for influencing individual decision-making and follows concrete steps from integrating risk awareness into recruitment, setting the tone from the top, and establishing clear, consistent policies that reward positive behavior, correct errors, and punish transgressions. The fact is, however, that a company with a vibrant risk culture that embraces core values will not need to rely entirely on the rules, instead tapping into the human impulse to do the right thing.

NOTES

1. Lam, James. "Five House Rules for Managing Risky Behavior," *Harvard Business Review*, June 13, 2012.
2. "Fifty-eight Percent of Employers Have Caught a Lie on a Resume, According to a New CareerBuilder Survey" (press release), CarreerBuilder, 2014. Retrieved from http://www.careerbuilder.com/share/aboutus/pressreleasesdetail.aspx?sd= 8%2F7%2F2014&id=pr837&ed=12%2F31%2F2014.
3. Vincent, Roger. "Yahoo CEO Resigns Over Resume Discrepancy," Los Angeles Times, May 14, 2012.
4. Miner, John B. and Capps, Michael H. *How Honesty Testing Works*, Praeger, 1996.
5. Lord, Mimi. "Capitalizing on Inertia: Automation Boosts Retirement Savings," TIAA-CREF Institute, 2006.
6. Flying in general exemplifies the availability bias. Many people think they are more likely to die when flying than when driving, when the reality is the exact opposite. This is likely a combination of greater news coverage about plane accidents and the psychological impact of imagining a plane crash.
7. If you are still confused by the result, try reasoning with frequency instead. The disease affects 0.001% of the US population, which means that 3,000 people have the disease. If tested, all 3,000 would receive positive diagnoses. But a specificity of 99.9% means that if everyone in the United States (population 300 million) were to be tested, 300,000 people without the disease would be told they did. Of the 303,000 people with positive test results, only 3,000 have the disease, and our initial worry over the positive test result seems premature.
8. Kahneman, Daniel and Tversky, Amos. "Prospect Theory: An Analysis of Decision under Risk, *Econometrica*, 47(2), pp. 263–291, March 1979.
9. "If You See Something, Say Something" is a trademark of the U.S. Department of Homeland Security. See https://www.dhs.gov/see-something-say-something.
10. Zolkos, Rodd and Bradford, Michael. "BP Disaster Caused by Series of Risk Management Failures, According to Federal Investigation of Gulf Spill, "*Business Insurance*," September 18, 2011. Retrieved from http://www.business insurance.com/article/20110918/NEWS06/309189982.

CHAPTER 7

The ERM Framework

INTRODUCTION

In managing something as complex as a large corporation, or even a single function within such an organization (including ERM), it's easy to miss the forest for the trees. That is, one can quickly lose track of the big picture by getting caught up in the details. At the other end of the spectrum, too broad a view can lead one to overlook something important. In order to establish a structured approach, businesses have been implementing management frameworks that encapsulate the big ideas of a complex topic while breaking them down into discrete components. Early frameworks, such as the BCG Matrix (1968) and Porter's Five Forces (1979), focused on competitive analysis and strategy formation. Others, notably the Balanced Scorecard developed in 1987, focused on performance management and reporting. However, none of these frameworks directly address risk.

In this chapter, we'll begin by examining the nature and usage of frameworks in general. We'll next consider why organizations need a workable ERM framework that can coexist alongside (or within) these broader frameworks. Then we'll establish criteria to evaluate the usefulness of an ERM framework. I'll also offer my own take on an ERM framework that I think many companies can adapt for their own use.

THE NEED FOR AN ERM FRAMEWORK

I hope the previous chapters have made it clear why ERM is so important in today's business climate, but why do we need an ERM framework? Why can't current management structures simply incorporate risk management? Big companies have been functioning for a long time without ERM models, so it's a fair question.

The first part of the answer is that a framework is a communication tool. We use frameworks to transmit ideas in other areas of the business world; it only makes sense to use one for something as complex as ERM—especially since it remains a poorly understood topic outside the practice of risk management itself. Effective ERM requires a great deal of coordination and collaboration horizontally—among departments—and vertically, within organizational units. A simple framework helps each cohort visualize its role. For example, the three lines of defense against risk—business units, corporate management, and the board—are most effective when each understands the entire defensive structure. (We'll examine the lines of defense in complete detail in the next chapter.) An ERM framework also aids communication within a business over time, irrespective of executive turnover. It establishes a consistent basis for evaluating the company's risk management efforts and those of other companies in order to establish industry standards.

Frameworks help manage complexity as well. The number of risks that face organizations is ever-growing: strategic, financial, operational, reputational, legal- and compliance-related, and more recently, cybersecurity. These manifold challenges are interconnected, often in subtle ways that require careful analysis. Organizational complexity also factors into the equation, including meeting the needs of multiple business units and control functions, internal audit, and external regulators. In addition, an organization must have multiple lines of defense that interact dynamically even as they respond to risk events in real time. With this Byzantine level of complexity—not to mention the high stakes involved—organizations need a guiding framework to ensure that no one is duplicating effort and nothing slips through the cracks.

Strategic Frameworks

When designing a framework for ERM, it is helpful to look at management frameworks that have endured over time to determine the qualities that made them successful. Here are four strategic frameworks—three familiar, one quite new—that can serve as benchmarks for our own efforts.

BCG Matrix Figure 7.1 shows the BCG Matrix. This simple four-part matrix, created in 1968 by the Boston Consulting Group, illustrates the value potential of different business units across market growth (which consumes cash) and market share (which generates cash).[1] A star business unit is one that experiences both high growth and high market share. Cash cows are those that require little cash input yet hold onto market share nonetheless. By categorizing business initiatives in this way, a company can determine where to invest for the future. Note that the matrix does not offer a solution, but simply a clearer depiction of the issue at hand.

Porter Five Forces Figure 7.2 shows the Porter Five Forces model. Michael Porter of Harvard University devised this framework in 1979 to represent

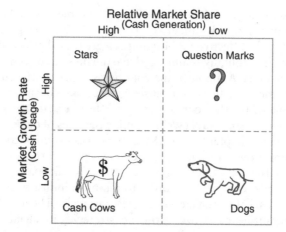

FIGURE 7.1   BCG Matrix
Bruce Henderson, *"The Product Portfolio."*
Retrieved December 26, 2016

The Five Forces That Shape Industry Competition

FIGURE 7.2   Porter's Five Forces
Michael E. Porter, "The Five Competitive Forces that Shape Strategy," *Harvard Business Review*, January 2008, p. 86–104

the competitive threats to a company within its industry.[2] Porter saw this framework as a more rigorous alternative to SWOT (strengths, weaknesses, opportunities, treats) analysis. Each of these forces affects a company's ability to serve its customers and make a profit. Two competitive threats (substitute products or services and new entrants) and two supply-chain forces (the bargaining powers of suppliers and customers, respectively) exert continual pressure, while a third competitive threat, established rivals, is both central and cyclical.

The Balanced Scorecard The Balanced Scorecard (Figure 7.3) was introduced by Bob Kaplan and David Norton in 1992 as a technique for evaluating management performance based on the organization's vision and strategy.[3] Its greatest innovation is including non-financial elements alongside financial ones, which makes it perennially relevant to today's holistic view of business leadership. At its heart is the vision and strategy

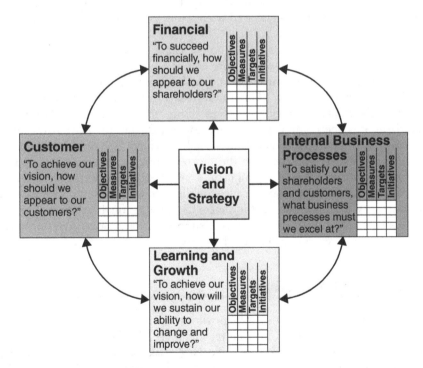

FIGURE 7.3 The Balanced Scorecard
Kaplan, Robert S., and Norton, D. P. (1992). "The Balanced Scorecard—Measures That Drive Performance," *Harvard Business Review* (January–February): 71–79

	Disruptive Innovation	Sustaining Innovation
Revenue Performance	Transformation Zone: Horizon 2	Performance Zone: Horizon 1
Enabling Investments	Incubation Zone: Horizon 3	Productivity Zone: Horizon 1

FIGURE 7.4   Moore's Four Zones
Geoffrey A. Moore, "Zone to Win," Diversion Books, November 3, 2015

of the organization, which inform the other elements of the framework: financial, customer, internal processes, and learning and growth. The Balanced Scorecard is valuable also for its structure, which emphasizes feedback loops in which measured results spur continuous improvement.

Moore's Four Zones   In his 2015 book, *Zone to Win*, Geoffrey Moore sets out a framework to help mature companies with a growing problem: defending themselves against paradigm-shifting technology that disrupts their incumbent franchises.[4] The framework (Figure 7.4) follows a portfolio model, allocating strategic resources along three investment horizons: Horizon 1 is the coming fiscal year; horizon 2, one to three years; and horizon 3, three to five years. Established franchises live on the sustaining side of this matrix and focus on the shortest horizon. Emerging businesses gestate in Horizon 3 as they might in a venture capital portfolio: Weaker ones fail quickly and inexpensively while stronger bets win additional resources. When an investment in that stage shows enough promise to bring to scale, it can move into Horizon 2 supported by greater investment to propel it into a revenue-producing business.

ERM FRAMEWORK CRITERIA

As you can see, one obvious problem with these frameworks is that they do not explicitly address risk. For that reason, there have been several attempts over the past few years to create a workable risk management framework. In doing so, however, we must not forget the lessons these enduring models offer. Like them, an ERM framework must be simple, comprehensive but not repetitious, balanced and integrated, flexible, and, of course, effective. Here's a closer look at each of these criteria:

Simple: When it comes to guiding principles, simplicity is key. Simple ideas can be communicated clearly and applied with accuracy. If a framework is overly complicated, it will be difficult to communicate, to implement, and to evaluate. Take the example of a roadmap. Drivers need enough detail to get their bearings and determine which turns to take. But if a map is cluttered with unnecessary information such as terrain and other details, it will be difficult to follow. Likewise, a strong ERM framework should provide enough structure to guide highly detailed decisions, but not be so comprehensive as to cloud the decision-making process. I believe a good rule of thumb for any framework is 5 +/− 2 (i.e., 3–7) components because research studies have shown that is the sweet spot for human memory.

Mutually Exclusive, Collectively Exhaustive (MECE): This attribute is composed of two parts that complement one another. First of all, the components of a good ERM framework are *mutually exclusive*, meaning that each is unique with no overlap. Second, the framework should be *collectively exhaustive*. It should be comprehensive enough to apply to every part of the organization and account for every eventuality. Returning to the roadmap example: A map should be exhaustive enough to be useful for any driver, whether a tourist, a road-tripper, or a businessperson. Creating separate maps for each driver's purpose would be inefficient, as it would generate a great deal of duplicate information. A strong ERM framework should be informative and applicable to every level of management without containing redundancies.

Balanced and Integrated: An ERM framework shouldn't overemphasize any aspect of risk management at the expense of others. An unbalanced framework could lead to a breakdown in communication or inadequate preparation for a certain type of risk. In addition, it must be integrated into the context of the organization. A framework may be flawless in theory, but if it clashes with the well-oiled operations of the existing management structure, it simply won't work. Each element of the model complements the others while also supporting the organization as a whole. A strong framework should resemble an auto engine, with each piece fitted precisely with the next to work in harmony, while also working with other components (steering wheel, accelerator) that the vehicle relies upon.

Flexible: Risk is by its nature unpredictable. Industry dynamics, business models, and disruptive technologies are constantly changing. Just as ERM processes must protect against unforeseen risk, so too must the framework encompass the unknowable while still embracing the organization's long-term vision. A strong ERM model will be broad and inclusive enough to remain relevant through changes in business plans and market conditions. While particular ERM strategies and defensive plans will evolve as an organization does, the framework should be a flexible template to guide that evolution.

Effective: Of course, we all care about the bottom line. An ERM framework isn't any good if it doesn't actually prepare an organization for negative events or bring opportunities to light. The effectiveness of a framework reflects its impact within the organization. This criterion should be applied judiciously, however, as the effectiveness of a framework relies heavily on how well it is implemented (which has its own challenges for evaluation). The effectiveness of an ERM framework can be measured by the extent it is integrated into business and risk decisions, as well as its contribution to producing the desired business outcomes.

CURRENT ERM FRAMEWORKS

While I believe that each organization should customize its own ERM framework, there's certainly no reason to reinvent the wheel every time. For that reason, a broadly accepted, standardized model is a worthy goal. Two such models are in use today internationally and across industries: the COSO ERM framework, and the Australia/New Zealand framework (AS-NZS), also known as ISO 31000. The two frameworks take very different approaches to risk management and are suited to different kinds of organizations. The COSO framework, frequently used by large corporations, is highly structured and detailed. ISO 31000 is less prescriptive and more process based.

The COSO Framework

The most widely used ERM framework globally comes from the Committee of Sponsoring Organizations of the Treadway Commission (COSO). Formed in the mid-1980s to help companies comply with new federal anti-fraud legislation, COSO is a joint initiative of five major U.S. accounting industry organizations, including the Institute of Management Accountants (IMA), the American Accounting Association (AAA), the American Institute of Certified Public Accountants (AICPA), the Institute of Internal Auditors (IIA), and Financial Executives International (FEI). In cooperation with PricewaterhouseCoopers, COSO published a framework for internal control in 1992, which it adapted in 2004 as an integrated ERM framework. The COSO framework was meant to be robust in its approach to risk and readily usable by management teams as they identify, assess, and manage risk.[5] The main distinguishing quality of this framework is its thorough inclusion of all possible risk levels and responses. In fact, it is so extensive that its complexity can work against it, making it unwieldy for some businesses.

In the spirit of full disclosure, I have been a vocal critic of the COSO 2004 ERM framework, both as a conceptual framework and as it is applied in ERM programs. My major conceptual criticisms centered on its complexity and that some of the components are not MECE (two of the key criteria discussed above). My major practical criticisms involve its application in risk assessments and the use of probability and severity ratings in prioritizing risks. Moreover, I do not believe the framework adequately addresses risk/return tradeoffs and the management of unexpected variance in business performance. However, I do believe the framework has contributed net benefits in ERM with respect to promoting awareness of ERM at the management and board levels as well as linking ERM to entity objectives.

Despite my known criticisms of the framework, the chairman of COSO, Bob Hirth, graciously invited me to participate in an advisory committee chartered to update and improve the framework. The new framework is scheduled to be released in 2017 after a comment and revision period. Out of respect to the work of the advisory committee and working groups, I will reserve comment until the new framework is published in its final form. At this point, I will say that the new framework addresses many of my critical comments. In the rest of this section, I will refer to the 2004 framework.

The Structure The concept behind the COSO ERM framework is a set of four basic entity objectives (See Figure 7.5). The framework is a cube-shaped matrix that breaks down these objectives in terms of control components and the organization's business structure. One dimension of the framework provides four categories of entity objectives:

1. **Strategic:** high level, mission-oriented goals
2. **Operations:** effective and efficient resource usage
3. **Reporting:** reliable information and communication
4. **Compliance:** conformity to laws and regulations

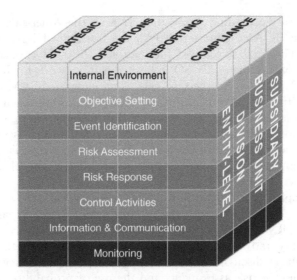

FIGURE 7.5 The COSO ERM Framework
"Enterprise Risk Management—Integrated
Framework," *Committee of Sponsoring
Organizations of the Treadway Commission,*
September 2004

The second dimension of the framework is a list of eight ERM components. While these elements could be considered sequential, COSO avoids such a view, instead emphasizing their interconnected nature. These include:

1. **Internal Environment:** shaping company culture, ethical values, risk perception and appetite
2. **Objective Setting:** creating goals within the four categories listed above
3. **Event Identification:** distinguishing between internal and external risks and opportunities
4. **Risk Assessment:** evaluating risk based on likelihood and impact
5. **Risk Response:** deciding whether to avoid, accept, reduce, or share risk
6. **Control Activities:** establishing procedural precedent to ensure appropriate response
7. **Information and Communication:** capturing and sharing information to support informed decisions
8. **Monitoring:** continually evaluating and optimizing business and risk processes

Finally, there is a third dimension to the framework in which all four objectives and eight components above are broken down by the structural elements of the organization itself:

1. Entity-Level
2. Division
3. Business Unit
4. Subsidiary

The idea behind the framework is to create a complete taxonomy of risk management, permitting evaluation and analysis at a granular level. For example, how optimized is the company's risk assessment when it comes to operations at the business unit level? What is the division-level internal environment surrounding regulation compliance? As you can see, a full implementation of the COSO framework is both broad and detailed.

Current Use In 2010, about 55% of U.S. organizations of various sizes and in numerous industries were using the COSO framework, with only 2% using the next most popular one.[6] COSO is a leading voice when it comes to compliance with legal codes. When the United States passed the Sarbanes-Oxley Act of 2002, which expanded internal control requirements for public companies, COSO was quick to publish an updated internal controls framework that incorporated the new legislation.[7] Companies that use some version of the COSO framework include Newell Rubbermaid, Alliant Energy, Mirant, and TD Ameritrade.

The COSO ERM framework is especially popular among very large corporations and banks, which must comply with extensive legal codes and face particularly complex, high-stake risks. However, the complexity that draws large organizations to this framework can be an obstacle for small to mid-size companies. Of 460 organizations polled in 2010, over 76% had a moderate or significant concern that the framework was overly theoretical, while 26% felt that the cube illustration was unnecessarily complicated.[8]

Referring back to our five initial criteria for an ERM framework, COSO is neither simple nor MECE. Consider the overlap between control activities and risk response or between information and monitoring. What's more, the sheer size of the matrix inevitably results in numerous similar or identical cells. How does the intersection of reporting and objective-setting truly differ from the confluence of information and strategic objectives? While certain corporations may need that level of nuanced detail in their ERM processes, it is difficult to grasp and to communicate to stakeholders.

The COSO ERM framework is also not very flexible when it comes to evolving needs. It is designed to account for any possible eventuality or change in business plan, so in that sense it has the potential to fit the needs of any business. But its rigid structure may result in a lot of management waste. It is like a one-size-fits-all life jacket: workable for big businesses, but awkward and unwieldy for smaller ones. And when it comes to a practical ERM model, we are looking for a well-tailored suit.

Nor is COSO as effective as it could be. The framework doesn't fully address the relationship between risk and reward. Remember that risk is a bell curve that indicates the relative probability of *all* outcomes, upside, downside, and neutral. The peak of the bell curve merely represents the likeliest of these outcomes. Visualizing risk in this manner offers opportunities to tweak the curve's shape to increase the likelihood of favorable results (for instance by reallocating resources) and reduce not only the likelihood of negative ones but their severity as well (for example, via risk transfer). With its strong emphasis on assessment and governance, COSO gives short shrift to actual risk *management*.

Finally, I have concerns about how many companies are using the COSO framework for their risk assessments. Most simply plot each risk against its probability and severity. While this has the virtue of simplicity, it essentially collapses the risk bell curve into a single point. Many companies compound this error by applying mathematics to their qualitative analyses, for example, multiplying severity rating by probability rating to create an overall risk "score." A healthcare company I once worked with had used an even more baffling equation: probability rating plus severity rating divided by 2. Their only reasoning? That a consultant had recommended that years before!

As discussed above, the new COSO framework will address many of these shortcomings. My purpose here is not to beat a dead horse. And the transition from the old to new framework will take time. Nevertheless, it is important for companies that are currently using the old framework to understand its potential pitfalls.

Australia-NZ Model (AS/NZS) aka ISO 31000

In 1995 a group of government and private-sector organizations from New Zealand and Australia assembled to develop and publish a generic and flexible model for risk management. They hoped that it could be adapted to fit the needs of any industry. Their efforts were successful, and the model slowly spread into the northern and western hemispheres. It was even revised and adopted by the International Organization for Standardization (as ISO 31000) in 2009.[9] The framework was updated slightly in 1999 and again in 2004.

The Structure Whereas COSO emphasized the interconnection of all aspects of risk management, the AS/NZS ERM model is a linear process

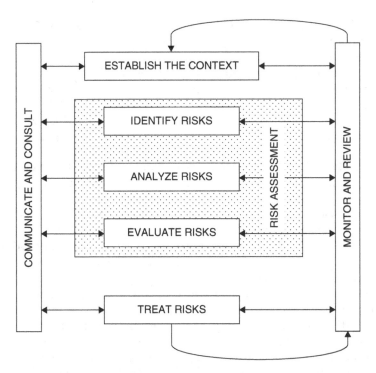

FIGURE 7.6 The Australia-NZ Model (ISO 31000)
Standard AS/NZS ISO 31000:2009, Risk Management—Principles and Guidelines

(see Figure 7.6). COSO urges a continual evaluation of one component in terms of the others; the AS/NZS model is cyclic and iterative. There are seven interconnected elements in the AS/NZS framework. The basic cycle of the model begins with establishing the risk context and progresses through identification, analysis, evaluation, treatment, and monitoring/reviewing before returning to establishing context. The monitoring and reviewing step also influences each stage of the ERM process, as does the first component of the framework, communicating and consulting.

1. **Communicate and Consult.** Communicating with internal and external stakeholders at each stage in the process is central to this model.
2. **Establish the Context.** Context includes business objectives, risk appetite, and criteria for evaluating risk.
3. **Identify Risks.** Identify where, when, why, and how events could prevent, degrade, delay, or enhance the achievement of business objectives.
4. **Analyze Risks.** Determine likelihood and consequences; identify and evaluate the effectiveness of existing controls.

5. **Evaluate Risks.** Prioritize risks by measuring them with the pre-established criteria and consider the potential benefits and adverse outcomes.
6. **Treat Risks.** Develop and implement specific cost-effective strategies and action plans for increasing potential benefits and reducing potential costs.
7. **Monitor and Review.** Monitor the effectiveness of the risk management program to ensure that it is operationally sound and cost-effective.

Current Use   Like COSO, AS/NZS has found widespread use around the globe. In addition to ISO's version, nearly identical frameworks are in use by London's Institute of Risk Management, the U.S.-based Institute of Management Accountants, and the U.S. Department of Energy. As its designers intended, there is some variation among implementations. In fact, they considered the framework a template that each organization would fill out according to its needs.[10] The result is an intuitive structure based on a set of processes and principles applicable to any organization.

While the AS/NZS framework meets many of our criteria for a strong ERM framework, it could be more balanced. Three of the seven components have to do with risk assessment while there is very little guidance about actually dealing with risks or making risk-informed business strategy and policy decisions. The similarity among the three risk-assessment components (identify, analyze, and evaluate) makes it less MECE than we'd like.

Lam's ERM Framework (2003)

In my 2003 book, I recommended a model ERM framework that combined the simplicity of AS/NZS with the rigor of COSO. The structure consists of four interconnected layers, each with one to three elements for a total of seven components. See Figure 7.7 for my 2003 ERM framework. Let's examine the levels and components of that framework.

Level 1: Risk Governance

Corporate governance sits at the top of the entire framework. It ensures that the board of directors and management have established the appropriate organizational processes and corporate controls to measure and manage risk across the company.

Level 2: Risk Origination and Management

Line management integrates risk management into the revenue-generating activities of the company, including business development, product and relationship management, risk-based pricing, and so on.

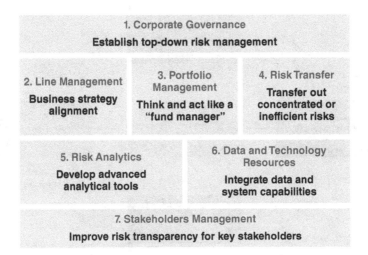

FIGURE 7.7 Lam's ERM Framework (2003)

Portfolio management aggregates risk exposures, incorporates diversification effects, and monitors risk concentrations against established risk limits.

Risk transfer mitigates risk exposures that are deemed too high, or are more cost efficient to transfer to a third party than to hold in the company's risk portfolio.

Level 3: Risk Analytics and Data Management

Risk analytics provides the measurement, analysis, and reporting tools to quantify the company's risk exposures as well as track external drivers.

Data and technology support the analytics and reporting processes.

Level 4: Communication and Relationship Management

Stakeholder management includes meeting stakeholder expectations and communicating and reporting the company's risk information to its key stakeholders. As with corporate governance, stakeholder management encompasses the breadth of ERM and serves as the model's foundation.

AN UPDATE: THE CONTINUOUS ERM MODEL

My own thinking has evolved since the publication of my first ERM book. Based on work with client organizations across various industries and

FIGURE 7.8 The Continuous ERM Model

different maturity levels, I've come to believe that a simplified framework, with no greater than 4–5 components, would be more intuitive and useful. The continuous ERM model I describe in Chapter 3 is a refinement of this earlier framework. Here, I've reduced the number of components from seven to four, and illustrate the cyclical, iterative nature of continuous ERM using feedback loops. Figure 7.8 shows the updated ERM framework. It is important to note that the four components specifically address four fundamental questions related to risk management:

1. **Governance structure and policies:** *Who* is responsible to provide risk oversight and make critical risk management decisions?
2. **Risk assessment and quantification:** *How* (ex-ante) will they make these risk management decisions in terms of analytical input?
3. **Risk management:** *What* specific decisions will they make to optimize the risk/return profile of the company?
4. **Reporting and monitoring:** *How* (ex-post) will the company monitor the performance of risk management decisions (i.e., a feedback loop)?

Governance Structure and Policies

Governance structure and policies address the question of who (i.e., individuals, functions, or committees) is responsible for making risk management decisions, and what policies provide incentives, requirements, and constraints (e.g., risk tolerances) for the decision makers. Governance structure and policies should include the following:

Risk Governance How should the board provide effective risk oversight?

- Should the board consider establishing a separate risk committee, or assign risk oversight responsibility to the audit committee or the full board?
- Should the board consider adding a risk expert to assist in risk issues, similar to the addition of financial experts to oversee financial issues?
- Should board members be more engaged in the risk management process?

Companies should address these questions regarding the board's governance structure, risk expertise, and its role in ERM to enhance the board's effectiveness in providing risk oversight. As a recent example, UBS announced that it added one CRO and two CFOs to the board, and investors reacted favorably, sending the stock price up seven percent in late trading. At the same time, board members should be fully engaged in the risk management process. This includes debating risk tolerance levels, challenging management on critical business assumptions, and holding management accountable for the risk–return performance of past decisions.

ERM Policy Companies should establish an ERM policy to support the risk oversight activities of senior management and the board. One of the most important components of an ERM policy is the delineation of specific risk tolerance levels for all critical risk exposures, known as the risk appetite statement (RAS). These risk tolerance levels enable the board and corporate management to control the overall risk profile of the organization. Other key components of an ERM policy typically include:

- Board and management governance structure
- Summaries of risk committee charters
- Risk management roles and responsibilities
- Guiding risk principles
- Summaries of risk policies and standards
- Analytical and reporting requirements
- Exception management and reporting processes

Risk-Compensation Linkage The design of incentive compensation systems is one of the most powerful levers for effective risk management (including risk culture), yet until very recently companies have paid insufficient attention to how incentives influence risk/return decisions. For example, when earnings growth or stock price appreciation drives incentive compensation, as is typical, corporate and business executives are effectively motivated to increase risks in order to drive up short-term earnings and stock price. To better align the interests of management and investors, long-term, risk-adjusted financial performance should drive incentive compensation systems. There are several ways to achieve this:

- Incorporating risk management performance into incentive compensation
- Establishing long-term risk-adjusted profitability measurement
- Using vesting schedules consistent with the duration of risk exposures
- Applying clawback provisions to account for tail risk losses.

Risk Assessment and Quantification

Risk assessment and quantification processes address the question of how analytical tools and processes support risk management decisions. Risk assessment and quantification tools for ERM include:

- **Risk assessments** that identify and evaluate the key risks facing the organization, including estimations of the probability, severity, and control effectiveness associated with each risk.
- **A loss-event database** to capture systematically an organization's actual losses and risk events so management can evaluate lessons learned and identify emerging risks and trends.
- **Key risk indicators (KRIs)** that provide measures of risk exposures over time. Ideally, KRIs are tracked against risk tolerance levels and integrated with related key performance indicators (KPIs).
- **Analytical models** that provide risk-specific and/or enterprise-wide risk analyses, including value-at-risk (VaR), stress-testing, and scenario analyses. One of the key objectives of these models is to provide loss estimates given an organization's risk portfolio.
- **Economic capital models** that allocate capital to underlying risks based on a defined solvency standard. These models often support risk-adjusted profitability and shareholder value analyses.

While the above tools can provide useful information, organizations should be aware of potential pitfalls. One of the key lessons from financial crises is that major risk events are usually the result a confluence of interrelated risks rather than any single risk on its own. To avoid the silo approach to risk analysis, companies need to integrate their risk assessment and quantification processes, as well as focus on critical risk interdependencies. Currently, many companies employ valuable tools, but they are typically utilized independently rather than in a holistic manner. They may use value-at-risk models to quantify market risk, credit-default models to estimate credit risk, and risk assessments and KRIs to analyze operational risk. Going forward, companies must integrate these analyses to gain a broader perspective.

Risk models are only as reliable as their underlying assumptions. Prior to the financial crisis of 2008, many of the credit models used were based on the assumption that years of rising home prices and benign default rates would continue in the future. Moreover, credit and market risk models often assume some level of diversification benefits based on historical default and price correlations.

However, the financial crisis has also provided strong evidence of the risk management adage that price correlations approach one during market stresses (i.e., global asset prices dropped in concert). In other words, the benefit of diversification may not be there when it's needed most. Companies should stress-test the key assumptions of their risk models to understand how sensitive results are relative to these assumptions.

Risk Management

Risk management addresses the decisions and actions companies have to optimize their risk/return. As discussed in Chapter 3 and further elaborated in Chapter 16, key risk-response decision points include:

- Risk acceptance or avoidance
- Risk mitigation
- Risk-based pricing
- Risk transfer
- Resource allocation

Typically, the risk management function does not handle the above decisions, but rather supports business and corporate decision-makers by providing risk/return analyses and tools. Moreover, the risk function should offer an independent assessment of critical business/risk issues.

The role and independence of the risk management function is a critical issue. Should the risk function be a business partner and actively participate in strategic and business decisions, or take the role of a corporate overseer and provide independent oversight? Can the risk function balance these two potentially conflicting roles? A related issue is whether the chief risk officer (CRO) should report to the CEO or to the board, or both.

One organizational solution may be to establish a solid reporting line between the CRO and CEO, and a dotted reporting line between the CRO and the board. On a day-to-day basis, the risk function serves as a business partner advising the board and management on risk management issues. However, under extreme circumstances (e.g., CEO/CFO fraud, major reputational or regulatory issues, and excessive risk taking) the dotted line to the board becomes a solid line such that the CRO can go directly to the board without concern about his or her job security. Ultimately, to be effective the risk function must have an independent voice. A direct communication channel to the board is one way to ensure that this voice is heard.

Reporting and Monitoring

The risk reporting and monitoring process addresses the question of how critical risk information is reported to the board and senior management, and how risk management performance is evaluated.

Currently, a general sense of dissatisfaction exists among board members and senior executives with respect to the timeliness, quality, and usefulness of risk reports. Companies often analyze and report on individual risks separately. These reports tend to be either too qualitative (risk assessments) or quantitative (VaR metrics). Risk reports also focus too much on past trends. In order to establish more effective reporting, companies should develop forward-looking, role-based dashboard reports, customized to support the decisions of the individual or group, whether that is the board, executive management, or line and operations management. ERM dashboard reports can integrate qualitative and quantitative data, internal risk exposures and external drivers, and key performance and risk indicators.

In order to evaluate the performance of the ERM program itself, organizations need to establish metrics and feedback loops based on measurable objectives. The objective of risk management could, for instance, be defined as to minimize unexpected earnings volatility. In this case, the purpose of risk management is not to minimize absolute levels of risks or earnings volatility, but to minimize unknown risks or drivers of earnings volatility.

DEVELOPING A FRAMEWORK

In addition to organizing the processes underpinning ERM, frameworks can be a powerful communication tool. This is particularly true in cases where the risk culture of an organization has not reached full maturity or, as is too often the case, there is no real risk culture at all. For that reason, the first step in developing a workable ERM framework for one's organization is to assess not only the risk processes already in place, but also the current risk culture. Let's review some of the key risk culture drivers in light of how they might inform an ERM framework:

- **Risk awareness:** How are employees made aware of the risks involved in their day-to-day decision-making? And how can that process be improved? An efficient risk framework should enhance risk awareness.
- **People:** Who is in charge of disseminating risk-related information? Where do their roles intersect with the roles of decision-makers across the organization? The framework should provide guidance as to the necessary risk-related roles.
- **Skills:** Each component of the framework will require certain skills. Does the framework make those clear? What systems must be in place to develop these capabilities?
- **Integrity:** This speaks to how well employees and managers internalize risk awareness and response, which in turn is a product of how fully risk is integrated into key processes. The framework should, therefore, be closely integrated with the broader strategic framework of the organization, so that the two reinforce one another rather than conflict.
- **Incentives:** A framework should elucidate the behaviors that best support the risk management goals of the company. Incentive programs and compensation schemes should reinforce those behaviors.
- **Tone from the top:** In order for the company's board members, CEO, and other business leaders to express their commitment to risk management, that tone must be ingrained in the ERM framework. What's more, the framework should inform the roles that senior management and the board play in risk management.
- **Communication:** Is the ERM framework effective as a communication tool? Does it clarify the role of risk in day-to-day decision-making? And does it illuminate the lines of communication that must be open in order for ERM to be fully effective?
- **Change management:** While the framework itself will not directly address change management, it should offer some guidance as to how it might take place. For example, it would provide discrete components of ERM, some of which may be more challenging to implement than others. This could help prioritize where to begin with implementation.

Adapting the Continuous ERM Framework

The goal of the Continuous ERM Model is to capture the strengths of the frameworks above in a single template that is flexible enough to accommodate the needs of organizations across industries. It is designed to meet the five criteria of an enduring framework: simplicity, MECE, balance and integration, flexibility, and effectiveness. Ultimately, it is a theoretical abstraction that should lead to real applications of ERM programs. For example, the application of this framework in a small non-profit is going to look very different from implementation in an international bank. It is important for the CRO (or equivalent position) to assess the needs of the organization, then choose and adapt an ERM framework that is tailored to those needs. The scope and complexity of the framework should match that of the organization. The components of the framework should be balanced to reflect the priorities of the organization. As the company works to adapt the framework to meet the organization's needs, it must keep in mind not only the aspects of risk culture discussed above, but also the "hard," numerical aspects of ERM. While the framework will not enumerate specific metrics used to measure performance, it will provide guidance as to what those metrics might be, and, more importantly, it will establish a reporting and monitoring structure to make sure those metrics and their accompanying analysis reach those who need them in a timely manner.

From Framework to Standards

As the company implements a framework, it will begin establishing precedents to inform best practices and goals to strive for as an organization. These can in turn form the basis for an ERM development roadmap. A clear vision for continual ERM improvement is key to staying ahead of the curve when it comes to risk. In order to do so, companies should use the framework to answer the following questions:

1. **Where are we?** The feedback loops and monitoring protocols established in the framework should reveal the current status of the organization's ERM efforts.
2. **What are the best-in-class practices to strive toward?** A good framework should help make apples-to-apples comparisons with competitors and even companies in other industries. Those comparisons, along with the knowledge gained from experience, should help evaluate where the organization could be based on its size, industry, and complexity.
3. **What do we need to do in order to reach our ideal state?** Once the risk team has established the starting point and goal, it can begin creating the roadmap: Do policies need updating? Does the risk culture need to change? Who must take action?

What does the process of establishing standards look like? Imagine this situation: A company uses a VaR model to determine market risk on a monthly basis as part of the risk assessment and quantification components of its framework. To take standards to the next level, the company can measure exposure more frequently. The best practice would be continuous, real-time monitoring, but this "Olympic-level" precision may not be necessary or cost-effective for less complex organizations, such as a regional bank. That's what I mean by customizing best practices based on the size and complexity of the organization. If daily measurement is sufficient, continuous monitoring would be overkill. This means that in order to achieve best-in-class practice, the company must shift from monthly to daily reporting. The ERM framework is a tool to close this gap. It allows companies to organize their current set of standards, get the needed reports, and create a roadmap to best-in-class practice.

CONCLUSION

In this chapter, we looked at how frameworks can offer a high-level view of key business processes such as strategic planning and execution. We examined the criteria that make a framework both simple enough to understand but flexible and sophisticated enough for large, complex organizations. Then, we focused our attention on the available ERM frameworks, including my own, the Continuous ERM Model. And finally, I discussed ways in which companies can adapt one or more of these models to fit their needs. Establishing such a framework is the first step in creating an ERM program. It is the cornerstone upon which companies will build out a comprehensive risk management approach that will inform every aspect of decision-making and strategic direction.

NOTES

1. Reeves, Martin, Moose, Sandy, and Venema, Thijs. "BCG Classics Revisited: The Growth Share *Matrix*," Boston Consulting Group, 2014. Retrieved from https://www.bcgperspectives.com/content/articles/corporate_strategy_portfolio_ management_strategic_planning_growth_share_matrix_bcg_classics_revisited/.
2. Porter, Michael E. *Competitive Strategy: Techniques for Analyzing Industries and Competitors*, Free Press, 1998.
3. Kaplan, Robert S. and David P. Norton. "The Balanced Scorecard—Measures that Drive Performance," *Harvard Business Review*, January–February 1992.
4. Moore, Geoffrey. *Zone to Win: Organizing to Compete in an Age of Disruption*, Diversion Books, 2015, pp. 34–37.

5. *Enterprise Risk Management—Integrated Framework*. Committee of Sponsoring Organizations of the Treadway Commission (COSO), 2004. Retrieved from www.coso.org.
6. Beasley, Mark, Bruce Branson and Bonnie V. Hancock. *COSO's 2010 Report on ERM: Current State of Enterprise Risk Oversight and Market Perceptions of COSO's ERM Framework*, Organizations of the Treadway Commission (COSO), 2010.
7. Ibid.
8. Ibid.
9. *ISO 31000: Risk Management*, ISO, 2015 *Joint Technical Committee OB-007 Risk Management*. Risk Management Standards, Standards Australia International and Standards New Zealand, 1995
10. Ibid.

Governance Structure
and Policies

The Three Lines of Defense

INTRODUCTION

Nations have armies, diplomats, and border patrols to protect their citizens. Football teams have offensive lines to protect their quarterback, and defensive tackles, linebackers, and safeties to prevent the other team from scoring. The fact is that no entity can depend on a single line of defense to protect itself. Rather, a tiered approach is the most effective and efficient, and enterprise risk management is no exception.

Each of the structures I describe above has internal and external defense structures that can be viewed as a pyramid, the base of which are the "front lines," which thwart the most obvious attacks. The next level both oversees that broad base and captures more elusive threats, and at the top, a highly refined cadre manages and monitors the lower levels while combating the threats that have penetrated the other lines. Take the human immune system, which has three lines of defense:

1. **External defenses:** These are a combination of physical and chemical barriers—skin, mucus membranes, and fluids such as tears and sweat—that prevent many foreign agents from penetrating the outer layer of the body. These defenses are nonspecific, meaning that they are designed to thwart a variety of threats.
2. **White blood cells:** Leukocytes (white blood cells) circulate throughout the body. If a pathogen penetrates the first line of defense, these nonspecific defense mechanisms encounter them and attempt to abolish them by engulfing and destroying them.
3. **Antibodies:** If a pathogen penetrates the nonspecific leukocyte barrier, they stimulate a specific immune response. Antibodies are proteins secreted by a specific type of lymphocyte, whose specific shape matches that of the antigen. The antibody combines with the antigen, rendering it inactive.

Note that the defense lines become more specialized and narrowly focused as one moves within the concentric circles of defense. Having antibodies on the outside of the body, for example, would be ineffective because of the essentially infinite number of antigens they would face. Better to have low-maintenance passive built-in systems. At the same time, these layers repel a diminishing number of threats.

Just like the human body, corporate entities embracing enterprise risk management have three lines of defense against risk. In this chapter, we'll begin by examining the most popular view of these three lines of defense, and where I think this methodology falls short. I'll then propose some adjustments to this model, and examine the roles of the board, senior management, and business units. And finally, I'll illustrate how these three lines of defense work together to reduce threats and enhance opportunities for the organization as a whole.

COSO'S THREE LINES OF DEFENSE

In the 1990s, the Committee of Sponsoring Organizations of the Treadway Commission (COSO) produced the widely adopted guidance for internal control over financial reporting. And in 2001, the commission turned its attention to enterprise risk management, and produced its first ERM framework a few years later. In 2004 a triple defense system for companies was put forth by COSO:

1. Business and operating units.
2. Risk and compliance functions
3. Internal audit

Since its introduction, this model has been adopted not only by the audit and financial communities, but by government regulators such as the Federal Reserve and the Office of the Comptroller of the Currency (OCC), as well. In fact, the OCC codifies the roles and responsibilities of each of the three lines of defense in the final version of its *Guidelines Establishing Heightened Standards for Certain Large Insured National Banks, Insured Federal Savings Associations, and Insured Federal Branches.*

Let's take a closer look at each of these defensive lines.

First Line: Business and Operating Units

As is the case with an army at war, an organization's first line of defense is its "boots on the ground," that is, the operational or business units that conduct the company's affairs on a day-to-day basis. These units include not only profit-generating units such as sales teams, client service teams, and manufacturing units, but also back-office functions such as human resources, IT, as well as myriad other operating units large and small. This line manages the organization's risks by implementing and maintaining effective internal control procedures day in and day out. It encompasses mid-level and front-line managers who are responsible for identifying control breakdowns and inadequate processes, and for fixing whatever problems they find. It also involves the front-line employees themselves—sales and customer service reps, production workers, bank tellers—who follow these processes.

In other words, simply by following best practices as standard operating procedure, these units are reducing risk. And by continuously improving processes and adapting to new circumstances, they become more and more adept at thwarting threats.

Take the example of financial fraud. Two basic tenets of fraud prevention are *segregation of duties* and *segregation of authority*. Segregation of duties involves circumscribing any individual employee's roles, responsibilities, and access to financial records, assets, and systems. In an accounting department, for instance, one employee opens and logs incoming payments from customers, while another records these payments in the company's records. These two independent sets of records can then be compared to ensure that all incoming payments are properly recorded.

Segregation of authority means that one worker, such as a supervisor, must review and sign off on the work of another. To continue the accounting example, the employee responsible for recording a disbursement would not be the same person who has the ability to authorize the disbursement, thus reducing the opportunity for fraud or embezzlement.

As the first line of defense, the business and operating units are the ultimate owners of their own risk, responsible for measuring and managing it on a day-to-day basis.

Second Line: Risk and Compliance Functions

The second line of defense consists of the risk and compliance functions,[1] which approach the goal of risk management in two related yet distinct ways. As we have seen in previous chapters, the risk function establishes processes and procedures to ensure that the organization operates within its target risk appetite, monitors the company's overall risk profile, and recommends action when risk falls outside the tolerance levels established by the board and management. The compliance function has a narrower focus, monitoring operations to ensure that the firm is adhering to statutory and regulatory requirements. At its most mature level, the risk function will actively oversee risks of every variety, including strategic, financial, credit, market, reputational, operational, and more. Similarly, compliance will involve itself in different areas depending on the industry, but may include customer protection, data-security and privacy, environmental safety, and other regulated areas.[2]

The scope and complexity of the second line of defense varies depending upon a number of factors such as the size of the company and the industry in which it operates. Smaller companies may relegate second-line responsibilities to the financial or operational functions. In larger companies—particularly those in heavily regulated industries—these functions might be headed by a chief risk officer (CRO) and chief compliance officers (COOs) who report to senior management or directly to the CEO.[3]

Third Line: Internal Audit

The third line of defense in the COSO framework is internal audit. This function provides independent assurance of the second line of defense as well as the first line of defense.

As internal audit reviews controls and risk management procedures, it identifies problems and reports its findings to the audit committee of the board and to senior management.[4] What distinguishes internal audit from the other two lines of defense is its high level of independence and objectivity, due to the chief audit executive's direct reporting line to the board. Thanks to its distinct responsibilities and independent positioning, internal audit is able to provide reliable assurance on the effectiveness of the organization's overall governance, risk management, and internal control processes.

It's a common misunderstanding to conflate this third line of defense with the functions of the other two.[5] After all, who better than an auditor to help establish first-line controls or perform second-line risk management activities? But given internal audit's role as a failsafe, and its oversight of the first and second defense lines, commingling its functions with the other two roles can compromise internal audit's objectivity and limit its overall effectiveness.

PROBLEMS WITH THIS STRUCTURE

Unfortunately, this structure fails to address several issues, many of which have come to the fore following the 2008 financial crisis.

Lack of Board Oversight

First, where does the board fit into all of this? Is it the fourth line of defense? Such an implied structure would suggest that the board oversees internal audit, which in turn oversees risk and compliance. But that is not how boards are expected to, or should, function. In the COSO three lines of defense framework, the board only appears relative to the auditing function—that is, the internal auditors report to the board as well as to senior management. But this underplays the ultimate governance and oversight position that the board holds in key areas. A company's board of directors serves five key functions:

1. **Strategy:** Simply put, is the company pursuing the right strategy and executing appropriately? The *executive committee* may focus on these issues, but they are usually taken up by the full board as well.
2. **Management:** Do we have the right CEO and executive management team? Are we paying them appropriately? Are our incentive structures aligned with shareholder interests? Do we have a succession plan in place? The *compensation committee* is responsible for these areas.
3. **Board effectiveness:** Do we have a diverse and effective board? Are the committees and individual directors contributing in a meaningful way? Do we have the right skills and experiences? The board's *nominating and governance committee* is responsible for these areas.
4. **Audit:** Are the company's books and records accurate? Has the company implemented the proper internal controls? Is it meeting public-disclosure and SEC filing requirements? The board's *audit committee* oversees these functions.
5. **Risk and compliance:** Is the company properly managing its risk and complying with laws and regulations? In the past, this has often been the purview of the audit committee, but increasingly boards are establishing a separate *risk committee* to focus exclusively on these issues.

It became clear during the 2008 financial crisis that boards had not been paying nearly enough attention to this fifth function. In the wake of the crisis, regulators and external stakeholders are placing full responsibility for overseeing the risk and compliance functions squarely on the board's shoulders, insisting that the board ensure those functions are in place and operating effectively.

In COSO's framework, internal audit is at the top of the defense hierarchy. But this structure is inconsistent with how corporate oversight is practiced: internal auditors, after all, have a mandate to audit the work of the risk function, but they do not hold administrative authority over CEOs, executive leaders, CROs, COOs, or their staffs. Internal audit is part of the solution—a tool employed by the board—but it's not the whole story in terms of the third line of defense.

The economic crisis of 2008 and subsequent downturn exposed a serious lack of effective risk oversight by corporate boards, especially in the banking industry. In my 2003 book, *Enterprise Risk Management*, I made ten predictions about the future of risk management, among which was that as ERM became the industry standard corporate boards would have a central role to play. My hypothesis was that new financial disasters would continue to highlight the pitfalls of the traditional siloed approach to risk management, and as a result, external stakeholders would hold boards of directors responsible for risk oversight and demand an increasing level of risk transparency.

I also predicted that as boards of directors recognized their responsibilities to ensure appropriate risk management effectiveness, the risk oversight responsibilities of the audit committee would shift to a dedicated risk committee.[6]

These two predictions have largely come to pass, though not exactly as I'd predicted. The level of board involvement in ERM has increased significantly over the past several years.[7] This higher level of awareness and engagement has become most pronounced since the global financial crisis. Numerous surveys reveal that risk management has overtaken accounting issues as the top concern for corporate boards—a strong indication that boards are finally getting the message. In a 2010 COSO survey, only 28% of respondents described their ERM process as "systematic, robust and repeatable with regular reporting to the board,"[8] while the 2011 Enterprise Risk Management Survey by the Risk Management Society (RIMS) showed that the majority—80%—have built or plan to build an ERM system, even though only 17% have fully implemented one.[9] Clearly, while there is a much higher level of attention paid to ERM, many boards are working diligently to enhance their risk governance and oversight capabilities, including risk appetite and reporting, board expertise and education, and assurance of risk management effectiveness.

This increased attention to risk has led a number of leading institutions to establish risk committees. An acquaintance of mine, a director of a large energy firm who is on the company's audit committee and its risk committee (she currently chairs the former, and had previously chaired the latter), provided me with a succinct distinction between the two:

> "*The audit and risk committees have very different mandates, and different lenses through which they see the world,*" she told me. "*The audit committee is charged with thinking inside the box. They make sure that you are in compliance with both the spirit and the letter of rules and standards that authorities have established—SEC rules, FASB standards, Sarbanes-Oxley (SOX) requirements and so on. You don't want to the audit committee to be creative.*"
>
> "*The risk committee, on the other hand, is charged with thinking outside the box. They're not focusing on what goes on day to day, but rather on the improbable but highly consequential events*

or risks that might occur. You want them to see around corners, to be creative," she concludes.

In the final analysis, I believe companies operating in volatile, risk-intensive, and highly regulated industries should at least consider a risk committee. But one size doesn't fit all. Depending on the board composition, ERM maturity, and overall philosophy to risk governance, it may be appropriate for the audit committee or the full board to provide risk oversight. Ultimately, the board is responsible and it should ensure that all risk oversight responsibilities are appropriately delegated to the committees given their unique charters.

In many respects, the global financial crisis was the ultimate "stress test" for companies around the world. Many failed, and even those with established ERM programs reported mixed results. A 2009 Deloitte survey of global financial institutions found that just 36% had an ERM program in place, with an additional 23% in the process of implementing one and a similar portion planning to create one. Those who considered themselves "extremely effective" in managing major risk categories were well in the minority. To wit: Just 6% gave themselves highest marks for managing operational risk.[10] The financial crisis also revealed the weaknesses of silo-based risk management. Highly interrelated risks like those that threatened giants such as AIG and Goldman Sachs cannot be isolated and managed independently. And finally, the crisis pinpointed the importance of "soft" issues such as culture, values, and incentives. When a company explicitly or tacitly creates a culture of excessive risk, it is all but impossible for even the best risk management program to succeed.

Audits Are Episodic

Another shortcoming of the COSO structure comes from the episodic nature of audits. Certainly annual or even biannual reviews are a critical component of the defense structure. But regulation such as Sarbanes-Oxley and Dodd-Frank has made the *ongoing* accuracy of financial information a top priority. For one thing, company leaders must individually certify the accuracy of that information. In addition, penalties for fraudulent financial activity were raised significantly. And finally, these regulations increased the oversight role of boards of directors and the independence of the outside auditors who review the accuracy of corporate financial statements.

As a result, two distinct roles have emerged: periodic audit and continuous monitoring. The latter is the responsibility of the risk and compliance functions that comprise the second line of defense, overseen by the board's risk committee. In a continuous monitoring scheme, management constantly assesses key business processes, transactions, and controls, permitting ongoing insight into the effectiveness of internal controls and risk management. It would be inaccurate to suggest that internal audit oversees these functions. Rather, both internal audit and risk functions are overseen by the board, each reporting to their respective committee.

Auditors Are Outside the Command Structure

The third weakness in the COSO defense structure is that it does not accurately reflect the administrative role of internal audit. Consider the corporate structure: The board oversees management (including the risk function), which in turn oversees the various business units. Internal audit, however, serves a distinct function outside this structure: It has a mandate to audit the risk function, but does not have direct supervisory authority over it. For that reason, auditors are not well positioned to drive change when necessary. What's more, as risk management becomes more comprehensive and complex, the accounting and process lens of auditors does not fully encompass the breadth of risk issues handled by the quantitative analysts and compliance professionals whose work they review.

In fact, a 2011 paper by the IIA Research Foundation found that 25% of internal auditors failed to meet the role in ERM as envisaged by IIA standards.[11] This is consistent with a 2010 IIA Global Internal Audit Survey, which found 57% of internal audit functions perform audits of ERM processes while 20% intend to grow their ERM audit activities over the next five years.[12]

THE THREE LINES OF DEFENSE REVISITED

The three lines of defense comprise an effective overall model, but as you can see, some adjustments are in order. Taking into consideration the short-comings mentioned above, I propose the following definitions:

> **Third line:** Board of Directors (and internal audit)
>
> **Second line:** CRO and ERM Function (and corporate management)
>
> **First line:** Business and Operating Units (and support functions)

Figure 8.1 provides a summary of the three lines of defense model. The most obvious change here is the replacement of internal audit with the board of directors as the third line of defense. But there are other subtle though significant differences as well. These adjustments also reflect how boards and management teams provide risk oversight and mitigation in real life. Specifically, this new framework highlights how the three lines of defense interact and reinforce one another, and it has the additional benefit

3rd Line of Defense	**Board of Directors (and Audit)** • Establish board risk governance and oversight processes • Approve risk policies; link strategy, risk, and compensation • Accountable for periodic review and assurance of controls
2nd Line of Defense	**CRO and ERM Function (and Corporate Management)** • Establish and implement risk and compliance programs • Execute risk policies and standards, risk appetite and tolerances, and reporting processes • Accountable for ongoing risk monitoring and oversight
1st Line of Defense	**Business Units (and Operating Functions)** • Assume risk to generate profits and growth • Execute customer management, product pricing, P&L plans • Ultimately accountable for business/risk management

FIGURE 8.1 Three Lines of Defense Model

of being mutually exclusive and collectively exhaustive (MECE). That is, its components are mutually exclusive to avoid overlaps while they are also collectively exhaustive to ensure that the framework is comprehensive.

Discussing the broad roles of board, management, and business units in ERM is all well and good, but in practice, decisions fall to specific committees, functions, or individuals. These decision makers can be at the board, corporate management, or business and functional unit level, so let's take a deeper look at the roles of each in this new scheme.

The Board: The Last Line of Defense

The central difference between my framework and that developed by COSO is that instead of internal audit holding the last line of defense, the board itself takes this position (albeit supported by internal audit). This single change addresses many of the shortcomings of COSO's framework.

The board holds the critical responsibilities of corporate governance and risk oversight. As such, it is not enough to rely on internal audit. An audit function may not have the skills, experiences, or mandate necessary to perform this high-level function. Consider the failure of banks such as Lehman Brothers in 2008. While these institutions had internal audit functions that audited risk and compliance processes, they did not capture the subtle, inherent dangers of credit exposures to the housing market. This shows how internal auditors may be too focused on putting the company's risk processes through stringent tests to see the bigger picture—which can potentially lead to devastating consequences.

I would argue that given the weaknesses of the COSO framework revealed by the economic crisis of 2008, corporate boards have a central and primary role in ERM.

First, recent regulations have placed the responsibility of corporate governance and risk oversight squarely on the board's shoulders: In December 2009, the SEC established rules that require disclosures in proxy and information statements about the board governance structure and the board's role in risk oversight, as well as the relationship between compensation policies and risk management. Additionally, Dodd-Frank requires that a board-level risk committee be established by all public bank holding companies (and public non-bank financial institutions supervised by the Federal Reserve) with over $10 billion in assets. This committee is responsible for ERM oversight and practices, and its members must include, according to the law, "at least one risk management expert having experience in identifying, assessing, and managing risk exposures of large, complex firms."[13]

Beyond the corporation's walls, stakeholders are clearly interested in and benefiting from effective governance and ERM. To wit: Standard & Poor's (2010) found that North American and Bermudan insurers with "excellent ERM" had better stock performance than those with "weak ERM." In 2008, the former fell 30% while the latter dropped 60%. In 2009, stocks of strong ERM companies gained 10% while those of weak ERM insurers fell by the same percentage. At the same time, rating agencies, led by S&P, have established ERM criteria for financial and non-financial corporations that will be applied in their rating processes.[14]

So the board is central. But what, exactly, is its role in risk management? The board of directors is responsible for establishing risk governance structure and oversight processes; reviewing, challenging, and approving risk policies; and overseeing strategy execution, risk management, and executive-compensation programs. It is a complex mandate, and for that reason many boards may need to augment their skill set by bringing aboard directors with solid risk experience, and by creating a risk committee that is separate and distinct from the audit committee.

Key business decisions for the risk committee include:

- Establishing the statement of risk appetite and risk tolerance levels, as well as other corporate risk policies
- Reviewing specific risk assessments and focus areas, such as cyber-security, anti–money laundering, third-party oversight, and business contingency planning
- Reviewing and approving management recommendations with respect to capital structure, dividend policy, and target debt ratings

- Reviewing and approving strategic risk management decisions, including major investments and transactions
- Overseeing the overall development and effectiveness of risk and compliance programs

This complex and comprehensive mandate can be broken down into three primary functions: *governance*, *policy*, and *assurance*.

Governance At the top of the board's responsibilities is to establish an effective governance structure to oversee risk, which requires the following steps:

1. **Define risk oversight responsibilities across the full board and various committees.** A top priority in establishing an enterprise risk management structure is clarifying responsibilities. While the full board generally retains overall responsibility for risk oversight, a growing number of organizations are establishing risk committees. Based on the 2010 COSO report, 47% of board members at financial services organizations indicated that they had a risk committee, versus 24% at nonfinancial services firms. As discussed earlier,[15] such a committee is required by Dodd Frank Section 165 for banks.
2. **Build risk experience and expertise among board members.** Even as boards are being held more accountable for risk management, they acknowledge that they don't have the expertise to execute: A majority of respondents (71%) to the COSO survey acknowledged that their boards "are not formally executing mature and robust risk oversight processes." In fact, fewer than 15% of board members were fully satisfied with the board's processes for understanding and challenging the assumptions and risks associated with the business strategy.[16] It is imperative, therefore, that the board include members with deep experience and ability in risk management. In the past, this skill set was clearly lacking in many boards, reducing their ability to see the levels of risk their companies were taking on.
3. **Define responsibilities held by the board and management.** This new framework makes clear the division of responsibilities between the board and management. Nonetheless, the risk governance structures at the board and management levels should be fully aligned.
4. **Integrate strategy and risk management.** For many companies, risk management has been an afterthought, when in fact it should be an integral part of strategic planning. The board must consider how much risk it is willing to take on to achieve its strategic goals. Monitoring the organization's strategy and execution has long been the purview of boards. As boards become more active in ERM, the integration of strategy and risk is a logical and desirable outcome.

5. **Assure independence for the chief risk officer.** Independent risk management is a core tenet of ERM.[17] The board must ensure that risk management is independent of the business and operational activities of the organization. Moreover, under exceptional circumstances (e.g., excessive risk taking, major internal fraud, and significant business conflicts) the chief risk officer should be able to escalate risk issues directly to the board without concern about his or her job security or compensation. The same holds true for the chief compliance officer.

Policy Risk governance allows the organization to implement risk management and oversight, but the board also needs an instrument for communicating its expectations and requirements.[18] That is the role of risk management policy. While it is management's responsibility to develop and execute risk management policies, the board must challenge and approve them and monitor ongoing compliance and exceptions.

An ERM policy should provide explicit tolerance levels for key risks. It should effectively communicate the board's overall risk appetite and expectations, and make clear the linkage between risk and compensation policies. A robust risk management policy should also include a statement of risk appetite, and it should articulate the company's goals for strategic risk management. We'll take a more complete look at risk policy in Chapter 12, but here's a basic breakdown:

Statement of Risk Appetite Articulating the company's risk appetite is an essential element of establishing the ERM policy. Companies should specify the amount of risk that they are willing to take on in pursuit of strategic and business objectives in terms of risk appetite and tolerance. The development of a suitable risk appetite statement (RAS) is an important aspect of governance and risk oversight, since it helps employees throughout the corporate hierarchy make risk-based decisions. A typical risk appetite statement is organized by the company's major risk categories (for example, strategic/business risk, market risk, credit risk, operational risk, reputational risk, etc.), each defined by unique metrics. The RAS then assigns a range of acceptable values within which the company should operate. Not only does this help to integrate risk into strategic planning, it also allows the company to track its risk exposures against tolerance levels over time.[19]

Strategic Risk Management The board has always had oversight responsibility for the company's strategy and its execution (which is why they're often populated by former CEOs). But following the lessons learned from the financial crisis and regulatory expectations, boards must now focus on risk oversight as well. It is logical—and perhaps inevitable—that these two functions will converge over time. You can see why with a glance at the familiar bell curve: Considering a company's strategic risk, the middle part of the curve is the expected enterprise value produced by the strategy, but on either side are strategic uncertainties and business drivers that could move the enterprise value higher or lower. With strategy and risk thus part of a single continuum, it only makes sense to consider them in a fully integrated fashion. In addition, numerous empirical studies indicate that when companies suffer a significant drop in market value, the majority of the time it is due to strategic risk, and not financial or operational risks.[20]

Assurance   The third responsibility of the board is to ensure that an ERM program is in place and operating effectively. It does this through monitoring and reporting, independent assessments, and objective feedback loops. To fulfill its mandate to oversee ERM, the board must rely on management to provide critical information through communications and reports. Board members often criticize the quality and timeliness of the reports they receive. The standards that they want but may not be getting to their satisfaction include:

- **A concise executive summary** of the enterprise risk profile, as well as external business drivers.
- **Streamlined reports**, including a focus on key board discussion and decision points.
- **An integrated view** of the organization, versus functional or silo views.
- **Forward-looking analyses**, versus historical data and trends.
- **Key performance and risk indicators** shown against specific targets or limits.
- **Actual performance** of previous business/risk decisions, as well as alternatives to, and rationale for, management recommendations for board decisions.
- **Sufficient time** allotted for discussions and board input, versus management presentations.

Later in this book we'll look at how ERM dashboards can help meet these standards.

Second Line of Defense: CRO and ERM Function (and Compliance)

The second line of defense consists of the chief risk officer (CRO) and the ERM and compliance functions.[21] This line of defense falls within corporate management, and as such supports the CEO and the executive management team. The CEO, then, is critical to the success of ERM efforts. If the CEO is not on board with risk, the CRO will be fighting an uphill battle. But with the engagement of the CEO, the CRO can work through the full executive committee to manage risk across the enterprise. For example, the CRO would work with the CFO to quantify and control financial risk, or with the head of HR to see that hiring and performance management have a positive effect on the organization's overall risk profile.

The second line of defense supports corporate management by establishing the infrastructure and best-practice standards for ERM. This includes developing risk policies and procedures, analytical models, and data resources and reporting processes. And finally, the ERM and compliance functions are held accountable for ongoing risk monitoring and oversight— particularly safeguarding of the company's financial and reputational assets and ensuring compliance with laws and regulations.

Rise of the CRO You may have noticed that unlike COSO's, this framework makes specific mention of the CRO. I believe that the CRO will play an increasingly central role in enterprise risk management, and the rise of this position among global corporations confirms its importance: A 2013 survey by Deloitte found that 89% of global financial institutions had a CRO or equivalent position. Moreover, 80% of the institutions indicated that their CROs reported directly to the CEO or the board (up from 42% in 2006).[22] What's more, CRO positions are being filled by executives with significant line experience, and many CROs are becoming CEO prospects. We'll take a fuller look at the chief risk officer role in Chapter 11. Beyond financial institutions, companies in other risk-intensive industries should consider appointing a CRO or at least designate a de-facto CRO.

Oversight of Business Units One of the risk function's primary duties is to establish and implement risk and compliance programs. These include policies that will guide and constrain the decision-making processes of the business units. You might say that the second line of defense is the connective tissue between board-level strategy and front-line implementation. Specific responsibilities include:[23]

- Risk management development, monitoring processes and implementing the company's overall risk management
- Monitoring operations and ensuring that all business functions are implemented in accordance with established risk management policies and standard operating procedures

- Developing analytics and models that quantify enterprise and specific risks, including correlations and interdependencies
- Monitoring and reporting to departments with highest accountability for the company's overall risk exposure

Key business and risk management decisions for this function include allocating financial and human capital resources to business activities that produce the highest risk-adjusted profitability, implementing organic and/or acquisition-based growth strategies, and establishing risk transfer strategies to reduce excessive or uneconomic exposures. Clearly, the execution of these strategies would require the support and collaboration of the entire executive management team.

Enterprise-Wide Scope A critical aspect of the ERM function is that it has an enterprise-wide perspective. An increasing number of studies have shown that stronger corporate governance and ERM programs are statistically associated with better financial performance and shareholder return.[24]

Prior to the late 1980s, companies practiced risk management in operational and functional silos. The objective was mainly to develop cost-effective insurance and hedging strategies and minimize financial and operational write offs.[25] In the years following, companies began to manage financial risks (i.e., credit, market, liquidity) in a more integrated manner and apply economic capital techniques. (We'll detail these techniques in Chapters 13 and 15.) This led to more cost-effective risk oversight functions and efficient allocation of capital resources. Since the mid-1990s, ERM has continued to increase the reach of risk management to include strategy and business risks.

First Line of Defense: Business Units (and Support Functions)

As is true in the COSO framework, the first line of defense is made up of the business and operating units, including all profit centers and support functions such as IT and HR. They perform day-to-day business processes and support operations, and as such are at the forefront of risk management. Each business unit or function is ultimately accountable for measuring and managing the risks they own or share with other units. For example, business units must assume risk in order to generate profits and growth. In this process, they make daily decisions about which risks to accept and which to avoid. Of course, these decisions should be in line with the company's risk appetite, which is established by the board of directors.

Business units are responsible for executing customer-management, product-development, and financial plans, as well as monitoring and mitigating resulting risks at a tactical level. Moreover, they are accountable for product pricing. By incorporating risk in the pricing process, the firm can be fully compensated for the risks that it chooses to take on. Risk responses include:

- *Acceptance or avoidance*: Increase or decrease a specific risk exposure through its core business, M&A, and financial activities.
- *Mitigation*: Establish risk-control processes and strategies in order to manage a specific risk within a defined risk tolerance level.
- *Pricing:* Develop product and relationship pricing models that fully incorporate the "cost of risk."
- *Transfer*: Execute risk transfer strategies through the insurance or capital markets if risk exposures are excessive and/or if the cost of risk transfer is lower than the cost of risk retention.
- *Resource allocation*: Allocate human and financial resources to business activities that produce the highest risk-adjusted returns in order to maximize firm value.

BRINGING IT ALL TOGETHER: HOW THE THREE LINES WORK IN CONCERT

So far, we've focused on the roles and responsibilities of each line of defense. But the added value of this framework is how these functions work together.

That wasn't always the case. Historically, business units were largely left to their own devices. Risk management, if it existed at all, came in the form of intermittent monitoring and reporting. It was only during a crisis that management would try to address risk on a hands-on basis. As for boards, many were little more than ceremonial bodies that convened meetings, received reports, and rubber-stamped management strategies and financial statements without significant review or challenge.

All that has changed under the modern ERM framework. Business units are still at the forefront of innovation—introducing new products, establishing new markets—but they have a new partner at the risk management level. Led by the CRO, risk and compliance experts serve an oversight and consultative role, providing analytics to business units, helping them incorporate the cost of risk into their pricing, and offering tools and processes to help them make better decisions day to day.

The first and second lines of defense work well together because they have different perspectives on the same processes and data. While business units are focused on what they expect based on planning, budget, and other criteria (in other words, the center of the bell curve), risk experts focus on the unexpected—the long tails of the curve.

The roles in this relationship must remain in balance, however. When the risk function partners with business units, it naturally cedes some of its objectivity. That's where the board and internal audit comes in. It can maintain its independence precisely because the risk management team has assumed the consultative role.

At the other end, the CRO (and similarly, the CCO) maintains a clear reporting relationship with the board, even as he or she serves the CEO. This role's independence is strengthened when the board (or its risk committee) participates in the hiring, firing, performance-evaluation, and compensation decisions regarding the CRO and CCO. These two roles should also have a clearly defined relationship, including the ability to request executive sessions in the absence of the CEO and executive management.

CONCLUSION

A framework consisting of three defensive lines provides a solid bulwark against negative risk impact. The COSO framework includes three lines composed of business units, management, and internal audit. This, however, can lead to some important gaps. What's more, it excludes the board entirely. That's why I propose a framework in which internal audit is replaced by the board, which nonetheless utilizes the audit function in its role overseeing the other lines of defense. These lines have clearly delineated roles and responsibilities, allowing them to work in concert for the good of the organization. In doing so, the board, management, and business units can move beyond a defensive stance to adopt a strategic perspective that takes advantage of opportunities even as it mitigates downside risk.

NOTES

1. "Risk Management: Easy as 1 ... 2 ... 3," *Tone at the Top*, The Institute of Internal Auditors, February 2013.
2. "The Three Lines of Defense in Effective Risk Management and Control," The Institute of Internal Auditors, 2013.
3. Ibid.
4. Ibid.
5. Ibid.
6. Lam, James. "Back to the Future," *Risk Management Association Journal*, Volume 89, August 2010.

7. McNish, Rob et al. *Getting to ERM: A Road Map for Banks and Other Financial Institutions*, McKinsey & Company, 2013.

8. Beasley, Mark S., Bruce C. Branson, and Bonnie V. Hancock. *COSO's 2010 Report on ERM: Current State of Enterprise Risk Oversight and Market Perceptions of COSO's ERM Framework*, Committee of Sponsoring Organizations of the Treadway Commission, 2010.

9. *2011 Enterprise Risk Management Survey*, RIMS, 2011.

10. Global Risk Management Survey: Sixth Edition, Deloitte Touche Tohmatsu, June 2009. Retrieved from http://www.ucop.edu/enterprise-risk-management/_files/deloitte_globalrskmgtsrvy.pdf.

11. Sobel, Paul. *Internal Auditing's Role in Risk Management*, The Institute for Internal Auditors Research Foundation, 2011.

12. Ibid.

13. U.S. Congress. *Dodd-Frank Wall Street Reform and Consumer Protection Act*, H.R. 4173 (111th), 2010.

14. "S&P: North America, Bermuda Insurers Enhancing Enterprise Risk Management Efforts," *Insurance Journal*, May 2, 2011. Retrieved from http://www.insurancejournal.com/news/international/2011/05/02/196878.htm.

15. Beasley, Mark S. et al., *COSO's 2010 Report on ERM*.

16. Ibid.

17. Lam, James. "The Role of the Board in Enterprise Risk Management," *RMA Journal*, April 2011.

18. Ibid.

19. Lam, James. *Enterprise Risk Management from Incentives to Controls*, 2nd edition, Wiley, 2014.

20. Ibid.

21. "Risk Management: Easy as 1...2...3," *Tone at the Top*, February 2013.

22. Global Risk Management Survey, Eighth Edition: "Setting a Higher Bar." Deloitte Touche Tohmatsu Limited, 2013.

23. Alijoyo, Antonius, *The Essentials of Enterprise Risk Management for Directors and Commissioners*, Indonesian Institute of Commissioners and Directors, n.d.

24. Lam, James. *Enterprise Risk Management from Incentives to Controls*, 2nd edition, Wiley, 2014.

25. Ibid.

CHAPTER **9**

Role of the Board

INTRODUCTION

In the aftermath of the financial crisis of 2008, boards of directors have taken a much more active role in risk governance and oversight. This is partly the result of regulation, but it also makes solid business sense, which is why the trend appears to be gaining steam as stakeholder expectations continue to rise. Boards are growing more cognizant of how ERM can benefit the organization, improve relations with key stakeholders, and satisfy heightened regulations worldwide.

Among the key groups that provide independent risk monitoring—boards, auditors, regulators, rating agencies, and institutional investors—the board of directors is unique in its direct responsibility for ensuring sound risk management and the degree of leverage it has for doing so. At most organizations, corporate management bends over backward to satisfy board demands. By asking tough questions and establishing high expectations for ERM, the board can set the tone from the top and effect significant change in the risk culture and practices of an organization.[1]

Studies indicate that boards are recognizing the importance of ERM and are making significant changes as a result. For one thing, the world is getting riskier. According to a 2013 survey by the Association for Financial Professionals (AFP), 59% of firms face greater earnings uncertainty relative to five years earlier.[2] Respondents also expect risks to increase in the next two years. In another study that same year, Accenture found that risk management was a higher priority for 98% of those surveyed.[3] As boards face new threats like cybersecurity and emerging technologies, they rely on ERM to ensure that all of the key elements of effective risk management are in place. As part of this trend, board-level risk committees and joint audit and risk committees are becoming more prevalent in firms across the globe. Additionally, companies are increasingly integrating ERM into business strategy and decisions.

While boards feel that their companies have made progress in ERM, they see plenty of room for improvement. Gaps remain, for instance, between risk assessments and risk-based decision making. There is a universal need for better risk management practices and qualified board members to assist in oversight. And boards are concerned that they are not yet fully equipped to assume their new fiduciary duties to evaluate enterprise risk, set appropriate policies and risk appetite, and monitor ERM effectiveness. As a result, directors who understand regulatory requirements and have the expertise to oversee complex risks are in great demand.

This chapter will focus on the role of the board, with the support of the risk and audit committees, in ERM oversight. To ensure the effectiveness of ERM, boards are reexamining governance structure and roles; risk policies and limits; and the process of monitoring and reporting. With respect to ERM oversight, this chapter will examine three central questions:

1. What key regulatory requirements must directors consider as part of their risk governance and oversight?
2. What are current board practices for ERM?
3. What can boards do to oversee more effectively ERM and the key risks facing their organizations?

REGULATORY REQUIREMENTS

Recent regulations by the SEC, Financial Stability Board (FSB), and the Basel Committee have ratcheted up minimum standards of corporate governance. In response to deficiencies revealed during the 2008 financial crisis, these organizations established new guidelines that stress the role of risk governance structures and policy in improving ERM. The regulations address governance issues such as board composition, responsibilities, independent risk management practices, and the integration of strategic plans and risk management. While most of these regulations come from the financial services industry, where risk practices and regulations are more advanced, boards in other industries can gain valuable insights and ideas from them. Let's examine some of these requirements across the globe.

Board Responsibility: Capital Requirements Directive IV (CRD IV), the implementation of Basel III in the Eurozone, addresses board composition and the need for independent risk management. It vests in boards the ultimate responsibility for effective risk management. Under the directive, banks must establish suitability criteria for directors and create policies for board diversity with regard to age, professional background, and gender. Banks must also elevate the status of independent risk management and ensure that the chief risk officer (CRO) has direct access to the board. CRD IV also addresses capital shortfalls with additional systemic risk buffers, higher minimum capital ratios, and higher risk weightings on counterparty exposures.[4]

Prioritizing Risk Management: In the United States, the Office of the Comptroller of the Currency (OCC) released heightened expectations for risk frameworks and the role of independent risk management in 2014. The additional OCC standards require public holding companies (and public non-bank financial institutions supervised by the Federal Reserve) with more than $10 billion in assets to establish appropriate stature for an independent risk committee and internal audit. Integration of strategy and risk management, long a recommended best practice for boards, is now mandatory. Boards must develop a strategic plan and update it regularly to reflect changes in the organization's risk profile.[5]

Since the Dodd-Frank Act was signed into law in July 2010, board-level risk committees have become more prevalent. Dodd-Frank requires large financial institutions to establish a board risk committee responsible for ERM oversight and practices, and to include among its members at least one experienced risk management expert.[6]

Compensation Policies: In 2014, an additional Dodd-Frank requirement took effect: Boards must review compensation policy to ensure incentives do not encourage excessive risk-taking. CRD IV also addresses compensation policy as it relates to risk management. The relationship between compensation and risk culture is also enshrined in the 2013 extended FSB guidelines as well as the 2014 OCC guidelines. OCC stresses the importance of maintaining a proper risk culture through compensation policies that reward compliance. The FSB standards address the relationship between compensation policies and adherence to risk appetite statements.

Risk Appetite Statements: Recent regulations also strengthen the board's role in drawing up effective risk appetite statements and communicating risk management expectations to management, staff and shareholders. Both the FSB and OCC have delineated board responsibilities for monitoring and approving risk appetite statements. The OCC requires independent risk management to update systematically a comprehensive risk appetite framework, which the board must approve. In addition to addressing the linkage between risk appetite statements and compensation, the FSB requires the board to review the risk appetite framework to ensure it remains consistent with the organization's short and long-term strategy and business and capital plans.[7]

Additionally, the National Association of Corporate Directors' (NACD) Advisory Council on Risk Oversight has identified "next practices" for boards. Echoing OCC and FSB guidelines, the NACD suggestions include developing risk appetite statements with management to "reflect the 'overlay on strategy and risk.'" Rather than be involved in detailed strategy, boards "need to connect management's assertions to what the strategy is, then have them intelligently identify the risks."[8] A framework developed with management, clearly outlining how much risk the board is willing to accept in pursuit of strategic objectives, also provides shareholders greater transparency.

Greater Transparency: New disclosure rules seek to enhance compensation practice and board accountability to shareholders. FSB's Pillar III, issued in July 2011, proposes principles for proper compensation practices and requires the disclosure of compensation policies. SEC rules adopted in December 2009 require disclosures in proxy and information statements regarding board governance structure and the board's role in risk oversight. Companies must describe the relationship between compensation policies and risk management, as well as the extent to which executive compensation may lead to excessive risk taking.

In March 2014, the National Association of Insurance Commissioners (NAIC) implemented Own Risk and Solvency Assessment (ORSA), a regulatory reporting requirement for large insurers[9] in the United States. ORSA Summary Reports require descriptions of the insurer's ERM framework and assessments of risk exposure, risk capital, and solvency positions under normal and severe stress scenarios. The new ORSA reporting requirement thus encourages forward-looking assessments and reinforces good risk management practices.

All of these regulations will profoundly affect risk management practices by enhancing senior management's accountability and laying ultimate responsibility for ERM oversight squarely on the board. New and emerging requirements also highlight the need for qualified directors to ensure that effective risk governance structures and policies are in place.

CURRENT BOARD PRACTICES

Recent studies suggest that boards are improving governance structure and policy to guide the ERM practices of their organizations. Increasingly, for instance, boards in industries beyond banking and capital markets are adopting ERM programs. A 2013 global study by Accenture found that more than half of companies surveyed in the energy (61%) and insurance (55%) industries have adopted an ERM program.[10]

Even as boards continue to recognize the need for more effective governance structures, companies are reexamining the composition and independence of the board itself. According to a 2013 PwC survey of corporate directors, 55% of boards had a separate CEO and chair while 47% of the remainder were considering the separation of these roles. In addition, a growing number of boards have committees dedicated to overseeing risk management practices. Many have instituted standalone risk committees while others have created hybrid ones overseeing both audit and risk.[11]

According to Accenture's study, 97% of organizations employ a CRO or other senior executive to direct the risk management function. When it comes to risk, boards are not just looking at governance structure, but also policy and culture, even though only 26% feel they have achieved success in those areas "to a great extent." As a result, 60% of boards discussed setting "the tone from the top," in the 12 months preceding the study, and 46% increased their interaction with management to reduce fraud risk.[12]

One significant development in recent years is the institution of so-called clawback policies among Fortune 100 companies. These provisions allow firms to recoup incentive payments previously made to employees in the event of a financial restatement or revelation of ethical misconduct. The rise of clawback policies may also reflect growing stakeholder expectations and the onset of increased regulation in this area, such as new SEC requirements. I should note, however, that in practice clawback provisions are rarely triggered and few cases have attracted significant notice. Most notable is Wells Fargo in the aftermath of its cross-sell scandal. In September 2016, the board clawed back $41 million from CEO John Stumpf and $19 million from community banking head Carrie Tolstedt.

Despite these advances, boards remain skeptical of ERM's ability to create value. Fewer than one in three believe that their ERM programs have enhanced long-term profit growth, though 80% cite that as an important goal.[13] To close the gap, boards are augmenting their ranks with risk experts in an effort to better incorporate risk management into strategic and business decisions.

On the whole, boards are taking an active role in improving ERM oversight and looking for ways to enhance their practices. Before we discuss how boards can improve ERM oversight, let's examine a case of flawed governance structure.

CASE STUDY: SATYAM

Satyam Computer Services was once the largest software company in India. Considered a leader in India's burgeoning IT sector, Satyam garnered the attention of major investment groups such as Aberdeen and Morgan Stanley.[14] In 2008, the company received the World Council's Golden Peacock Award for excellence in corporate governance.

Just a year later, Satyam's chairman, B. Ramalinga Raju, admitted that the company's balance sheet inflated cash and bank balances by $1.44 billion, understated liabilities by $300 million, and reported nonexistent accrued income of $86 million.[15] Raju also admitted that previously announced acquisitions totaling $1.6 billion were nothing more than "the last attempt to fill the fictitious assets with real ones."[16] The companies in question were, in actuality, owned and managed by members of Raju's family.

The public was shocked by Satyam's fall from the pinnacle of corporate governance practice, but should it have been? The company's own Form 20-F filing with the Securities & Exchange Commission, dated August 2008, revealed serious governance issues:

> We do not have an individual serving on our Audit Committee as an "Audit Committee Financial Expert" as defined in applicable rules of the Securities & Exchange Commission. This is because our board of directors has determined that no individual audit committee member possesses all the attributes required by the definition "Audit Committee Financial Expert."[17]

Why was the board so ineffectual? For one thing, the company had no nominating and governance committee to appoint the necessary experts. In fact, Satyam's board had just three committees: Audit (which the company admitted lacked financial experts), Compensation, and Investor Grievances. Second, though the chair and CEO were technically separate positions, they were held by brothers, a clear conflict of interest.

This lack of proper governance was undoubtedly intentional. Raju and his brothers exercised a dominant position on the board and regularly put family interests above those of stakeholders. They could easily introduce questionable strategic plans in order to cover their tracks without fear of challenge. In summary, Satyam suffered three key governance issues:

1. Board members were not qualified to oversee executive management. Few had financial backgrounds.
2. The board lacked independence and objectivity, due to the family relationship between CEO and chair and the combined power of the Raju brothers to influence decisions.
3. The company lacked transparency and accountability. Rather than enhance accountability, the board's governance structure allowed the Raju brothers to operate against the interests of shareholders.

THREE LEVERS FOR ERM OVERSIGHT

While not involved in day-to-day business activities, boards have ultimate responsibility for an ERM program that creates value for the organization. What can they do to oversee ERM and the key risks facing the organization? The answer is GPA: *Governance, Policy, and Assurance*:

Governance: The board must establish an effective governance structure to oversee risk. Issues to consider include: How should the board be organized to oversee ERM? What is the linkage between strategy and risk management? How can the board strengthen the independence of the risk management function? How can the capital structure of the organization best conform to its risk profile, including its dividend policy and target credit ratings?

Policy: The board must approve and monitor an ERM policy that provides explicit risk tolerance levels for key risks. Do risk management policies and tolerance levels effectively capture the board's overall risk appetite? What is the relationship between risk policies and compensation policies?

Assurance: Finally, the board must establish processes to ensure the effectiveness of the company's ERM program. What are the performance metrics and feedback loops used to evaluate ERM? How can management improve the structure and content of board reports? How should that assurance be disclosed to investors, rating agencies, and regulators?

In the previous chapter, we discussed the GPA model in the context of the three lines of defense. Let's examine these board levers in greater detail in terms of regulatory expectations and board risk oversight practices.

Governance

A fundamental step in ERM oversight is to establish an effective risk governance structure at the board level. Risk governance delineates the oversight roles and decision points for the board and its committees, as well as its relationship with management.

To exercise its responsibility, the board needs directors with the expertise to provide independent analysis of the company's strategy, its execution, and the risks it takes on. The board must act objectively and in the best interests of the organization's stakeholders. Charged with recruitment and training of board members, the Nominating and Governance Committee should seek candidates with demonstrated industry and risk management expertise. Mandates such as Dodd-Frank require boards to establish risk committees that include a qualified expert, but boards would do well to look beyond regulatory checklists. Rather, they should appoint directors who can add strategic value to the company. For example, bank boards should consider the following criteria for a risk expert:

- An understanding of risk governance and management practices at financial institutions, including board risk oversight, risk policy and appetite, monitoring and assurance processes, and risk reporting and disclosure requirements.
- Experience as chief risk officer, and/or actively supervising the chief risk officer of a large, complex financial institution.
- Knowledge of banking regulations and standards, such as Dodd-Frank, Basel II and III, SEC, ORSA, OCC, FSB, and Federal Reserve requirements.
- Experience in the identification, assessment, and management of the key risks faced by financial institutions, including strategic, business, market, liquidity, credit/counterparty, operational, IT, cybersecurity, and systemic risks.
- Knowledge of ERM, including assessment of cross-risk interdependencies and aggregate risk profiles.
- Ability to oversee the CRO's implementation of the ERM program and lead and/or advise the board on major risk governance and policy issues, as well as guide and/or challenge management on recommended risk strategies, plans, and assumptions.
- Experience in overseeing and/or executing applications of key risk management tools, including value at risk, economic capital, risk-adjusted pricing and profitability models, risk-control assessments, stress testing, and scenario analysis.
- Understanding the usefulness and limitations of risk management tools, including a solid grasp of derivatives and hedging strategies.

The board should discuss whether the CEO or an independent director should also serve as chair of the board. The chair leads the board, which holds the responsibility of management oversight, while the CEO is directly responsible for management. A split CEO and chair eliminates the possibility of a conflict of interest. This structure also supports the board's primary responsibility for oversight without excessive involvement in day-to-day management. Despite these advantages, most major U.S. banks (for example, J.P. Morgan and Morgan Stanley) retain combined CEO/chairs with relative success. In cases where the board retains a combined CEO/chair, it usually designates a lead independent director (LID) to assume overall responsibility for oversight of the CEO and management. Advocates of a combined CEO/chair argue that the individual in such a position has a superior understanding of the organization, but critics cite the importance of board independence for objective decision-making. Whatever the structure, the composition of the board should support the flow of information between senior management and directors and enhance the board's ability to carry out its oversight responsibilities.

Risk Committee of the Board While the full board retains ultimate responsibility for risk oversight, a growing number of organizations have established a separate risk committee to oversee ERM processes. This committee reviews reports from executive management and provides the full board with data and analysis regarding the organization's risk profile and emerging risks. Consider the typical components of a risk committee charter:

- **Purpose:** Introduces the objective of the committee and gives a concise statement of responsibility in oversight.
- **Composition and Meeting:** Includes the number of members on the committee and qualification requirements such as expertise and experience. It might include a statement of regulatory requirements for risk experts as well.
- **Responsibilities and Duties:** Covers the responsibilities of the committee in terms of ERM and reporting duties for management and the CRO (if applicable). May include a description of how the risk committee coordinates with the audit committee to ensure internal audit meets risk-governance requirements. If the company has a CRO, the charter should define that role. Lastly, it should outline the requirements and responsibility for reviewing management reports.

The risk committee should review its charter regularly and update it to reflect regulatory requirements and the needs of the organization.

Audit Committee The audit committee charter is complimentary to that of the risk committee. The audit function provides evaluations that assist the risk management processes. While internal audit does not aid in the development of risk management processes it can play an important role in assurance. Internal audit assesses reporting of key risks and ensures that the risks are properly evaluated. As internal audit directly reports to the audit committee, the risk committee and audit committee should interact to enhance the organization's review of risk management while remaining independent of one another. For companies with joint audit and risk committees, it is critical that each mandate receives proper allocation of time and attention, and that membership includes both distinct skill sets.

Responsibilities of the Board vs. Management Boards and management often express a need for more clarity in terms of roles and responsibilities. In theory, at least, the board and management serve distinct functions that may be likened to the legislative and executive branches of the U.S. government. The board, like Congress, represents the interests of shareholders and other stakeholder groups while management operates the company in the same way that the White House executes policy. But in the real world, as in politics, roles and powers may overlap. A board with poorly defined responsibilities may encroach on management's purview or, in the other extreme, fail to examine and challenge management's decisions. Figure 9.1 outlines the alignment and key differences between board and management responsibilities with respect to each aspect of ERM implementation.

ERM Component	Executive Management	Board of Directors
Risk Governance	Establish management structure and roles	Establish board structure and roles
ERM Vision and Plan	Develop and implement	Support vision; track progress against plan
Risk Tolerance Levels	Establish and conform	Debate and approve
Risk Policies	Develop and implement	Approve and monitor
Business and Risk Strategies	Formulate and execute	Challenge key assumptions; monitor execution
Critical Risks	Manage and measure; optimize risk/return	Provide input and oversight
Risk Reports	Provide context, analysis, and key points	Monitor key exposures, exceptions, and feedback loops
Risk Analytics	Provide qualitative and quantitative analyses	Obtain ERM assurance; conduct board assessments

FIGURE 9.1 Executive Management and Board Responsibilities for ERM

There is one area in which board and management should work in perfect concert: setting the "tone from the top" and fostering a culture of integrity and honesty across the organization. While boards should encourage intelligent risk taking, they must also demand zero tolerance for unauthorized and unethical behavior. One way to do this is to ensure the independence of the risk management function, allowing risk managers to carry out their responsibilities without fear of reprisal. In practical terms, this means there ought to be a direct line of reporting from the risk function, headed by the CRO or equivalent, to the board, ideally represented by its risk committee.

The CRO would still be on the CEO's executive committee, but under exceptional circumstances (for example, excessive risk taking, major internal fraud, or significant business conflicts), the CRO should be able to escalate risk issues directly to the board without concern about his or her job security or compensation. Such stature resonates with the entire company and empowers risk management functions to promote good risk practices.[18] See the E*TRADE Financial case study in the next chapter for more discussion on this topic.

Value-Creation from Integrating Strategy and Risk Monitoring strategy has long been the purview of boards, so as boards become more active in ERM, it makes sense that strategy and risk management will become increasingly integrated. In fact, strategic risk management is key to a successful ERM program. It preserves and creates value for the organization, and it may uncover opportunities the organization has failed to exploit. Let's examine how this worked for the Danish toymaker LEGO.

A 2013 article in the *Wall Street Journal* highlighted LEGO's success in strategic risk management. Just a decade earlier, however, the company confronted near-bankruptcy because of strategic missteps.[19] At the time, LEGO faced emerging competitors, changing demographics, and the maturing of its lucrative Star Wars and Lord of the Rings licensed product lines. In 2006, senior director of strategic risk management Hans Laessoe saw the need for dramatic change. He began by identifying LEGO's major strategic risks and projecting them forward using Monte Carlo simulations; active risk and opportunity planning; and scenario analysis. Among his discoveries was that in some cases the organization was actually too risk averse. As a result of his efforts, LEGO managed an average growth of 21% and a profit growth of 34% over 2007 to 2013 despite a stagnant overall toy market.[20]

In an effort to take similar advantage of prudent risk opportunities, today's boards are pushing management to integrate risk management more fully into strategic planning. We'll take a closer look at this synergy in Chapter 15, but for now suffice it to say that senior executives will need to rethink their approach. They must make sure that strategic initiatives are consistent with the organization's risk appetite, and adapt them as its risk profile shifts. They should develop contingency plans so that the company can change course to avoid unforeseen obstacles or seize new opportunities. And they must see risk controls not as impediments to business activity but integral to value creation. Before they can do all that, however, companies must set forth clear policies around risk management.

Policy

A company's ERM policy sets out board expectations for risk management and oversight. Executive management formulates and implements the policy while the board of directors reviews, challenges, and approves it. The adoption of a formal, organization-wide risk policy will help avoid these common problems:

- Absence of explicit limits or tolerance levels for key risks
- Lack of standards across different policies for various types of risk (credit, market, operational, etc.)
- Insufficient reporting and monitoring of policy exceptions and resolutions
- Gaps in key risk governance, oversight, and reporting components
- Stale procedures that fail to capture risk and may indeed obscure a developing issue

The most important risk policy is the risk appetite statement (RAS). This document is critical to risk oversight because it helps employees throughout the corporate hierarchy make risk-savvy decisions. Risk appetite statements are not meant to capture *all* material risks—that would make them too unwieldy. Rather, they provide an overall view of the company's preferred risk profile and identify how to achieve and maintain it. (We'll examine risk appetite statements more fully in Chapter 12.) A clearly defined RAS offers guidance to management as it executes strategy, and provides the board with a benchmark as it exercises its oversight.

Risk policy will naturally inform policy in other areas. For example, the board and management should examine compensation policy to ensure that it does not reward excessive risk. In fact, recent history has shown that the causal link between compensation policy and risk should be one of the board's top concerns. As the saying goes, people don't do what you tell them to do; they do what you pay them to do. Therefore, the board and its compensation committee should ensure that risk management receives sufficient weight in performance evaluations and incentives. By incorporating

ERM into compensation plans, the board can have a far-reaching impact not only on management actions, but on employee behavior at every level of the organization as well.

The examples below, taken from J.P. Morgan, show how a well-thought-out compensation policy can incorporate risk management:

Examples from J.P. Morgan's Compensation Policy Below is a statement from J.P. Morgan's bonus recoupment policy regarding potential actions for the clawback of bonuses.[21]

> *Appropriate action could include actions such as termination, reducing compensation in the year the restatement was made, seeking repayment of any bonus received for the period restated or any gains realized as a result of exercising an option awarded for the period restated, or canceling any unvested equity compensation awarded for the period restated. Consideration may also be given to whether or not any one or more of such actions should be extended to employees who did not engage in misconduct that contributed to the restatement.*

In addition to the bonus recoupment policy, incentive awards are subject to clawback and other provisions described in the Firm's most recent proxy statement. From J.P. Morgan's 2014 Proxy Statement.[22]

> *We have put in place rigorous and extensive clawback/recoupment provisions on both cash incentives and equity awards, which enable us to reduce or cancel unvested awards and recover previously paid compensation in certain situations*
> *. . . . Incentive awards are intended and expected to vest according to their terms, but strong recovery provisions permit recovery of incentive compensation awards in appropriate circumstances. We also retain the right to reduce current-year incentives to redress any prior imbalance that we have subsequently determined to have existed.*

Assurance

In order to know whether ERM is working effectively, organizations need to establish assurance processes, including monitoring and reporting, performance metrics, objective feedback loops, and independent assessments. At the same time, however, board members often report that the risk reports they currently receive are not as timely or useful as they'd like.

Boards can influence management practices by demanding clear, concise reporting, helping to select key performance indicators, and determining the appropriate reporting frequency. What would such reports look like? Consider these best practices:

- A concise executive summary of business/risk performance, as well as external performance drivers
- A focus on key points for board discussion and decision-making, uncluttered by extraneous detail
- Forward-looking analyses versus historical data and trends
- Key performance and risk indicators shown against specific targets or limits
- Sufficient time for board input and discussion

These criteria can be even more effectively addressed with role-based dashboard reports. These are single-screen displays that present summary risk and performance information while allowing users to drill down to supporting data as necessary. By tapping into existing business systems on a real-time basis, modern dashboard programs facilitate communication with timely and relevant content. Ideally, this will include qualitative and quantitative data, internal risk exposures, external drivers, and key performance and risk indicators. Chapter 19 will focus exclusively on these important new tools.

All this information gathering is of little use unless it allows the board not only to monitor activity but also to support continual improvement. In the past, companies could declare their ERM efforts a success if they achieved development milestones and didn't experience regulatory violations, losses, and other negative events. These metrics are still necessary but no longer sufficient. Instead, they must be augmented by feedback loops that drive improvement. Earnings-at-risk analysis, which I discuss in Chapter 20, is one such feedback loop. Another is the ERM scorecard, which allows the board to measure effectiveness in the following terms:

- **Achievement of ERM development milestones:** These might include instituting an ERM policy, setting risk tolerance levels, drafting a risk appetite statement, etc.
- **Lack of regulatory/policy violations or other negative events:** Directors and executives could include "no surprises"—such as regulatory violations and fines, risk limit breaches, customer or reputational events—as a key success factor in ERM.
- **Reduction of total cost of risk:** The sum of expected loss, unexpected loss (or the cost of economic capital), risk transfer costs, and risk management costs equals the total cost of risk.

- **Performance-based feedback loops:** These include minimizing unexpected earnings volatility, minimizing variances between ex-ante risk analytics (e.g., risk assessments and models) and ex-post risk results (actual losses and events), and contributions to shareholder value creation.

Just as boards retain independent auditors to review and provide assurance for the financial statements, they should also retain an independent party to review and provide assurance for the ERM program. The assessment should evaluate ERM components relative to industry best practices and/or progress against plan. Internal audit can also provide assurance and monitor risk management processes. The board should conduct a self-assessment of its role in ERM as well. I will discuss risk reporting and monitoring processes in more depth in Chapters 18, 19, and 20.

Assuring that ERM processes are effective is important not only for the board, but also for the organization's other stakeholders. Through proxy statements and annual reports, the board communicates information regarding the company's performance to stakeholders. Regulators, including the FSB and SEC, require information on governance structure, policy, and assurance processes to be included in proxy statements. These requirements enhance communication with stakeholders and keep the board accountable for oversight of the organization.

CONCLUSION

With growing uncertainty and ever-increasing stakeholder expectations, board responsibilities in ERM oversight are not without challenges. Boards are not involved in day-to-day enterprise activities, and they have limited time to review materials and meet with management. Nonetheless, the board, with the support of its committees, is charged with overseeing risk management and ensuring such processes create value for the organization. As we discussed, the board has three key levers for doing so: a well-thought-out governance structure to organize risk management and oversight activities; risk policies to articulate the board's expectations in regard to risk appetite and tolerance; and assurance processes and feedback loops to gauge the effectiveness of the ERM program. With these tools, the board can effectively implement its ultimate responsibility for risk management to regulators, shareholders, and other stakeholders.

NOTES

1. Lam, James. "The Role of the Board in Enterprise Risk Management," *RMA Journal*, April 2011.

2. *2013 AFP Risk Survey: Report of Survey Results*, Association for Financial Professionals and Oliver Wyman, 2013.
3. *Accenture 2013 Global Risk Management Study: Risk Management for an Era of Greater Uncertainty*, Accenture, 2013.
4. European Parliament. *Regulation (EU) No 575/2013 of the European Parliament and of the Council of 26 June 2013 on Prudential Requirements for Credit Institutions and Investment Firms and Amending Regulation (EU) No 648/2012 (1)*, 2013.
5. U.S. Office of the Comptroller of the Currency, Department of the Treasury. OCC *Guidelines Establishing Heightened Standards for Certain Large Insured National Banks, Insured Federal Savings Associations, and Insured Federal Branches; Integration of 12 CFR Parts 30 and 170*, 2014.
6. U.S. Congress. Dodd-Frank Wall Street Reform and Consumer Protection Act, H.R. 4173 (111th), 2010.
7. *Principles for an Effective Risk Appetite Statement*, Financial Stability Board, 2013.
8. *Summary of Proceedings*: National Association of Corporate Directors, Advisory Council on Risk Oversight, 2013.
9. *ORSA Summary Report Guidelines Draft*, National Association of Insurance Commissioners, 2014.
10. *Risk Management for an Era of Greater Uncertainty*, Accenture, 2013.
11. *Boards Confront an Evolving Landscape: PwC's Annual Corporate Directors Survey*, Pricewaterhouse Coopers, 2013.
12. *Risk Management for an Era of Greater Uncertainty*, Accenture, 2013.
13. Ibid.
14. Christy, John. "India's Enron," *Forbes,* January 27, 2009.
15. Basilico, Elisabetta, Grove, Hugh, and Patelli Lorenzo. "Asia's Enron: Satyam (Sanskrit Word for Truth)," *Journal of Forensic & Investigative Accounting* 4(2), 2012.
16. Bellman, Eric, and Range, Jackie. "Satyam Probe Scrutinizes CFO, Audit Committee," *Wall Street Journal*, January 14, 2009.
17. Behan, Beverly. "Governance Lessons from India's Satyam," *Bloomberg Businessweek*, January 16, 2009.
18. Lam, James. "The Role of the Board in Enterprise Risk Management," *RMA Journal*, April 2011.
19. Hansegard J. "Building Risk Management at Lego," *Wall Street Journal*, August 5, 2013.
20. Læssøe H. "Three Examples of Value from @Risk in Decision Making at the LEGO Group" (Presentation), The LEGO Group, 2014.
21. *Corporate Governance Principles,* JP Morgan Chase & Co., n.a. Retrieved from http://www.jpmorganchase.com/corporate/About-JPMC/corporate-governance-principles#recoupment.
22. *Definitive Proxy Statement*, JP Morgan Chase & Co., 2014. Retrieved from http://www.sec.gov/Archives/edgar/data/19617/000001961714000321/jpm 2014definitiveproxy.htm#s468f86f88217403fa97210cda20ddb27 (accessed 1 July 2014).

CHAPTER 10

The View from the Risk Chair*

INTRODUCTION

In September 2012, I received a call from an executive recruiter representing the Board of Directors of E*TRADE Financial. He said the company was looking for a new director "with risk in his or her DNA." On November 14, 2012, I was appointed to the Company's Board, and also named Chair of the Risk Oversight Committee (ROC) and a member of the Audit Committee. Serving on a public company board had long been one of my professional goals, so this was a joyous occasion.

The general public may know the Company best for its Super Bowl commercials featuring a cute talking baby. Today, our advertising campaign features the popular actor Kevin Spacey. Perhaps this change is a good metaphor for the evolution of the company from an Internet darling to a mature S&P500 company.

TURNAROUND STORY

E*TRADE has an interesting turnaround story. Having executed the first-ever electronic trade by an individual investor more than 30 years ago, the company was an early digital disrupter, commonly known as a FinTech today. But in the 2007–2008 period, the Company found itself on the brink of collapse due to sizable, ill-timed investments in mortgages and other asset-backed securities that deteriorated during the economic crisis. This set off a series of events that—over the course of five years—led to troublesome capital position, activist investor pressure, and intense regulatory scrutiny. The Board and management team worked tirelessly to save the Company during those difficult years. While their good efforts

---

*This chapter was first published as a book excerpt in the September/October 2016 issue of NACD Directorship. This case study is also recommended in the NACD Director Essentials: Strengthening Risk Oversight.

provided a line of sight to better financial performance, there was still much work to be done to improve our regulatory standing and risk management capabilities. The purpose of this case study is to discuss the key initiatives that we had implemented to establish a robust ERM program.

Based on the Company's results to date, I believe we are moving in the right direction. In November 2012, the stock was trading around $8, we were undercapitalized and losing money, our debt ratings were B–/B2, and we operated under the tight regulatory restraints of memorandums of understanding (MOUs) from the OCC and the Federal Reserve. Since that time, E*TRADE has achieved solid profitability, reduced its corporate debt burden, de-risked the balance sheet, and established a far stronger capital position. In 2015, the MOUs were lifted, and we announced the first stock buyback program in over eight years. As of September 30, 2016, the stock closed at $29, and our debt ratings are BBB–/Baa3.

Of course, no company should ever rest on its laurels when it comes to risk management. We continue to face challenges such as enhancing cyber-security and improving our business drivers through organic and acquisitive growth. In the rest of this chapter, I will discuss the role of the board in risk oversight in the context of my experience at E*TRADE. In partnership with my board and management colleagues, we have established what I consider to be a best-in-class enterprise risk management (ERM) program, including an innovative first-of-its-kind performance feedback loop for ERM.

THE GPA MODEL IN ACTION

Prior to E*TRADE, I had served on the boards of two private technology companies, one of which I founded and served as president and vice chairman. I also worked as a senior risk advisor to U.S. and international boards across a wide range of industry sectors, including banking, insurance, asset management, healthcare, technology, and not-for-profit. Based on my experience, I created the GPA framework to develop the three key components for board risk oversight, as discussed in the previous chapter.

It is management's role to manage risk, and the board's role to govern and oversee. By addressing the fundamental elements of board risk oversight, the GPA framework has been useful in my prior work as a board advisor. The E*TRADE appointment was my first opportunity to apply it at a public company as a director and risk committee chair.

TOP PRIORITIES FOR THE RISK OVERSIGHT COMMITTEE

As the incoming Chair of the Risk Oversight Committee (ROC), I focused on addressing the regulatory requirements and expectations as set forth in the MOUs, as well as overseeing the build-out of a comprehensive ERM program. After an initial assessment, I outlined five top priorities for the ROC. I reviewed them with the other ROC members, the chairman, the CEO, and the chief risk officer (CRO) to gain their acceptance and support. Relative to the GPA framework, priorities #1 and #2 address governance, #3 addresses policy, and #4 and #5 address assurance. The five priorities are as follows:

Establish a Strong ERM Agenda

Board time is limited and precious so I wanted to make sure the ROC spent it productively. I worked with the CRO and committee members to establish an annual calendar. This calendar included agenda items required by charter, policy, law, or regulatory guidance. It also included deep dives into specific risks, such as credit and cybersecurity, as well as capital adequacy and stress-testing results.

In the past, the ROC focused mainly on financial and regulatory risks, but I wanted our scope to include strategic and operational risks as well. Independent studies of the largest public companies have shown time and again that strategic risks account for approximately 60% of major declines in market capitalization, followed by operational risks (about 30%) and financial risks (about 10%).[1] As such, it is imperative that any ERM program encompass strategic and operational risks.

The MOUs placed significant constraints on the Company, so their resolution was mission critical for the ROC. At each meeting, the chief compliance officer provided a status update on our progress in addressing all of the MOU requirements. We also sought to engage our regulators and to develop good relationships with them outside the boardroom, so the chairman, CEO, and I scheduled regular one-on-one meetings with them.

The ROC also received regular updates on our progress against the ERM roadmap. This multi-year roadmap included specific milestones and work plans to develop our risk and compliance (2nd line of defense) and internal audit (3rd line of defense) capabilities. It also included a risk culture program that encompassed training, executive town halls, and an annual risk culture survey.

Strengthen Independent Risk and Compliance Oversight

The independent reporting relationship between internal audit and the audit committee is a long-established standard in corporate governance. This is not always the case with risk and compliance functions. Yet, as we learned from the economic crisis and other corporate disasters, the independence of oversight functions is a critical success factor.

When I first joined E*TRADE, there were reporting lines between the ROC and the CRO and chief compliance officer, but other than a Power-Point chart, there was no documentation on what those lines really meant. I worked with the CEO and General Counsel to adopt the following section in the ROC Charter to formalize the independent reporting relationships between the ROC and the CRO (and separately the chief compliance officer).

> Evaluation of the Chief Risk Officer. At least annually, the Committee, in consultation with management of the Company, shall evaluate the performance of the Company's Chief Risk Officer and shall:
>
> a) Have, following consultation with management of the Company, the authority to retain and to terminate the Chief Risk Officer; and
>
> b) Provide input to Company management and the Compensation Committee of the Board with respect to the compensation structure, annual performance goals and incentives for the Chief Risk Officer.
>
> Management of the Company must obtain the Committee's approval prior to making any organizational reporting change, material changes to overall compensation and/or hiring or termination decisions with respect to the Chief Risk Officer.

Enhance Risk Policies, with a Focus on the Risk Appetite Statement

Risk policies should not be tombstones. They should be living documents that explicitly communicate the organization's risk management processes, guidelines, and risk tolerances. At E*TRADE, we had over a dozen risk policies for different types of risk (e.g., strategic risk policy, credit risk policy, operational risk policy, etc.). However, they didn't always share consistent structure, content, or process for renewal and board approval. For example, some had clearly defined risk metrics and risk tolerance levels while others did not. In the first cycle of annual policy renewal and approval, we established a set of guidelines for all existing and new risk policies. These guidelines created common standards such as risk oversight and management responsibilities, risk tolerance levels, and exception management and reporting processes.

More importantly, we developed a comprehensive risk appetite statement (RAS). The RAS establishes the types and levels of risk that we are willing to accept in pursuit of our business strategy. In my opinion, the RAS is the most important risk policy of all, because it provides the key risk limits and tolerance levels for the overall organization. For each risk type, we defined our core objectives with qualitative statements and supported them with quantitative risk tolerance levels. Each type of risk also has a defined governance structure with respect to its management at the operating units (1st line of defense) and its oversight at the risk and compliance functions (2nd line of defense). Moreover, the company communicates the RAS to every employee in order to support a common risk culture.

Improve the Quality of Risk Reports

The quality of risk reports the board receives substantially influences the quality of its discussions and decisions. Initially, the ROC package mainly consisted of lengthy PowerPoint presentations, granular risk assessments, and detailed metrics. However, it was not always clear where committee members should focus their attention or whether the risk metrics were within acceptable levels.

In order to improve the quality and effectiveness of risk reporting, I worked with the CRO to develop a standard "CRO Report" to provide a concise summary of the Company's risk profile. A week prior to each ROC meeting, we receive the CRO Report along with the ROC package. The CRO Report includes the following information:

- **Executive Summary.** The report appropriately begins with an overview of E*TRADE's aggregate risk profile and key risk exposures for the overall organization. It also draws the ROC's attention to the meeting's key discussion and decision points.
- **New Risk and Loss Events.** This section provides a summary of material risk and loss events, including initial loss estimates and root-cause analysis. These events may involve business practices; policy exceptions; regulatory issues; IT and cybersecurity events; and financial and operational losses.
- **Follow-up on Prior Risk and Loss Events.** Any resolutions or updates from previously reported risk and loss events are provided.
- **Emerging Risks.** This section identifies emerging risks that may impact the organization, as well as risk trends and developments for the industry.
- **Risk Assessments and Metrics.** In this section, the CRO, with input from the functional risk leaders, provides a summary of the major risk areas. Each summary includes expert commentary, as well as a risk appetite dashboard for the key risk metrics against risk tolerance levels. It also explains any deviations from risk tolerance levels, indicated by yellow (warning) or red (negative) signals. The types of risks include:
  - Strategic
  - Market
  - Interest Rate

- Liquidity
- Credit/Counterparty
- Operational
- Cybersecurity
- Reputational
- Legal, Regulatory, and Compliance
- Capital Adequacy

- **Progress Against the ERM Roadmap.** This section provides an update on the key accomplishments, progress to date, and major initiatives relative to the ERM Roadmap.
- **Terms and Definitions.** The report concludes with a glossary of technical terms, performance and risk metrics, and acronyms used.

Establish an ERM Performance Feedback Loop

How do we know if risk management is working effectively? This is a fundamental question that every board should address. The most common practice is to evaluate performance based on the achievement of key milestones or the lack of negative events. However, I believe qualitative milestones or negative proofs, though necessary, are not sufficient measures of success.

A performance feedback loop is a critical tool to support continuous improvement by adjusting a process (e.g., ERM) according to the variances between actual and desired performance. In order to establish a performance feedback loop for ERM, a company must first define its objective in measurable terms. I believe the objective of ERM is to minimize unexpected earnings volatility.[2]

In my first meeting with E*TRADE's CRO, I made clear that of the five ROC priorities, the ERM performance feedback loop is probably the most challenging but also the most valuable. It took about a year for the CRO, in collaboration with the CFO, to implement this innovative technique. The resultant analysis is affectionately known internally as the "Lam Report." By comparing ex-ante earnings-at-risk analysis to ex-post earnings attribution analysis, we are able to monitor the earnings impact of changing trading volumes, interest rates, credit performance, and other risk drivers. We can also isolate unexpected earnings volatility as a performance feedback loop for our overall ERM program.

CONCLUSION

These five ROC priorities provide the foundation for effective board risk oversight. Today, I am honored to serve on a board that is diverse, engaged, and effective. In my career, I have worked on over 50 ERM engagements as

CRO, board advisor, and now risk committee chair. E*TRADE has made the most significant progress in a relatively short three-year period. In retrospect, I believe several factors contributed to the rapid development of ERM at the Company. These factors included a good partnership between management and the board, effective leadership by the CRO and chief compliance officer, sufficient commitment of time and resources to the ERM build-out, and a focus on instilling a strong risk culture throughout the Company.

As I said earlier in this chapter, I believe that we are moving in the right direction, but no company should ever rest on its laurels when it comes to risk management. E*TRADE will continue to face new risks, whether operational, cyber, or strategic. Yet with the right framework and the proper focus from the executive team down to the frontline employee, E*TRADE and its board are ready to face these challenges. Going forward, we are building on our heritage as a digital disruptor, and innovating in a manner that embraces risk.

NOTES

1. James Lam, *Enterprise Risk Management: From Incentives to Controls*, 2nd edition, Wiley, 2014, pp. 434–436.
2. In addition to unexpected earnings volatility, a company may also strive to minimize unexpected changes in enterprise value and cash flows. It is important to note that the goal is not to minimize *absolute* levels of risks, but simply those from unknown sources.

CHAPTER 11

Rise of the CRO

INTRODUCTION

The 2008 financial crisis and subsequent scrutiny of corporate governance have put chief risk officers in the spotlight. I was interviewed by the *Wall Street Journal* for an article[1] aptly titled "Cinderella Moment: The Credit Crisis Means Chief Risk Officers Are Finally Being Listened To. But How Long Will It Last?" The article discussed the rise of CROs, their organizational prominence, and the abundant resources that they were receiving. It also discussed their key challenges in shaping corporate culture and establishing objective performance feedback loops. CROs have come a long way but they must demonstrate that they can add value as a member of the executive team.

In the past, CROs came mainly from risk management backgrounds, such as market risk, credit risk, corporate compliance, and internal audit. Reaching the CRO position was seen as the capstone for a risk management career. Today, many CROs come from business backgrounds and bring a much broader perspective to their jobs (i.e., they see the whole bell curve and not just the downside). Instead of a capstone, CRO positions can now be steppingstones toward the corner office and even the boardroom. Matt Feldman, whose profile is featured later in the chapter, represents this new class of CROs.[2]

Once only discussed in a financial industry context, chief risk officers are expanding into other highly regulated industries such as pharmaceuticals, energy, and insurance. But with greater exposure comes greater responsibility and accountability—the role has expanded beyond the purely technical. Increasingly, CROs are becoming integral to value creation and overarching business strategy. As companies continue to evolve their approach to risk management, the criteria they use to appoint a risk leader is evolving as well.

ERM is still a relatively young discipline, and the role of CRO remains fluid. The exact function of the chief risk officer can differ depending on the current circumstances of the company. If the firm's ERM program is mature, for example, the CRO's goal is likely to integrate risk into high-level strategy. If the company is recovering from a crisis, however, he or she might focus on guiding it toward stability. These are crucial tasks, and certainly comprise a portion of a CRO's duties. But without a clear overall vision of the role, any ambiguity could hinder any chief risk officer's effectiveness.

In a 2014 Harvard Business School working paper, Anette Mikes tracked the chief risk officer of a large toymaker for three years. At the onset of the study, this CRO's "responsibility concerned the design and facilitation" of the ERM program,[3] such as automating a number of critical processes. By the end, however, he had gained full support from upper management to focus on strategic risk oversight and value creation. For this reason, he referred to his function not as ERM, but as Strategic Risk Management (SRM). The evolution of the CRO's role was marked by key learning points—a project-based collection of risk information, a greater understanding of the importance of language, and the introduction of "act" issues (those accompanied by an agreed-upon and detailed action plan).

This study is a good example of what I mean by the fluidity of a chief risk officer's role. Even if the functions and goals are clear in the beginning, they will inevitably shift over time as the risk management process matures. To add to this dynamism, previous literature on the chief risk officer focused mainly on the banking industry. Translating strategies from a large financial institution to companies in other industries is difficult at best and may not always work.

In this chapter, I will provide a more comprehensive review of how chief risk officers work in the financial sector and beyond. We will touch on the rise of the chief risk officer before diving into key roles and responsibilities. And I will discuss potential pitfalls and challenges before laying out detailed steps for those starting a new tenure as CRO. My hope is that this chapter will guide companies to examine relevant criteria when selecting the right chief risk officer, and provide new CROs with a roadmap to success. At the end of the chapter, we will review the profiles and career paths of six current and former CROs.

HISTORY AND RISE OF THE CRO

The role now held by chief risk officers originated in the 1990s in the banking sector, where the initial focus was mainly on financial risks. During this time, risk management was expanding rapidly. Coinciding with advances in information technology, ERM practices developed sophisti-cated knowledge-based systems and quantitative risk-assessment tools.

For example, quantitative tools such as VaR and economic capital enable companies to measure financial risks across products, asset classes, and business units.

I came up with the title *chief risk officer* in 1993 when I was working for GE Capital. I was tasked with setting up a new capital markets business with specific responsibilities for the middle-office and back-office operations. The middle office included credit, counterparty, market, and liquidity risks. In my fist week on the job, I asked my boss what title I should put on my business cards. He simply said to come up with one that is appropriate for my responsibilities. My inspiration came from the technology side. At that time, GE Capital and other companies were appointing chief information officers (CIOs) whose job was to integrate different technologies and also to elevate IT to the executive level. I thought, why not create a CRO position to integrate multiple risk categories, and at the same time elevate the risk management agenda to the executive level? As the newly appointed CRO, I would be responsible for designing and implementing an ERM program. I held the CRO title at GE Capital and subsequently at Fidelity Investments.

Growing Popularity

Risk management came into sharp focus after the economic meltdown of 2008, when companies prioritized the development of comprehensive ERM frameworks. The value of CROs has risen worldwide as executives were appointed to guide and implement those frameworks.

Increased regulation has also aided the rise of the CRO. The Federal Reserve Board approved a rule in February 2014 that requires U.S. bank holding companies with assets of $10B or more to establish board-level risk committees.[4] As a result, 71% of surveyed institutions in the United States have such a committee, compared to 39% in Europe and 37% in Asia-Pacific. Notably, the prevalence of risk committees has proven to be a good indicator for the appointment of CROs.

Ongoing regulatory changes in Europe suggest that the percentage of financial institutions with risk committees (and CROs) will likely increase in the next few years. For instance, Article 44 of Solvency II requires insurance companies to have a risk management function that reports to the board. As of November 2012, 84% of insurers have CROs or intend to bring on a CRO.[5] On the financial side, Lee Guy, formerly of Barclays, joined Morgan Stanley as their European chief risk officer in July 2014.

While ERM in the United States and Europe is more mature than elsewhere, Asia-Pacific is not far behind. Already, 61% of surveyed institutions in the region increased board oversight of risk management after the financial crisis.[6] For example, OCBC Bank named Vincent Choo Nyen Fui as their new chief risk officer in August 2014. In a statement released by the bank, OCBC's CEO pointed to increased volatility and operational risks as key drivers for the appointment.[7]

As with any significant new development, there has been some skepticism about the increasing influence of CROs. For one thing, adding a new C-suite position challenges the existing executive structure. Critics have argued that other executives, such as the CEO or CFO, should already perform the responsibilities of a CRO. Each company department has different risks, that argument goes, and it's up to the CFO to manage those risks. Appointing a CRO, skeptics conclude, would cause redundancy.[8]

The best response to these critics is that the growth of ERM in both complexity and scope naturally leads to the need for a CRO independent of the CFO and even, to some extent, of the CEO. With more companies interested in developing their ERM systems, there is a greater need for risk leaders to implement them. Just as CIOs became more prominent with information technology advances in the early 1990s, CROs are now in the spotlight because of an increased focus on risk. Indeed, despite some pushback, companies have been adding CROs at a growing rate globally. Of 86 large institutions surveyed in 2012, 89% have CROs, up from 65% in 2002 and 86% in 2010.[9]

It should come as little surprise that CROs are most prevalent in highly regulated sectors and/or those industries with the highest risk profiles, such as finance and energy. For example, the three largest company categories in global consultancy CEB's Risk Management network are energy (18%), financial services (13%), and insurance (9%).[10] Obviously, regulatory pressures drive a need for ERM. For the same reason, the CRO role has expanded to other industries subject to intense regulation, such as pharmaceuticals, telecommunications, and health care. Perhaps not every company needs a full-time CRO, but I believe that any risk-intensive company should at least evaluate the position.

A CRO'S CAREER PATH

The risk management profession has expanded in many ways. In the past, risk managers could only aspire to become experts within a narrow risk function. Generally speaking, risk used to be a career path one fell into, not something one aspired to. Now, however, more and more people seek out risk concentrations as part of their higher education. The career ceiling for risk professionals has been all but lifted. CROs go on to become CFOs, CEOs, board members, and managing partners. For example, Paul Gallagher, who previously served as the head of risk at BNP Paribas Fortis and

CRO at ABN AMRO, became the latter institution's CEO in 2013. Likewise, Goldman Sachs recently added CRO Craig Broderick to its management committee, the first time in its history that the company has elevated a CRO to that level.

A look at how CRO compensation has grown over the past few years also serves as an indication of the position's growing importance. Today a CRO generally earns as much as a CFO—up to $10 million annually at large financial institutions compared to $500,000 in 2001.[11] In the last five years, the average CRO salary has increased 7.5% across all industries, to $184,000.[12] The rise in salary is a product of the overwhelming demand for CROs and evidence that firms are placing greater emphasis on risk management.

THE CRO'S ROLE

Just as the importance of risk management has fueled the rise of the CRO, so too has the CRO's growing prominence expanded the profession's responsibilities. As a leader for overall risk management, the CRO is responsible for creating, implementing, and managing a risk management function across the organization. This broad, organization-wide mandate differs significantly from the traditional approach to risk management, which operates within functional silos and tends to treat each risk individually, without considering interrelationships or aggregation. For this reason, it is imperative that the CRO have the support of the board and senior management in order to be effective.

A successful chief risk officer should have a clear vision of his or her general responsibilities before accepting the job, whether they are to reinvent the risk wheel or to support an existing foundation. The CRO will then need to identify direct reports and information channels. Beyond the required technical credentials, today's chief risk officer needs a firm grasp of soft skills, such as the ability to communicate priorities, shape culture, and influence others.

Today's CROs have numerous responsibilities, including:

- Providing overall leadership and vision for enterprise risk management, including addressing change management requirements
- Establishing integrated risk management across separate business units in the organization
- Overseeing the risk-taking activities of the organization, including organic and acquisition growth opportunities
- Developing risk analytical and data-management capabilities

- Implementing board- and corporate-level reporting in all risk areas and regulatory compliance
- Developing risk management policies and quantifying firm-wide risk appetite
- Communicating the company's risk profile to key stakeholders, including regulators, stock analysts, rating agencies, and business partners

This new, broader role faces three interrelated challenges that any CRO must work to overcome: reporting structure and collaboration, measuring and communicating the value of ERM efforts to key stakeholders, and making risk management an integral part of corporate culture. Let's look at these in detail one at a time:

Reporting Structure and Collaboration

For the uninitiated, CROs have a reputation for being naysayers—little more than in-house regulators. This is a bias that nearly every new CRO must overcome. But successful CROs are actually value creators who operate as partners to the board and senior management. The great challenge of a newly installed CRO, then, is to communicate this value to stakeholders from the board down to line workers. As a CRO gains trust and influence within the company, the role will naturally expand into operations, business development, and strategic decision-making. An effective CRO must be the consummate diplomat, forging relationships upward, laterally, and downward. To take just one example, a strong relationship with the CFO is a key driver of success. It allows the CRO to drive value generation rather than mere cost savings. A successful partnership between the CRO and CFO can implement more holistic risk management, promote a clear vision of global strategy, and support business growth and profitability.

So what does an optimal reporting structure look like? A CRO at a large financial institution generally acts as an independent member of management with a direct reporting line to the CEO. This can often cause friction among C-suite members, especially if the CRO, CFO, and CEO have different views on balancing risk and profit generation. Let me be clear that a little difference of opinion is healthy. What we have to be wary of is conflict that halts progress and innovation. These nonproductive tensions within the C-suite are one of the biggest obstacles to developing the CRO role to its fullest capacity.

One solution is to establish a dotted-line relationship between the CRO and the risk committee or audit committee of the board. An added benefit of this reporting structure is that it will increase the independence of the CRO. For a dotted-line reporting structure to work, it is important that the organization establish a few ground rules, including risk-escalation and communication protocols, as well as the role of the board and management in hire/fire decisions, annual goal setting, and compensation programs for the CRO (and chief compliance officer). The CEO also needs to buy into this reporting structure.

Even with these adaptations, there remains considerable ambiguity when it comes to the CRO's position within an organization. Many CROs outside the financial sector, for instance, still report through the CFO.[13] However, CFOs often have operational responsibilities such as treasury functions and sometimes IT and HR. It would be difficult for the CRO to provide independent oversight over these functions.

Communicating the Value of ERM

We have already considered that companies who adopt ERM programs receive both intangible and quantifiable benefits. These benefits can be traced back to the CRO. In other words, the value of the CRO is inextricably linked to that of ERM itself.

Often, a CRO's ability to mitigate risk and reduce regulatory issues are the sole measures of his or her success. But the CRO must challenge this approach and show that there can be a working balance between risk and profits. For instance, the CRO can offer alternative perspectives to enrich high-level decision-making. A successful CRO not only manages risk but also uncovers opportunities for growth. By identifying risks and exploring sustainable competitive advantages, the CRO creates impact not only by preserving value but also by developing strategies that create value anew.

The clearest way to evaluate ERM and the CRO role is to measure success with objective metrics. This is already the case for disciplines including IT. Companies can measure a CIO's success using metrics such as the percentage of projects that met or exceeded expectations, for example. By contrast, ERM is rarely evaluated via quantitative measures. It's not that such metrics don't exist; rather that they are rarely employed. In reality, there are several effective tools for evaluating the success of a company's risk management program. Examples include the minimization of *unexpected earnings volatility* or the maximization of *risk-adjusted profitability*. Other tools include key performance indicators (KPIs) and key risk indicators (KRIs) that can compare a company's risk profile (actual risk level) against its risk appetite (target risk level). The typical board may not be familiar with all of these metrics, so simply presenting them is not sufficient. The CRO must educate the board and persuade it of their usefulness.

Bear in mind that while these metrics are quantitative, they are nonetheless dependent upon an individual firm's business model and approach to risk. For example, the World Bank uses a software tool to analyze operational risk based on detailed questionnaires. Risks are scored and aggregated to expose areas of concern.[14] Such a questionnaire would look quite different, however, when deployed at a healthcare provider or energy firm. In other words, the specific metrics used, and the way they are analyzed, will inevitably vary from firm to firm. With that said, I believe that there should be some quantitative measures of value in place.

Instilling a Risk Culture

What gets measured get managed, so implementing the appropriate risk metrics will lead to changes in decision-making and behavior. However, the CRO must go beyond quantitative metrics to effect culture change through risk awareness and education programs. As ERM continues to mature, the goal becomes less about creating risk infrastructure and more about fostering a risk-intelligent culture.

History tells us that the biggest hurdle to change is usually a cultural one. The risk function is often seen as the police force or naysayer, putting the brakes on innovation. A clear example of what happens when a company doesn't buy into risk culture is the collapse of Lehman Brothers. Although the company had talented bankers and sophisticated analytics, senior management repeatedly ignored then-CRO Madelyn Antoncic's warnings of impending disaster. While the board seemed to value her input during a strong economy, they turned a deaf ear when the economy weakened and the firm had to take greater risks to meet earnings expectations. In particular, CEO Dick Fuld chose to disregard Antoncic's warnings about the bank's risky exposure to mortgage-backed securities. She was sidelined for months as executives continued to engage in high-risk bets. Despite Antoncic's protests, the bank raised its risk limits from $2.3 billion to $3.3 billion. When she was fired in 2007, the company raised the limit to $4 billion. Lehman Brothers famously collapsed shortly after, in 2008.

Clearly, in order for a CRO to implement change, the board and CEO must be supportive. The board must prioritize the CRO as a key C-suite executive with an independent voice. The CEO must set the tone at the top, embracing ERM so that the company as a whole embraces it as well. Only with this support in place can the CRO promote a risk-aware culture throughout the entire organization.

At the same time, the CRO must forge relationships laterally across senior management and the heads of other business groups. Managing risk can't just be the CRO's job. Risk has to be a firm-wide concern, and senior executives must not only understand its value but also accept ownership for risks that fall under their purview.

The CRO must spearhead this buy-in. As we will discuss in the next section of this chapter, this is why CROs need strong soft skills such as the ability to motivate change. Implementing culture change is arguably one of the toughest challenges in a CRO's journey.

HIRING A CRO

What does the ideal CRO look like? The many CROs I have worked with come from diverse backgrounds, including business, risk, legal, audit, and finance. There is no clear path to becoming a CRO; history has shown that great candidates can come from different disciplines. Nonetheless, there are a few criteria to look for when appointing a CRO. First, he or she should have core technical skills. Moreover, there are crucial soft skills such as leadership, the ability to influence others, and excellent communication. Whether hard or soft skills are more critical depends on the ERM maturity and culture of the organization. Let's take a look at these skill sets in greater detail:

> **Technical Skills.** The CRO should have technical skills in order to develop the analytical frameworks and risk assessment tools across the risk areas:
>
> - Core risk, financial and quantitative modeling skills
> - Experience in strategic, business, credit, market, and operational risks
> - Knowledge of compliance and regulatory requirements in the relevant industries
> - A solid foundation in strategic planning and capital management
> - A deep understanding of the business and competitive landscape
> - Critical-thinking and problem-solving abilities
>
> A firm should look for a CRO who has at least 15 years of risk and/or industry experience. Direct experience in risk management or finance functions is a plus, but the more important criterion is knowledge of the industry's customer base, value proposition, and regulatory environment. Having experience in the firm's most crucial risk function is also desirable. A company that faces market risk wouldn't want to bring in a CRO who has never dealt with it, for example.
>
> **Leadership:** The second skill set to look for revolves around leadership. A CRO must be a trailblazer for change, identifying opportunities and strategies to drive business growth and long-term goals. Specifically, a CRO needs to:

- Drive innovation and change.
- Manage diverse risk teams.
- Lead the implementation of various tracks in the ERM program.
- Have credibility with and the trust of C-suite executives, the board, and regulators.
- Provide thought leadership and introduce new management approaches.

It's one thing to be able to analyze and summarize risk; it's quite another to have the credibility to influence business decisions and effectively improve processes. A leader with a seat at important meetings gains visibility and the opportunity to include risk in the conversation. At the same time, however, anyone in the CRO role is likely to receive heavy pushback, particularly if risk management is a relatively new concept in the organization, and especially if they are the company's first CRO. A chief risk officer needs to stand firm in his or her beliefs and have the courage to provide objective opinions. In times of doubt, the CRO must lead by example, ensuring that risk management teams have the skill and capacity to be effective. It's easy to lead when everything is going smoothly, but has this candidate successfully led a team through a crisis?

Evangelism: The third skill set centers on the ability to convert skeptics into believers. CROs must motivate change. Though they are responsible for risk oversight, they need to influence others in order to do so, even as they encounter strong resistance. A candidate whose resume includes technical aptitude and leadership skills still may not be the best choice if he or she can't influence others. The evangelistic skills to look for are:

- Self-awareness and authenticity
- The ability to persuade management to "buy-in"
- A desire to provide risk-related guidance on strategic business decisions
- The capacity to deliver timely and practical advice to individual risk owners
- A willingness to promote a positive risk-aware culture

A CRO who must change a culture that may have been decades in the making faces a tough challenge with much at stake. Culture change is often the biggest hurdle to the success of an ERM program. If individual managers don't understand why they must take responsibility for their business unit's risk, the battle could be lost. For these reasons, a CRO candidate should have a history of influencing others and implementing change. If they have been successful in the past, it is much more likely that they will be successful in the future.

Communication: The last skill set to look for in a CRO relates to communication. This isn't just the ability to speak well or even to listen carefully. It means having a high EQ and the ability to engage others through timely and transparent dialogue. Communication is often the most important tool for driving culture change and raising awareness. Specifically, a CRO needs to:

- Listen to the board, senior management, key stakeholders, and all other levels of the firm to understand their needs and expectations.
- Deliver concise and direct information supported by facts and data.
- Simplify complicated risk information using language that is understandable to someone who has little to no risk background.
- Engage key stakeholders to build trust and value within the organization.
- Have an understanding of complex business issues and the ability to explain them to others.

The CRO needs to set a clear vision for the firm and communicate top priorities for implementing that vision. An additional benefit of excellent communication is an engaged, collaborative team. A strong CRO will include business-unit managers as early as possible in the implementation process to garner valuable feedback and win their support. As managers seek out the collaboration of other employees, they will be better positioned to integrate risk tools in their day-to-day activities.

A *Harvard Business Review* study listed "translation" as a top competency for risk management chiefs.[15] Effective communication, the researchers found, begins with removing technical jargon from reports and deliverables to make them more understandable and to better engage one's audience. The repercussions for failure can be dire: In the study, the group that used technical jargon to suggest economic capital forecasting as a tool for aggregating risks was shut down. An effective CRO will help others understand ERM tools, interpret the results, and drive action.

A CRO'S PROGRESS

What do a new CRO's first few months look like, and how do priorities change over time? A successful ERM process is deliberate, planned, and fluid. Most importantly it takes time. Depending on the current structure of the firm, a CRO's journey to strategic business partner could even take a few years, but he or she should be making a positive difference well before that. A CRO's path may involve four fundamental phases: uncovering risk appetite, developing tools, embedding culture, and creating value.

1. Uncover the Firm's Risk Appetite, Strategy, and Goals

A new CRO's first task is to understand the ins and outs of the business. Before jumping into program development, a CRO should be clear on not just the organizational dynamics of the company and its operations, but also the mission and values it supports. Some appropriate questions to ask might be:

- What does the short- and long-term strategic landscape look like? Plugging directly into the company's competitive position and strategic goals helps focus priorities and emphasizes to others the link between risk management and strategy.
- How does risk strategy fit into business objectives? Again, the answers to this question in a company without a strong risk culture may be vague and subjective. It is the CRO's job to strengthen the relationship between risk and strategic objectives.
- What makes this company tick? What are the driving principles and values? Who are the decision makers and influencers at the company, on the board?
- What are the company's risk appetite and limits? These may be new concepts, so the CRO might need to interpret highly qualitative responses into quantitative measures.

While engaging others in the organization to gauge sentiment toward risk, the CRO should also assess the company's risk absorption capacities prior to any risk-management efforts. Here's where an effective stress-testing program can help. The results of a stress test can help a CRO understand the firm's risk profile and define its risk appetite, as well as identify, plan, and set risk strategy. They also provide an excellent tool for demonstrating the need for ERM.

2. Develop an Appropriate Risk Framework

Next, a CRO should develop a framework that includes the definition of roles and responsibilities, implementation of various risk management tools, and documentation of risk policies. Using tools such as risk-assessments, key risk indicators, loss-event databases, risk analytics, and scenario analyses, a

CRO can create an effective risk infrastructure that supports ongoing ERM operations. In this stage, a CRO's goals are to:

- Implement a risk framework that integrates the firm's strategy and risk appetite, using key metrics that tie specific risks to business objectives.
- Assign clear roles and responsibilities for risk management throughout the organization.
- Create transparent processes and procedures for evaluating, measuring, managing, and reporting risk.
- Incorporate risk management practices into performance evaluation and compensation plans.

A note on this last goal: Revising compensation plans to reflect risk management results is a relatively new concept. It comes from the need, exposed during the financial crisis, to better link risk responsibility with performance. Especially in risk-intensive institutions, risk officers should provide feedback during executives' annual reviews. Either the CRO or CEO should bring up risk assessment when the conversation moves to bonus appropriation.[16]

A new CRO settling into his or her job will naturally revisit and revise steps 1 and 2 as new challenges come into play. There will likely be some process of trial and error as the CRO develops proper risk management tools and receives feedback. In the end, the CRO should take the firm's ERM to a level of maturity that is appropriate for the size and complexity of the business. On the way, a clever CRO can create a virtuous cycle of continuous improvement: The more understandable and rhythmic the framework, the easier it becomes to drive culture change.

3. Embed Risk into the Firm's Culture

The third and most important step in a new CRO's journey is embedding risk into the firm's culture. Risk culture is the bridge between risk assessment and value creation. It also means integrating risk into the first line of defense with respect to business and operational decisions. It can make or break a new ERM program. Sustainable culture change begins with improvements in risk practices from Steps 1 and 2. Once an operational system is in place, the CRO can focus more on promoting positive risk culture.

A CRO should work to embed a strong risk culture by:

- Working with the board and CEO to set the tone from the top, emphasizing the importance of risk management in achieving the company's strategic objectives
- Developing strategies alongside managers that balance revenue generation with intelligent risk taking

- Holding workshops and training programs to instill a common risk taxonomy and vocabulary among employees
- Having one-on-one meetings with managers and executives to address specific concerns
- Creating a positive learning environment with sufficient training and education
- Conducting annual risk culture surveys to gauge where the company is relative to target risk culture attributes

It is important to note that risk culture is not an input or lever that management can control directly. Risk culture is an outcome or consequence that is derived from the many ERM components that we have discussed throughout the book. If a company doesn't have the desired risk culture, it must change one or more of these components.

4. Become a Strategic Business Partner

Earlier in this chapter, we briefly touched on CROs becoming strategic business partners. This is the fourth and final stage of a CRO's journey. Once a CRO has established an operative ERM framework and nurtured a strong risk culture, he or she can devote more time to business strategy.

The best CROs are not only facilitators of good risk management practices. They are also key members of strategic decision-making who have formed strong relationships with the CEO and executive team. A CRO should engage with other members of the C-suite and provide opportunities for value creation.

CROs will know they are at this stage when:

- Risk is integrated into decision-making within the C-suite and across business units.
- There are measured improvements in the ability of the company to reach its strategic goals.
- The CRO and other risk officers have high visibility with upper management.
- Dialogue between board members naturally involves risk; members are comfortable with the language of risk management.
- The CRO may suggest increasing risk when good risk/return opportunities are present and the company has excess risk capacity.
- The organization, particularly senior management and the board, fully understand the value of the CRO.

I believe that the true value of a CRO reaches full realization at this stage. Once CROs have established the elements of a full-fledged ERM program, they can create value by promoting risk-informed decisions. In practice, it takes time, patience, and flexibility to reach this stage.

Chief risk officer is a relatively new position, particularly outside the financial sector. But it has quickly proven to provide significant value to organizations across the globe. There is no common path to becoming a CRO, and the role may shift depending on the maturity of a company's risk program. Nonetheless, great CROs share a few common attributes. They are technically knowledgeable not only in their own field, but in the business in general. The have strong leadership qualities and the ability to communicate well and influence others. These so-called "soft" skills are particularly important when it comes to developing a risk-aware culture across the organization and becoming a strategic partner who contributes shareholder value and helps steer the direction of the company.

CHIEF RISK OFFICER PROFILES

Over the next few pages, you'll meet six prominent ERM practitioners, all of whom are or once were chief risk officers. Each of these professionals took a separate path to becoming a CRO, with backgrounds such as theoretical mathematics, commodity trading, and policymaking, and they work in different industries. But while their experiences are widely varied, they share a few commonalities. Each, to one degree or another, had a hand in defining their role as CRO. Some were even the first to hold that position in their organizations. Each felt that the most important skills they brought to the job were strong leadership, communication, and collaboration with their peers. While all are highly proficient, technical abilities seem to take a back seat in their narratives. As you read their stories, think about where each of these professionals came from—and where their careers in risk management ultimately took them.

Paymon Aliabadi, EVP and Chief Enterprise Risk Officer, Exelon

The Importance of Change Management   Paymon Aliabadi's journey to risk management began more than 25 years ago at Pacific Gas & Electric (PG&E), where he was among the first wave of gas traders in the United States. His job was to optimize PG&E's gas contracts, and he innovated this task by taking risk (in the form of Value at Risk) into consideration before the advent of sophisticated software platforms to do so. Other traders quickly adopted the spreadsheet that Paymon created to calculate VaR. This eventually led to the development of an entire book about risk that was distributed throughout the company's gas department, and which Paymon would later present to the company's board.

In 1998, the energy sector began a period of restructuring. PG&E moved away from a trading model to a merchant business, acquiring pipelines, developing merchant assets, and building a national footprint through partnerships with companies such as Shell and Bechtel. Risk became a more prominent focus for the company, which asked Paymon to become PG&E's corporate risk manager. With its enterprise-wide approach to credit aggregation, credit exposure, and aging bad debt, the position made Paymon a prominent player in ERM. In addition, the company tasked him with creating and deploying a proprietary ERM system.

In 2013, Chris Crane, CEO of Exelon, approached Paymon about joining the $27.4 billion energy provider as CRO. Crane made it clear that Exelon wanted to implement a risk management framework across the enterprise, a novelty at a time when active risk management was typically limited to the trading floor. The company was concerned about growing risks from new endeavors such as fracking and shale gas, and so established the goal of installing a best-in-class framework that would reduce negative surprises.

Paymon knew that the buy-in of senior management and the board would be key to his success at Exelon. At the time, CROs in the energy sector did not typically have broad authority, but rather reported to the CFO, leaving risk management dependent upon the financial function and subject to its priorities. He asked for assurances from Crane that he and the board would support, sponsor, and champion risk management, to which Crane agreed.

Implementing a New Risk Management Framework Through Restructuring

Paymon's first act as CRO was a 90-day plan to lay the groundwork for an enterprise-wide ERM program. He spent the first few weeks meeting with teams across the company to better understand its various lines of business and overall corporate culture. Then, he laid out the foundational elements, budgeting, staffing, and scheduling for phases of ERM implementation.

One of Paymon's goals was to integrate risk into day-to-day operations. He established an eight-person ERM operations group tasked with creating risk-management positions embedded in key functions. He formed a seven-member analytics group, and transferred 10 employees from trading to enterprise credit roles. Additionally, he established that each of Exelon's operating committees would include a director of risk management. These accomplishments didn't occur overnight. It took between nine months and a year to create and fill the new positions.

Before Paymon's arrival, the risk management committee was a cumbersome 50- to 60-person operation whose deliverable was a lengthy monthly report. Paymon often found himself chasing down initiatives raised at this committee's meetings only to discover little follow-through. At Paymon's recommendation, a smaller group of senior executives has replaced this committee, meeting biweekly to make decisions and take action. The group is armed with a standing agenda and a project template with metrics, established standards, and next steps for maximum efficiency.

Taking a Pause to Clearly Define ERM Value Eighteen months after his first day as CRO, Paymon had filled all of the risk management senior positions and decided to take stock. He reached out to different teams in Exelon for feedback on Exelon's ERM implementation. He found that Exelon's trading group implemented risk management most effectively, with well-defined roles and clearly established processes. However, the broader organization had little understanding of risk and how it affected performance. Many divisions, such as the Utilities and Generation Companies group, had only recently implemented risk management policies. There was a sense that the new, company-wide emphasis on risk management was moving too quickly, leaving many individuals behind.

Paymon's inquiries led him to realize that he needed to focus on change management. At this stage, Exelon had already made good progress against its benchmarking models but there was a concern that further improvement could face roadblocks. "We wanted to take a momentary pause to the extent appropriate, invest some time in education, and explain best-in-class risk management to every stakeholder."

One of the biggest challenges in earning this buy-in, says Paymon, was getting an impatient management to recognize that speed of execution is not the only success metric. Implementation required an investment in training and communication that can't help but impact daily operations. "Risk management is a very fuzzy concept, and as you start to explain to folks some of the principles, it gets very technical," he argues. "It is important to balance the speed of execution and change-management education."

His goal during this pause was to demonstrate ERM's value proposition in order to generate a base of support from stakeholders to build upon in the future. Paymon engaged consultancies to help with the ERM roadmap and provide coaching for the senior leadership. This work made clear how ERM could support and drive business strategy, add value, and foster partnerships. I give Paymon a lot of credit for thinking outside the box to address a common stumbling block in ERM implementation through this thoughtful approach to stakeholder engagement.

What's Next in Energy? Looking forward, Paymon sees risk management continuing to increase its focus on supporting strategic growth, rather than merely reducing negative risk. People are uncomfortable with uncertainty, he reasons, so one of the educational tasks that the risk group must take on is letting management know that it's okay to move forward without complete information—as long as you've established contingency plans and a process of evaluating progress. Certainly, he notes, there will continue to be an emphasis on compliance. But in the energy sector, he sees two key areas of focus: operations and innovation.

On the operational side, high-profile negative events such as the 2010 PG&E San Bruno failure,[17] the BP Gulf of Mexico oil spill, and recent spills off the California coast, have led to increased public and regulatory scrutiny that demands more rigorous risk management. Paymon sees the utility part of the energy industry getting closer and closer to being compliance focused like the banking and financial industry.

However, the future of energy production promises tremendous change and innovation for the industry. Future CROs in the energy space will need to focus more on strategic risk as emerging technology such as renewables and micro-grids promise seismic shifts in business models. What renewable energy projects should companies invest in? How will they manage inevitable failures and dead ends? Should companies reduce strategic risk by holding off investing in new technology until it proves its worth, or might such caution put them behind the innovation curve?[18] This, along with the growth of analytics, drives how risk committees need to react with future trends.

Advice to Aspiring CROs   Finally, I asked Paymon what advice he would give to aspiring CROs. Here's what he told me:

> *Understand business fundamentals and the space you're working in. Having actually been in the business and managing the business earns you credibility, respect, and trust. The second thing is emotional intelligence. If you're too aggressive, you can wear out your welcome. If you're too passive you can be pushed over. The key is building relationships and having strong people skills.*
>
> *Then, you need to have that fine skill of being operationally focused on the one hand while able to quickly change pace and become very strategic. You need to take strategic and fuzzy concepts and information, and translate them into actions, programs, and tactical steps.*

The biggest hurdles new CROs are going to face are not the technical aspects, Paymon concludes. Culture, change management, and education are as important as modeling risk. ERM is still a relatively new field, he emphasizes, and it needs time and collective experience to mature. As you take out your new, shiny fleet, you want to make sure the rest of your sailors are behind you.

Matt Feldman, CEO, Federal Home Loan Bank of Chicago

From CRO to CEO When Matt Feldman became CEO of the Federal Home Loan Bank (FHLB) of Chicago in 2008, he broke the perceived career ceiling for chief risk officers. Matt served as the bank's chief risk officer from 2004 to 2006, and prior to his appointment as CEO, few expected risk professionals to reach that level.

Matt's earlier tenure as CRO was marked by a vastly improved relationship with the bank's regulator, the Federal Housing Finance Board, which had been problematic when he stepped into the role. He used his 15-year experience at Continental Bank, where he had interacted with regulators around the world, to repair that relationship with open communication, transparency, and responsiveness.

Focusing on Change

From the outset, Matt saw FHLB Chicago's problem as demanding transformative, not incremental change, which he says requires assuring that people, systems, and stakeholders are all focused on the same outcomes so that the organization is moving in one direction. As CRO, he realized that he had to align the bank's culture to bring risk management into the decision process.

As CEO, Matt committed to open communication with the Board of Directors and providing the board access to a much larger group of executives than had previously been the case. A highly engaged and well-informed board with a large group of executives who had direct access to the board was key to the transformation of the Bank. This same open approach to communications was essential for the Bank to gain credibility with its members, which are both the owners and primary customers of the Bank, as well as with other important constituencies, such as the other FHL banks and the regulators of the members.

The Bank faced a number of challenges as it sought to recover from its own challenges as the Great Recession unveiled new, significant risks for the Bank and its member institutions. Matt had learned about how vulnerable large financial institutions can be from his experiences at Continental Illinois and the Chicago FHLB was no exception. At its lowest point, the bank's market value (marked-to-market value) of equity was negative $740 million.

With the transformation that occurred, the Bank achieved a positive change in market value of over $5 billion.

Recovering from the Brink

Matt began his tenure as CEO by creating a new senior executive team with executives promoted from within the Bank. He continued to build management's relationship with the board by opening new communication channels so that the board had a better understanding of what was going on throughout the company. To better align senior management with strategic goals, he based compensation on key performance measures. Until the bank was profitable, none of the executive team would receive incentive compensation, and he deferred his own incentive compensation even further—until the bank paid a dividend. "I thought this was an important statement to make to the membership that our interests were aligned," he recalls. "We were not going to receive incentives for *improving* the bank. We were going to receive incentives for *fixing* the bank."

Having served in both roles, Matt emphasizes that CROs and CEOs must work together. While technical skills are important for CRO candidates (particularly to earn the respect of subordinates) an ability to communicate effectively is essential. What's more, CROs must maintain an organization-wide perspective, with the same fundamental understanding of the business as the CEO. That is not to say that there can be no difference of opinion, he cautions, only that a CRO should understand how to manage risk within the broader business context. Those skills, Matt argues, make CROs good candidates for the top position. "There is no reason to believe that a CRO need end their career as a CRO," he says.

The best general advice for success and ability to grow in an organization, Matt tells me, is this:

> *Try to follow your passion, so that even on bad days you don't have any qualms about getting up in the morning and arriving at work with a spring in your step. Focus on making meaningful contributions to the organization. Don't limit yourself to simply fulfilling your job description. If you see a need for change, try to handle it in a helpful, not obstructive manner. Guide rather than hammer the organization into the place you'd like to see it. Sometimes that requires a little more patience, and often requires a lot more pain. It is wildly more effective if you do it that way.*

Excellent advice from one of ERM's most successful practitioners.

Susan Hooker—Former CRO of Assured Guaranty

ERM as a Multidisciplinary, Cross-Functional Role In many ways, Susan Hooker's career in risk management has paralleled the evolution of ERM itself. She began with credit risk. After receiving an MBA in finance, Susan started working in a start-up operation with Financial Security Assurance (now part of Assured Guaranty Corp.), the first mono-line financial guaranty company to focus outside the municipal area. In this role, she proposed underwriting standards for new products, developed initial corporate financial models, put reinsurance programs in place to syndicate the company's underwriting risk, and informed decisions on the company's financial operations as a whole. This required her to delve deeply into the underwriting operations behind the company's business-generation efforts, the firm's financial operations and information systems, and the legal, rating agency, and regulatory constraints that the company faced.

Over time, Susan took on successive roles at different organizations that touched on risk management across markets and at all stages of a company's life cycle: expanding financial guaranty operations to London for both Financial Security Assurance and Assured Guaranty; becoming chief underwriting officer of Assured Guaranty; and re-underwriting portfolios and adjusting the mix of business lines as executive vice president at RVI Group. Most recently until 2015, she served as CRO of ACA Financial Guaranty managing the run-off of its book of business following the 2008 financial crisis. Susan says her big takeaway from these experiences was that chief risk officer is a multidisciplinary, cross-functional role that requires a clear understanding of how ERM fits into the organization's strategy and operations as a whole.

Managing Credit Risk and Satisfying Rating Agencies Financial guaranty companies insure principal and interest payments under various types of debt obligations and Susan's main responsibility at Assured Guaranty and at ACA Financial Guaranty was managing the risk of payment defaults in the insured portfolio. At the front end, with Assured Guaranty, this meant establishing clear underwriting standards and applying them consistently to new business opportunities. At the back end, with RVI and ACA, she re-underwrote existing risk portfolios to identify weaknesses and direct loss mitigation efforts. She also focused on assessing the companies' capacity to cover insured liabilities, examining asset–liability risk characteristics and ensuring capital and liquidity resources are adequate to meet claims. In addition, Susan directed remediation efforts with non-performing credits, set loss reserves, adapted to new regulatory requirements, and put proper risk systems in place. Much of her focus was on tracking market developments that influenced portfolio risk. "New types of investors targeting distressed debt were creating new dynamics in loss mitigation," she says. "It is important to understand the differing motivations of investors, and to be alert as the market introduces new instruments that can be used to hedge portfolio risk."

Ratings agencies such as Moody's and Standard & Poor's are key players in the financial guaranty business. The value of financial guaranty policies depends on maintaining high credit ratings that can reduce interest costs for bond issuers. In order to continue to write business, guaranty firms must satisfy these agencies that they have sufficient capital to support portfolio risk. For this reason, credit agencies serve as de facto regulators. As CRO, Susan was responsible for demonstrating capital adequacy to rating agencies.

The Importance of Managing Cross-Functional Relationships One of Susan's accomplishments at Assured Guaranty was developing a risk management framework that would allow the company to move successfully from what had been almost exclusively a reinsurance operation to an operation that could encompass primary business on the municipal and non-municipal side, as well as international operations. This required developing a deep understanding of the different stakeholders within the company so that she could make a realistic assessment of the resources required to broaden operations and obtain buy-in from these constituencies.

As Assured Guaranty's chief underwriting officer, Susan reported directly to the CEO. Overall management of the company was conducted through several C-level management committees. Susan led the committees that focused on risk-related decision-making, for example, those that established loss reserves, underwriting policies, transaction approval, and credit remediation. Multiple levels of approval were required before any proposal was brought to a management committee and one of Susan's critical roles was to keep an open dialogue with different functional areas (finance, legal, marketing) to identify concerns and smooth the way for ultimate committee approval. Understanding the different priorities and goals of each different functional area was key to her success at Assured Guaranty.

When talking about the challenges of engaging staff to risk management practices, Susan says that "there was significant pushback due to a lack of understanding of the changing market dynamics and the need to continually reassess long-held views. So, trying to get people to acknowledge that analytical tools and practices need to change at different stages in a company's life cycle was difficult. For example, risk management for an active underwriting operation required a very different approach than at a company in wind-down mode, and some people were not be able to make that transition."

Looking for Growth in the CRO Role Susan agrees with me that CROs have seen their roles grow in the past ten years, which she compares with an earlier growth in the CFO role. "I'm hoping that there will be an equal importance placed on the CRO role, which will mean that future CRO candidates must be truly multidisciplinary," she says.

Specifically, Susan believes that an aspiring CRO should be able to communicate clearly across disciplines and cut through jargon to clarify technical concepts. For example, it is critical for the CRO to get their technical experts on board to support the CRO's initiatives. Those experts are quantitative innovators and serve as a third-party check to risk strategy. "As a CRO, you always need to look for the next and the new, but you can't fall into the trap of going with the crowd and assuming that the next biggest risk of your industry as a whole is indeed the most relevant for your company," she says.

She also feels that risk management must shed its gatekeeper reputation. "It doesn't help to just say no," she says. "A CRO needs to help people understand the source of discomfort with any given business or operational proposal so they can work together to figure out ways to mitigate the risk. Just pointing out problems isn't enough. You have to go the next step and figure out how the problems can be overcome."

A good lesson is looking at the opportunity side of risk management.

Merri Beth Lavagnino, CRO, Indiana University

Bringing Risk Management to Academia If you had asked Merri Beth Lavagnino five years ago where she'd be today, she would never have said risk management. With 30 years of experience in higher education, Merri Beth has traced an unconventional journey to the CRO's office that reflects a strategic mindset and passion for her vocation.

In her previous post as Indiana University's chief privacy officer, Merri Beth had been tasked with establishing IT policy and complying with data protection laws, a natural fit given her IT background. When the university sought to create a centralized compliance office, they put Merri Beth in charge of the project. Soon after, the board was looking for a new chief risk officer. When the university finished their nationwide search, they found that many applicants had extensive ERM knowledge but little to no background in higher education. They didn't know the business, and they didn't know the university. So, they turned to Merri Beth in 2013, and she accepted the challenge.

Different Mission, Different Metrics The structure of Indiana University's ERM function is different from what we might see in the corporate world. First, Merri Beth's focus is only on strategic ERM and associated risk mitigation for the university rather than the full gamut of risk management. Indiana

University has a separate group to handle insurance, loss control, and claims. Individual business units and subject-matter experts handle operational risk management. Merri Beth manages the work of the Enterprise Risk Management Committee, which sets priorities, requests action, and monitors results.

Risk management is still a new concept in academia, and Merri Beth faced challenges that she says arose from a prejudice against so-called corporate approaches. ERM's reliance on accurate measurement of metrics and their impact against the bottom line, for example, raised hackles. But Merri Beth argues that metrics, though different from the ones a corporation may use, are nonetheless important. "The university's primary goal is to be an outstanding undergraduate and graduate institution," she says, "but what does outstanding education look like? How do you measure it?"

Accordingly, one of Merri Beth's proudest accomplishments was the creation of a set of risk metrics that reflected an academic institution's unique mission. The ERM Committee focused primarily on strategic risk, developing measurements for risks including likelihood, and severity of impact on academic quality, incoming student quality, public perception of the university, net revenue and expense, safety, and distraction from the mission/turmoil. As you can see, many of these seem purely qualitative. For example, the academic quality metric includes measures of faculty recruitment and retention as well as the quality of faculty, teaching, and research. Merri Beth established a ratings scale based on professional consensus that applied numerical values to these otherwise subjective criteria. A rating of 1 means that a specific factor posed little risk. At the top of the scale, a rating of 5 means that the situation has potential long-term consequences and the University risks damaging its status as an elite educator.

Most of IU's strategic risks are unique to higher education, as compared to corporate risks. For example, one of the biggest risks the university faces is competition from high school and community college credit as alternatives to first- and second-year curricula. If students choose to take dual credit courses in high school, they will likely skip introductory courses such as Biology 101. This could impact tuition income, and if this trend grows, curriculum adjustments to respond to a disproportionally larger proportion of juniors and seniors could cause reductions in staff for first- and second-year programs and services, and growth of those serving third and fourth years. Another risk has gained national attention in recent years: sexual assault. Merri Beth and Indiana University are tackling the problem with increased focus and resources aimed at mitigating the risk of sexual assault on campus.

Gaining Acceptance and Trust through Communication Communication is a key weapon in Merri Beth's battle for the hearts and minds of academia. Her office publishes a monthly environmental scan newsletter, *The Risky*

Academy, and distributes it to about 200 of the University's ERM participants. Articles illuminate trends affecting risk in higher education. A recent issue reported, for instance, that "64% of responding NCAA athletic trainers and team physicians said that concussed athletes had sought premature clearance to play, while nearly 54% felt pressure from coaches." Items are categorized by risk area (athletics, research, student life, etc.) for easy scanning, but Merri Beth hopes that readers will look beyond their own field to better understand risks to the entire university. That in turn should increase the maturity and effectiveness of their day-to-day and long-term decision-making.

Despite these successes, Merri Beth acknowledges that academic culture is not going to change overnight. She still faces pushback when it comes to defining risk appetite, for example. She thinks she'll wait out the current ERM cycle before raising the subject again, perhaps substituting the term *risk principles* or *boundaries* for the corporate-sounding *risk appetite.* In addition, because so much of enterprise risk in higher education centers on strategy, Merri Beth feels that the chief risk officer and the chief strategy officer could work more closely. "I'm interested in continuous strategic planning and continuous risk management," she says. "Strategy and risk management work best when they work hand in hand. CROs will have to increase their skillset in communication in order to connect with different stakeholders within the university."

To new risk practitioners, Merri Beth offers this advice: Build a strategic mindset. Understanding how to manage risk across the entire organization and forging a strategic vision are more important than acquiring technical knowledge. That, she adds, will come with research and practice.

Merri Beth is a trend setter in academia, where she is demonstrating that ERM can add value in strategic risk management.

Bob Mark, CEO, Black Diamond Risk

Making Risk Transparent Bob Mark is the CEO of Black Diamond Risk, a provider of corporate governance, risk management consulting, risk software tools, and transaction services. He has over 20 years of experience in risk management, previously serving as the CRO of Canadian Imperial Bank of Commerce (CIBC) and as partner in the Financial Risk Management Consulting division of Coopers & Lybrand (C&L). An ERM pioneer, Bob received the GAARP Risk Manager of the Year award in 1998.

Bob's journey to the risk management space began when he was a PhD student in applied math at New York University. Already interested in the use of mathematics in the financial space, Bob eventually focused on trading and risk management under the guidance of his thesis advisor, Ed Thorp, author of *Beat the Dealer: A Winning Strategy for the Game of Twenty-One.* As one of the early quantitative minds in risk management, Bob was driven to discover how quantifying trading risk could help reduce it.

Balancing Risk with Growth When CIBC decided to create the position of chief risk officer, they sought a candidate with market experience—someone who understood risk, who would take action, and who could use aggressive expansion tactics in the treasury area. CIBC, one of Canada's five Tier 1 banks, was in the midst of an aggressive strategy that included increasing market share and expanding into new capital markets. What's more, they were growing by leaps and bounds in derivatives. For these reasons, the bank was looking to up its risk-management game, and Bob delivered. During his 10 years at the bank, CIBC led innovation in the use of risk management techniques. Following the Basel Committee's adoption of Basel I in 1988, CIBC was among the first banks in the world the governing body approved for all areas of market risk detailed in the accord. Under Basel I, banks were required to categorize their exposures into various asset classes, which were then used to establish an overall risk multiplier. The Basel Committee not only approved CIBC for all asset classes, but they also assigned it the lowest multiplier among member banks.

Creating Risk Transparency One of Bob's top priorities as CRO was to make CIBC's risk more transparent to the board and management. That meant educating these groups in identifying and prioritizing risks. Luckily, he had a direct reporting line to the CEO, and sat on the board's management committee. Early on in his tenure, Bob enumerated the bank's top 10 risks and took the time to explain why they were important and what potential effects they could have. He recalls an occasion when those risks became manifest, on a day when the markets moved dramatically and the bank saw significant losses. "I remember going to the board and describing [the root causes behind] the loss," he says. "Things went wrong in a variety of places, but 93% of those losses could be attributed to the top 10 risks I'd outlined previously. I remember the CEO saying, 'You know what? We're not happy that we lost money, but we're very happy that the risk was made transparent.'"

Essentially, despite the losses, the bank's management committee understood that they entered into the situation with their eyes open thanks to Bob's analysis. This is a great illustration of a point I've been making throughout this book: Risk management doesn't equal zero risk. Rather, it means taking smart risks, and being prepared for potential negative consequences.

Getting CIBC's board and management to understand risk in these terms didn't happen overnight. When Bob first arrived at the bank in 1994, its risk function consisted of 100 or so relatively inexperienced employees. By

1997, his staffed numbered 700. But Bob didn't just increase headcount. He notes that one of the biggest challenges was finding—and keeping—the experienced practitioners he was looking for. At the time, risk professionals were not highly compensated, but Bob understood that their value grew with experience, and that he would need to convince the board that they had to be compensated accordingly. How? By showing that risk management could positively impact the bottom line. Although driven in no small part by quantitative application and analytics, Bob's success speaks to a softer side of ERM: collaboration, risk culture, and transparency, as well as the power of persistence.

Finally, I asked Bob what advice he would give to aspiring CROs. Here's what he told me:

> A CRO has multiple stakeholders and you need to see the world from the vantage point of these stakeholders. Stakeholders include shareholders, the board, the management committee, business units, the risk team and regulators.
>
> Clarity of thought is essential to be an effective CRO. Success hinges on your ability to effectively communicate and partner with all stakeholders in order to make the risk transparent.
>
> At some point in your career it is important for you to work in a revenue generating function .You must think of managing risk in both defensive and offensive terms since risk management and risk taking aren't opposites, but two sides of the same coin. If you see the world from the perspective of a business unit that is making choices about risk in relation to reward, then you can more effectively (in your role as a CRO) help your company manage their performance from a risk-adjusted return perspective.

Jim Vinci, Former Chief Investment Officer, Sierra Vista Advisors

Prioritizing Risk on the Front Lines   Risk management has long been central to Jim Vinci's career, but lately it has become a matter of life and death. Jim once served as chief risk officer or partner at large financial institutions including Lehman Brothers, PricewaterhouseCoopers, Paloma Partners, and Mount Kellett Capital Management. But a change of heart made for a rewarding and dramatic career change.

In 2011 while chief investment officer of Sierra Vista Advisors, Jim joined his town's volunteer ambulance corps. His initial motive was to give back to his community in his spare time. He soon discovered, however, that he enjoyed the work—so much in fact that in 2013 he left his 30-year Wall

Street career to enroll in the paramedic training program at New York's St. John's University. He recalls a day in Queens in 2012 when he responded to a woman in traumatic cardiac arrest and intubated her in the middle of the street. The moment he felt her pulse return, he knew this was what he wanted to do full time.

Jim sees many parallels between his CRO days and being a paramedic. There is a similar sense of urgency and accomplishment when overcoming challenges. One of his toughest as chief risk officer was gaining buy-in for risk management within the organization. He compares the role of a risk manager to that of a hockey team's goalie. A goalie can't possibly block every shot if the team's defensive line is ineffective, he explains. Similarly, a risk manager can't be expected to mitigate every risk if front-line managers fail to prioritize risk management in the first place. "You have to find a balance," he says. "There has to be some level of buy-in and support."

At Lehman Brothers, Jim focused on market risk and leverage while making a point of showing the C-suite how risk measurement can benefit shareholders. When he moved to PwC, he advised clients on risk issues and consulted with management to craft market-risk measurement and capital allocation methodologies. Jim considers his holistic approach to business as one of the most important drivers of success. You can't be a good risk manager, he argues, unless you understand the bottom line and how the business operates.

Jim applies this balanced mentality toward his day-to-day work as a paramedic, which combines business considerations, emergency medicine, and no small degree of selflessness. Whether risk management or healthcare, Jim's enthusiasm is clearly contagious: Not long ago, his daughter followed his career path by becoming an emergency medical technician.

NOTES

1. Davy, Peter. "Cinderella Moment: The Credit Crisis Means Chief Risk Officers Are Finally Being Listened To. But How Long Will It Last?" *Wall Street Journal*, October 5, 2010.
2. L.A. Winokur. *Breaking Through: The Rise of the RISK Executive*, GARP Risk Professional, February 2009. Retrieved from http://digitalresearch.eiu .com/risksandrenewables/report/section/part-ii-managing-and-mitigating-renewable-energy-risk.
3. Mikes, Anette. *The Triumph of the Humble Chief Risk Officer*, Working paper No. 14-114, 23 May 2014.
4. U.S. Board of Governors of the Federal Reserve System, Press Release, February 18, 2014. Retrieved from http://www.federalreserve.gov/newsevents/press/bcreg/20140218a.htm.

5. *The Role of the Chief Risk Officer in the Spotlight*, Towers Watson, 2014.
6. *Remaking Financial Services: Risk Management Five Years After the Crisis*, EY, 2013.
7. "OCBC Bank Appoints New Chief Risk Officer" (Press Release), OCBC Bank, May 16, 2014. Retrieved from https://www.ocbc.com/assets/pdf/media/2014/may/140516_media%20release_ocbc%20chief%20risk%20officer.pdf.
8. "Chief Corporate Frustration," *Treasury & Risk Management*, March 2002.
9. Global Risk Management Survey, Eighth Edition: "Setting a Higher Bar," Deloitte Touche Tohmatsu Limited. 2013, p. 11.
10. Mello, Jim. "Does Your Company Need a Chief Risk Officer?" (Blog Post), *CEB on the Go*, June 30, 2014. Retrieved from https://www.executiveboard.com/blogs/does-your-company-need-a-chief-risk-officer/.
11. Green, Jeff. "Risk Officer Rises to $10 Million Job After Market Meltdown," *Bloomberg News*, July 11, 2011. Retrieved from http://www.bloomberg.com/news/articles/2011-07-11/risk-officer-rises-to-10-million-job-after-derivatives-meltdown.
12. *2013 Risk Management Compensation Survey*, RIMS, 2013.
13. Pergler, Martin. *Enterprise Risk Management: What's Different in the Corporate World and Why*, McKinsey Working Papers on Risk, Number 40, December 2012, p. 8.
14. *The Evolving Role of the CRO*, Economist Intelligence Unit, May 2005.
15. Mikes, Anette, Matthew Hall, and Yuval Millo. "How Experts Gain Influence," *Harvard Business Review*, July 2013.
16. GRM Survey, Eighth Edition, Deloitte, p. 12.
17. In 2010, a PG&E gas pipeline in San Bruno exploded and leveled the California suburb. It was reported to be the result of an unintentional control system cyber-failure, causing the pipeline to over-pressurize and rupture. https://www.aga.org/final-ntsb-accident-report-san-bruno-pipeline-rupture-sept-26-2011.
18. Economist Intelligent Unit, "Managing the Risk in Renewable Energy," http://digitalresearch.eiu.com/risksandrenewables/report/section/part-ii-managing-and-mitigating-renewable-energy-risk, 2011.

CHAPTER 12

Risk Appetite Statement

INTRODUCTION

In recent years, many companies have scrambled to meet the stringent post-recession regulatory requirements by instituting new ERM plans or augmenting existing programs. However, regulatory compliance is not enough. In order for ERM to create value, companies must seamlessly integrate risk practices into the organization's day-to-day business processes at every level. A key lever for this is to implement a comprehensive risk policy that establishes metrics, exposure limits, and governance processes to ensure enterprise-wide risks are within acceptable levels.

At the heart of such a policy is the *risk appetite statement* (RAS). An RAS is a concise document that provides a framework for the board of directors and management to address fundamental questions with respect to strategy, risk management, and operations, including:

- What are the strategies for the overall organization and individual business units? What are the key assumptions underlying those strategies?
- What are the significant risks and aggregate risk levels that the organization is willing to accept in order to achieve its business objectives? How will it establish governance structures and management policies to oversee and control these risks?
- How does the company assess and quantify the key risks so that it can monitor exposures and key trends over time? How does it establish the appropriate risk tolerances given business objectives, profit and growth opportunities, and regulatory requirements?
- How does the organization integrate its risk appetite into strategic and tactical decision making in order to optimize its risk profile?
- How will the company establish an ERM feedback loop and provide effective reporting to the board and senior management?

Corporate directors may well recognize the need for a formal statement of risk appetite, but according to a 2013 National Association of Corporate Directors (NACD) study, only 26% of companies actually have one.[1] In this chapter I'll offer a set of guidelines, best practices, and practical examples for developing and implementing an effective RAS framework. Specifically, we'll look at the requirements of a risk appetite framework; the process of developing, implementing, and refining an RAS; and the monitoring and reporting processes that will ensure ongoing observance. We'll conclude with a practical example of an RAS that includes illustrative metrics and tolerance levels for key risks.

WHAT IS A RISK PROFILE?

A basic risk profile can be expressed in qualitative terms (low, moderate, high). At a more advanced level, a risk profile has a strong quantitative component that can be captured in a "bell curve" with a full range of probabilities and outcomes. In essence, the risk profile becomes a risk/return profile that quantifies expected performance, downside risk, and upside risk. It is also important to understand the shape of the risk/return profile, which may have a normal or asymmetrical distribution. The risk/return profile differs by risk type and business activity. For example, credit risk in the lending business has limited upside (loan margin) and significant downside (loan principal). Interest rate and foreign-exchange risks in the treasury function have a more normal distribution because interest rates and exchange rates can equally move for or against the company. Strategic risk in the corporate research and development (R&D) budget or a venture capital fund has limited downside (value of the investment) but significant upside (many multiples of the investment). The core objective of ERM is to optimize the shape of the risk/return profile of the organization.

REQUIREMENTS OF A RISK APPETITE STATEMENT

A well-developed risk policy in general and an RAS in particular must have the following attributes:

1. It is a key element of the overall ERM framework, specifically the governance and policy component.

2. It is aligned with the business strategy and expressed with quantitative risk tolerances.
3. It reinforces the organization's desired risk culture and is aligned with risk culture levers (e.g., tone from the top, people, training, etc.).
4. It produces better risk-adjusted business performance, and thus enhances the organization's reputation with key stakeholders.

Figure 12.1 provides an overview with these key attributes and the linkages between ERM, risk appetite, risk culture, and reputation.

A risk appetite statement is a board-approved policy that defines the types and aggregate levels of risk that an organization is willing to accept in pursuit of business objectives. It includes qualitative statements and guidelines as well as quantitative metrics and exposure limits. The RAS is implemented through a risk appetite framework, which includes the common language, policies, processes, systems, and tools used to establish, communicate, and monitor risk appetite. The risk appetite framework should incorporate the following elements:

Risk capacity (also known as risk-bearing capacity) represents a company's overall ability to absorb potential losses. Risk capacity can be measured in terms of cash and cash equivalents to meet liquidity demands and in terms of capital and reserves to cover potential losses. Companies in highly regulated industries, such as banking, may define their risk capacity conservatively as the capital set aside to absorb potential losses under adverse scenarios. This may be the capital that would permit them, for instance, to pass regulatory stress tests. Other companies, such as technology startups, might have a more aggressive definition of risk capacity that encompasses the capital and resources that could be lost to a point just shy of insolvency in a relatively short timeframe (e.g., until the next round of funding). The commonality among these calculations, however, is that they represent the *absolute maximum loss* a company is able (not simply willing) to take on. Risk capacity should also take into consideration an organization's skills, tools, and performance track record in managing risks. Consider two companies with similar risk profiles and capital levels: The one with superior risk management would have greater risk capacity.

Risk profile is a snapshot of an organization's risk portfolio at a specific point in time (past, present, or future). It is crucial for the risk profile to align with the business model and strategy of the organization. For example, one company may choose to be a low-cost provider, in which its risk profile is driven by low profit

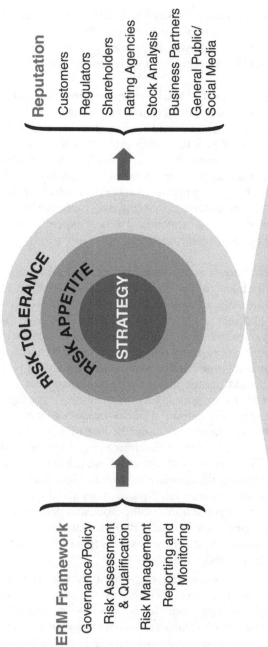

ERM Framework

Governance/Policy

Risk Assessment
& Qualification

Risk Management

Reporting and
Monitoring

RISK TOLERANCE

RISK APPETITE

STRATEGY

Reputation

Customers

Regulators

Shareholders

Rating Agencies

Stock Analysis

Business Partners

General Public/
Social Media

RISK CULTURE

| Tone from the Top | Talent Management | Training Programs | Risk Culture Surveys | Incentive Programs |

FIGURE 12.1 Key ERM Linkages

margin (i.e., weak pricing power) and significant operational risks (e.g., cost control, supply-chain management, and scale economics). Conversely, another company could choose to be a high-quality, value-added provider, where its risk profile is driven by a high profit margin and significant strategic and reputational risks (e.g., product innovation and differentiation, customer experience, and brand management). The current risk profile of an organization is determined by all of the underlying risks embedded in its business activities, whereas the projected or target risk profile would also include business-plan assumptions.

Risk-adjusted return provides the business and economic rationale for determining how much risk an organization should be willing to accept. In fact, an organization should not be willing to accept any risk if it is not compensated appropriately. Conversely, if the market is providing a higher than expected return, then an organization should be willing to increase its risk appetite (while still considering its risk capacity as discussed previously). At the inception of any business transaction, the risk originator must establish an appropriate risk-adjusted price that fully incorporates the cost of production and delivery as well as the cost of risk (i.e., expected loss; unexpected loss or the cost of economic capital; insurance and hedging costs; and administrative costs). I cannot emphasize enough the importance of risk-adjusted pricing! Although every business takes risks, it has only one opportunity to receive compensation for them: in the pricing of its products and services. In addition to pricing, organizations use a range of tools—Economic Value Added (EVA®),[2] economic capital (EC), and risk-adjusted return on capital (RAROC)—to measure risk-adjusted profitability, evaluate investment and acquisition opportunities, and allocate capital and other corporate resources. It is important that these tools accurately account for risk.

Risk appetite represents the types and aggregate levels of risk an organization is willing to take on to actively pursue its strategic objectives. It should fall within the broader umbrella of risk capacity and, in the best possible scenario, will align closely with the organization's current risk profile. A high risk appetite will consume a greater portion of risk capacity, while a low risk appetite will consume a smaller portion, thus providing a greater buffer zone and reducing the vulnerability of the organization's capital and resources. A company's risk profile should closely resemble its risk appetite. In reality, however, it is very challenging for companies to have a clear understanding of their enterprise risk profile, which may be masked by risk assessments created in organizational silos, poorly understood correlations, and inadequate analysis of earnings and value drivers. Gaining a full understanding of a company's risk profile—and, subsequently, its risk appetite—is what makes an RAS particularly valuable. When a company's risk profile is out of sync with its risk appetite, management should make course corrections to bring the two closer in line.

Risk tolerance is often used as a synonym for risk appetite, but in practice it is quite different and plays an important role in the risk appetite statement. Risk tolerances are the quantitative thresholds that allocate the organization's risk appetite to specific risk types, business units, product and customer segments, and other levels. Certain risk tolerances are policy limits that should not be exceeded except under extraordinary circumstances (hard limits) while other risk tolerances are guideposts or trigger points for risk reviews and mitigation (soft limits). Whereas risk appetite is a strategic determination based on long-term objectives, risk tolerance can be seen as a tactical readiness to bear a specific risk within established parameters. Enterprise-wide strategic risk appetite is thus translated into specific tactical risk tolerances that constrain risk-acceptance activities at the business level. Risk tolerances are the parameters within which a company (or business unit or function) must operate in order to achieve its risk appetite. Once established, these parameters are communicated downward through the organization to give clear guidelines to executives and managers and also to provide feedback when they are exceeded. For this reason, risk tolerance should always be defined using metrics that are closely aligned with how business performance is measured (i.e., key risk indicators should be closely related to key performance indicators).

Establishing risk tolerance levels is one of the major challenges in developing an RAS framework, but it is essential to its success. There are many ways to determine risk tolerances. It is up to each organization to decide which ones work best. Table 12.1 offers some approaches that an organization may take to determine risk tolerance levels. Please note that these approaches are not mutually exclusive. Sometimes, a blended approach is best. For example, one may initially set a risk tolerance level using statistical analysis (95% confidence level observation) and then adjust it up or down according to management judgment.

TABLE 12.1 Approaches to Establishing Risk Tolerance Levels

1. Board and management judgment
2. Percentage of earnings or equity capital
3. Regulatory requirements or industry benchmarks
4. Impact on the achievement of business objectives
5. Stakeholder requirements or expectations
6. Statistics-based (e.g., 95% confidence level based on historical data)
7. Model-driven (e.g., economic capital, scenario analysis, stress-testing)

While the main purpose of an RAS framework is to establish limitations on risk, it also provides other important benefits, including:

- Developing a common understanding and language for discussing risk at the board, management, and business levels.
- Promoting risk awareness and enforcing the desired risk culture throughout the organization.
- Aligning business strategy with risk management to provide a balance between financial performance and risk-control requirements.
- Quantifying, monitoring, and reporting risks to ensure that they are within acceptable and manageable levels.
- Embedding risk assessments and risk/return analytics into strategic, business, and operational decisions.
- Integrating risk appetite with other ERM tools, including risk-control self-assessments (RCSAs), key performance indicators (KPIs) and key risk indicators (KRIs), economic capital, and stress-testing.
- Meeting the needs of external stakeholders (e.g., regulators, investors, rating agencies, and business partners) for risk transparency; safety and soundness; and environmental and social sustainability.

DEVELOPING A RISK APPETITE STATEMENT

The development of the RAS is an important early component of ERM program deployment. It provides significant strategic, operational, and risk management benefits because it informs risk-based decision making for the board of directors; executive management; risk control and oversight functions (risk, compliance, and internal audit); and business and operating units. The implementation requirements for an RAS depend on the size and complexity of the organization; the business and regulatory environment in which it operates; and the maturity of its ERM program. The following provides some general guidelines for developing an RAS and for refining it on a continuous basis.

Step 1: Assess Regulatory Requirements and Expectations

As part of a larger ERM effort, an RAS offers far greater value than merely meeting regulatory requirements. Nonetheless, aiding the process of meeting such requirements is a significant benefit. Whether or not it is actually required by specific laws, regulations, or industry standards, an RAS offers a systematic and holistic approach to controlling risk exposures and concentrations. Successful deployment of an RAS can address the requirements of several common regulatory schemes. Consider the following examples from the financial services industry:

- **U.S. Securities & Exchange Commission (SEC).** As part of a global collaborative effort of 12 supervisory agencies from 10 countries, the SEC issued a report in December 2010 that evaluated how financial institutions have progressed in developing risk appetite frameworks, including IT infrastructures and data aggregation capabilities.[3]
- **U.S. Federal Reserve (Fed).** The Fed's Consolidated Supervision Framework for Large Financial Institutions, released in 2012, directs that each firm's board of directors, with support from senior management, should "maintain a clearly articulated corporate strategy and institutional risk appetite." It further stipulates "that compensation arrangements and other incentives [be] consistent with the corporate culture and institutional risk appetite."[4]
- **Financial Stability Board (FSB).** In November 2013, the FSB enhanced its regulatory guidance on ERM and the RAS framework. This regulatory guidance included key terms and definitions and, more important, established regulatory expectations for the board.[5]
- **U.S. Office of the Comptroller of the Currency (OCC).** In 2014, the OCC set forth guidelines for financial institutions that include "a comprehensive written statement that articulates the bank's risk appetite, which serves as a basis for the risk governance framework."[6]
- **Own Risk and Solvency Assessment (ORSA).** Instituted by the National Association of Insurance Commissioners (NAIC) in 2014, ORSA affirms that "a formal risk appetite statement, and associated risk tolerances and limits, are foundational elements of risk management for an insurer; understanding of the risk appetite statement ensures alignment with risk strategy by the board of directors."[7]

While these regulations are focused on banks, insurance companies, and other financial institutions, organizations in other industry sectors can benefit from the standards and guidelines they provide. Moreover, all companies should understand the RAS framework expectations established by global stock exchanges, rating agencies, and other organizations such as the National Association of Corporate Directors (NACD), Committee of Sponsoring Organizations of the Treadway Commission (COSO), and the International Organization for Standardization (ISO).

Step 2: Communicate the Business and Risk Management Benefits of the RAS

Senior management must set the tone at the top and communicate the critical role that the RAS plays in the risk-management process. This communication should come from the CEO, CFO, CRO, and other senior business leaders and be directed at key internal stakeholders. Such communication may take place in town hall meetings, workshops, corporate memos, or e-mails. It should clearly articulate the support from the board and corporate leaders and provide the implementation steps, expected benefits, regulatory requirements, industry standards, and business applications of the RAS for key stakeholders. Additionally, internal stakeholders who are responsible for developing and implementing the RAS framework should receive appropriate training.

Step 3: Organize a Series of Workshops to Develop the RAS

With the appropriate communication and training completed or well underway, the organization is ready to develop the RAS. The executive sponsor (e.g., the CRO or CFO) of the RAS should organize a series of workshops with risk owners (e.g., business and functional leaders) to develop the risk appetite metrics for their organizational units while the CEO and key executive team members develop those for the overall enterprise. The purpose of these workshops is to develop the RAS with input from all of the risk owners by addressing the following questions sequentially:

- **Business Strategy:** What are the business strategies and objectives for each business unit or function? What are the key assumptions underlying these strategies?
- **Performance Metrics:** What are the KPIs that best quantify the achievement of these business or process objectives? What are the performance targets or triggers for these KPIs?

- **Risk Assessment:** What are the key risks that can drive variability in actual vs. expected performance?[8]
- **Risk Appetite:** What is the company's appetite for each of these key risks? What are the KRIs that quantify the exposure levels and/or potential loss? What are the limits or range of tolerances for these KRIs?

Figure 12.2 provides a diagram of the logical flow of these questions in the context of a risk/return bell curve. Unfortunately, many companies break down this logical flow by separating the strategy and ERM components. These companies generally define strategic objectives and KPIs as part of strategic planning (Steps 1 and 2 in Figure 12.2) and provide reporting to the executive committee and the full board. Separately, they perform risk assessments and develop KRIs as part of ERM (Steps 3 and 4) and provide reporting to the ERM committee and the risk or audit committee of the board. The integration of strategy and ERM (integrating Steps 1 through 4) provides much better analysis, insights, and decision-making, including the alignment of KPIs and KRIs for the RAS framework. In other words, don't dissect the bell curve and look at return and risk separately!

These workshops might take place over the course of a few months. By the end of this step, the executive sponsor should be satisfied with the quality of the initial risk-appetite metrics and risk tolerance levels. The key objective of these workshops is to develop an initial set of KPIs and KRIs with their performance targets and risk tolerances, respectively. Some of the proposed metrics might be aspirational, and the risk owners will need time to flesh them out with real-world data. A subset of available metrics will be the basis of a prototype RAS and dashboard report in the next step.

Step 4: Develop and Socialize a Prototype RAS and Dashboard Report; Produce a Final RAS Based on Board and Business Feedback

Based on the output from Step 3, the team can produce a prototype document for the RAS to generate discussion and kick off what will become an iterative process. This document should include the RAS framework, a dashboard report with risk appetite metrics, and the RAS itself with qualitative statements and quantitative risk tolerances. (For more, see "Examples of Risk Appetite Statements and Metrics," below.)

The executive sponsor can use this prototype document to socialize the prototype RAS and obtain input from corporate and business executives as well as select members of the board of directors (e.g., chairs of the risk and audit committees). Based on management and board feedback, the team can then produce a final RAS framework and dashboard report.

Integrating Strategy and ERM

1. Define business strategy and business objectives

2. Establish KPIs and performance targets based on expected performance

3. Identify risks that can drive variability in performance (risk assessments)

4. Establish KRIs and risk tolerances for critical risks

5. Provide integrated monitoring with respect to 1–4

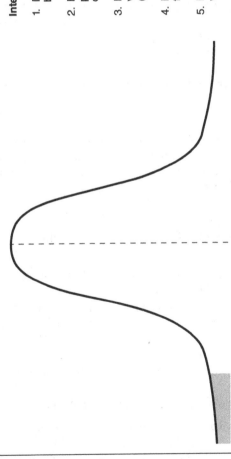

Downside Risk   **Expected Performance**

Distribution of Outcomes

FIGURE 12.2 Distribution of Outcomes

Step 5: Obtain Executive Management Approval

At this stage, the RAS is ready for management consideration. The executive team should take the time to discuss and vet the RAS thoroughly. This discussion may lead to changes in the risk appetite statement, metrics, and/or risk tolerance levels. Once this is complete, the executive committee or ERM committee would issue final approval.

Step 6: Obtain Board Approval

The RAS should next be reviewed by the full board of directors, who will similarly discuss and challenge it. A key objective in this step is to establish a concise set of risk-appetite metrics and risk tolerance levels that are appropriate for board-level oversight and reporting. Final approval may come from the risk committee, audit committee, or the full board. Nonetheless, the full board should review the RAS in the context of the overall corporate strategy.

Step 7: Communicate the RAS, including Roles and Responsibilities

After management and the board approve the RAS, management should communicate it to all employees. This is because everyone plays a role in risk management and should understand the organization's overall risk appetite and tolerances. This communication should define risk ownership as well as the roles and responsibilities for implementing the RAS framework. (See "Roles and Responsibilities" for details.)

Step 8: Review and Update Current Business Plans and Risk Policies

Ideally, the RAS would be closely aligned with the development of business plans and risk policies. The business world is dynamic and fluid, and the RAS must be responsive to significant changes in the competitive environment, regulatory guidance, risk-adjusted return opportunities, and the organization's risk profile and risk capacity. As such, the RAS, business plans, and risk policies should be "living documents" that are regularly reviewed and updated given key changes in the organization's business environment.

Step 9: Provide Ongoing Monitoring and Reporting

In order for the board and executive management to provide effective governance and oversight of the RAS framework, including the key risk exposures and concentrations of the organization, the ERM team must establish risk dashboard reports and monitoring processes. (See "Monitoring and Reporting" below for an example of an RAS dashboard report.)

Step 10: Provide Annual Review and Continuous Improvement

In addition to off-cycle reviews that ensure the company's risk appetite is responsive to significant changes in the business environment, the company should conduct a formal review of the RAS at least once a year. This formal annual review includes proposed changes to the RAS framework and risk tolerance levels, alignment with business plans and risk policies, and management and board approvals.

Moreover, the organization should look for opportunities to improve the RAS framework on a continuous basis. These enhancements may include economic capital models, stress-testing and scenario analysis, technology solutions and reporting tools, broader coverage of risk, exception management plans, and integration into strategic and business decisions.

ROLES AND RESPONSIBILITIES

The process of developing, implementing, and renewing a comprehensive RAS framework should involve key stakeholders from every level of the organization. Figure 12.3 provides a summary of the main roles and responsibilities for the business units, executive management, and the board. The RAS itself should document specific roles and responsibilities for carrying out the risk policy, including reporting and exception-management processes.

The "three lines of defense" model described in Chapter 8 offers a lens through which to view the risk governance structure and roles defined in the RAS:

1. **Business units (first line of defense)** are ultimately responsible for measuring and managing the underlying risks in their area of business (i.e., profit centers) or functional units (i.e., support functions such as HR or IT). In effect, they are the "risk owners." Business units represent the first line of defense because they are closest to risk acceptance and mitigation activities. They also have first-hand knowledge and experience in managing the risks that they face, including potential business impacts.

    As active participants in the workshop meetings discussed previously in Step 3, the business and functional leaders are also responsible for defining their strategies and aligning them with the appropriate risk appetite and tolerance levels. Once the RAS is established, they must report policy exceptions to the CRO and/or executive management. The business and functional units are ultimately accountable for

Board of Directors (with Audit support)
- Review, challenge, and approve the RAS framework
- Provide risk governance and independent oversight
- Accountable for overseeing the effectiveness of the RAS, with audit support

Executive Management (with Risk and Compliance support)
- Establish corporate strategy, RAS framework, and reporting
- Monitor aggregate risk exposures against risk tolerances
- Accountable for communicating the RAS, reinforcing the risk culture, and optimizing the enterprise risk/return profile

Business Units and Functions (i.e., risk owners)
- Establish business strategies, metrics, and risk tolerances
- Report policy exceptions to executive management
- Accountable for managing the business within defined risk appetite

BOARD OF DIRECTORS

EXECUTIVE MANAGEMENT

BUSINESS UNITS

FIGURE 12.3 Key Roles

how well their businesses and operations perform vis-à-vis the risk tolerances established in the RAS.

2. **Executive management with the support of risk and compliance functions (second line of defense)** is responsible for developing and communicating the RAS framework. The CRO (or equivalent) should lead this effort. The CEO, with the support of the executive management team, establishes the overall corporate strategy and ensures that business-unit strategies are aligned. Executive management is also responsible for defining the risk appetite and risk tolerances at the enterprise level and providing ongoing reporting to the board and other key stakeholders (e.g., regulators, rating agencies, institutional investors).

   The CRO and the ERM team are responsible for developing analytical and reporting tools to measure and monitor aggregate risk exposures against risk tolerances. They also must provide business context, expert analyses, and root causes for any risk tolerance breaches. Executive management is ultimately accountable for how well it optimizes the risk/return profile of the organization and for the strength of its risk culture.

3. **The board with the support of internal audit (third line of defense)** is responsible for reviewing, challenging, and approving the RAS framework. Once the framework is in place, the role of the board shifts to providing independent oversight. The risk or audit committee may take the lead in this ongoing process. It is also the responsibility of the risk or audit committee to step in when it sees exposures that are consistently above risk tolerances or if a business or functional unit does not demonstrate a strong risk culture. These failures may require a "deep dive" to investigate and correct. On the other hand, if risk limits and tolerances are never exceeded (i.e., no policy exceptions over an extended period of time), then the board may reasonably question whether the RAS tolerances are too high or lax to be effective.

   The board is ultimately responsible for ensuring that an effective ERM program is in place, including a robust RAS framework. To fulfill this critical fiduciary responsibility, the board must receive timely, concise, and effective risk reporting from management, usually in the form of an RAS dashboard. This dashboard should clearly highlight any risk metric that falls outside its associated tolerance (e.g., by showing it in a "red zone") and include commentary that explains the root causes for the policy exception along with management's plans and timeframe for remediation. We'll give a fuller introduction to the RAS dashboard below, with a complete discussion to follow in Chapter 19.

MONITORING AND REPORTING

The venue and timeframe for RAS monitoring will vary based on the business, function, and organizational level. For example, IT may monitor tactical risk metrics and warnings on a real-time basis in its data center "war room" where performance and risk indicators are displayed across multiple interactive screens. A business unit, and the ERM function, may monitor key business and risk metrics on a weekly basis, with more formal monthly or quarterly reviews. Executive management and the board would monitor the RAS based on their committee schedules.

An effective RAS dashboard reporting process should be structured to produce consistent reports at various levels of the organization. Bear in mind that the number and types of metrics would likely vary with the target audience. Figure 12.4 provides an illustrative example of an RAS dashboard reporting structure. The report is organized into five primary risk categories: strategic/business, financial, operational, compliance, and reputational. Each risk category has a set of risk metrics assigned with tolerances or ranges that act as limits or guidelines for acceptable risk exposures. In this example, these metrics are tracked over the previous four quarters.

Figure 12.5 shows an illustrative RAS dashboard report with specific metrics and tolerance levels for each major risk type. It is important to note that the RAS is meant to capture only the most critical risks. Otherwise, it would be far too unwieldy to be effective. By pinpointing the most useful risk metrics, the RAS aims to provide an overall, holistic view of the company's risk profile. For instance, it should identify key risk indicators (KRIs) that link to the main drivers of short- and long-term performance. These KRIs can alert management to the potential for unacceptable business outcomes and trigger corrective actions.

As an alternative or complement, the RAS metrics can be organized into separate reports by major risk type. This way, the risk executive responsible for that area can provide business context and expert commentary along with the RAS metrics. This reporting structure integrates qualitative and quantitative information, as well as allows for a greater number of RAS metrics.

An effective RAS should provide a "cascading" structure of risk exposures and limits at the board, executive-management, and business-unit levels. This structure allows users to drill down to underlying exposures to answer specific questions and issues (e.g., "What business activities make up our strategic risk exposure to China?"). Similarly, it aggregates business-level exposures upward to the enterprise level (e.g., "What is our total net credit exposure to Goldman Sachs across the entire enterprise?"). The level of detail visible for each metric depends on the needs of the specific

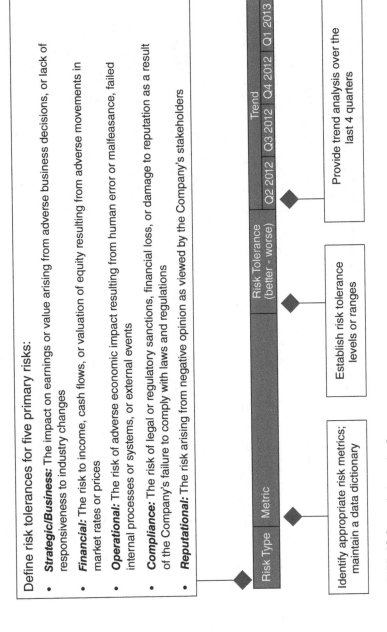

Define risk tolerances for five primary risks:

- **Strategic/Business:** The impact on earnings or value arising from adverse business decisions, or lack of responsiveness to industry changes

- **Financial:** The risk to income, cash flows, or valuation of equity resulting from adverse movements in market rates or prices

- **Operational:** The risk of adverse economic impact resulting from human error or malfeasance, failed internal processes or systems, or external events

- **Compliance:** The risk of legal or regulatory sanctions, financial loss, or damage to reputation as a result of the Company's failure to comply with laws and regulations

- **Reputational:** The risk arising from negative opinion as viewed by the Company's stakeholders

Risk Type	Metric	Risk Tolerance (better - worse)	Trend			
			Q2 2012	Q3 2012	Q4 2012	Q1 2013

Identify appropriate risk metrics; maintain a data dictionary

Establish risk tolerance levels or ranges

Provide trend analysis over the last 4 quarters

FIGURE 12.4 Risk Appetite Structure

Risk Appetite Statement Dashboard Report (Illustrative Draft for Discussion)

Risk Type	Metric	Risk Tolerance (better - worse)	Trend Q1 2013	Q2 2013	Q3 2013	Q4 2013
Strategic/ Business	ROE	12-10%				11.2%
	ROA	1.50-1.00%				1.55%
	Market-to-Book Ratio	1.5-1.0x				1.75x
	Diversification Benefit (%)	> 20%				
	New Loan Growth (per quarter)	$1.0B				$1.3B
	New Deposit Growth (per quarter)	$500mm				$684mm
	Tier 1 Leverage Ratio					12.40%
	Tier 1 Risk-Based Capital Ratio					21.10%
	Total Risk-Based Capital Ratio					21.90%
	Unexpected Earnings Volatility	< 20%				
Financial	% Loan Delinquency (30+)	0.5-1.0%				
	Credit Over-Concentration as % of Tier 1 Capital					
	NII Sensitivity (Year 1)	3-5%				
	EVE Sensitivity (+100bp)	6-8%				
	Liquidity Coverage Ratio (90 days)	150-120%				
	Material Exceptions to Financial Risk Policies and Limits	0				
Operational	# of Cyber Incidents with Business Impact	0 - 2 - 5	0	0	1	
	% of High Risk Operational Control Issues	< 10%	0	0	3	
	Operational Losses as % of Total Revenue	< 1%				
	% of Failed Business Transactions	NA				
	% of Ineffective Key Controls	NA				
	# of Cyber Incidents with Business Impact	5 - 10	0	0	0	0
Compliance	# of High Severity Compliance Issues	0	0	0	0	0
	# of Outstanding Fair Lending/CRA Issues					
	% of Compliance Areas Deemed Effective	90% - 80%				
Reputational	Retention of High Potential Key Managers					
	Employee Satisfaction and Engagement					
	Regulatory Ratings					
	Lending Customer Satisfaction					
	Deposit Customer Satisfaction					
	# of Significant Legal, Ethical, and Reputational Events					
	Cumulative 5-Year Stock Return vs. Comparables	120 - 80				

FIGURE 12.5 Risk Appetite Structure, Key Metrics

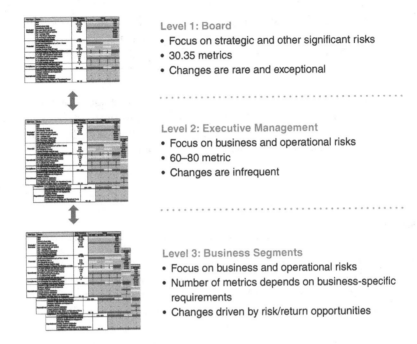

Level 1: Board
- Focus on strategic and other significant risks
- 30.35 metrics
- Changes are rare and exceptional

Level 2: Executive Management
- Focus on business and operational risks
- 60–80 metric
- Changes are infrequent

Level 3: Business Segments
- Focus on business and operational risks
- Number of metrics depends on business-specific requirements
- Changes driven by risk/return opportunities

FIGURE 12.6 Cascading and Dynamic RASs

audience (i.e., board, corporate management, or business unit). Figure 12.6 provides an illustration of cascading risk appetite statements at the three levels of the organization. As shown, the RAS would be at its most dynamic at the business level, where managers may choose to make changes based on risk/return opportunities while respecting board- and management-level risk tolerances.

Certain types of risk metrics will naturally aggregate across the organization while others are unique to specific business and operational units. Since the board and executive management RAS reports are focused on strategic and enterprise-wide risks, they should focus on aggregate risk metrics, such as:

- **Earnings,** including earnings-at-risk and unexpected earnings variance.
- **Value,** including shareholder value-added and market/book ratios.
- **Loss,** such as actual losses, operational loss-to-revenue ratios, stress-testing, or scenario-based losses.
- **Cash flow,** such as cash-flow-at-risk and liquidity-coverage ratios.
- **Financial risk,** including aggregate market risk and credit/counterparty risk exposures.

- **Number of incidents,** such as policy exceptions, cyberattacks with material business impact, and legal and regulatory issues.
- **Key stakeholder metrics,** such as retention of high-performance employees or levels of customer engagement and satisfaction.

Finally, the RAS should provide a "common language" for the ERM program. This would consist of a glossary of relevant business or technical terms and acronyms as well as a data dictionary that describes each risk metric, how it is calculated, where the underlying data is generated, and why it is included.

EXAMPLES OF RISK APPETITE STATEMENTS AND METRICS

The following sections provide examples of risk appetite statements, performance and risk metrics, and risk tolerance levels for the following risk categories: enterprise-wide risk, strategic risk, financial risk, operational risk, legal/compliance risk, and reputational risk. For simplicity, each risk appetite statement is paired with one or two example metric(s) and risk tolerance level(s). In practice, there may be a number of risk metrics and risk tolerances for each risk appetite statement.

Enterprise-Wide Risk Management

The objective of our ERM program is to minimize unexpected earnings volatility and maximize shareholder value. The following risk appetite statements, metrics, and risk tolerances are in support of this overarching objective:

> **Business Objectives:** We will integrate our ERM program into our business decision-making, and design our risk-mitigation and management strategies to enhance the likelihood of achieving our business objectives. *Metric: Any shortfall between actual vs. expected performance of our top strategic objectives will be less than 10%.*

> **Investment-Grade Debt Rating:** We will maintain our capital adequacy and debt coverage to achieve an investment-grade rating from all major rating agencies. Moreover, we will maintain surplus capital and liquidity reserves to support future growth and buffer against economic uncertainties. *Metric: Debt ratings from the major rating agencies will be at least investment grade; surplus capital and liquidity will exceed 15% of total requirements.*

Unexpected Earnings Volatility: We will perform earnings-at-risk (ex-ante) and earnings attribution (ex-post) analyses and target unexpected earnings variance to be a reasonable portion of total earnings variance. *Metric: Monthly unexpected earnings variance (i.e., earnings variances from unexpected sources) will be less than 20% of total earnings variance.*

ERM Maturity: We will continue to develop our ERM capabilities to ensure that our program remains best-in-class. Based on the size and complexity of our business, we will achieve an "excellent ERM" assessment from independent third parties within three years. *Metric: Completion of the three-year ERM roadmap initiatives and milestones will be at least 90% in the monthly tracking report.*

Risk Culture. All employees are expected to understand the risks associated with the business activities in which they are engaged. Every employee is accountable for operating within risk appetite standards and tolerances. *Metric: Annual risk culture surveys will exceed defined target levels.*

Strategic Risk Management

We strive to diversify our business portfolio to mitigate exposures to macroeconomic changes. Our business units will only pursue investment opportunities and business transactions that are consistent with the overall corporate strategy and our defined core competencies. We will focus our marketing efforts and technology initiatives to enhance significantly customer experience.

- Corporate Diversification: Our growth strategies (organic growth and M&A) will be formulated to create economic value and diversification benefit. *Metric: Diversification benefit will exceed 30%.*[9]
- Strategic Alignment and Core Competence Focus: We will focus on business investments that are consistent with our overall strategy and core competencies. *Metric: Investment capital to support noncore businesses will be less than 10%.*
- Customer Experience: We strive to offer a superior customer experience both online and in service centers. *Metric: Customer satisfaction will exceed 80% in both channels.*
- Risk-Adjusted Profitability: We will achieve an overall risk-adjusted return on capital (RAROC) that exceeds our cost of equity capital (Ke), resulting in a positive economic profit for the aggregate business and our shareholders. *Metric: Enterprise RAROC will exceed Ke by at least 2%.*

Financial Risk Management

We take financial risks in order to support our core business activities. We cannot predict the direction of financial markets and therefore do not speculate on markets to generate income. We manage our liquidity position in a conservative manner for both expected and stressed business conditions.

- **Interest Rate Risk:** Our treasury department aims to manage interest rate risk within board-approved limits. *Metric: Maximum impact on income given a 100bp parallel shift in rates is 7%.*
- **Credit Risk:** Our lending activities are based on strong underwriting standards and "know your customer" principles. *Metric: Net credit losses will be less than 1% of average loan balances.*
- **Liquidity Risk:** We manage our liquidity position to ensure that we can meet our cash obligations even under liquidity stress tests. *Metric: Maintain a liquidity coverage ratio of at least 200% under the likely scenario and at least 110% under the stressed scenario.*
- **Hedging Effectiveness:** We use derivatives for hedging purposes and never to speculate. We use only permitted derivative products, and each hedge transaction must decrease the earnings sensitivity of the overall risk position. *Metric: Hedge effectiveness ratio will exceed 80%.*

Operational Risk Management

We establish and test internal control systems to prevent, detect, and mitigate operational risk exposures. Each business unit is required to identify and assess its operational risks and ensure that they are measured and managed effectively.

- **Operational Losses:** We measure and track operational losses and incidents across the organization to identify root causes, mitigate risks, and ensure that losses are within acceptable levels. *Metric: Operational loss/revenue ratios should be less than 1% for all business units.*
- **Talent Management:** We strive to establish and maintain a talented workforce, especially through the professional development and retention of high-potential employees. *Metric: Retention rate of high-potential employees will be at least 90%.*
- **Third-Party Vendor Management:** We rely on business partners and third-party vendors to provide critical services. For that reason, we seek to minimize high-risk third-party vendor relationships. *Metric: High-risk third-party vendor relationships must be exited within one year, or a viable, fully tested contingency plan must be in place.*

IT/Cyber-Risk. We manage our IT infrastructure to ensure system availability and capacity to meet business requirements as well as to protect against natural and manmade threats, including cyberattacks. *Metric: Number of IT events with material business impact will not exceed two per month. Recovery time for critical-system failures will be within one hour. Automated patching program should exceed 90% of known vulnerabilities.*

Legal/Compliance Risk Management

We will conduct our business within the confines of all laws and regulations. Every employee is held accountable for maintaining the highest ethical standards.

Ethics Policy: We have zero tolerance for violations of our corporate ethics policy. We will respond to all exceptions to our corporate ethics policy based on the severity of the violation, including termination, bonus clawback, and legal actions. *Metric: An action plan will be established for all significant ethical violations within 30 days.*

Open Regulatory Findings: The number of open regulatory findings will be maintained within an acceptable level. *Metric: Active regulatory findings will be fewer than 15.*

New Legal Matters Opened: The number of new legal matters opened will be maintained within an acceptable level. *Metric: New legal matters opened each month will be fewer than five.*

Legal and Compliance Cost: We will control the direct cost for resolving legal and compliance issues, including fines, settlements, penalties, and outside legal and regulatory advisory expenses. *Metric: Total legal and compliance cost in the last 12 months will be less than $10 million.*

Reputational Risk Management

Our reputation is extremely valuable, and it is every employee's responsibility to safeguard and enhance it. The board, CEO, and senior management will ensure that the level of reputational risk the company assumes is managed effectively.

Customer Perspective: We will enhance our customers' experience when doing business with us and address any issues in a timely and effective manner. *Metric: Acknowledge customer complaints within 24 hours, and resolve legitimate complaints within five business days.*

Employee Perspective: We will strive to be the employer of choice in our industry and maintain a high level of employee satisfaction. *Metric: Annual survey of employee satisfaction will be greater than 90%.*

Shareholder Perspective: We will deliver superior shareholder returns and create significant shareholder value by allocating capital to the highest risk-adjusted return opportunities. *Metric: Stock performance will be in the top quintile against our peer group.*

General Public and Media Coverage. We will closely follow coverage of our company in the press, social media, and other public forums to monitor reputational risk levels. *Metric: We have zero tolerance for headline risk associated with unacceptable business practices, privacy breaches, and internal fraud.*

The risk appetite statement is a foundational component of an effective ERM program. It establishes a board-approved policy that aligns the organization's risk tolerances with strategic objectives, risk profile, and risk-management capabilities. For the board, executive management, and business and operational staff, the RAS addresses a central question: "How much risk are we willing to accept to pursue our business objectives?" A risk appetite framework defines what key types of risk a company faces and sets tolerance levels to serve as guides and limits for decision-making at every level. To develop an RAS, a company must begin by assessing regulatory requirements before developing and socializing a prototype, obtaining management and board approval, and finally communicating the policy throughout the organization. A well-developed RAS framework will have a cascading structure based on the three lines of defense (business unit, management, board) so that each organizational level understands its responsibility and so that risks can be properly aggregated across the company.

The only thing certain in business is uncertainty. The RAS is an essential tool for any organization that strives to pursue its business strategy while managing all of its significant risks. By establishing strategic priorities and risk boundaries for all employees, a robust RAS that is communicated effectively can also have a profound impact on an organization's risk culture.

NOTES

1. *2012–2013 NACD Public Company Governance Survey*, National Association of Corporate Directors, 2013.
2. EVA® is a registered trademark of Stern Stewart & Co.
3. Securities & Exchange Commission. *Observations on Developments in Risk Appetite Frameworks and IT Infrastructures*, 2010.

4. Board of Governors of the Federal Reserve. *Consolidated Supervision Frameworks for Large Financial Institutions*, 2012.
5. *Principles for an Effective Risk Appetite Framework*, Financial Stability Board, November 12, 2013.
6. U.S. Treasury Department, Office of the Comptroller of the Currency. *OCC Guidelines Establishing Heightened Standards for Certain Large Insured National Banks, Insured Federal Savings Associations, and Insured Federal Branches; Integration of 12 CFR Parts 30 and 170*, 2014.
7. *Own Risk and Solvency Assessment (ORSA) Guidance Manual*, National Association of Insurance Commissioners, 2014.
8. This analysis may be provided by the risk-control self-assessment (RCSA) process.
9. One measurement of diversification benefit is the net reduction of economic capital requirements when correlation effects across business units are factored in. In other words, the economic capital requirement for the overall corporation is less than the sum of its parts.

Risk Assessment and Quantification

CHAPTER 13

Risk Control Self-Assessments

INTRODUCTION

An initial step in ERM is to identify, assess, and prioritize an organization's key risks. The risk control self-assessment (RCSA) is a common tool that is well established in regulatory guidance and industry frameworks. Companies across all industry sectors use RCSAs for identifying, mapping, and controlling risks that threaten strategic and other objectives.[1] Companies that integrate RCSA into the daily activities of their business units will also find it easier to adhere to the growing body of stakeholder expectations and regulatory requirements.

By its very nature, RCSA implementation will vary depending upon a company's specific needs. There is, however, a common process and methodology that all RCSAs follow. We'll begin this chapter with a short overview of risk assessment and the benefits it offers. Next, we'll examine how companies can implement RCSA process and methodology such as identifying risks, evaluating existing controls, and developing risk mitigation strategies. We'll look at the short- and long-term post-RCSA processes to get the most out of the results and increase future efficiency with an emphasis on common pitfalls and practical solutions. We'll conclude the chapter by examining how to incorporate risk assessment into the business process through strategic planning and review.

RISK ASSESSMENT: AN OVERVIEW

The objective of risk assessment (or RCSA) is to identify, evaluate, and prioritize an organization's key risks to enable more informed business and risk management decisions. Risk assessment principles are well established in industry frameworks such as COSO ERM, the Dey Report, the Turnbull Report, and ISO 31000.

Risk assessments generally include the following key steps:

1. Establish the business context with respect to organizational objectives and regulatory requirements.
2. Identify the key risks that may negatively (or positively) impact the achievement of business objectives.
3. Evaluate the key risks in terms of probability (likelihood of occurrence) and severity (financial and reputational consequences).
4. Evaluate the effectiveness of controls associated with the key risks.
5. Determine the risk management strategies, including accountabilities and action plans.
6. Prioritize the top risks for further analyses, quantification, and risk mitigation.
7. Provide ongoing reporting and monitoring.

The key benefits of risk assessment include:

- Enhanced awareness and transparency of the key risks facing the organization
- More efficient cross-functional knowledge transfer
- Improved risk analytics and quantification processes
- Enhanced reporting to the board and management
- Improved business performance through risk-based decision making

While most organizations have implemented risk assessment programs for many years, common obstacles may prevent them from achieving the full benefits. These obstacles include:

- Lack of senior management sponsorship and/or business unit support for the risk assessment program
- Inconsistencies in the risk assessment standards that are used over time; and/or the quality of input throughout the organization
- Inability to develop an overall risk profile due to the vast amount of qualitative data, which may be difficult to aggregate, prioritize, and quantify
- Lack of integration with other ERM processes and/or business activities and operations
- Difficulty in showing tangible business benefits other than compliance with regulatory and corporate requirements

RCSA METHODOLOGY

Risk assessment is the process of identifying, evaluating, and prioritizing key risks related to the achievement of business objectives. Each organization should customize its risk assessment methodology for its own particular business scope, operating complexity, and risk management maturity. However, there are common industry processes and practices for risk assessment. Figure 13.1 provides an overall process map of the four phases of risk assessment.

The first phase **sets the foundation.** This should include senior-level sponsorship for risk assessment to ensure business unit participation and candor. Other elements include organizing and planning, establishing a risk taxonomy, developing risk assessment tools, and providing education and training.

The second phase involves **risk identification, assessment, and prioritization.** This includes establishing the context in terms of business objectives and regulatory and policy requirements. During this phase, the RCSA team conducts risk assessment interviews and/or workshops in order to identify, evaluate, and prioritize key risks. It enables many companies identify their top risks.

The third phase consists of **deep dives, risk quantification, and management.** In this phase, the company performs in-depth analyses (i.e., deep dives) of the top risks identified at the enterprise-wide level. The RCSA team then establishes key risk indicators (KRIs) and risk tolerance levels for each of these top risks. In addition, the team develops and implements specific risk management strategies, including accountabilities and action plans.

The fourth phase involves **integration of RCSA into business and ERM processes.** Risk assessment should not be a standalone exercise. Companies should integrate it with other ERM and business management processes, such as strategic planning, business activities, operational processes, and board and management reporting.

With respect to the overall risk assessment process, common pitfalls and practical solutions include:

- **Lack of an overall methodology and plan.** As illustrated in Figure 13.1, the plan should not only address risk identification and assessment, but also how to aggregate the results and report them to management and the board, how risk assessment information supports business and risk management decisions, and how risk assessment meshes with other business and ERM processes. Without an overall methodology and plan that clearly establishes the desired outcomes, it is difficult to aggregate and apply the vast amount of data that risk assessment generates.
- **Insufficient prioritization of risks.** Risks are not equally important, so a "one size fits all" approach is unlikely to be fully effective. The objective of risk assessment should not be to identify and assess *all* of the risks facing the organization (in fact, such a list would be infinite). Rather, the objective is to identify and assess the *key* risks, and to quantify, report, and manage the most critical enterprise-level risks.

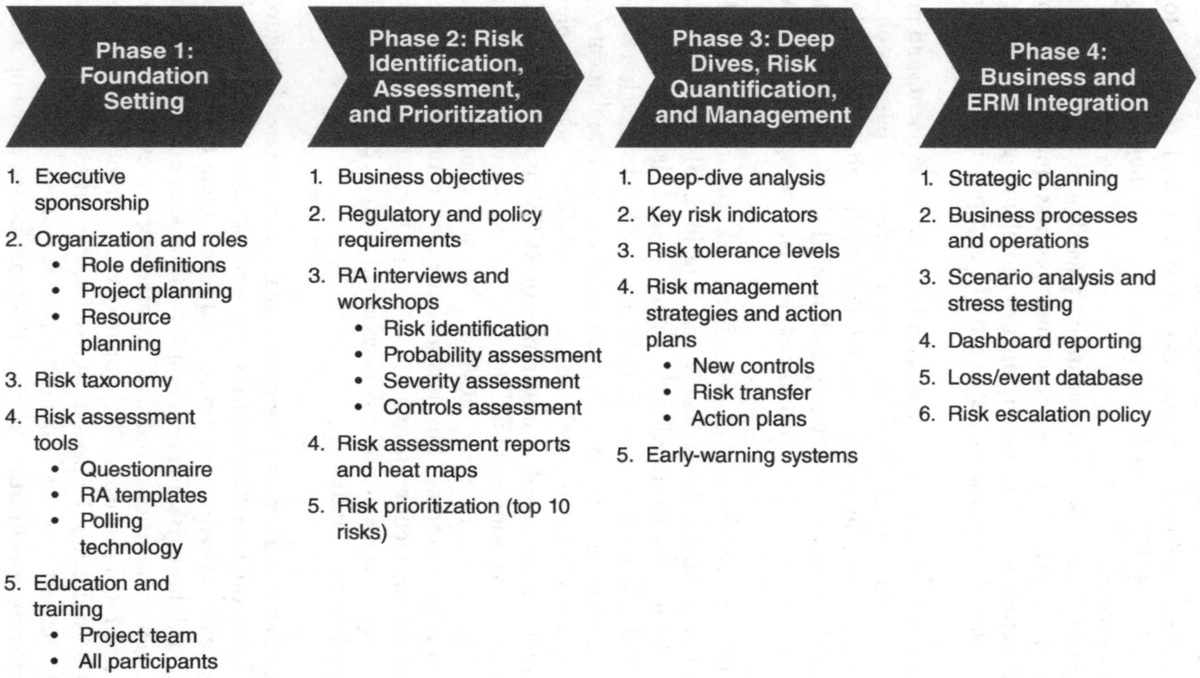

Phase 1: Foundation Setting

1. Executive sponsorship
2. Organization and roles
   - Role definitions
   - Project planning
   - Resource planning
3. Risk taxonomy
4. Risk assessment tools
   - Questionnaire
   - RA templates
   - Polling technology
5. Education and training
   - Project team
   - All participants

Phase 2: Risk Identification, Assessment, and Prioritization

1. Business objectives
2. Regulatory and policy requirements
3. RA interviews and workshops
   - Risk identification
   - Probability assessment
   - Severity assessment
   - Controls assessment
4. Risk assessment reports and heat maps
5. Risk prioritization (top 10 risks)

Phase 3: Deep Dives, Risk Quantification, and Management

1. Deep-dive analysis
2. Key risk indicators
3. Risk tolerance levels
4. Risk management strategies and action plans
   - New controls
   - Risk transfer
   - Action plans
5. Early-warning systems

Phase 4: Business and ERM Integration

1. Strategic planning
2. Business processes and operations
3. Scenario analysis and stress testing
4. Dashboard reporting
5. Loss/event database
6. Risk escalation policy

FIGURE 13.1 RCSA Methodology—Process Map

- **Siloed view of risks and controls.** Risk assessments should not represent only one organizational point of view, regardless of whether that point of view is from business units, corporate functions, or control functions such as audit or risk management. Effective risk assessments originate from a cross-functional view of risk. For example, business units may provide useful bottom-up assessments of their businesses, products, customers, and distribution channels while senior executives offer a top-down assessment of risks that may impact strategic and enterprise-wide objectives. At the same time, audit and risk management offer independent assessment of control effectiveness and risk interdependencies across the organization. At some companies, even board members participate in risk assessment by providing unique perspectives on regulatory, industry, and business issues.

Let's discuss the four phases of RCSA in greater detail.

PHASE 1: SETTING THE FOUNDATION

The foundation-setting phase provides the essential support elements for risk assessment, including senior executive sponsorship, organization and planning, key documents and tools, and education and training. The absence of any of these elements may hinder the efficiency and effectiveness of the risk assessment process.

Executive Sponsorship

At the start of the risk assessment cycle, a senior-level sponsor (e.g., CEO, CFO, or CRO) should communicate the board's and executive management's commitment to the risk assessment process, its key objectives and expected benefits, and the expected timeline, along with primary milestones. Given the time constraints and other priorities business managers face, it can be difficult to get their full and candid input without high-level sponsorship. The project sponsor and other corporate leaders should lead by example, engaging in the risk assessment process with candid and thoughtful input.

Organization and Roles

The implementation team should produce an overall plan to define tasks, accountabilities, and deadlines. Key roles may include an RCSA manager to execute specific tasks and delegate responsibilities; subject matter experts to provide technical expertise; trained facilitators to assist in managing meetings and workshops; and risk analysts to capture, organize, analyze, and report on results. Together, these roles will constitute the RCSA project team.

Risk Taxonomy

Having a common language is key to an effective discussion. This is particularly true in risk management, since each company will have its own hierarchy of risks, depending on its business model, industry, and many other factors. Therefore, establishing definitions and categories of risks to facilitate discussion is crucial to running a successful RCSA. As much as possible, these categories should be common to all business units and functional areas in order to facilitate aggregation across the organization. In this regard, it is important to align the risk taxonomy with the business language used in the organization.

A popular way for companies to classify risk is according to operational events, a system the Basel Committee endorses. For example, a company might establish a broad category of employment-practice events with further subcategories such as employee relations, workplace safety, and diversity.

Other companies choose cause-driven or impact-driven classification. Under the former, risks are classified according to the root cause of operational losses. However, this method can run into difficulty when there are multiple root causes for a loss, or when the cause is unclear. The impact-driven method classifies risks by the financial impact of operational losses. While the classification itself poses few challenges, it may leave companies with an insufficient understanding of root causes. I believe the cause-driven method, despite its challenges, is the preferred method. Management can only address root causes (e.g., employee training), but not consequences (e.g., employee errors).

In addition to this taxonomy, it is often helpful to have a glossary of key terms (e.g., probability, severity, tolerance, etc.). This can help avoid unnecessary confusion and ensure the entire company is on the same page.

Risk Assessment Tools

The RCSA project team should employ the tools that facilitate the risk assessment process in the most effective and efficient way. Typically, assessment tools fall into two categories: short-answer surveys and open-ended interviews. The former is most appropriate for gathering aggregate data during staff workshops. The latter can provide a fuller and more contextualized discussion of risk issues. Polling a large group of operational personnel requires a standardized question/answer template while the detailed input of senior executives and board members is best captured by open-ended questions. Figure 13.2 shows an example of an executive questionnaire.

In the past, the available technology could support either of these tools, but rarely both in a sufficiently integrated fashion. Modern cloud-based technologies not only support both assessment approaches, but are also able

1. Please summarize the scope of the business or operating unit that you are representing.
2. Review the key short-term and long-term business objectives for your business unit.
3. Looking back, discuss the major losses, incidents, or near-misses that concerned you the most.
4. Looking forward, identify the main risks faced by the company and your specific business unit, including estimated probabilities and consequences.
5. Discuss the key controls associated with these main risks (e.g., risk policy and tolerance levels, processes and systems, risk mitigation strategies).
6. Discuss the metrics and reporting associated with these main risks.
7. Identify other relevant issues that we have not discussed.

FIGURE 13.2 Top-Down Executive Questionnaire

to integrate them seamlessly, making data aggregation easier and less error prone—and, in many cases, completely automated in real-time.

Education and Training

A knowledgeable staff is essential to a company's success in risk assessment. The project team should be conversant in best practices for implementing risk assessments, analyzing and aggregating risk assessment results, and providing analyses and reports to management and the board. Other participants must understand the role of risk assessment, why the risk assessment is being done, what the value is to the business, how they can best participate and contribute, and how they can apply the results to mitigate risks and enhance business performance. A well-planned and executed training program can achieve both these goals.

Common Pitfalls and Practical Solutions

- **Lack of senior management participation.** As part of the project planning process, senior executives should commit their time to participate in the process. Senior management should not only be the "audience" for the risk assessment in terms of receiving the final risk assessment reports, it should be an active participant. In addition to communicating executive sponsorship, senior management can provide useful input on key risks and controls. As with any enterprise-wide initiatives, there is a high correlation between senior management engagement and success in risk assessment.

- **Inappropriate resource planning and allocation.** A critical success factor in the implementation of risk assessment is having the right level and mix of professional resources. On the one hand, some companies only allocate minimal, part-time staff resources to conduct risk assessments. Inadequate resources may result in inaccurate or superficial assessments of risks and controls. On the other hand, it is possible to over-allocate professional resources. At one mid-size bank, a team of more than 20 full-time risk staff and consultants worked on an annual risk assessment that took nine months to complete. The result was an overly bureaucratic process that drained corporate and business unit time and resources. Moreover, the end product was several thick binders of risk assessment information that was ultimately of little use.
- **Insufficient preparation.** Risk assessment is not an ad-hoc process that companies can implement on the fly. It requires thoughtful planning and organization. The development of risk assessment tools and training programs should be a fundamental step. For most companies, risk assessment is an ongoing annual process that requires significant corporate and business unit time and attention. Thus, thoughtful preparation can go a long way to ensure that the risk assessment process is efficient and effective.

PHASE 2: RISK IDENTIFICATION, ASSESSMENT, AND PRIORITIZATION

Once the foundational groundwork has been laid, the project team is ready to execute. The key deliverables in this phase include top-down risk assessments from senior executives, bottom-up risk assessments from business and operating units, risk assessment reports and heat maps, and the prioritization of enterprise-level risks.

Business Objectives

A key tenet of ERM is to identify, assess, and manage risks in the context of business objectives. Part of strategic and business planning is establishing key objectives at the corporate and business unit levels, each associated with a key performance indicator or KPI (e.g., market share, operating efficiency, earnings growth, etc.). In turn, key risks may impact the achievement of these business objectives and variability in the KPIs. These key risks are associated with key risk indicators or KRIs (e.g., product/service quality problems, operational risk metrics, unexpected earnings volatility, etc.). Associating key business objectives and KPIs with key risks and KRIs provides the basis for integrated performance reporting and management.

In pursuit of business objectives, businesses must also comply with regulations and corporate policies, another key objective of ERM. In risk assessment, it is useful to summarize the regulatory requirements and guidelines, as well as corporate policies and associated risk tolerance levels (if available) for each key risk.

Identifying Risk

Before cataloguing risks via surveys, interviews, and workshops, it is important to understand the status of each risk within the current environment. This is best defined in terms of inherent risk, controls, and the resultant residual risk.

Inherent Risk Inherent risk refers to the risk exposure of an event prior to consideration of any controls or mitigation efforts. Inherent risk is typically assessed along four attributes,[2] which can be defined qualitatively or quantitatively:

1. **Probability:** the likelihood of a risk event
2. **Impact:** the extent to which a risk event will affect the company in terms of financial, security, employee, or reputational impacts
3. **Vulnerability:** the susceptibility to a risk event
4. **Speed of onset:** the length of time between the occurrence of a risk event and the point at which it affects the company

These attributes are often interrelated. For example, the more vulnerable a company is to a risk event, the greater its impact. Similarly, multiple risk events can have an aggregate impact on the company. That is why having a documented taxonomy is so important. A company can evaluate its risk interactions by grouping individual risk events into broader categories and studying their aggregate effects. For example, individual risk events relating to distribution, sourcing, and vendor relationships would fall under a broader category of supply chain risk.

Controls How well a company manages its risks and their interdependencies depends on how effective its controls are at mitigating unwanted effects of risk events. Controls may be preventative, detective, or corrective:

1. Preventative controls are intended to stop a risk event before its occurrence.

2. Detective controls are intended to identify a risk event after its occurrence.
3. Corrective controls are intended to minimize the impact and close the vulnerability.

It's easy to see how preventative controls might be preferable to detective or corrective ones, but the former may not always be possible. A good example is cybersecurity, where it is nearly impossible to prevent 100% of cyberattacks, so the cybersecurity program must have effective detective and corrective controls.

Some controls are manual while others can be automated. If a control involves both automated and manual components, it should be classified as manual. For example, a software system may produce a daily exception report that an employee must review before reporting and resolving each item. Because it requires the employee's involvement, this would be considered a manual control.

The risk management team should regularly evaluate the design and effectiveness of controls and recommend changes when warranted. For this reason, the RCSA process should include a testing protocol to assess the effectiveness of the control, identify gaps in the control environment, and produce a corrective plan for timely remediation if necessary. Evaluating design ensures that the control is performing as intended while evaluating effectiveness makes sure the control is operating or being operated appropriately. Evaluation usually involves a thorough walkthrough of the control. Considerations during the evaluation should include:

- Is the control effectively mitigating its intended risk?
- Is the control performing correctly and when appropriate?
- Is the control properly situated within the business process?
- Is there adequate segregation of duties?
- Do individuals who perform the control have the requisite knowledge required? Are they aware of the ultimate objective of the control?
- Is the input required by the control accurate?
- What is the likelihood of control failure?
- Can the control be made more efficient?

Residual Risks Once a company has assessed inherent risks and controls it can then determine the residual risk of individual events—that is, the risk exposure of an event after taking controls and mitigation efforts into consideration. While the purpose of identifying inherent risk is to determine which risk events require the most attention and resources for mitigation, residual risk is a closer measure of the actual risk exposure a company faces and the effectiveness of existing controls. Residual risk is what a company considers when it chooses to mitigate, avoid, transfer, or accept risk.

Risk Assessment Interviews and Workshops

As discussed previously, it is useful to conduct interviews using open-ended questions when working with senior executives on risk assessments. In addition to identifying key risks associated with corporate objectives (i.e., top-down risk assessment), these interviews can gather important institutional knowledge about business strategy and culture, lessons learned from previous risk events, and the kinds of KPIs and KRIs that senior executives find most useful. For business unit teams, it may be more appropriate to organize workshops to develop bottom-up risk assessments. During the interviews and workshops, participants identify risks or risk events, and assess probability, severity, and effectiveness of controls through the use of polls or surveys. They may also decide on risk treatment, such as avoidance, mitigation, transfer, or acceptance.

Risk Assessment Reports and Maps

The interviews and workshops may result in a large number of risk assessments. It is the responsibility of the project team to aggregate and report on these results. Risk assessment reports generally provide the following information for each risk:

- Description of the risk or risk event
- Assessment and rating of probability (or likelihood)
- Assessment and rating of severity (or impact)
- Assessment and rating of control effectiveness
- Responsible person(s) and oversight committees
- Management response and action plans

In addition to risk assessment reports, heat maps (or "risk maps") can help visualize the risk assessment information. On a heat map, risks are plotted against probability along the y or vertical axis and severity along the x or horizontal axis. An alternative methodology is to plot risks according to their severities and effectiveness of controls. Attention should then be focused on risks with high severity and low control effectiveness. Regardless of the methodology used, it is important to note that risk assessments and heat maps are generally not considered by board members and senior executives as actionable information that can support board- or executive-level decisions. Rather, they should be viewed as initial risk assessment and visualization reports that can support further analyses and modeling. In other words, risk assessments and reports are "start products," not "end products."

Risk Prioritization

Based on the aggregate risk assessment results, the company should identify its most critical risks (e.g., top-10 risks). This is not to say that the company should only pay attention to 10 risks. In fact, each business unit or functional area may identify their own top risks and collectively monitor all of the key risks recorded in the risk assessment process. However, it is useful to establish a priority list of enterprise-level risks. For example, one large asset management firm reported over 700 risks. It would be impractical for executive management or the board to review and monitor such a large number of risks. Instead, the project team should identify the top-10 risks for the company based on the risk assessment information and confirm their analysis with executive management.

Common Pitfalls and Practical Solutions

- **Lack of clear business objectives or risk policy constraints.** Most companies have a clear sense of regulatory requirements and guidelines. However, some companies have not clearly defined their business objectives, and/or have not established explicit risk tolerance levels. For these companies, it may be difficult to assess risks in the context of business objectives and policy constraints. In some instances, the company develops business objectives and risk policies in parallel with the risk assessment process. In other instances, this management issue is recognized as a risk of its own.
- **Defining risks in terms of consequences rather than root causes.** Companies often define risks based on consequences instead of root causes. This can create frustration in determining the appropriate risk treatment because consequences are not directly controllable. For example, a company cannot decrease production errors or customer complaints directly, but it can increase process automation and staff training. Another example would be that a company cannot determine its debt rating, but it can manage the company's capital structure and interest coverage capabilities given their target debt rating. The last example is that a company cannot control foreign exchange (FX) rates, but it can control its FX exposures and monitor volatility.

■ **Inconsistent estimates of probability and severity.** What is the probability and severity of a risk event? The answers depend on the timeframe and more importantly how the company defines *worst case*. Any risk can be conceptualized and, with adequate data, quantified as a bell curve. The bell curve represents a range of probabilities and severities. When assessing the probability and severity of a risk event, different people may be thinking of different levels of worst case. To address this issue, the project team should establish clear guidelines with respect to the worst case, as well as the timeframe for the risk assessment. For example, companies that calculate value-at-risk across products or economic capital across business units always harmonize the probability level (e.g., 95% or 99%) and timeframe (e.g., 1 year) that they use in their models. That is the only way they can produce apples-to-apples results. ERM teams implementing RCSAs should consider this approach so the risk assessment results are consistent.

PHASE 3: DEEP DIVES, RISK QUANTIFICATION, AND MANAGEMENT

The top-10 risks identified in the previous phase represent the most critical risks facing the company. This list focuses management time and attention on the appropriate risks. Each of these key risks warrants further assessment, quantification, and management strategies.

Deep Dives

Deep dives are more granular risk assessments. Beyond the information gathered during Phase 2, deep dives may add risk assessments from the next level down in the organization, external benchmarking of the risk and related controls, process maps that clearly document the key business and operational flows, independent assessments from auditors and regulators, and control effectiveness testing. Overall, the purpose of deep dives is to gather more detailed and actionable information.

Key Risk Indicators

Peter Drucker was right when he said "What gets measured gets managed." For key risks, that means developing actionable KRIs that support the quantification and monitoring of top risks. In addition to measuring risk exposures, it is useful to track risk metrics related to control effectiveness (key control indicators) and leading indicators (early warning indicators).

Risk Tolerance Levels

Risk tolerance levels, as outlined in the company's risk appetite statement (RAS), provide benchmarks against which management can evaluate risk assessments and KRIs and represent the company's risk appetite on key risks. Examples of risk tolerance dimensions include market risk, credit risk, or liquidity risk limits; business performance targets and triggers; operational performance goals and limits; and other benchmarks for desirable and undesirable performance. Ideally, the company tracks KRIs against risk tolerance levels so management can clearly see if risk levels are within acceptable ranges.

Risk Management Strategies and Action Plans

Without strategies to reshape the company's risk/return profile, every process up to this point would be an intellectual exercise. Based on an assessment of key risks relative to business objectives and tolerance levels, management should decide on the appropriate strategy to address each one. These strategies will incorporate one or more of the four broad categories of risk response: avoidance, mitigation, transfer, or acceptance. Any risk acceptance should be followed by discussions of how to incorporate the total cost of risk into product pricing and/or performance measurement systems. The total cost of risk includes expected loss, unexpected loss (e.g., cost of economic capital), risk transfer costs, and administrative costs. To support the execution of risk-management strategies, the risk function should develop action plans (e.g., creating corrective actions, project change requests, and risk transfer strategies) with clear accountabilities and approval from management.

Early Warning Systems

Risks are inherently fluid, dynamic, and difficult to predict. Thus even the best risk assessment and quantification processes may not identify the next risk event that impacts the organization. Companies should develop early warning systems to indicate emerging risk issues before a risk event occurs. While KRIs are associated with specific risks, early warning systems provide a more generalized and comprehensive way for companies to foresee potential risk events. For example, a spike in employee absenteeism or customer complaints may hint at more significant operational risk issues. Or an uptick in credit spreads and price volatility may provide early warnings about capital markets turmoil. In conjunction with these early warning systems, companies should invest in preparedness with respect to early-action and crisis-management strategies. For example, in a financial market crisis, early actions may include contingent liquidity and capital plans to raise financial resources during the initial stages of the crisis when funds are still available. In a natural disaster, the crisis management program may include business contingency planning and recovery plans, as well as internal and external communication protocols.

Common Pitfalls and Practical Solutions

- **Failure to prioritize top risks.** The risk assessment process in Phase 2 will likely produce a large number of key risks that could impact business objectives. But a key risk for a business unit may not be a key risk for the company as a whole. It would be too burdensome to develop KRIs, risk tolerance levels, risk management strategies, and early warning systems for all of these risks. Thus the company must identify its top risks so management and the board can focus their attention appropriately. However, this does not preclude business units developing more granular analysis and action plans for their own key risks.
- **Insufficient quantification.** Information collected from risk assessments is largely qualitative. Even the probability, severity, and control assessment ratings usually represent numeric expression of qualitative inputs. In order to build confidence in the appropriate risk management strategies and actions, objective risk quantification must supplement risk assessments. This includes developing KRIs, risk tolerance levels, and early warning indicators.
- **Insufficient risk management strategies and action plans.** One of the biggest complaints about risk assessment is that the process does not result in value-adding strategies and actions. Companies spend significant time and resources to produce and review a large volume of risk assessment reports and heat maps, but these documents may sit on the shelf until the next assessment cycle. The end goal of risk assessment is not only to produce better information, but also to support more intelligent decision-making based on that information. It is critical to develop specific risk management strategies and action plans as part of the risk assessment process. Moreover, companies should integrate risk assessment into business processes and other ERM practices. We examine this integration further in the next section.

PHASE 4: BUSINESS AND ERM INTEGRATION

Risk assessment should not be a standalone process. It should be part of strategic planning and review processes, business processes and operations, and other ERM processes such as dashboard reporting, loss/event tracking, and risk escalation policies.

Strategic Planning

Companies must establish clear links between strategic planning and risk assessment. In fact, the integration of strategy and ERM is a key initiative as boards and executive management take a more active role in risk oversight. This integration offers significant benefits. The strategic planning process results in business objectives that should drive risk assessment. On the other hand, risk assessment illuminates key risk exposures and the cost of risk, both of which are essential in making risk/return tradeoff decisions during the strategic planning process. In addition to strategic planning, companies should also integrate risk assessment into strategy and business review processes. As companies execute their business strategies, they often organize strategy and business review sessions to consider new information such as competitive trends, customer data, and business performance. They can then update risk assessments and related monitoring processes with this new information.

Business Processes and Operations

Key business processes and operations should include risk assessment on a day-to-day basis. For example, the pricing of the company's products and services should fully incorporate the cost of risk. Risk assessments can also support other processes such as new product and business development, M&A transactions, project management, and capital allocation. Operational processes should also integrate risk assessment analysis. For example, a process map can depict where key risks (and actual errors and losses) may occur within an operational process. Management can then embed specific controls and risk-monitoring processes where they are most effective.

Scenario Analysis and Stress Testing

Companies should not only be concerned about the worst-case scenario of any single risk, but also the possibility of a more consequential scenario of multiple risk events, such as a failed product launch, an economic downturn, or a new competitive threat. Moreover, the company may stress test the combined failure of key controls, such as risk model error, incorrect data, and departure of key risk personnel. While less likely than a single risk event, the confluence of multiple risk events (i.e., the "perfect storm") may present the company with critical challenges worth preparing for.

Dashboard Reporting

The sheer volume of data from risk assessments, other ERM analytics, and business performance systems can be overwhelming. In order to provide senior management and the board with the appropriate information, I strongly recommend creating dashboard reports designed to support the specific decision-making and informational needs of corporate executives and board members.

At the board level, for example, these reports would provide a concise executive summary of business/risk performance as well as external performance drivers. They would focus on key board discussion and decision points, providing forward-looking analyses of organization-wide performance, including key performance and risk indicators shown against specific targets or limits. And they would offer actual performance data on previous business/risk decisions as well as rationale for management recommendations. A modern dashboard system, which we'll examine more thoroughly in Chapter 18, can also provide drill-down capabilities to underlying data and analysis when desired.

Loss/Event Database

Every risk loss or event represents a valuable learning opportunity, but only if the risk team captures and reviews them systematically. Companies should develop and maintain a loss/event database to capture all material losses and incidents. This database can inform postmortem analyses in terms of root causes and needed controls, reveal key risk trends and emerging patterns, help address risk issues before they become major problems, and close a feedback loop on the efficacy of risk assessments and dashboard reporting. Based on my experience, developing a loss/event database is a low-cost but high-value ERM initiative.

Risk Escalation Policy

Risk events do not occur on a regular interval, but in real time. Thus, annual risk assessments—even if they are updated monthly or quarterly—may not support timely alerts or management responses. A risk escalation policy can mitigate this problem by establishing specific notification triggers for material losses or events (e.g., losses above a certain threshold, risk events that impact a certain number of customers, etc.). A lesson learned from previous corporate disasters is that bad news does not always travel up the organization. A risk escalation policy establishes the explicit expectation and specific criteria for communicating risk events on a timely basis.

Common Pitfalls and Practical Solutions

- **Integration occurs only in back-end reporting.** Some companies simply provide consolidated reports of various business and risk management processes. However, integrating risk assessment with other ERM and business processes should not only occur on the back end. It should involve integrated planning and analysis in the front end on an ongoing basis in terms of performance and risk monitoring as well.
- **Insufficient change management.** At most companies, the integration of risk management with strategy and business activities requires significant changes in organizational processes. Each organizational unit may have well-established policies and procedures for its business. To implement the necessary change, the RCSA team should establish a clearly defined change agenda. This includes change-management strategies to align goals, overcome barriers, and measure and track success.

ERM AND INTERNAL AUDIT COLLABORATION

As the risk landscape increases in complexity, it is becoming more and more important to increase collaboration and coordination efforts between the ERM program and the company's internal audit function. An innovative way to accomplish this is through the use of the RCSA process. RCSA data and outputs can provide points of comparison between ERM risk focus areas and those of internal audit, thus providing an added level of structure and assurance.

A simple first step to sync a company's RCSA process to its internal audit program is to map RCSA risk focus areas to those in the internal audit universe. This allows both ERM and internal audit to better understand their risk and audit review coverage at any given moment. Such an approach provides the ERM team additional perspective on controls and risk mitigation processes while it offers a quasi-independent evaluation of audit scope and priorities. For example, risk assessments can inform risk-based audit plans while audit findings can validate control effectiveness ratings.

The mapping process should take place after the completion of RCSA as well as during the annual internal audit plan-setting period. By coordinating efforts between ERM and internal audit, the organization can ensure that there is a consistency in approach and a focus on the risks that truly are impactful.

NOTES

1. *Risk Management Assessment Framework: A Tool for Departments.* HM Treasury (United Kingdom), 2009. Retrieved from https://www.gov.uk/government/uploads/system/uploads/attachment_data/file/191516/Risk_management_assessment_framework.pdf.
2. Curtis, Patchin and Mark Carey, *Risk Assessment in Practice.* Deloitte & Touche LLP. Sponsored by the Committee of Sponsoring Organizations of the Treadway Commission, October 2012.

CHAPTER 14

Risk Quantification Models

INTRODUCTION

Risk assessments, as discussed in the previous chapter, provide qualitative information with respect to the identification, evaluation, and prioritization of key risks. Risk models, the topic of this chapter, provide quantitative information with respect to the amount, shape, and sensitivity of those key risks. Risk models have long been applied in financial and insurable risk fields, such as financial risk management and actuarial science.

Risk models help manage risk by breaking it down and expressing it in mathematical terms. Models differ in methodology, assumptions, input data, and complexity, but all produce fundamentally similar output—a probability distribution or "bell curve."

The models we'll discuss in this chapter quantify three broad categories of risk: market, credit, and operational. Strategic risk models will be discussed in the next chapter. Because statistical modeling is a highly technical subject, entire books are written on a single type of risk modeling. The purpose of this chapter is to provide a high-level overview of several commonly used models in risk management. While CROs and ERM practitioners do not need to be quants, they should have a general understanding and familiarity with the risk quantification models.

> Market risk models examine the exposure to potential loss due to changes in market prices (i.e., interest rates, FX rates, equity prices, and commodity and energy prices). The most common market risk model remains *Value-at-Risk (VaR)*. However, the 2008 financial crisis exposed many weaknesses in the model, so risk managers have replaced or augmented it with *Expected Shortfall (ES)*, which addresses some of its shortcomings. We'll also look at *Asset/Liability Management (ALM)* models, designed to measure interest rate risk due to mismatches in asset and liability rate sensitivities.

Credit risk models come in four flavors: *credit scoring*, which estimates the expected default frequency at a point in time; *credit migration*, which examines how the credit quality of exposures changes over time; *credit exposure*, which estimates the loan equivalent exposure of credit transactions, and *credit portfolio* models, which assess the risk/return profile of a portfolio of credits.

Operational risk models represent potential loss from inadequate or failed internal processes, people, and systems, or from external events. The most common of these is the *Loss Distribution Approach (LDA)*, which estimates separate distributions for loss likelihood and loss severity and aggregates them. Causal models, which directly link loss outcomes with the drivers of the business, may be evolving into best practice.

In addition to these models, this chapter will look at how firms can implement and maintain an effective model risk governance program, which includes creating a model inventory, performing validation, and establishing data governance.

MARKET RISK MODELS

Market risk is the exposure to potential loss from changes in market prices. Shifts in equity or commodity prices, interest rates, and foreign exchange rates can all have negative consequences for a firm's financial position. The degree and type of market risk exposures vary by industry and company, but financial institutions are particularly vulnerable to this type of risk. They may participate in proprietary trading or market-making activities, and have exposure to interest rate changes due to asset/liability duration mismatches.

Value-at-Risk

Developed in the early 1990s, Value-at-Risk (VaR) remains one of the most common market risk models. VaR measures the potential loss of market value for a position or portfolio for a given confidence level and holding period. It performs best for liquid trading securities over short holding periods. The model provides a standardized measure of market risk by translating the riskiness of an entire portfolio into currency terms. VaR is interpreted with three main data points: a holding period, a probability, and a loss amount.

For example, suppose that the five-day VaR of a trading portfolio is $10 million at the 99% confidence level. The model predicts a loss no greater than $10 million within the next five trading days 99% of the time, which leaves a 1% chance that a loss greater than $10 million will occur. The three main methodologies for calculating VaR are the parametric approach, Monte Carlo simulation, and historical simulation. Each model uses different assumptions and methodologies to produce a loss estimation:

Parametric VaR   The parametric approach, sometimes called the variance-covariance approach, is the simplest method for calculating VaR. Its simplicity comes from the fact that it makes two basic assumptions about the risks and returns. First, risk factor returns are assumed to be normally distributed and linearly correlated, which allows the model to calculate the distribution of risk factor returns directly from their variances and covariances. Similarly, it assumes that asset returns are linearly related to risk factor returns, which is true for some securities but not for many others, particularly those with optionality.

   Though a useful tool when the assumptions are reasonable, the parametric approach may produce inaccurate results for portfolios containing options or other securities with skewed return distributions (e.g., mortgages).

Monte Carlo Simulation   The Monte Carlo simulation retains the first assumption of the parametric approach, that is, a normal distribution of risk factor returns. But rather than assuming linearity between assets and risk factors, Monte Carlo re-prices the portfolio under a large number of random scenarios. The model therefore accounts for optionality, and can correctly price both linear and nonlinear instruments. The large number of iterations required make Monte Carlo simulation the slowest method of calculating VaR. However, the use of randomly generated scenarios makes this technique especially useful for modeling securities that are path-dependent, such as structured derivatives and mortgage loans and securities.

Historical Simulation   The historical simulation approach uses observed price data to calculate the effect on the value of a portfolio. The method does not rely on either of the assumptions used by the parametric model. For this reason, historical VaR produces better estimates of the actual distribution of risk than the other methods, but its predictions are based solely on past events—a crucial weakness for highly volatile markets. Historical VaR cannot predict market conditions that have not been observed, making it impractical for new securities.

Weaknesses of VaR   VaR is a useful metric when used by risk managers who understand how to apply it correctly. However, its assumptions make it unreliable under certain conditions. First of all, VaR is a poor measure of "tail" risk, since it assumes normally distributed risk factor returns within a preset confidence level. As a result, VaR leads to an underestimation of extreme losses. For this reason, portfolios routinely experience "VaR breaks"—losses beyond the confidence interval—far more often than the model predicts.

And finally, VaR performs poorly in stressed markets. VaR accounts for the risk reduction (or diversification) effect of imperfect correlation between securities in a portfolio. During market turmoil, however, prices of dissimilar securities (equities, corporate bonds, and commodities, for example) often move together to a significant degree. In addition, liquidity often dries up in a crisis, making it difficult to unwind a portfolio quickly. VaR models generally do not account for these effects.

The financial crisis of 2008 exposed the weaknesses of VaR, which failed to determine appropriate capital (and liquidity) requirements during the extreme market turmoil. Subsequent developments have focused on models that address these shortcomings. In May 2012, the Basel Committee on Banking Supervision published a consultative document advocating the use of *expected shortfall*.[1]

Expected shortfall (also known as conditional VaR, represents the expected losses in a portfolio for a risk event beyond the VaR confidence level. Unlike VaR, expected shortfall takes into consideration extreme market conditions. In fact, the ratio of expected shortfall to VaR provides a useful estimate of how much the tail of a distribution curve is skewed.

Asset/Liability Management Models

Asset/Liability Management (ALM) measures the risk that banks face due to duration mismatch between assets and liabilities. This disequilibrium can cause loss due to changes in interest rates or liquidity. ALM is a good choice to model illiquid portfolios and structural positions (such as a bank's balance sheet). By contrast, the assumptions behind VaR models do not take into account low liquidity, nonlinearity of customer behavior, or embedded options.

Compared to VaR, ALM models offer more sophisticated interest-rate and foreign-exchange modeling since they can incorporate different yield curve and FX movements. They are also more accurate than VaR for long holding periods. This is because ALM models are more flexible, to capture the effects of risk-factor relationships that emerge over longer periods of time, such as deposit flows and pension liabilities.

ALM models can also account for embedded options and path-dependent products. The bulk of traded products have relatively simple relationships to risk factors such as interest rates and foreign exchange rates. However, the on- and off-balance-sheet positions of banks, insurance companies, and other financial intermediaries may include illiquid asset and liability positions with more complex relationships to these risk factors. For example, assets such as U.S. residential mortgages effectively bundle prepayment options with debt, which creates a complex relationship to interest rates. ALM models are designed to capture this complex behavior and appropriately value the change in assets and liabilities attributable to risk factors.

CREDIT RISK MODELS

Credit risk is the economic loss suffered due to the default of a borrower or counterparty. Credit risk management is the identification, quantification, monitoring, and control of credit risk at both the transactional and portfolio level. These include *credit-scoring models*, which estimate the expected default frequency of a borrower or counterparty at a specific point in time; *credit migration models*, which focus on how the credit quality of exposures changes over time; *credit exposure models*, which estimate the Loan Equivalent Exposure (LEE) of credit transactions, and *credit portfolio models*, which assess the risk/return profile of a portfolio of credits and take the impact of diversification into account.

Credit-Scoring Models

One key input when measuring credit risk is the likelihood that a given credit exposure will default over a given period of time—this is often called the Expected Default Frequency (EDF). The most common analytical tool used to estimate EDF are credit-scoring models, including empirical models, expert models, and Merton-based models:

- **Empirical models** analyze the historical default experience for similar credit exposures. For example, an empirical model might analyze income, outstanding debt, and length of employment to predict the default frequency of a credit card customer. Fair Isaac's FICO score is an empirical model applied to a consumer borrower base.
- **Expert models** attempt to capture the judgment of credit experts in the form of a model. In most cases, credit experts are senior individuals within the organization who have strong credit-assessment skills.
- **Merton-based models** use the Merton model of a firm's capital structure combined with market information to develop the implied default rates of companies. Under the Merton model, a firm defaults when its asset value falls below the value of its liabilities. A company's default probability then depends on the amount by which assets exceed liabilities and the volatility of those assets.

Credit Migration Models

The credit grading models described above are useful for developing a point-in-time estimate of the default frequency of a company or entity. However, credit quality can and does change over time. If an institution has long-term credit exposures, it must understand how credit quality can change in the future. The problem is complicated by credit migration—the fact that companies' fortunes and creditworthiness will likely change from one year to the next. Thus the EDF, per annum, of a long-term exposure is not necessarily equal to the one-year EDF. It would be the same only if creditworthiness remained constant. Similarly, short-term credits such as money market instruments may have different EDFs than one-year exposures. The primary objective of credit migration models is to attach cumulative default probabilities over a number of years to internal grades. Two common approaches underlie credit migration models depending on how one sources and/or uses the relevant data:

- **Cohort study:** Under this approach, the credit portfolio is divided into cohorts based on origination year, geography, and risk grade. Then, one can estimate multiyear EDFs by using the multiyear cumulative default rates observed historically for different grades of credit. Like the historical method of calibrating the one-year EDF, however, cohort studies suffer from a lack of reliable data. This is particularly true for longer time periods, as many grading scales have limited track records. Nonetheless, credit card and mortgage lenders often use the cohort study approach because marketing programs and product features vary each year and can have a material impact on the credit performance of each cohort.
- **Migration matrices:** An alternative approach to estimating multiyear EDFs is through the use of migration matrices. This method observes the rates at which grades change—in other words, the rates at which credits migrate between grades. Migration rates are much higher (and thus, easier to measure accurately) than default rates, particularly for higher-quality credits. Together with the previously calibrated EDFs for each credit grade, a table of migration probabilities produces a complete series of long-term EDFs. The rating-to-rating migration matrix approach is more commonly used for corporate borrowers and counterparties.

Counterparty Credit Exposure Models

The use of financial instruments, such as foreign exchange forwards, forward rate agreements, swaps, and other derivatives, generates potential credit risk exposure. The credit risk arises when market conditions move in one party's favor, so the contracts that it has engaged in have a positive mark-to-market value or replacement cost. If the other party to the trade (the counterparty) defaults and cannot honor its obligations, the first party is exposed to the current mark-to-market amount.

Because this exposure is contingent upon the default of a counterparty, one can usually use a credit risk framework to evaluate the risk. Unlike many forms of credit risk where the exposure is known (such as term loans), the exposure to a counterparty is driven by market risk factors such as interest rates or foreign exchange rates. Analytical models must estimate potential exposure to a counterparty. The simplest approach uses a percentage of the notional contract value as the expected exposure for calculating credit risk, potentially varied by contract type and term. This approach is crude, and can substantially over- or underestimate risk. One improvement uses the present market value of the contract, although this does not take into account the potential for greater (or lesser) exposure in the future. But one can calculate potential credit exposures for most instruments using formulas based on price volatility and contract maturity. Formula-based approaches work well for single-payment contracts, such as foreign exchange forward contracts or forward rate agreements, but they generally do not work well for multiple-payment contracts such as interest rate swaps. In these cases, a Monte Carlo simulation approach, which estimates the expected and maximum credit exposures given a wide range of potential rate and price movements, is more accurate.

Credit Portfolio Models

The credit risk models discussed so far have focused on the assessment of individual credit risk exposures. Credit portfolio models aggregate the credit risk of individual exposures to determine how losses may behave at the portfolio level. The three general approaches include financial, econometric, and actuarial models.

- **Financial models** rely on the Merton model of a firm's capital structure, which assumes that a firm defaults when its asset value falls below the value of its liabilities. A borrower's default probability depends on the likelihood that the value of assets will drop below the value of liabilities, which is in turn a function of asset price volatility. Asset values are usually modeled in a log-normal distribution, which means changes in asset values are normally distributed. One can then express the default probability as the probability of a standard normal variable falling below some critical value, representing the point at which the value of liabilities exceeds the value of assets. One can estimate the distribution of possible losses in the portfolio through Monte Carlo simulation.

- **Econometric models** attempt to model the default rate for a borrower (or group of similar borrowers) in terms of the behavior of macroeconomic variables. Put simply, the default rate of each sector (representing a group of similar borrowers) is determined by changes in macroeconomic variables such as interest rates, gross national product, unemployment rates, and so on.
- **Actuarial models** employ mathematical techniques that are commonly used for loss distribution modeling in actuarial literature. CreditRisk+, a standard-setting actuarial model developed by Credit Suisse Financial Products, relies on an analytical, closed-form formula for default risk. The formula takes average default rates and volatilities as inputs and provides a distribution of credit portfolio losses as the output. It requires relatively little data and can be calculated much faster than the computation-heavy Monte Carlo simulations used by other risk models. The main problem with this approach: It assumes the bank already has useful default data.

OPERATIONAL RISK MODELS

In contrast to market and credit risk, operational risk defies simple explanation. In fact, when operational risk was first introduced as a new concept in ERM in the 1990s, it was defined as the collection of risks that are *not* credit or market risks. Basel II defines operational risk as "the risk of loss resulting from inadequate or failed internal processes, people and systems or from external events."[2] Operational risk management is evolving rapidly and becoming increasingly important. For some technology- and process-intensive businesses, operational risk is sometimes considered the most important risk type.

Operational risk is uniquely difficult to model. The operational risk bell-curve is heavily skewed so that highly frequent but very small losses predominate. These high-probability losses are nearly irrelevant, however. The vast majority of aggregate operational risk losses are due to events that are exceedingly rare but devastating. Operational risk models attempt to quantify the risks associated with these extreme events.

A research report published by Milliman in 2013 identifies four types of operational risk models used by modern financial institutions. These include basic indicators and standard formulas, scenario analysis, a loss-distribution approach, and a causal approach.[3]

> **Basic indicators and standard formulas** are simple models that represent operational risk with a single input. Both the Basel II basic-indicator and standardized approach fall into this category, with annual gross

income representing operational risk. While straightforward, these methods are simplistic and do little to convey anything meaningful about operational risks or the control environment.

Scenario analysis is a top-down, what-if process measuring the impact that a particular event (or combination of events) will have on the enterprise.[4] In the context of operational risk management, scenario analysis combines quantitative data with the expertise of senior managers. Risk managers develop a wide variety of adverse scenarios, and managers give opinions on the size and likelihood of losses in each set of circumstances. This data is then aggregated to produce a quantitative estimate of operational risk.

Loss Distribution Approach (LDA), now standard practice in the banking industry, is a statistical method for calculating an aggregate loss bell curve from frequency and severity distributions of broad risk categories, adjusted for how losses might be related. This loss distribution can be applied to assess capital sufficiency using a risk analytic such as VaR.

Causal models rely on a web of connections that map effects back to their direct causes. Each connection is assigned a conditional probability, resulting in a Bayesian network that can be analyzed quantitatively. By focusing on risk drivers, causal models can account for complex and nonlinear relationships among root causes. This leads to greater understanding of loss events and helps identify areas for effective risk mitigation. Causal models can take longer to implement, however, and require more detailed operational understanding. Traditional statistical approaches may be more appropriate for organizations that are not operationally complex.

Basel II

Basel II allows for three different methodologies to calculate operational risk capital charges:

The Basic Indicator Approach requires banks to hold operational risk capital equal to a fixed percentage of their three-year average positive annual gross income.

The Standardized Approach is similar to, but more granular than, the basic indicator approach. Operational risk capital is determined by the revenues and multipliers of eight standardized business lines.

Advanced Measurement Approaches (AMAs) determine the regulatory capital requirement based on a bank's own internal models based on the following tools:

- **Internal Loss Data (ILD):** a record of the enterprise's actual previous losses.
- **External Loss Data (ELD):** information on operational losses experienced by other enterprises within the industry.
- **Scenario analysis:** a way to estimate how possible future events might affect the enterprise.
- **Business environmental and internal control factors (BEIFCs):** measures of specific types of operational risk within an enterprise.

Basel II does not endorse any particular model, but it establishes guiding principles. In order for a bank to use AMA, its model must pass a regulatory review. When a bank qualifies to use a more complicated approach, its regulatory capital requirements often decrease. This provides an incentive to implement AMA models.

2016 Proposed Revised Approach According to Basel III In response to a critical review of the AMAs, in March 2016 the Basel Committee proposed removing it from the regulatory framework. Further, the organization proposed that the revised operational risk capital framework rely on a single non-model-based method for the estimation of operational risk capital, which is termed the Standardized Measurement Approach (SMA). The SMA builds on the simplicity and comparability of a standardized approach while embodying the risk sensitivity of an advanced approach. The intent behind this standardized combination of financial statement information and a bank's internal loss experience is to allow for consistent and comparable measurements of operational risk capital measurement.

MODEL RISK MANAGEMENT

Enterprises, particularly large financial institutions, have come to depend on ever more complex quantitative risk models. Basel and Solvency II regulations, as well as guidance issued by the Fed and OCC in the United States, are key drivers of this trend. Regulatory scrutiny now focuses on the governance programs that oversee risk modeling. But as with many aspects of risk management, companies shouldn't consider model governance simply a matter of compliance. Rather, a well-implemented program can enhance a firm's risk management process overall.

Model governance attempts to maximize the value a firm derives from risk models, encompassing all the technology, expertise, and methods needed to support this goal. Model governance can be thought of as an effort to control model risk—the pitfalls that can arise from the use of models.

Model Risk

Reliance on quantitative models creates a type of operational risk called model risk. Model risk is the possibility of undesirable outcomes due to decisions based on model outputs, which can include errors in strategic decision-making, reputational damage, and financial loss.[5] Model risk falls into three categories:

- Errors within the model that cause it to produce misleading output
- Lack of data governance
- Improper use or misapplication of the model

This type of risk increases with the complexity and number of models used, the weight they are given during decision-making, the impact of those decisions, and the degree of uncertainty about inputs or assumptions they incorporate. In addition, there is risk that the models themselves are not appropriate to the firm's circumstances, or that governance policies and procedures are ineffective or absent.

Internal Model Errors Each quantitative risk model depends upon a particular methodology to process input data with the intent of producing useful and comprehensible output. But the computations underlying the model are often highly complex and opaque to the end user. By definition, quantitative models require some simplification of reality in order to produce useful output. However, the assumptions must be reasonable if the model is to be valid. Errors may result from faulty design or poor implementation, such as applying theory improperly, using incorrect formulas, or relying on invalid assumptions. New research findings and market conditions can also render a model obsolete.

Internally flawed models may produce misleading output that undermines the decision-making process. Once a model has been implemented within an institution, such flaws may not be apparent during routine use but come to light only in the aftermath of a preventable loss. As we will discuss later, effective model validation is important to catch internal errors before they cause any damage.

Lack of Data Governance As the saying goes, "garbage in, garbage out." Quantitative risk models rely on accurate input data. If the data provided is incorrect, the model's output will be useless or, worse, misleading no matter how sophisticated or theoretically valid the model may be. Even a perceived lack of data integrity decreases the value of model outputs by reducing confidence in the model. Enterprises should therefore prioritize data governance to mitigate model risk.

Model Misuse Because risk models rely on certain assumptions to work, applying them to a situation they weren't designed for can lead to serious error. Even theoretically sound models can fail when analysts use them outside their designed context, or under conditions in which their assumptions are invalid. Misuse may take the form of applying a model that is inappropriate for the situation, or interpreting a model's output incorrectly. Decision makers can avoid either outcome if they have a clear understanding of a model's limitations.

Components of a Model Governance Program

The scale and complexity of a model governance program should be proportional to an enterprise's model risk. Nonetheless, all model governance programs should include an inventory of models, validation methods and reporting, and data governance. These three core components ensure that there exists a sufficient level of control and oversight such that the key models and their related outputs can be relied upon by the risk program and the organization, especially in the facilitation of strategic decision-making.

Model Inventory A model inventory is simply a list of all models used by an enterprise, including those in development or recently discontinued. Each entry should include a definition of the model, its purpose and use, its risk rank (high, medium, low),[6] the inputs it requires and the output it produces, as well as key assumptions it depends on. In order to maintain efficacy, the release date, version number, and last update should also be noted, as well as a schedule for periodic validation.

Model Validation To control model risk, an enterprise must be certain that its models are free of internal errors and that they are used appropriately. The validation process involves testing a model's reliability and performance. One can think of validation as a way to identify, catalog, and manage a model's limitations.

The joint guidance document published in April 2011 by the Federal Reserve Board (FRB) and OCC (SR 11-7 / OCC 2011-12) specifies three elements for a comprehensive model validation process:

1. **Conceptual evaluation,** which reviews the theoretical basis upon which a model was designed. This will often involve a review of the documentation produced during the model's original development and

subsequent revisions, and an examination of its underlying assumptions and mathematical methods in light of current research and industry practice. Quantitative tests under a variety of conditions will confirm that the model performs as expected.

2. **Ongoing monitoring** ensures that models continue to function properly. Changes in market conditions or the firm's business activities can cause models to stop producing reliable output. This necessitates the periodic reevaluation of model performance. The appropriate frequency of monitoring depends on the type and risk rank of the model. Those tasked with monitoring should make sure that end users are applying its output correctly and that results continue to be relevant and reliable. They should also benchmark output against estimates or the results from alternative models (also known as challenger models). Discrepancies warrant further investigation, though they do not always indicate a problem with the model.

3. **Outcomes analysis** assesses model output by comparing it to actual results. It attempts to measure how well a model performs with real-world data and examines the variation between a model's predictions and actual outcomes. Alternatively, back-testing evaluates model predictions against observed data from a previous time period. In either case, significant deviations from expectations may be a sign of problems that require more detailed examination.

The risk function should implement and prioritize model validation according to each model's risk ranking, and submit high-risk models to comprehensive, well-documented and frequent validation. If the company uses models supplied through third-party vendors, these should undergo validation as well. Vendors typically manage their models externally without providing full transparency into their methodology. Nonetheless, they should be able to demonstrate conceptual soundness through documentation and their own validation results, which should explain the model's limitations and assumptions.

An important concept in the FRB's and OCC's guidance document is "effective challenge," in which the analysts performing validation are objective as well as competent. Ideally, this means that those who are validating a particular model were not involved its development or use. Practically, however, model developers and users are often the only ones technically capable of performing a validation. In that case, an independent party could review their work separately.

Validation Reports Once a model undergoes validation, the risk function should document results and create a report to summarize the findings.

According to the Model Risk Management Guidance (AB 2013-07), published by the Federal Housing Finance Agency (FHFA) in November 2013, a model validation report should include analysis of a model's input data and assumptions, its theoretical basis, its code and mathematics,[7] and its output reports.[8]

This framework is consistent with the one provided by the OCC and the FRB. The first three areas are part of the evaluation of conceptual soundness while evaluation of the output combines information that is obtained during both ongoing monitoring and outcomes analysis. In addition to these elements, a model validation should explain the model's purpose and use; how it was tested; the limitations imposed by its assumptions and other factors; and its performance over a range of scenarios.

If the validation process uncovers problems, the report should also include recommendations for remediation such as redeveloping the model, augmenting it with alternatives, establishing restrictions on its use, or abandoning it altogether. Bear in mind, however, that any significant changes to a model would require revalidation.

In addition to validation, models should undergo reviews at least annually, and high-risk models may require review more frequently. Annual review can be less extensive than model validation of a new or altered model. The review should test model performance and compare the assumptions and limitations with any changes in the business segment or industry. Annual review should also reexamine model risk and determine whether a risk rating change is warranted. In many cases, regulators require models to be reviewed by an independent third-party. Even if an independent review is not mandatory, it serves as an effective independent attestation to the validity and accuracy of the models, as well as a critical evaluation of the underlying assumptions within each key model.

Data Governance Data governance encompasses the accessibility, integrity, and security of the organization's data. This enterprise-wide function oversees all of the company's data assets. To manage model risk, data governance must be effective at safeguarding model input data. This can present challenges, because the data often inhabits the intersection between the IT department and the business unit using the model, leaving unclear which department bears responsibility for its integrity. Data governance may typically rest with IT, but end users in the business unit may have custody of the data during model validation. End users often move data from its original source into other computing systems for ease of use, too, which can compromise its integrity. Organizations must develop clear policies to control access to model data and ensure its integrity.

THE LOSS/EVENT DATABASE

In addition to the risk quantification models and model governance practices described above, a mature ERM program will also utilize additional risk measurement tools as part of its overall approach and strategy. These tools provide added insights and measurement capability to the ERM program.

It is often said that those who don't learn from past mistakes are destined to repeat them. In the world of ERM, risk is constantly and continuously rearing its ugly head, many times in an unforeseen and unpredictable fashion. Therefore, it is critical to have a process for logging and documenting risk events and associated losses as they occur. This loss/risk event database is a key component for enhancing a company's ERM efforts on an ongoing basis. It also serves as a historical archive of realized risk and the losses both directly and indirectly attributable to those risk events.

A loss/event database is relatively simple to implement, but to be effective, it must capture the right data. For example, the database must include both the expected and unexpected losses that result from each event, and incorporate root-cause analysis. Key elements of each record in a loss/event database include:

- A detailed description of the risk event
- Duration of the event
- Impacted business units/functions/risk areas
- Detailed overview of the existing management control/risk mitigation efforts in place at the time the event took place
- A detailed description of the loss, captured in a quantitative form and broken out into expected vs. unexpected loss

The risk data and metrics contained within a loss/risk event database serve multiple purposes. First, they allow the organization to quantify real losses due to unmitigated risk events. This can help identify trends that affect the overall effectiveness of an ERM program. Second, the loss/risk event database creates a historical record of realized risk. This allows the ERM function to evaluate potential controls and risk mitigation strategies to act as barriers to future risk realization in the same or similar risk areas. Third, the loss/risk event database is a key driver of the feedback loop, which I will discuss in Chapter 20. The database serves as a reference to review existing risk-assessment processes and controls to ensure that future related risk is effectively anticipated, assessed, and mitigated as necessary.

Finally, the loss/risk event database can serve as an empirical attestation to the value proposition of the ERM program. By documenting risk events and the realized losses from those events, the risk program can assess and quantify mitigation strategies. By viewing these risk event losses in terms of inherent vs. residual risk, the ERM program can evaluate its own performance and make adjustments as necessary.

When implemented correctly, a loss/risk event database can serve as a key input to a number of ongoing processes and enhancements within the ERM program as well as a historical record of realized risk events and losses from which the organization can derive lessons learned and future opportunities for risk mitigation.

EARLY WARNING INDICATORS

A final arrow in the ERM measurement quiver deserves mention here, though it will receive a thorough review in Chapter 18. These are early warning indicators. In the case of most risks, it is possible to devise a leading indicator that suggests a risk may be rising just around the corner. Early warning indicators are a subset of key risk indicators (KRIs), similar in concept to key performance indicators (KPIs) familiar to any businessperson. The significant difference between KPIs and KRIs is that while the former tells us about actual performance, the latter tells us about variables that can impact our future performance. As such, early warning indicators are critical metrics to monitor, track, and report.

MODEL RISK CASE STUDY: AIG

The fall of global insurance giant AIG during the 2008 financial crisis illustrates the importance of model risk management. AIG's liquidity problems came as a result of its credit-default swaps (CDSs) portfolio. AIG's financial products unit had sold CDS—a type of derivative that offers insurance against the default of an underlying debt security—on billions of dollars of debt. The CDS portfolio exposed AIG to three types of risk:

- **Default:** the losses from repaying counterparties in the event of underlying debt default
- **Collateral:** the increases in collateral demanded by counterparties if the underlying debt securities were downgraded or lost value
- **Write-down:** the potential accounting write-downs to AIG's books in the event of a decrease in market value of the CDS

AIG priced the CDSs it sold using quantitative models developed by Yale finance professor Gary Gorton. Based on extensive historical data, the models focused solely on the risk of default, ignoring risks from both collateral calls and write-downs. This was by design, and it was a limitation that AIG management was aware of. The models should have been used only as a tool to price CDS contracts. Yet AIG used them as an assurance of the financial stability of the entire business. By using the models outside of their intended context, AIG failed to account for the collateral and write-down risk of the CDS business, nor did the company maintain sufficient capital to meet collateral calls. These risks were considered too late, as noted in an October 31, 2008, article in the *Wall Street Journal*:

> *The problem for AIG is that it didn't apply effective models for valuing the swaps and for collateral risk until the second half of 2007, long after the swaps were sold, AIG documents and investor presentations indicate. The firm left itself exposed to potentially large collateral calls because it had agreed to insure so much debt without protecting itself adequately through hedging.*[9]

AIG's financial position deteriorated under increasing collateral calls, until September 15, 2008, when the company was saved from bankruptcy by a bailout from the Federal Reserve.

AIG's demise demonstrates the importance of a properly implemented model governance program. An effective validation process examining their limitations and assumptions would have shown that the models were being used inappropriately. AIG's ineffective model governance led to significantly increased model risk, with eventual disastrous consequences.

Risk models can be a useful tool to quantify an enterprise's market, credit, or operational risk. Models must be used in the right context, however, and in a manner consistent with their limitations and assumptions. By limiting model risk, effective model governance helps utilize these important tools to their fullest potential. Used appropriately, quantitative models can greatly assist management. They can quantify risk/return trade-offs, enabling sound business decisions; be used to develop risk-based pricing, which fully incorporates the cost of risk; and measure risk exposures to ensure they do not exceed prescribed limits. Whatever the specific application, quantitative models are an indispensable part of making decisions about risk. In the next chapter, we'll examine how these and other tools can help organizations develop and achieve their strategic goals.

NOTES

1. *Operational Risk—Supervisory Guidelines for the Advanced Measurement Approaches*. Basel, Switzerland: Basel Committee on Banking Supervision, 2010.

2. *International Convergence of Capital Measurement and Capital Standards.* Basel Committee on Banking Supervision and Bank for International Settlements, 2006. Retrieved from http://www.bis.org/publ/bcbs128.pdf.

3. Corrigan, Joshua and Paola Luraschi. *Operational Risk Modelling Framework,* Milliman, 2013.

4. Long, Robert. *Stress Testing and Model Governance,* Federal Deposit Insurance Corporation, 2013.

5. Versace, Michael. *EMEA Banking: Model Governance Framework,* IDC Financial Insights, 2012.

6. The risk rank is an estimate of model risk based on a particular model's relative business or regulatory impact. Typically, risk ranks are broad, qualitative categories (e.g., high, medium, and low). Transparency is prioritized for higher risk models. Higher risk ranks are expected to receive more frequent and thorough model validation. Key assumptions for models in this category should be well-documented and updated frequently.

7. When these elements are unavailable (e.g., for vendor models), the report should compare model output with similar models or appropriate equations.

8. *Advisory Bulletin AB 2013-07: Model Risk Management Guidance,* Federal Housing Finance Agency, 2013.

9. Mollenkamp, Carrick, Serena Ng, Liam Pleven, and Randall Smith, "Behind AIG's Fall, Risk Models Failed to Pass Real-World Test," *Wall Street Journal,* October 31, 2008. Retrieved from http://www.wsj.com/articles/SB122538449722784635.

Risk Management

CHAPTER 15

Strategic Risk Management

INTRODUCTION

As a member of the board of directors or senior management, which risks should you be most concerned about?

Recent business headlines have focused attention on Federal Reserve interest rate policy, economic slowdown in China, declining oil prices, Middle East instability, international and domestic terrorism, and cybersecurity.

In its *Global Risks Report 2016*, the World Economic Forum identified five top worldwide risks with the greatest potential impact:

1. Failure of climate change mitigation and adaptation
2. Weapons of mass destruction
3. Water crises
4. Large-scale involuntary migration
5. Severe energy price shock

It is the job of those tasked with risk oversight or risk management to consider these macro-risks, but more importantly, to optimize their company's risk-return profile based on the interactions of these macro-risks and the specific risks that are unique to their industry and business model.

The nature, level, and velocity of risks have changed in the past and will continue to change in the future. One risk in particular that should always be at the forefront of risk management is strategic risk. Strategy provides the overall plan for an organization to achieve its core mission and increase value to its key stakeholders (e.g., customers, employees, shareholders, regulators, etc.). Strategic risk can result throughout the strategy development and implementation processes, including:

- Design and development of the corporate strategy, such as alignment with the core mission and values, business-unit strategies, and operating budgets

- Implementation of the corporate and business-unit strategies to achieve key organizational objectives
- Actions and reactions from customers, suppliers, and competitors, as well as the impact of emerging technologies
- Resultant risks (which can be strategic, operational, or financial risks) from the execution of corporate and business-unit strategies, including the utilization of risk appetite and risk capacity

This chapter will provide a set of guidelines, best practices, and practical examples for measuring and managing strategic risk, such as:

The importance of strategic risk—particularly given the typical high failure rate of strategic initiatives and empirical studies that show the impact of strategic risk exceeds the impact of all other forms of risk combined

Measuring strategic risk using economic capital, shareholder value-added, and other risk-adjusted performance measures

Managing strategic risk through strategic planning, risk appetite, new business development, mergers and acquisitions (M&A), and capital management processes

THE IMPORTANCE OF STRATEGIC RISK

One of the most important responsibilities—perhaps the most important responsibility of the board of directors and senior management—is setting the company's strategic direction in order to maximize shareholder value. To do so, executives must be able to anticipate key trends and future opportunities. But of course no matter how confident you may be, the future is not foreseeable. In other words, strategy involves risk. In this chapter, we will take a look at how the practice of strategic risk management arose as ERM matured over the past decades. We will examine the role risk analysis and management can have in strategic planning. We will also show ways companies can measure and manage strategic risk. We'll conclude with several case studies involving familiar multinational corporations that reveal how they manage strategic risk.

As senior management gathers to set strategic priorities, it is faced with a daunting task. Each decision is, in essence, a wager that bets the company's available resources on informed predictions about macroeconomic, industry, and market trends. They are betting on the company's core competencies and its ability to find areas of growth even as it tries to avoid visible and unforeseen pitfalls. How large a bet management and the board are willing to make depends on the size of the organization, its maturity, and how capable the company is of facing the risks and opportunities before it. A winning bet will increase shareholder value, while ill-advised or bad bets may reduce value or, in the worst case, destroy it entirely.

Strategic Decisions Have a High Failure Rate

Strategic decision-making is fraught with danger. Research studies indicate that the failure rate for strategic initiatives is up to 70%.[1] In addition, there is an abundance of case studies and examples that illustrate strategic decision-making gone awry. Just Google "examples of bad strategic decisions" and you'll get over 2 million results. One of my favorites is 24/7 Wall Street's "The Worst Business Decisions of All Time." In mini–case study form, it highlights eight of the worst decisions by what were at the time Fortune 500 firms.[2]

In response to a 2009 McKinsey survey that asked senior executives about their most recent strategic decisions, respondents indicated three predominant problem areas:

1. Executives tended to dramatically overestimate their organization's ability to execute the strategy chosen.
2. Corporate leaders didn't adequately foresee competitive responses nor did they ensure complete alignment between the chosen strategic direction and their team members' incentives.
3. Due to common decision-making biases, executives limited their field of vision for the strategic options by not considering viable alternatives.[3]

Why do some companies get strategic decision-making right while others do not? Is it as simple as one executive's "gut" being better than another's? Or is one organization just naturally better positioned to come out on the right side of a strategic decision? I argue it goes much deeper than either of these reasons. And strategic risk management is center stage.

Risk Embedded in Strategic Decision-Making

Strategic risk can take various forms. One is simply pursuing the wrong strategy, such as overinvestment in a new product or a pursuit of the wrong acquisition candidate. Even with the right strategy, failing to execute effectively remains another risk. For example, a company might make the right acquisition but fail to integrate it effectively.

There is also the risk of inaction or not responding to key market trends. Outside factors, such as customer trends and emerging technologies, may render the existing strategy ineffective or outdated. This has become increasingly common in an age when mobile devices are replacing desktop computers, which themselves had replaced mainframes. In these cases, being on the wrong side of technological evolution can destroy considerable value. But if you're the disruptor, you can actually use these same opportunities to create enormous value. Finally, strategy execution will likely impact the overall risk profile of the company, including second-order strategic risks, operational risks, and financial risks. A well-implemented ERM program will consider all of these risks.

Companies ignore strategic risks at their peril. Independent studies of the largest public companies have shown time and again that strategic risks account for approximately 60% of major declines in market capitalization, followed by operational risks (about 30%) and financial risks (about 10%).[4] Yet, in practice, many ERM programs downplay strategic risks or ignore them entirely. There are some historical reasons for that. When companies began to develop formal ERM programs in the early 1990s, they focused almost exclusively on financial risk, due to some high-profile losses stemming from derivatives and the fact that financial risk (i.e., interest rate risk, market risk, credit and counterparty risk, and liquidity risk) is more readily quantifiable.

In the mid-1990s, several disasters related to unauthorized trading at financial firms shifted attention toward operational risks, which are harder to measure. The difficulty in measuring these risks lies in the nature of operational glitches, the vast majority of which are commonplace, but financially insignificant. On the rare occasions when operational controls do break down, the consequences can be devastating—and not only for banks. One example is the 2010 Deepwater Horizon catastrophe. In addition to the damage and impact of the oil spill itself, the event also inflicted enormous financial and reputational damage on BP, Transocean, and Halliburton.

But if the goal of ERM is to enable management to identify, prioritize, and manage key risks, programs ought to give the highest priority to strategic risks, followed by operational. The financial risks that dominate ERM today should actually come a distant third.

What Is Strategic Risk?

Strategic risk can be defined as any risk that affects or is inherent in a company's business strategy, strategic objectives, and strategy execution. The list includes:

- Consumer demand
- Legal and regulatory change

- Competitive pressure
- Merger integration
- Technology change
- Senior management turnover
- Stakeholder pressure

Other risks may qualify for particular companies depending on the nature of their business. Siemens, the European conglomerate, captures this sentiment in its broad definition of strategic risk: "everything, every obstacle, every issue that has the potential to materially affect the achievement of our strategic objectives."[5]

It is important to distinguish between operational and strategic risk. A company that has unmatched manufacturing processes will still fail if consumers no longer want its products. Whether they knew it or not, even the most efficient buggy-whip makers faced an existential threat in 1908 when Henry Ford introduced the Model T. In more recent times, Apple transformed the competitive landscape for cellular handset makers the day it launched the first iPhone. Good operations mean doing things right while good strategy means doing the right things. Long-term success requires doing both well under uncertainty.

The ability to recognize and manage strategic risks is critical to the sustainable success of any company. The rest of this chapter explains how to consider strategic risks in the planning process, how to measure these risks, and how to apply the results in practice.

MEASURING STRATEGIC RISK

At one time, strategic risk was measured solely in qualitative descriptors. But the latest yardsticks developed to measure financial risk—economic capital and risk-adjusted return on capital (RAROC)—can be applied to operational and strategic risks as well. This paves the way for strategic risk management to become a top priority for ERM practitioners—the next frontier in the challenge to control and manage enterprise risks.

In order to evaluate the effectiveness of strategic risk management, an organization must first determine the measures of success for the execution of its strategy, such as product innovation, enterprise earnings, return on equity, and intrinsic value. The next step is the identification and assessment of key strategic risks, which may include regulatory approvals, product pricing, sales effectiveness, and market share. While the overall strategy is meant to increase the expected value of the measures of success, strategic risks may drive variability in the same measures for better or worse.

Economic Capital

Risk identification and assessment is the first step, but a company must measure risks before it can manage them. Economic capital is a common currency whereby any risk can be quantified, thus making it one of the best available metrics.

Firms in any industry hold capital for two primary reasons: (1) to fund ongoing operations and investments and (2) to protect against unexpected losses. Unlike book capital, which is an accounting measure that represents the sum of invested capital and retained earnings, economic capital represents the amount of capital required to absorb unexpected loss. A simple example can illustrate the difference between book capital and economic capital: A company that increases its risk exposures, say, by increasing foreign exchange exposures or operational risks, will not instantaneously increase its book capital. Its book capital will reflect this shift over time only as the company experiences actual losses or retained profits. But its required economic capital will immediately increase as soon as its risk exposures increase.

A comparison between book capital and economic capital, while they are different, is very useful for determining capital adequacy. A company is overcapitalized if its book capital is above economic capital, and it is undercapitalized if the reverse is true. It is also important to note that book capital is a financial indicator of past performance, whereas economic capital is a forward-looking indicator of future performance. Strategic risk is about the future performance of the overall organization.

For strategic risks, the calculation of economic capital is forward-looking: the capital required to support new product launches or potential acquisitions, for example, or to withstand anticipated competitive pressure. The basic process is:

1. Generate standalone distributions of changes in the enterprise's value due to each source of risk.
2. Combine the standalone distributions, incorporating diversification effects.
3. Calculate the total economic capital for the aggregate distribution at the desired target solvency standard.
4. Attribute economic capital to each risk based on the amount of risk generated.

Risk-Adjusted Return on Capital (RAROC)

Dividing the anticipated after-tax return on each strategic initiative by the economic capital generates risk-adjusted return on capital (RAROC). If RAROC exceeds the company's cost of capital (Ke, or cost of equity capital), the initiative is viable and will add value; if RAROC is less than Ke, it will destroy value. But the decision whether to back an initiative should not depend on a single case reflecting the expected value. The company should run the numbers for multiple scenarios to see the distribution of results in both more and less favorable circumstances or in combinations of better and worse conditions over time. The final decision will depend on the specific company's risk appetite.

RAROC can be calculated for an institution as a whole or separately for each of its individual activities. Because the amount of economic capital that is required to support each of the enterprise's activities is proportional to the risk generated by that activity, economic capital can be used as a standard measurement of risk. Combining the economic capital required to support the risks of an activity with the activity's expected economic returns yields a ratio that represents the amount of return the institution expects per unit of risk involved.

The primary use of RAROC is to compare the risk–return trade-offs of different, and potentially quite diverse, strategic decisions. Economic capital/RAROC analysis works for organic growth initiatives as well as potential acquisitions. For example, a company with excess capital can determine if it is in the best interest of shareholders to buy back stock, grow the core business, or make a strategic acquisition.

In addition to economic capital and RAROC, companies deploy other methodologies to measure and manage strategic risk, such as net present value (NPV) calculations based on risk-adjusted discount rates or EVA®[6] (Economic Value Added) models. The advantage of economic capital and RAROC models is that the analytical results are linked to risk exposures, earnings, capital management, and shareholder value.

MANAGING STRATEGIC RISK

Risk management has evolved from a loss minimization mission to one that also includes value creation. Figure 15.1 shows the evolution, as well as how ERM could impact each of the value drivers for a company (such as revenue, expense, and growth strategies). In this section, we will discuss examples of increasing shareholder value through the value drivers in strategic risk management.

The goal of strategic risk management is to optimize the long-term risk–return profile of the company. It informs decisions such as:

- **Risk acceptance or avoidance:** The organization can decide to increase or decrease a specific risk exposure through organic growth, its core business (new product and business development), mergers and acquisitions (M&A), and financial activities.

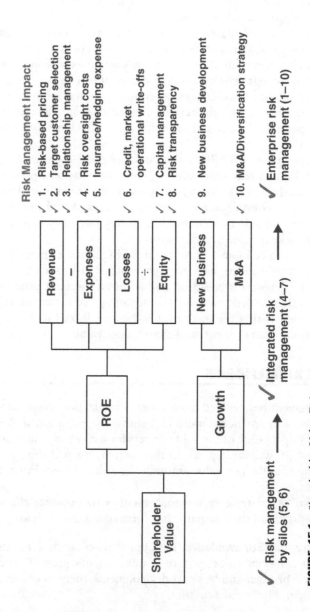

FIGURE 15.1 Shareholder Value Drivers

- **Risk-based pricing:** The pricing of a company's products and services represents the one opportunity to receive compensation for the risks it takes. Without question, pricing must fully incorporate the cost of risk.
- **Risk mitigation:** This involves the implementation of business and risk control strategies in order to manage strategic risk within defined tolerance levels.
- **Risk transfer:** If risk exposures are excessive and/or the cost of risk transfer is lower than the cost of retention, an organization can decide to execute risk transfer strategies through the insurance or capital markets.[7]
- **Resource allocation:** An organization can allocate human and financial resources to business activities that produce the highest risk-adjusted returns in order to maximize firm value.

Risk management is an ongoing process, and strategic risk is no exception. Though it presents its own particular challenges, monitoring strategic risk can give companies a critical heads-up to oncoming obstacles. This in turn offers the greatest possible latitude when it comes to adjusting strategic or tactical efforts in order to mitigate downside risk or take advantage of an unexpected opportunity.

Strategic Planning and Review

The start of the strategic risk management process is strategic planning. Several management frameworks help companies plan out their strategy. They may begin by analyzing their strengths, weaknesses, opportunities, and threats (SWOT) to determine where best to focus new initiatives. From there, many turn to one of the strategic frameworks I reviewed in Chapter 7. These include Kaplan and Norton's balanced scorecard to evaluate each initiative from different perspectives, including customers, internal processes, organizational capacity (knowledge and innovation), and financial performance. Some companies utilize Michael Porter's Five Forces model, which analyzes the effect on new initiatives of supplier power, buyer power, and competitive rivalry, threat of substitution, and threat of new entry. And then there's Geoffrey Moore's model for technology companies, The Four Zones to Win, in which strategic initiatives fall into one of four zones: incubation, transformation, productivity, and performance.[8]

These popular strategic planning tools provide structure to the process, but risk professionals have long recognized a major flaw: They do not fully take risk into account.[9] In the aftermath of the 2008 financial crisis, Kaplan himself acknowledged the shortcoming: " ... the measurement, mitigation, and management of risk have not been strongly featured in David Norton's and my work."[10]

Risk Appetite

The strategic initiatives that are approved—as well as the triggers for acceleration or corrective action—all depend on a company's risk appetite, which I discussed in greater detail in Chapter 12. ERM implementation requires a company to create a risk appetite statement that defines how much risk it will take in pursuit of its business strategy. For strategic risks, the risk appetite metrics typically reflect the potential impact on earnings or enterprise value arising from adverse business decisions or lack of responsiveness to industry changes.

Rigorous use of standard planning tools generates an expected value for each strategic initiative without regard to the distribution of outcomes around that value should the projected results fail to materialize. Yet every initiative involves risk, and risk is a bell curve centered on the expected value, either today or at some future date, with tails trailing off toward worse or better performance. Companies that ignore risk in the planning process forgo the opportunity to manage the shape of that curve.

For example, two initiatives with identical expected values may have quite different risk profiles. One may have a narrow bell curve, which implies a higher probability the expected outcome will occur, a low risk of failure, and little opportunity for an unexpected windfall. The other may have a fat bell, suggesting that an outcome other than the expected value is more likely. Planning tools give no guidance on how to choose between the two, and the "right" choice will not be the same in every case, because companies have different appetites for risk.

Determining the Optimum Risk Profile

Although risk always takes the form of a bell curve, not all bell curves are alike. Figure 15.2 shows how the bell curve can be used to capture strategic and other risks with respect to the expected value and value drivers.[11]

Interest rate risk or market risk can be plotted on an essentially symmetrical curve, as interest rates or market prices have an equal chance of moving with you or against you. On the other side of the spectrum, operational and compliance risk have a limited upside but large potential downside. After all, not having any IT, compliance, or legal issues simply means business as usual. But a major negative event, such as a security breach, IT downtime, or regulatory issue, can have tremendous downside consequences.

If managed well, strategic risk is unique in that its downside can be limited while its upside can be unlimited. A recent example is Uber, a disruptive technology company that is changing the ground transportation industry. Its valuation has gone from $60 million in 2011 to more than $50 billion in 2016. An asymmetrical bell curve with significant upside risk can describe

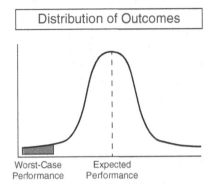

Examples:

1. Strategic risk. Enterprise value vs. value drivers

2. Business risk. Expected EPS vs. earnings drivers

3. Financial risk. Net interest margin vs. interest rate changes

4. Operational risk. IT performance vs. SPOFs (single points of failure) and cybersecurity

5. Regulatory risk. Regulatory standing vs. compliance requirements

FIGURE 15.2   Risk Bell Curves

any new product or business opportunity, whether that opportunity is part of a corporation's growth strategy or a venture capital firm's new investment.

Consider a decision tree that maps the probabilities and consequences of different decision paths.[12] This map not only provides a better picture of the risks and rewards involved, but also helps identify trigger points for action if the initiative lags behind expectations. Taken this way, the optimum strategic risk profile resembles a call option: limited downside exposure with unlimited upside potential. The sooner a company recognizes an initiative is in trouble, the sooner it can take corrective action—such as getting the initiative back on track, deploying risk mitigation strategies, or shutting it down altogether.

The objective to minimize downside and increase upside is the basis of real option theory. A *real option* is the right, but not the obligation, to undertake a business investment or to change any aspect of that investment at various points in time, given updated information. The beneficial asymmetry between the right and the obligation to invest under these conditions is what generates the option's value.

Venture capital firms take advantage of this asymmetry as part of their business model all the time. According to research by Shikhar Ghosh, a senior lecturer at Harvard Business School, about 75% of venture-backed firms in the United States fail to return investors' capital, and 95% fail to see the projected return on investment. That leaves a success rate of only 5%.[13] To maintain an ideal risk profile, the VC carefully stages the funding rounds in order to minimize its investments in the 95% of bad investments, and reap outsized returns on the 5% of good investments. This low "hit rate" is why one of the key criteria for VCs is a large potential market size. When they win, they need to win big.

Pharmaceutical companies take a similar portfolio approach. They invest in drug development internally, buy patents that look promising, or acquire entire drug companies. They can then continue to make limited, iterative investments in successful ventures and bow out of those that fail to achieve expected performance levels.

M&A Decisions

M&A transactions can have a profound impact on the strategic risk profile of companies. A good deal can help a company leapfrog its competitors while a bad one can set it back many years. The ERM function can support critical decisions in M&A by assessing the risk profile of the target company and the risk–return economies of the combined organization.

Traditional merger analysis is based on financial projections of the companies operating as independent entities as well as a combined company. Based on these financial projections, companies can estimate potential earnings dilution or accretion for a number of scenarios by manipulating variables such as acquisition price, expected revenue growth, and cost synergies. But traditional earnings dilution/accretion analysis does not adjust for risk. As such, it can lead to a decision with adverse strategic and financial consequences.

Let's examine how ERM can help a company make better M&A decisions. Figure 15.3 provides an example of an M&A analysis.

In this example, Company A is considering acquiring either Company B or Company C. To simplify this example, assume that both companies can be acquired for the same price. Based on traditional financial analysis, Company C appears to be more attractive because it has a higher RAROC and a higher market-to-book (M/B) ratio than Company B. In M&A parlance, acquiring Company C would be antidilutive (no earnings dilution) while acquiring Company B would be dilutive.

But this evaluation does not consider the effects of diversification benefits (i.e., risk correlations), which is one of the key reasons why companies turn to acquisitions. ERM incorporates risk correlation into its evaluation of the two potential acquisitions. The impact of the diversification benefits is evident in the economic capital line of the combined entities. Acquiring Company B would result in a 30% diversification benefit: The economic capital of A + B is 210 compared to 300 before the merger (200 for Company A and 100 for Company B). On the other hand, acquiring Company C would result in a 10% diversification benefit: The economic capital of A + C is 270 compared to 300 before that merger (200 for Company A and 100 for

	A	**B**	**C**		**A + B**	**A + C**
Revenue	100	50	50		150	150
Expense	50	30	25		80	75
Pre-Tax	50	20	25		70	75
Tax	20	8	10		28	30
Net Income	30	12	15		42	45
Economic Capital	200	100	100		210	270
RAROC	15%	12%	15%		20%	17%
M/B Ratio	1.00	0.67	1.00		1.50	1.20

* - Assumes Ke = 15% and g = 5%

FIGURE 15.3 M&A Analysis

Company C). As such, the acquisition of Company B would actually result in a higher RAROC and a higher M/B ratio for the combined company.

As this example shows, ERM can inform M&A decisions. The key is leveraging analytical tools such as economic capital and RAROC to evaluate alternative uses of capital—different acquisition candidates, organic growth (see risk-based pricing in the next section), and stock buybacks—and quantify their impact on shareholder value.

Risk-Based Pricing Decisions

A company can also grow organically by attracting new customers, introducing new products, and winning more business with current customers. To ensure a positive contribution to its strategic risk profile, the company must price its products appropriately. The most effective way for companies to ensure an appropriate return on the risks that they are willing to accept is to incorporate the cost of risk into their pricing methodologies. If the cost of risk is not fully reflected in the initial pricing (for example, if the product or transaction is underpriced relative to the risk), then there is nothing the company can do to recover its costs. Risks that are underpriced may increase revenue and growth in the short term, but over time they will destroy shareholder value. When quantifying the total cost of risk, companies should include:

- Expected loss (EL), or average loss per year over a business cycle
- Unexpected loss (UL), which can be defined as economic capital × Ke (cost of equity capital)

▪ Risk transfer costs (of hedging or insurance)
▪ Risk management costs (that pertain to maintaining staff, systems, etc.)

Figure 15.4 shows a numerical example of risk-based pricing, which is based on the same methodology used to calculate RAROC.

In the first column, "Calculate RAROC," the math works from top to bottom. We have a $100 million transaction and a 2.5 % margin, resulting in $2.5 million in revenue. We derive pre-tax net income of $1 million after subtracting risk losses (expected loss) of $500,000 and expenses of $1 million. Assuming a 40% tax rate, we calculate a net income of $600,000. In this example, we allocated $2 million in economic capital based on the transaction's underlying risks. Finally, we can calculate a 30% RAROC by dividing net income by economic capital.

This 30% RAROC metric can aid decision-making in two ways. First, it can support product and customer management strategy. If RAROC is greater than Ke, then the transaction or customer is creating shareholder value and the company should increase this business. Conversely, if RAROC is less than Ke, then the transaction is destroying shareholder value and the company should discontinue this business, increase price, or cross-sell more profitable products to the same customer to increase the overall RAROC of the relationship above Ke.

Second, RAROC can support business management and resource allocation. Companies can compare the RAROCs of different business

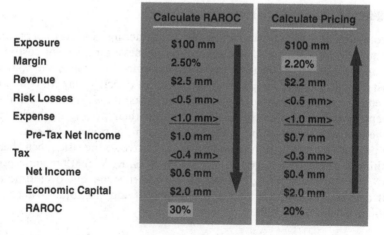

	Calculate RAROC	Calculate Pricing
Exposure	$100 mm	$100 mm
Margin	2.50%	2.20%
Revenue	$2.5 mm	$2.2 mm
Risk Losses	<0.5 mm>	<0.5 mm>
Expense	<1.0 mm>	<1.0 mm>
Pre-Tax Net Income	$1.0 mm	$0.7 mm
Tax	<0.4 mm>	<0.3 mm>
Net Income	$0.6 mm	$0.4 mm
Economic Capital	$2.0 mm	$2.0 mm
RAROC	30%	20%

FIGURE 15.4 Risk-Based Pricing

units against each other because they provide a universal risk-adjusted measurement of profitability. Other profitability measures, such as profit margin, return on assets (ROA), and return on equity (ROE), are not risk-adjusted, so comparisons could lead to false conclusions. For example, a business unit with marginally lower ROA and ROE might be more attractive than another business unit if the former has a substantially lower risk profile. RAROC analyses support management decisions regarding which businesses to grow, maintain, fix, shrink, or exit.

In our example, how should the company respond if a close competitor decides to introduce a discount pricing strategy by charging a 2.3% margin (instead of 2.5%)? Risk-based pricing can support that business decision. The Calculate Pricing column of Figure 15.4 demonstrates this. The math in this instance works backward, or from bottom to top. Say the company decides that it must achieve at least a 20% RAROC for this business. By applying the same methodology as above, but in reverse, it determines that a 2.2% margin would meet this minimum. As a result, management can safely lower the price to remain competitive.

For more than 20 years, banks have applied economic capital, risk-based pricing, and RAROC analysis in managing their businesses. Banks use these tools to measure risk-adjusted profitability and pricing for a wide range of products and services, including commercial loans, consumer loans, derivative products, and investment banking and brokerage services. But risk-based pricing is also a critical practice for nonfinancial companies. The Airbus case study below shows the potential pitfalls when strategic programs do not fully account for the cost of risk.

Case Study: Airbus

After five rocky years of delays and cost overruns for two high-profile product launches, European aviation giant Airbus acknowledged in 2010 that a large part of its problems related to the fact that it failed to account for risk in its pricing strategy.

At the time, two of Airbus's biggest programs—the A380 superjumbo jetliner and the A400M military transport plane—were years behind schedule and billions of dollars over budget. Several smaller programs also faced issues meeting deadlines and fulfilling customer requirements. Louis Gallois, CEO of Airbus parent the European Aeronautic Defence and Space Company (EADS), admitted that the company generated "insufficient" profit due to problems with the flagship programs. EADS CFO Hans Peter Ring added that the core issue was the difficulty in matching the heavy demands of customers against the ambitious financial returns expected by investors. "We are in a high-tech, complex business, and there is a lot of risk in our business. That won't change," Ring said in an interview with the *Wall Street Journal*. "The question is how to price risk. Obviously, in some cases we didn't price it right."

As it turns out, Airbus mispriced the risks given the operational complexities of these two programs. In selling the two-deck A380, it urged buyers to specify unprecedented levels of luxury onboard. The complexity of customizing planes with showers and private suites overwhelmed Airbus production systems. And in 2003, EADS signed a contract with seven NATO countries to deliver the A400M, the world's most sophisticated propeller-driven military transporter, under rigid contract terms normally used for simpler passenger jets. The project was more difficult than Airbus expected, and it quickly blew through the fixed-price budget. "The way we made our commitment for development and production of the plane under a fixed-price contract was not the right way," Ring said.

One key benefit of strategic risk management is early warning of potential problems. Alarms will sound if an initiative falls behind expectations, giving management the opportunity to redirect the effort, lay off risk, or, if results come in so far below target that nothing can salvage the project, to implement an exit strategy early on. The ability to "fail faster" will do more than almost anything else to improve a company's financial performance.

Lack of reliable metrics is no longer an obstacle to strategic risk management. Economic capital is a common currency in which any risk can be quantified, and the RAROC calculated in various scenarios allows management to determine which business activities will maximize shareholder value.

Although strategic risks pose the greatest threat to most companies, few have yet to incorporate strategic risk management into their ERM program. Strategic initiatives always involve risk, and some will not pan out as expected no matter how carefully planned. Companies that manage strategic risk skew the overall risk–return profile in their favor. They can ramp up initiatives that exceed expectations and spot potential losers in time to take corrective action before significant losses accumulate. Risk management should improve the percentage of successful initiatives as well as create a strategic risk profile similar to a call option, with its limited downside risk and unlimited upside potential.

APPENDIX A: STRATEGIC RISK MODELS

As discussed in the chapter, ERM can help management to optimize the company's strategic risk profile by investing in M&A and organic growth opportunities that will increase the upside while minimizing the downside by "failing faster" with losing investments and initiatives. Below are two excellent case studies on strategic risk management.

GE Capital

During the 1990s, GE Capital employed a version of real options in its Policy 6.0 program. Under this program, if an investment did not live up to expectations, management had the option to mitigate or exit, thus limiting exposure. For new products, new businesses, or mission-critical projects, Policy 6.0 represented a practical best-practice model for strategic risk management. It required a detailed analysis of strategic risks associated with any new initiative as well as quarterly reviews between business leaders and GE corporate executives to monitor and manage business performance relative to clear expectations. The major components of Policy 6.0 include:

- **Key Assumptions:** The new business must identify the key assumptions that support its feasibility, often including the most critical strategic risks such as business trends, customer needs, and disruptive technologies.
- **Monitoring Systems:** For each assumption, the business must identify monitoring systems for key performance indicators, key risk indicators, and early warning indicators. They must also specify the individuals responsible for oversight.
- **Trigger Points:** For critical metrics, the business must establish predefined positive, expected, and negative trigger points to initiate management actions or reviews in between the quarterly reviews. Breaches of significant thresholds may trigger immediate escalation and special reviews.
- **Management Decisions and Actions:** Positive trigger points signify results that are better than expected, which may prompt management to accelerate the business plan or take more risk. Negative trigger points give management the opportunity to initiate risk mitigation strategies or an exit strategy if key metrics and trends are well below expectations.

Similar to a VC firm, Policy 6.0 allowed GE Capital to continue or accelerate its investments that meet or exceed expectations while making timely corrective actions on investments that don't.

Duke Energy

In the late 1990s, the market for electric power went through wrenching changes when states began to deregulate utilities.[14] At a strategy session in July 2000, Duke Energy identified three possible scenarios for its future business environment:

- Economic Treadmill, in which U.S. economic growth would stagnate at 1% per year
- Market.com, in which the Internet would revolutionize the relationships between buyers and sellers
- Flawed Competition, in which uneven deregulation would continue in the energy industry, causing significant price volatility in different regions.

The timing proved prescient. Duke had appointed its first chief risk officer earlier that year, and the U.S. economy had begun the slide that would burst the Internet bubble.

Duke set early warning signals for each scenario: macroeconomic indicators, regulatory trends, technology changes, environment issues, competitive moves, and patterns of consolidation in the energy industry. It soon became apparent that "Flawed Competition" was the most likely outcome, enabling Duke to take evasive action against potential adverse consequences. Unlike many competitors, Duke scaled back its capacity expansion and concentrated on maximizing returns from its existing portfolio even if that meant shedding assets. Anticipating an oversupply of power generation in Texas in the coming years, Duke sold some new plant projects in the state before construction was complete.

Duke reaped the rewards of its foresight in subsequent years and continues to perform well relative to its competitors.

NOTES

1. Mark Hughes, "Do 70 Per Cent of All Organizational Change Initiatives Really Fail?" *Journal of Change Management*, November 2011, pp. 451–464.
2. "The Worst Business Decisions of All Time," 24/7 Wall St., October 17, 2012. Retrieved from http://247wallst.com/special-report/2012/10/17/the-worst-business-decisions-of-all-time/.
3. "Flaws in Strategic Decision-Making: McKinsey Global Survey Results," McKinsey & Company, January 2009. Retrieved from http://www.mckinsey .com/business-functions/strategy-and-corporate-finance/our-insights/flaws-in-strategic-decision-making-mckinsey-global-survey-results.
4. Lam, James. *Enterprise Risk Management: From Incentives to Controls, Second Edition*, Wiley, 2014, pp. 434–436.
5. *Exploring Strategic Risk*, Deloitte, 2013.
6. EVA is a registered trademark of Stern Stewart & Co.

7. For example, an acquirer may purchase insurance and/or issue a catastrophe bond to reduce an undesirable risk from a potential acquisition (e.g., product liability, natural disasters, or multiple events or triggers).
8. http://zonetowin.com/.
9. "A good case can be made that the balanced scorecard (or any other business reporting methodology) should include a risk assessment either as a separate category or as a part of each of the four performance components." James Lam, *Enterprise Risk Management, Second Edition*, John Wiley & Sons, 2014, p. 96.
10. Kaplan, Robert. "Risk Management and the Strategy Execution System," *Balanced Scorecard Report*, 2009.
11. For simplicity, a symmetrical or normally shaped bell curve is shown. But the specific shape of the bell curve (e.g., shape, skewness) will depend on individual risks faced by an organization.
12. The classic decision tree is a similar construct as a bell curve, except that it is displayed sideways and used to support decision making at critical junctures.
13. Gage, Deborah. "The Venture Capital Secret: 3 out of 4 Start-Ups Fail," *Wall Street Journal*, September 20, 2012.
14. Wysochi, Bernard, Jr. "Power Grid: Soft Landing or Hard?" *Wall Street Journal*, July 7, 2000.

CHAPTER 16

Risk-Based Performance Management

INTRODUCTION

As we have discussed throughout the book, risk is a bell curve with an expected value, a downside, and an upside. The objective of ERM is to optimize the shape of that bell curve. Risk-based pricing aims to achieve an appropriate return, or expected value, given the underlying risks of the business. A risk appetite statement and related tolerances, risk mitigation strategies, and risk transfer strategies are designed to control downside risks. Finally, strategic risk management is the lever to increase upside opportunity with respect to growth and innovation.

The purpose of this chapter is to discuss risk-based performance management for the key processes to optimize the risk profile and maximize value. Figure 16.1 shows the key relationships between risk, capital, and value creation. Risk-based performance management supports the value creation process by optimizing these interdependent relationships:

- **Shareholder value and enterprise-wide risks.** How much return did we achieve on risks? Corporate and business leaders are responsible for taking intelligent risks consistent with the company's risk appetite that will produce appropriate returns. Performance (KPI or output metric) is measured by risk-adjusted profitability, whereas as the key driver (KRI or input metric) is the difference between actual pricing vs. risk-based pricing. To the degree actual pricing is equal to, or great than, risk-based pricing, the return on risk is appropriate and value will be created.
- **Enterprise risks and economic capital.** How much capital do we need to support the underlying risks in the business? This view is from a debt holder perspective and is the primary focus of bond holders, regulators, and rating agencies. Performance can be measured by capital adequacy

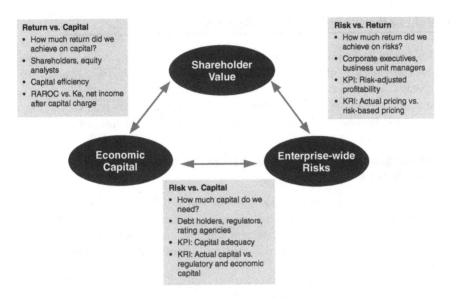

Return vs. Capital
- How much return did we achieve on capital?
- Shareholders, equity analysts
- Capital efficiency
- RAROC vs. Ke, net income after capital charge

Risk vs. Return
- How much return did we achieve on risks?
- Corporate executives, business unit managers
- KPI: Risk-adjusted profitability
- KRI: Actual pricing vs. risk-based pricing

Shareholder Value

Economic Capital

Enterprise-wide Risks

Risk vs. Capital
- How much capital do we need?
- Debt holders, regulators, rating agencies
- KPI: Capital adequacy
- KRI: Actual capital vs. regulatory and economic capital

FIGURE 16.1 Key Relationships Between Risk, Capital, and Value Creation

(and debt service coverage). Management can manage this relationship through the company's risk-based capital and dividend policy. To the extent actual capital is above regulatory capital and economic capital requirements, the company is sufficiently capitalized.

- **Economic capital and shareholder value.** How much return did we achieve on capital? This view is from a shareholder perspective and is the primary focus of stockholders and equity analysts. Performance is measured by capital efficiency, or to what degree management allocates capital to the highest risk-adjusted return opportunities (i.e., strategic risk management). Management can allocate capital efficiently by growing businesses where the risk-adjusted return on capital (RAROC) exceeds the cost of equity capital (Ke), resulting in positive net income after capital charge (NIACC).

Accordingly, companies need to take risk and its relationship with capital and value creation into account when thinking about performance management. Looking at performance management in this manner will not only give the board and management a better perspective on how to measure and improve company performance, but also help align individual performance with organizational objectives.

The first three sections of this chapter delve into how a company should consider performance management in regard to risk, capital, and value creation, respectively.

PERFORMANCE MANAGEMENT AND RISK

Many say performance and risk should be managed in an integrated manner because they are opposite sides of the same coin. I agree but would go further to say that risk management is a *key driver* of performance and both lie on the same bell curve. This section explores in detail why it is crucial for a company to align performance management with risk management.

Better Risk Management means Better Performance Management

In and of itself, improved risk management will lead a company to better performance by improving risk-adjusted profitability and lowering unexpected volatility.[1] Risk management uncovers advantageous opportunities for a company as well as the risks that could prevent it from achieving strategic goals.

Companies can begin by identifying and assessing the key risks associated with their strategy (as discussed in Chapter 13). Effective risk assessments (or RCSAs) create a solid foundation upon which to build detailed risk quantification methods, timely follow-up and risk mitigation strategies, and proper consideration of risks in business decisions. The top-down RCSA involves group or individual interviews with executive and senior management and establishes direction and company goals for risk assessment. The bottom-up RCSA utilizes staff workshops and other tools to promote accountability and communication throughout the company. Risk managers then report and prioritize the information they've gathered.

RCSAs ensure continuous improvement in the company's risk assessment process. Immediately following RCSA, for example, risk managers will conduct deep dives; identify key risk indicators, tolerance levels, and early warning signs; and develop strategies to manage newly identified risks. Over the long term, executives will follow up on the RCSA team's recommendations and continue to monitor them on an ongoing basis.

Integrating Performance and Risk

The concept of linking performance and risk with risk-adjusted metrics is well known to everyone in the investing world. Measures like the Sharpe Ratio, which measures expected return in excess of the risk-free rate for every unit of risk, are commonly used to answer the actionable question: Does the expected return justify this risk? Even the apparent star trader who in the short-term is generating returns far in excess of expectations will eventually harm his firm if his actions exceed the firm's risk appetite. Since returns are only sustainable when they operate in conjunction with sound risk-taking, returns are only as good as the risks implicit in them are tolerable.

Given that a company takes risks to generate growth and profits, it only makes sense to include risk in the measurement of business performance. Not reporting risk and other aspects of business together would be like separating revenue and expense reports. It is therefore unfortunate that many companies have traditionally measured returns without considerations of risk. These companies only look at sales, profits, and net income while at best looking at losses and events on the risk side separately.

Just as management can only assess profitability by combining revenues and expenses, it can only balance risk exposures and business opportunities by integrating risk and business reporting. This integration allows the company to accurately answer how much risk it is willing to accept in pursuit of business goals. In other words, what is the appropriate balance of risk and reward for the company? A well-considered answer to that question can prevent common pitfalls such as taking risks that are either too high or too low for the projected outcome.

PERFORMANCE MANAGEMENT AND CAPITAL

Performance and capital management are inexorably linked, and companies should strive to integrate the two when analyzing business operations. One concrete way to do this is to use risk-adjusted metrics when analyzing performance. In this section we'll examine the components of risk-based performance metrics.

Linking Risk and Capital

Capital is the wealth of a company in terms of shareholder's equity. Greater risk requires greater capital to offset potential loss, which means that the cost of capital increases with risk. In order to evaluate capital sufficiency, a company will often compare its actual capital (the amount that appears on the balance sheet) to its economic capital (EC), or the amount of capital necessary to overcome potential business, financial, and operational risks.

Economic Capital

Economic capital can be calculated for any type of risk and aggregated to produce a value for the company as a whole. These qualities make it the ideal "common currency" to evaluate risk across the organization and thus provide a realistic overview of a company's capital structure and allocation as well as its future needs. What exactly is economic capital? In more technical terms, it is the amount of equity required to cover unexpected losses based on a predetermined solvency standard.

Economic capital should not be confused with regulatory capital.[2] While both function as a company's buffer against potential losses, regulatory capital is stipulated by external regulation (i.e., Basel III) while EC is determined by the company in accordance with current economic conditions. The Basel Committee has taken some steps to better align regulatory capital with economic capital, but given that the former must in some sense be "one size fits all," the latter will always be the better measure of financial health and resiliency for the specific needs and idiosyncratic features of an individual company.

The basic steps for calculating economic capital are:

1. Establish a solvency standard for the overall company, as reflected in its target debt rating.
2. Measure the economic capital for individual risks based on the fundamental risk exposures and the solvency standard.
3. Aggregate the economic capital across individual risks, incorporating the correlation effects between risks.

The solvency standard is the desired creditworthiness of an organization, which can be inferred from its target debt rating. For example, an institution that has a target solvency standard of 99.9% would default, on average, only once every 1,000 years. This is roughly equivalent to an institution awarded an "A" rating by the debt rating agencies.

A higher solvency standard implies that more economic capital is held for a given level of risk. Put another way, the greater the risk that an institution bears, the greater the financial resources it must have in order to maintain a given solvency standard. A widely accepted theoretical framework for relating the amount of capital a company needs to hold against a given level of risk is based on Robert Merton's model of default, which states that a company's shareholders own the right to default on payments to debt holders and will do so if the value of the firm's equity (i.e., net assets) drops below zero. Debt holders charge shareholders for default risk by demanding a spread over the risk-free rate on the funds they provide. The probability of default is a function of the current level and potential variability (the probability distribution) of a firm's net asset value.

The calculation of an organization's economic capital is generally done "bottom up." That is, the economic capital is calculated separately for each type of risk and then aggregated, taking into account the effects of diversification, to come up with the overall economic capital for the entire enterprise. Economic capital also applies the same methodology and assumptions in determining enterprise value.

PERFORMANCE MANAGEMENT AND VALUE CREATION

Performance management should not merely focus on regulatory compliance or loss minimization, but should also enhance a company's ability to achieve business objectives and maximize shareholder value. Using economic capital in performance management builds a bridge between risk and value.[3] This section demonstrates the role economic capital plays in calculating risk-based performance metrics, which in turn support resource allocation and risk–return optimization. I should also point out that, unlike key risk indicators (KRIs), which measure downside risk or volatility, performance metrics measure *expected* performance.

We'll be looking at three specific risk-based performance metrics: net income after capital charge (NIACC), shareholder value added (SVA), and risk-adjusted return on capital (RAROC).

Net Income after Capital Charge

Think of net income after capital charge (NIACC) as a company's *economic* profit, or a firm's revenue after deducting its monetary costs and opportunity costs, which include the cost of risk:

$$NIACC = Net\ Income - Economic\ Capital\ Charge$$

$$= Net\ Income - (Economic\ Capital\ *\ Ke)$$

Net income is what a company makes minus its costs. Economic capital charge is the total amount of economic capital multiplied by the cost of equity (Ke). The cost of equity can be calculated using the Capital Asset Pricing Model (CAPM).

Shareholder Value Added (SVA)

Shareholder value added (SVA) is simply the discounted value of the NIACC—it represents the incremental value that is added (or subtracted if it is negative). Companies can use NIACC and SVA to evaluate business operations from short-term and long-term perspectives, respectively.

SVA is especially useful for business investments that have uneven income streams or long payback periods. NIACC would not accurately measure the economic contribution of such investments. Net present value (NPV) is a widely accepted metric to measure the financial return of businesses and investments. SVA can be considered as a risk-adjusted NPV while NIACC can be considered a measure of risk-adjusted net income. Next we will discuss RAROC, which is a measure of risk-adjusted ROE (return on equity).

Risk-Adjusted Return on Capital (RAROC)

A company creates value when it makes smart business decisions with its available capital and when it is properly compensated for the risks incurred. As a performance indicator, risk-adjusted return on capital (RAROC) helps a company optimize its risk-taking and maximize value creation. Management can determine RAROC for the company as a whole, but it is more useful to calculate a value for each business activity (e.g., product, customer, or business unit) in order to compare them to one another on an apples-to-apples basis. RAROC is the ratio of risk-adjusted return to economic capital. That is, it is the anticipated after-tax return on each strategic initiative divided by the economic capital:

$$RAROC = Risk - Adjusted\ Return/Economic\ Capital$$

Risk-adjusted return can be based either on net income or on expected return. Using net income in the calculation provides an indication of *actual* profitability while the use of expected return provides a measure of *normalized* profitability. This is particularly relevant when applying RAROC to credit risk-related activities, since expected rather than actual losses are typically used to calculate return.

The other component of RAROC, economic capital (EC), allows a company to allocate capital to activities on the basis of risk vis-a-vis the company's target solvency standard. Since the amount of economic capital that is required to support each of the company's activities is proportional to the risk generated by that activity, economic capital serves as a standard measurement of risk. Dividing an activity's expected return by EC yields a ratio that represents the amount of return the company expects per unit of risk it takes.

If RAROC exceeds the company's cost of capital (Ke, or cost of equity capital), the initiative is viable and will add value; if RAROC is less than Ke, the endeavor will destroy value. But the decision whether to back an initiative should not depend on a single case reflecting the expected value. The company should run the numbers for multiple scenarios to see the distribution of results in both more and less favorable circumstances or in combinations of better and worse conditions over time. The final decision will depend on the specific company's risk appetite.

The primary use of RAROC is to compare the risk and return of potentially quite diverse business activities. RAROC is particularly useful when capital is scarce, and a company needs to choose among potential investments. Using RAROC as a performance metric can clarify which operations are worth pursuing and which require greater consideration. It might reveal seemingly profitable operations to be excessively risky, or expose others as too capital-intensive to be worth the potential returns. Additionally, it helps to align the actions of individuals and business units with company-wide targets.

One drawback of using RAROC as a performance metric is that it does not capture the total amount of value that an activity generates. RAROC only provides a ratio or percentage on the expected return per dollar of risk capital in a single period. For example, suppose a business unit currently has a RAROC of 25%, well above the company's target of 15%. If RAROC were the primary performance metric, the unit would not want to generate additional business that did not meet or exceed its current RAROC of 25%, as the additional business would lower the average below its current level. This is obviously problematic because the company's management would like the subsidiary unit to pursue all opportunities that gave returns at 15% or more. As such, it is useful to supplement RAROC with NIACC and SVA analyses.

Key Relationships between Risk, Economic Capital, and Value Creation

Let's now take a look at how enterprise-wide risks, economic capital, and shareholder value are related. Recall that economic capital can be defined as the level of capital required to cover the risks that a company faces, more commonly known as its risk profile. The more risk the company takes on, the more economic capital is required to cover it. Economic capital in turn affects shareholder value in terms of return on that capital.

Value can thus be expressed in terms of RAROC as follows:

$$M/B = (RAROC - g)/(Ke - g)$$

where M = market value, B = book value, Ke = cost of equity capital, and g = annual earnings growth rate.

The advantage of economic capital and RAROC models is that the analytical results are linked to earnings, capital management, and shareholder value maximization.

Risk Transfer

Companies can also create capital efficiency by risk transfer. Management may find that risk exposures resulting from its M&A activities or core operations are deemed too concentrated or inefficient to retain.

Traditionally, risk transfer has been viewed by companies as a way to solve specific micro-risk issues. A firm's rationale for implementing risk transfers is either (1) the firm's exposures are too excessive and it needs to shed risk, or (2) it is more efficient financially for that risk to be taken on by a third party, such as a hedge fund or insurance provider. Within a company, for example, the treasurer may use financial futures and swaps to hedge interest rate and foreign exchange risk exposures while the insurance manager might purchase product liability and property and casualty insurance to protect against certain business and operational risks. Both the treasurer and the insurance manager have specific risk problems they seek to address through risk transfer. They will evaluate various proposals from product providers and then make a decision based on the best structure and price.

Even in a risk silo, however, the cost of risk transfer can be greatly reduced when individual positions are grouped into portfolios. For example, the treasurer can reduce hedging costs for interest rate risk by macro-hedging the overall balance sheet as opposed to micro-hedging individual assets and liabilities. Similarly, insurance managers have realized significant premium savings by taking advantage of internal diversification and transferring the residual risks using multiple risk, multiyear insurance policies.

ERM takes diversification a step further by integrating the risk silos into a firm-wide risk portfolio. The benefits of diversification, or internal hedges, can then be maximized by considering the volatility and correlation of all risk exposures. As such, the company can integrate its risk transfer activities and focus on its net risk exposures. Taking an ERM approach to risk transfer produces four key benefits:

- Incorporation of the full impact of diversification and thereby reducing the notional amount of coverage and cost of risk transfer
- Rationalization of various risk transfer strategies to avoid the over- and under-hedging of different risks
- Optimization of the limits and attachment points for insurance/ reinsurance policies as well as for the hedging structures for derivative transactions
- Minimization of risk transfer costs by arbitraging between traditional and alternative risk transfer products as well as between product providers

The economic capital and RAROC methodology for risk-based pricing is also a useful tool for evaluating the impact of different risk transfer strategies. For example, the economic benefits of executing any risk transfer strategy include lower expected losses and reduced loss volatility, and the economic costs include insurance premium or hedging costs as well as higher counterparty credit and operational risk exposures. In a sense, the company is ceding both risk and return, resulting in a ceded RAROC. Ceded RAROC indicates the degree to which the transfer reduces risk. It is calculated by dividing the incremental change in return by the incremental change in economic capital:

$$Ceded\ RAROC = \Delta\,Risk\text{-}adjusted\ Return / \Delta\,Economic\ Capital$$

In essence, it represents the effective cost of risk transfer. If the ceded RAROC is less than the cost of equity capital (Ke), then the risk transfer creates shareholder value. Conversely, if the ceded RAROC is more than Ke, then the risk transfer is destroying shareholder value.

SUMMARY

Aligning performance management with risk allows a company to conduct its activities based on targets that maximize value. As management adopts performance metrics and indicators that are in line with the company's long-term business goals, the following should be considered:

- Which business activities create the most value? Which ones destroy value?
- Have there been times when the company has been very successful or unsuccessful in delivering value to investors and other stakeholders? What were the root causes of those successes or failures? What lessons can they impart?
- Are business units accountable for their risk and performance management? Do they freely share information and best practices?
- Does the company assess existing and potential risks effectively? Are assessment results available and easily accessible to those who need them?
- How effectively is information resulting from risk and performance management incorporated into decision-making?
- Do the board and management actively promote a culture of risk-based performance management? Are there incentives in place for individuals to adopt this approach?

Prior to the economic crisis, many financial institutions compensated their traders based on the overall return of their trading activity. As a result, traders took greater and greater risks in search of bigger and bigger returns and had no incentive to consider risk. Imagine, instead, what would have happened if these companies had measured their performance using *risk-adjusted* metrics. Suddenly, high-risk trades would threaten compensation, and traders would have taken risk into account. This would have led to a more "risk-aware" culture that better aligned with the company's risk appetite.

Effective risk-based performance management requires more than simply reporting metrics and outcomes, though that is an essential first step. Management—and the organization as a whole—must learn from results and integrate them into every level of decision-making. Only when individual units act in harmony with the organization's overall risk appetite can a company execute its business goals effectively.

Good management is ultimately about turning ideas into action. In order to do so effectively, boards and management must define clear short- and long-term business goals and then determine which performance indicators are most relevant to those goals. It is up to the risk function to measure those indicators accurately and establish appropriate feedback loops and monitoring processes. This hard data is an essential tool to developing the "softer" side of ERM by incentivizing behavior and fostering a risk-aware corporate culture throughout the company.

To optimize its risk profile, a company should strive to integrate risk management into its business processes. Risk-adjusted performance management supports this integration, which in turn optimizes performance in areas such as pricing, resource allocation, and decision-making.

NOTES

1. Lam, James. Risk Management: *The ERM Guide from AFP*, Association for Financial Professionals, 2011.
2. *Range of Practices and Issues in Economic Capital Frameworks*, Basel Committee on Banking Supervision, 2009.
3. *From Compliance to Value Creation: The Journey to Effective Enterprise Risk Management for Insurers*, McKinsey & Company, 2014.

Risk Monitoring and Reporting

Integration of KPIs and KRIs

INTRODUCTION

A successful ERM program not only highlights risks that an organization faces and helps avert them, but also highlights opportunities the company can take advantage of to boost growth and value. This is only possible if one is able to peer into the future to see those risks and opportunities coming down the pike. But how? Likely you are familiar with the concept of key performance indicators (KPIs), which help managers determine how well they are progressing toward their goals. While KPIs are important in ERM programs to evaluate their performance, it is only through key risk indicators (KRIs) that one can tease out trends that may indicate future risk. The adage "what gets measured gets managed" is true not just of KPIs but of KRIs as well. If risk managers can measure risk, then and only then can they optimize business decisions around it.

I'll begin this chapter by defining indicators in general, and KPIs and KRIs specifically. Because they are better known, I'll explore KPIs in greater depth before looking at the role of risk measurement and reporting in ERM. We'll then turn to the task at hand: creating effective KRIs that a company can use to anticipate future risks. I'll then elaborate on how best to implement a KPI/KRI program within an ERM framework before concluding with some best practices.

WHAT IS AN INDICATOR?

To understand key indicators, we must first understand indicators themselves. An indicator is a specific type of metric that answers the question, "How are we doing?" in an actionable way. Often, indicators accompany benchmarks to measure success or failure in meeting certain goals. Indicators enable management and other decision-makers to assess the needs of the company and the progress toward intended outputs, outcomes, tactical goals, and strategic objectives.

Indicators are as varied as the activities they measure. One way of classifying indicators is by the stage of a process they are measuring. An *input indicator*, for example, might measure the human and financial resources assigned to a particular project, whereas an *output indicator* could measure the quantity of goods and services produced. Further downstream, an *outcome indicator* measures broader results achieved through goods and services.[1]

Another way to categorize indicators is according to the breadth of their relevance. A *macro indicator* might be relevant to understanding risk exposure based on macroeconomic trends, for example. A *common indicator* is relevant to everyone in the organization while a *specific indicator* would apply to a single business unit, function, or activity.[2]

KPIs are simply indicators specifically used to determine how well the company is performing against its business goals. They are *key* because they directly and significantly impact business performance. What's more, a KPI must be sufficiently specific to suggest actions that will lead to improvement. For example, total sales volume may be an important metric, but if it falls short of expectations, it doesn't provide any hint as to a cause or potential solution to the problem. By contrast, consider a company that has chosen to grow sales by focusing on a target market of midsize manufacturers in a certain geographic region. A KPI that measures the value of sales opportunities with that profile currently in the pipeline can reveal just how efficiently the sales team is working. It also hints at possible solutions, such as increasing the size of the sales team or drilling down to find potential sticking points in the sales process.

KRIs show how much risk is associated with a specific activity or investment. Companies may use them to monitor controls, risk drivers, and exposures in order to provide insight into possible risk events. The best KRIs can be tracked against risk tolerance levels and monitored alongside related KPIs and business objectives. While KPIs measure the result of past actions and events, KRIs are more forward looking. That allows time for rapid action should a company's risk profile threaten to surpass appetite. If KPIs help answer the question, "How are we doing?" KRIs answer the question, "Where are we going?"

Strategic frameworks such as Balanced Scorecard rely on KPIs to measure performance as it relates to strategy. In this model, a company uses performance indicators to monitor the implementation and effectiveness of its strategy as well as measure the gap between actual and target performance. This in turn helps determine the organization's effectiveness and operational efficiency.

Although the traditional Balanced Scorecard (BSC) does a good job of setting targets with KPIs, it does not directly address risk. Augmenting the BSC with KRIs for key risk measures can provide a more balanced view. This permits the scorecard to attribute specific risks to an objective, identify the possibility of future adverse impact, and act on early warning signs of adverse events. These measures aren't limited to the BSC approach, of course. Companies can implement both KRIs and KPIs with whichever strategic and ERM frameworks they choose.

USING KEY PERFORMANCE INDICATORS

KPIs fall into two broad categories: internal and external. Internal KPIs typically affect a company's performance only in a limited way, without material effect on the bottom line. Companies may use internal KPIs to improve internal processes, without the need to report to clients, shareholders, or even senior management. For example, the "bounce" rate of a website (those visits that leave without clicking any links) might be a helpful internal KPI for the goal of optimizing landing pages, but it's not something the CEO must necessarily keep abreast of as a sign of company health. External KPIs are those that impact the company's bottom line, and which deserve the attention of senior management. To take another example, the number of people following a consumer-goods company on Facebook is unlikely to be a useful external KPI, whereas the volume of product support requests, which could reflect serious quality issues impacting sales, would be an effective external indicator.

Good KPIs can be challenging to identify, but the following attributes can help guide the development:

1. **Quantifiable:** KPIs must be objectively measurable. This is non-negotiable, as it removes bias associated with subjective measures.
2. **Relevant:** When KPIs are tied directly to business objectives, they will typically provide information that is immediately actionable.
3. **Critical:** External KPIs should have a linear relationship with revenue, cost, or business objectives and directly impact the company's bottom line.
4. **Timely:** The best KPIs are not only quantifiable, they can also be measured quickly (preferably in real time) so that management can act on the data as soon as possible.

KPIs have been around a long time, and they have become embedded as standard operating procedure in many industries and numerous corporate functions. By way of illustration, the list below offers a few examples of common KPIs for each category of performance:

- **Financial:** Net Profit, Return on Investment, Price/Earnings Ratio
- **Marketing:** Market Share, Brand Equity, Search Engine Rankings
- **Operations:** Project Cost Variance, Time to Market, Process Waste Level
- **Internal:** Human Capital Value Added, Revenue per Employee, Employee Churn Rate
- **Sustainability:** Carbon Footprint, Energy Consumption, Waste Reduction Rate
- **Customers:** Net Promoter Score, Customer Retention Rate, Customer Profitability Score

When formulating KPIs, companies must not only determine their type and purpose, but also the source of the measure, ideal frequency of measurement, and a target value for each KPI. Once the monitoring process is in place, it must of course be maintained in order to keep the company on track. I find the best way to handle monitoring is to create dashboards that automatically display updated data in an accessible format adapted for various users throughout the organization. (We'll take a more detailed look at ERM dashboards in the next chapter.) Companies have a wide variety of KPIs to choose from, so it is best to focus on a few critical ones while monitoring the others less intently. Every organization is different, so each must begin by using its own scorecard and strategy as a guide in choosing the most effective KPIs to track.

BUILDING KEY RISK INDICATORS

While KPIs work like thermostats or electric meters, providing current and historical data to act upon, key risk indicators function more like smoke detectors. The purpose of a smoke detector is to alert residents to early signs of a fire so that they can escape safely before it is too late. KRIs serve a similar function. Good KRIs are based on warning signs that a company is headed in the wrong direction and could potentially lose value. KRIs also identify variables (e.g., interest rates, economic trends, business drivers) that can have a significant impact on future performance. These warnings will alert key executives early enough so that the company can adapt to the changes or avoid trouble altogether before it's irreversible. And since not all risks are bad risks, a company should also have KRIs that indicate potential opportunities as well as challenges.

Sources and Characteristics of Effective Key Risk Indicators

Like key performance indicators, KRIs should be quantifiable, critical, relevant, and timely so as to provide objective feedback to managers on business direction and help focus action. In addition, however, they should be predictive enough to act as early warning signs for possible changes in an organization's risk profile.

As part of a comprehensive ERM program, companies should develop a set of KRIs for each risk category they face. This is relatively easy for data that companies collect as part of doing business, but can present a challenge in other areas. For example, financial institutions usually have an abundance of data describing credit and market risk indicators, but little to support operational KRIs. By contrast, nonfinancial corporations may have significant insight into operational risk, but find it difficult to develop KRIs for financial or technology risk. All companies face the challenge of developing leading indicators that can effectively provide early warnings of potential future losses.

Business and Functional Units One final source of KPIs and KRIs deserves special note: the leaders of the company's business and functional units. While risk assessments might tease out some of the key risks facing each business or functional unit, there is no substitute for sitting down and interviewing their leaders. These interviews will not only add color to risks identified in assessments, but they may also uncover additional, often more significant, risks that need to be measured and monitored.

Consider the interview questions below for developing KPIs and KRIs for a business or functional unit. Questions 1 and 2 help to develop KPIs while questions 3 and 4 relate to KRIs. The last three questions should lead to a better understanding the business or functional unit's perspective on the overall ERM program, and identify opportunities for improvement going forward:

1. What are the key business or financial objectives based on the business strategy?
2. What key performance indicators (KPIs) best quantify the achievement of these objectives? What are the performance targets or triggers for these KPIs?
3. What are the risks that can drive variability in actual vs. expected performance?[3]
4. What are the key risk indictors (KRIs) that quantify the levels and/or potential loss of these risks? What are the risk limits or tolerances for these KRIs?

5. What are the worst-case scenarios for the business? (i.e., defined as "extremely unlikely, but possible" scenarios that may include the occurrence of one or more key risks, and possibly one or more control failures)?
6. How can the company improve its risk mitigation and management processes?
7. How can the company improve its risk reporting and monitoring programs for the board and management?

The meetings with business leaders should produce a good set of KPIs and KRIs, but the focus should be on quality rather than quantity. In addition to executive meetings, the risk team should consider other sources and characteristics of effective KRIs. See Figure 17.1.

While the development of useful KRIs is a significant challenge, there are some readily available sources, including:

- **Policies and regulations:** Regulations that govern the business activities of the company, as well as the corporate policies and limits established by management and the board, provide useful compliance KRIs. These indicators may include risk exposures against limits or compliance with regulatory requirements.
- **Strategies and objectives:** The performance metrics established by senior management to assess corporate and business strategies are another good source of KRIs. Note that performance metrics are designed to measure actual or expected performance, whereas KRIs should be designed to measure downside risk or performance volatility[4].
- **Previous losses and incidents:** Many companies have compiled loss-event databases that capture historical losses and incidents. These databases can provide useful insights on what processes or events have the potential to drive financial or reputational loss. The risk function can then develop KRIs to monitor them.
- **Stakeholder requirements:** The expectations and requirements of external stakeholders—customers, rating agencies, stock analysts, business partners—can help in the development of KRIs based on variables that are important to these key groups.
- **Risk assessments:** Risk assessments performed by the company—including audit assessments, risk-control self-assessments, and stress tests mandated by regulation such as Sarbanes-Oxley—can also provide valuable input on the business entities, processes, or risks requiring KRIs.

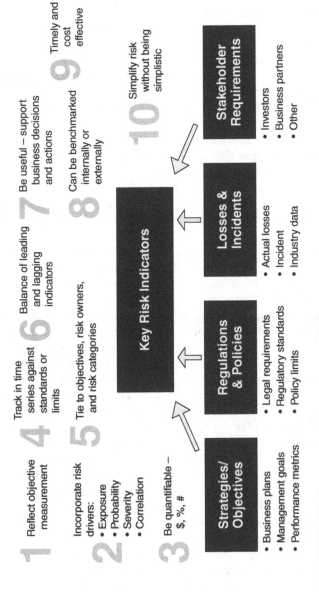

FIGURE 17.1 Sources and Characteristics of Effective KRIs

1 Reflect objective measurement

2 Incorporate risk drivers:
• Exposure
• Probability
• Severity
• Correlation

3 Be quantifiable – $, %, #

4 Track in time series against standards or limits

5 Tie to objectives, risk owners, and risk categories

6 Balance of leading and lagging indicators

7 Be useful – support business decisions and actions

8 Can be benchmarked internally or externally

9 Timely and cost effective

10 Simplify risk without being simplistic

Strategies/ Objectives
• Business plans
• Management goals
• Performance metrics

Regulations & Policies
• Legal requirements
• Regulatory standards
• Policy limits

Losses & Incidents
• Actual losses
• Incident
• Industry data

Stakeholder Requirements
• Investors
• Business partners
• Other

Key Risk Indicators

The sources above may produce a large number of KRIs. The risk team can narrow that number down by evaluating their effectiveness against the following 10 characteristics:

1. **Rely on consistent methodologies and standards.** Effective KRIs provide objective and consistent measurement of risk over time, which is enhanced by the use of standardized methodologies such as a validated model or process.
2. **Incorporate one or more of the four risk drivers: exposure, probability, severity, and correlation.**[5] As the main determinants of potential loss, these four risk drivers are especially helpful in measuring and tracking risks.
3. **Quantify by dollar amount, percentage, or number.** KRIs should be quantitative metrics that can be monitored and reported, both in terms of actual and projected performance.
4. **Track in time series against standards or limits.** Metrics need good benchmarks to support meaningful interpretation. KRIs should be reported relative to their trends against established performance goals and risk tolerances.
5. **Tie to objectives, risk owners, and standard risk categories.** KRIs should be aligned with the business objectives they can impact, the risk owners who are accountable, and categories in the risk taxonomy to support aggregate risk monitoring.
6. **Balance leading and lagging indicators.** Lagging indicators reflect actual performance and are more accurate while leading indicators reflect future performance and are more actionable. Effective risk and performance reporting should include a balance of both.
7. **Support business decisions and actions.** KRIs should be useful, and not just interesting or informative. That means they support risk-based decisions and actions at the business, corporate management, and board levels. A good acid test at the end of a report or meeting is if the company actually made any decisions that impact its risk profile.
8. **Benchmark internally and externally.** Managers need contextual information, such as internal and external benchmarks, to perform relative performance and risk analyses. How does our company compare to competitors and how do our business units compare to each other? For example, the loss-to-revenue ratio is effective because it can be easily benchmarked against other businesses.
9. **Are timely and cost effective.** KRIs that take too much time or resources to develop may not be as effective because they may be too stale to be useful and/or too expensive to generate regularly.

10. **Simplify risk without being simplistic.** Red, yellow, and green signals based only on someone's opinion are simplistic and subject to challenge. On the other hand, the same signals can be very effective in simplifying complex information if they are based on robust analytics and cross-functional analyses.

Finally, KPIs and KRIs should always be reported with expert commentary and analysis. The board and management is not only interested in what the risk managers see, but also what they think about what they see.

KPI AND KRI PROGRAM IMPLEMENTATION

The first step in implementing an effective key indicators program is to define business strategy and objectives, as well as specific performance targets and risk tolerances. The company's overall risk framework should provide some guidance in this respect, but if that framework is in development, one can still proceed with identifying key indicators. In fact, the work done here will also inform the framework, so they are both part of an iterative process. Regulatory requirements should also be included in this effort.

Next, the risk management function should map the decision-making process that leads to each goal or requirement. And then the team should focus on each of these decision points. It is generally more useful if we reverse the order of the typical input-processing-output paradigm, and instead think about decisions, supporting data and analyses, and input requirements:

- Who makes what decisions, whether an individual, function, or committee?
- How do we support those decision-makers with the right KPIs, KRIs, expert analyses, and reporting?
- How do we support the analyses and reporting with the right technology and data resources?

With this in mind, let's discuss the steps to identify, select, and report on the appropriate KPIs and KRIs.

Identification

Once the analysis and collection of strategies, objectives, and targets is complete, the team should turn its attention to the risk exposures that can impact each one. The task at this stage is to identify an indicator for each exposure. Remember that a risk indicator is not a historical measure, but has predictive qualities. For example, if the company's bottom line relies heavily on a certain commodity price, knowing the current price doesn't offer insights into its future movement. For that one must track a driver behind that commodity's future price. These could be as disparate as political stability, weather patterns, or supply-and-demand trends in key markets. Such indicators might identify current exposure levels, emerging risk trends, or past events that could present significant risk.

Risks can arise from business activities, corporate strategy, culture, or any combination of these sources. Since these will vary from company to company, few organizations will have matching risk exposure profiles. As a result, each company will wind up with a unique set of KPIs and KRIs. Since there is no "one size fits all," the risk function should plan on taking sufficient time to examine the company's exposures before identifying their key risk indicators and putting them in place.

Selection

The result of this research will be a broad set of risk indicators. Up to this point, the focus has been on quantity and inclusion. Now, however, the risk function must consider the "key" part of KRI by whittling this list down to those indicators that are truly significant and worthy of close monitoring. The implementation team should begin by evaluating each risk in terms of probability and severity. Then, they should look at how each affects strategic objectives. Mapping key risks to strategic initiatives lets management identify the most critical metrics that can serve as key risk indicators to help oversee the core strategic initiatives and business operations. Next, evaluate the effectiveness of controls associated with the key risks. Determine the risk management strategies (including accountabilities and action plans) for each key risk the process identified. Finally, the risk team should prioritize the top risks identified for further analyses, quantification, and risk mitigation.

Tracking and Reporting

In order to track KPIs and KRIs, it is necessary to determine trigger thresholds, or warning indicators that activate feedback loops. The organization may have already set tolerances for such triggers based on its risk appetite statement. If not, one can turn to industry best practice and internal surveys to set these thresholds. These warning levels should be submitted to the board for final approval, along with mitigation plans that address how to handle breaches.

The next step is to monitor each key indicator and make sure that it is available to the relevant decision-makers when they need it. Practically speaking, this means determining how to aggregate and report the data. Integrated dashboards (discussed in Chapter 18) are an ideal way to distribute this information. Dashboard reporting allows a company to aggregate data in one place and automatically build reports designed for individual decision-makers.

The final step is to determine how frequently to track indicators. This depends on both the accessibility of the data and its time sensitivity, and can range from continuous monitoring to weekly, monthly, or other periodic reports. Once the company's KPI and KRI programs are up and running, the risk function should revisit them on a regular basis to reassess their usefulness and accuracy.

BEST PRACTICES

Keep Stakeholders and Objectives in Mind

One of the most important things to keep in mind while developing KPIs and KRIs is the role of stakeholders. Stakeholders determine the trajectory of the organization, so it makes sense to include them in planning, and even in the earliest stages of identification. First, identify stakeholders, their needs or desires, and what metrics address these concerns.

Since ERM must align with organizational objectives, the mapping of KPIs and KRIs to business objectives is an important next step. Companies must ask the right questions to determine how well indicators and goals align. These steps will not only help develop metrics most relevant to the organization's objectives, but also make stakeholders more willing to help with the development and implementation of the measurement and reporting process.

Leverage Existing Metrics

Another best practice is to leverage existing metrics by repurposing them toward ERM goals. Companies already measure many KPIs and perhaps even a few KRIs that it can be brought to bear. This is both efficient and cost-effective, but it comes with a caveat to avoid the common management bias toward familiar measurement. If an existing indicator is no longer effective, the company should replace it or eliminate it altogether.

The risk team might also research and find external databases of KRIs and loss-events that may have been developed by industry groups or associations. These external sources of data could also inform the development of useful metrics.

Limit Indicators to the Most Relevant

Everyone in the organization will have an opinion as to which risks are the most important to monitor with KRIs. Those tasked with selecting indicators must take care to avoid bias by using objective measures such as risk likelihood and severity, and alignment to strategic priorities. Often, companies can choose among several KRIs to monitor a specific risk. In that case, the one with the strongest causal relationship to the risk will yield the most significant information. Throughout the selection process, it is important to document each KRI chosen including a definition and a description of how it is measured. Clarity is key.

Establish Monitoring and Reporting Frequencies Early On

In order to avoid ambiguity, it is important to determine early on how the company will monitor each key indicator, and how often. If possible, data collection should be automated so it does not rely on human intervention. A dashboard program can help aggregate data and compose reports. Choosing the proper frequency for aggregation and analysis means finding a balance between time sensitivity and the resources required—frequent enough to be useful, but not wasteful. Finally, it is worthwhile to review periodically KPIs and KRIs for continued usefulness, particularly following any shift in strategy or process. If, further down the line, the company determines that an indicator is no longer needed, or that others should be added, the framework should allow for such renewal. Continuous monitoring of key indicators will prove useful in the final product.

CONCLUSION

Key indicators of risk and performance are at the very heart of an effective ERM program. In this chapter, we looked at how KPIs help management answer the question, "How are we doing?" and how KRIs address, "Where are we going?" KRIs allow risk managers to "see around corners" and anticipate oncoming risks. By doing so, companies can take steps to mitigate these risks as well as take advantage of available opportunities. Effective KPIs and KRIs can support these essential if sometimes vexing decisions because they are quantifiable, relevant, and timely. Finding such indicators and determining which are the most relevant to the business is a multistep process that begins by identifying business unit–specific and organization-wide objectives and recognizing associated risks. It involves gathering all potential indicators and editing down this broad collection into a small, actionable set of measurements that merit ongoing monitoring. By tracking this focused set of key indicators, companies can not only see how they're performing against objectives, but also anticipate and mitigate future risks. In the next chapter, we'll discuss the ideal tool for efficiently communicating not only KPIs and KRIs, but contextual information and expert analysis in a straightforward, actionable format: the ERM dashboard.

NOTES

1. Horsch, Karen. "Indicators: Definition and Use in a Results Based Accountability System," *Harvard Family Research Project*, 1–4, 1997.
2. Gantt, Kristen L. and Tom Diminich. "Key Risk Indicators—Focusing on the Right Risks in Today's Environment," *Risk Business Americas*, 2010.
3. This is the focus of RCSA processes, discussed in Chapter 13.
4. Lam, James. "Emerging Best Practices in Developing Key Risk Indicators and ERM Reporting," *Cognos*, 2008.
5. Two of the most useful KRIs used in ERM—value-at risk and economic capital—can incorporate all four risk drivers.

CHAPTER 18

ERM Dashboard Reporting

INTRODUCTION

One of the key objectives of ERM is to promote risk transparency, both in terms of internal risk reporting and public disclosure. In a Deloitte survey of approximately 1,500 cross-industry executives,[1] 86 percent identified "risk information reporting" as of high or moderate priority, making it the most highly prioritized of 13 risk initiatives. What's more, this priority was followed closely by "risk data quality and management" (76 percent) and "operational risk measurement system" (69 percent). Clearly, these executives understand that establishing a robust risk measurement and reporting system is critical to ERM success.

One of the best ways to implement such a system is with an ERM dashboard. A dashboard differs from traditional risk reporting in a number of ways, which we will discuss more fully later in the chapter. Suffice it to say for now that a dashboard provides consolidated and timely reports of risk exposures or opportunities across an enterprise. These reports offer early warnings and support preemptive actions by the board and management as well as business and functional users.

However, the term *dashboard* is not a particularly accurate metaphor. For the most part, automotive dashboards tell the driver what has already happened and what is currently taking place. They indicate speed the car has reached, and how much fuel remains in the tank. They do have some helpful indicators of emergency situations—such as a drop in oil pressure or an engine problem. But these warnings typically come too late to take preventative measures, and the damage may have already occurred.

The "drivers" of a company will already have a good idea of what problems they currently face, or faced in the past. What they need is something to tell them what is *likely to happen in the future*. That is the goal of an ERM dashboard. In that sense, it is more like a navigation system than an automobile dashboard. It should act as a roadmap to the destination—a strong business outlook with plenty of new opportunities and minimal downside risks.

Many companies still approach risk reporting as though it were analogous to a car's speedometer. Far too often, they focus on past and current metrics rather than creating an advanced navigation system that displays not only past and current data, but also indicators of future events. Such a system would also provide operators with options for forestalling negative events while making positive outcomes more likely. This is the kind of dashboard required by a continuous performance-based risk management framework as discussed in Chapter 3.

But how to design a dashboard? Consider the ERM process as a pyramid of information and analysis. Data sources, analytics, models, and reports make up the pyramid's broad base while decision-making sits on top. To create a dashboard, one might be tempted to start from the bottom of the pyramid collecting available data sources and working upward toward analysis, reporting, and "navigation." But I recommend starting the design process from the top by defining the critical decisions that the dashboard will support. After all, a driver must first tell the car's navigation system where to go before it can produce directions. So asking high-level questions will be useful in determining the destination of the company: Who will use the information provided? What kind of decisions do they make? What information do they need to support these decisions? From there, we can determine the metrics, analyses, and reports required to support those decisions.

Basic Questions in Dashboard Design

When designing a dashboard reporting system, it is useful to start by articulating the key questions the dashboard is meant to address. For example, the ERM dashboard for the board and senior management may attempt to answer the following five basic questions:

1. Which If Any of Our Business Objectives Are at Risk? A company's risk appetite statement (RAS) defines risks according their effect on primary business objectives. The ERM dashboard should similarly organize risk information (e.g., quantitative metrics, qualitative risk assessments, early warning indicators) within the context of key strategic and business objectives. For each objective, the dashboard report might show green, yellow, or red indicators to signal that its achievement is on track, threatened, or off track, respectively. For objectives with yellow or red indicators, the board and management should then be able to drill down to the underlying analyses.

2. Are We in Compliance with Laws, Regulations, and Policies? The ERM dashboard should include a compliance monitor that shows at a glance the company's compliance status with key policies, regulations, and laws. Again, traffic-light signals would highlight whether the company is in full compliance (green), approaching violation (yellow), or in violation (red). Drill-down capabilities would again enable further analysis with respect to more detailed compliance metrics and reports.

3. What Risk Incidents Have Been Escalated? The ERM dashboard should be able to escalate critical risk incidents to the appropriate managers, executives, and board members in real time. In order to support this feature, the system must be able to capture risk incidents that meet a defined threshold (e.g., customer impact, financial exposure, reputational impact, etc.) throughout the company. Moreover, the ERM dashboard needs to have an embedded algorithm that would prioritize risk incidents and escalate them to the proper individuals. (This capability depends on establishing a clear risk-escalation policy that defines risk-reporting criteria across the organization, including ownership of specific risks, as I describe in Chapter 12.) The most critical incidents should prompt alerts that the appropriate individuals can receive via email, text, or other system for immediate response.

4. What Key Indicators Require Attention? A key goal of an ERM dashboard is to indicate potential problems and opportunities before they arise. For that reason, it should include KRIs that help predict such instances. In designing dashboards, companies must consider which quantitative metrics, KRIs and KPIs are most relevant to the decision-making needs of specific users, whether at the board, management, or business-unit level. As we discussed in Chapter 17, KPIs typically revolve around financial, marketing, operations, internal, sustainability, and customer performance. KRIs are typically derived from policies and regulations, strategies and objectives, previous losses and incidents, stakeholder requirements, and risk assessments. Ideally, each metric would include performance thresholds and/or risk tolerance levels to provide context for evaluation. KPIs measure our progress against targets while KRIs measure our risk against predetermined tolerances. For the most important metrics, the dashboard should provide trend analysis and expert commentary. Remember: KPIs and KRIs should answer "How are we doing?" and "Where are we headed?" while indicating where course corrections may be required along the journey.

5. What Risk Assessments Need Review? Risk assessment is an ongoing process. Top-down risk assessments, bottom-up risk/control self-assessments (RCSAs), regulatory examinations, and audit reports all take place on a regular basis. Given that these assessments include mainly qualitative information, the dashboard need only provide a summary of key findings and analyses. In addition, each summary should clearly indicate whether it meets board and management expectations (green), is near those expectations (yellow), or falls short (red). When more detailed review is necessary, the actual risk assessments and reports would be available via drill-down.

For a typical company, it might take days or weeks to gather the required information to answer these five questions on an enterprise-wide basis. The fundamental problem is that the information is stored in different systems, databases, spreadsheets, and reports. To further complicate things, the typical siloed approach to risk measurement uses static reports often limited to the risks facing a single business or functional unit. Compiling these static reports requires significant manual work, resulting in data integrity issues and less time for risk analysis and decision-making.

With an effective dashboard reporting system, the board and management should be able to answer all five of these questions in a few minutes. The dashboard would provide executive reporting of enterprise-wide risks, with drill-down capabilities to allow central monitoring of all key risks. The only way to accomplish this is to utilize a single, enterprise-wide system capable of gathering and analyzing this data. Such a system would have the following key attributes:

- A single point of access to all critical risk information—even if it resides in disparate risk systems and data sources
- Executive reporting of enterprise-wide risks combined with drill-down capabilities to more granular risk data and analyses
- Just-in-time risk information, whether real-time alerts or periodically compiled data such as monthly credit reports or quarterly risk assessments
- Integration of quantitative KPIs and KRIs with qualitative risk assessments, policy documents, and external market data
- Provisions for users to add commentary or analysis to the risk information presented

In Chapter 10 I offered a template for a periodic report from the CRO to the risk committee of the board. Now I'd like to augment that template with these additional best-practice guidelines:

- Every board reporting package should have an executive summary that:
  - Provides the overall context and "story" from the management team
  - Is concise, self-contained, and easy to understand (readable within an hour)

- Focuses board attention on key discussion and/or decision points
- Other board meeting and reporting standards
  - No presentation should be greater than an hour (including Q&A) or 30 slides (excluding appendices).
  - Each KPI or KRI should be tracked against a performance target or risk tolerance, respectively.
  - It should be clear at a glance whether a metric is above (green), below (red), or near (yellow) the defined management threshold level(s).
  - A concise narrative should be included with each chart.
  - Avoid using unnecessarily complex charts (e.g., 3-dimensional charts).
  - A glossary of technical terms and acronyms should be provided with each report or presentation.
- Hallmarks of success
  - Board reports and presentations become much shorter.
  - Board meetings become shorter and less frequent.
  - The ratio of presentation/dialogue goes from 80/20 to 50/50.
  - Each and every director leaves meeting with the same (or similar) top-5 key discussion or decision points.

TRADITIONAL RISK REPORTING VS. ERM DASHBOARD REPORTING

Traditionally, companies have reported risk on individual spreadsheets by manually gathering and compiling information from different areas of the company. They would then store this information in summary spreadsheets, databases, documents, or reports. Key problems with this approach include:

- Manually transferring information from one document to another leads to multiple versions of the same information and can easily create data inconsistency and inaccuracy.
- Once the information is exported from one system to a spreadsheet or other static report, it loses its context, history, and auditability, not to mention that it immediately becomes stale.
- Responsibility for data integrity and governance becomes unclear once there are multiple sources.
- The information buried in these reports is difficult to disseminate efficiently to the proper audiences, much less analyze and act upon.

- As businesses continue to grow, so does the amount of information they must gather. Reports become increasingly complex, and users charged with compiling and analyzing the data find themselves overloaded with details that might not be pertinent to their role.

Dealing with all of these issues time and again introduces significant inefficiencies to the risk reporting and data management processes. Two recent examples highlight the risk of clerical errors in spreadsheets. In April 2014, Bank of America incorrectly reported its capital ratios in a critical stress test thanks to an "incorrect adjustment" related to debts it had assumed from Merrill Lynch in 2009. Their mistake hurt their regulatory standing and dividend payout, and caused the biggest stock drop for B of A since 2012.[2] The infamous "London Whale" debacle at JPMorgan Chase & Co. in 2012 is another noted example of data-reporting mismanagement. Errors made by copying and pasting data from one spreadsheet to another were partially to blame for the $6.2 billion trading loss.[3]

These examples could have been prevented by using a cloud-based dashboard reporting system with built-in change management, data lineage, and audit capabilities. It is one of the few practical solutions to maintain the flexibility of spreadsheets, and allow better control of enterprise data, reduced chance of hidden errors, and improved data integrity.

ERM Dashboard Reporting

Let's have a look at the key ways a dashboard differs from legacy methods:

- **An integrated approach to analysis:** Traditional risk reporting provides information in silos such as risk types, business units, and functional units. ERM dashboard risk reporting allows for a more integrated approach by evaluating the impact of risk on enterprise-wide strategic objectives, or examining the impact of a single scenario (e.g. recession, counterparty default, or an extreme weather event) across all risk types and business units.
- **Forward-looking indicators:** Traditional risk reporting tends to focus on historical data and internal information. An ERM dashboard provides this information, but aggregates it and updates it automatically. This gives the risk function more time to focus on forward-looking analyses and early warning indicators, as well as external market data and macroeconomic trends.
- **Greater flexibility:** Traditional reporting involves a trade-off between volume and clarity. Board members and executives may want more concise analysis and reports (i.e., executive summaries) while business and functional managers require more granular information. The drill-down

capability of dashboard reporting eliminates this trade-off, allowing the board and executive management to view high-level risk information and analysis while also providing the more granular information needed by the business and functional units. What's more, live data can be analyzed by risk type, business unit, or strategic objective—indeed, in just about any way that would help pinpoint issues and address them quickly.

- **Decision-oriented approach:** While traditional risk reporting can handle what-if questions (such as the effect of falling commodity prices or rising interest rates), dashboard reporting can address more decision-oriented questions: So what if commodity prices go down? What should we do about it? An advanced ERM dashboard provides the real-time analytics that the board and management need to review current risk sensitivities as well as the impact of alternative strategies.
- **Interactive data:** Traditional reporting is akin to reading a book while dashboard reporting is similar to searching for information on Google. The ERM dashboard should be able to address key questions, as well as provide summary and detail information, in order to meet the decision-making needs of the individual using it. Today, few people would go to the library instead of using Google to find information. Similarly, the board and management should have access to an efficient ERM dashboard instead of going through stacks of reports to get critical risk information.

Additional Features

In addition to the above components of dashboard reporting, new features are surfacing that are becoming part of the reporting standard. An established dashboard program should incorporate the following elements to allow for the most streamlined and effective reporting:

- **Single-Source Publishing:** Software that allows the same data to be published in multiple places at once across a platform effectively eliminates duplicate content. Single-source publishing not only makes reporting more accurate, it also increases efficiency and frees up time for making important business decisions instead of managing data. This holds true not only for numeric data, but for text as well. This allows users to access the same written analyses from anywhere, thereby allowing the contextual information necessary for interpreting numeric data to travel with it. The same technology can also produce dynamic charts that automatically update as data is refreshed.

- **Collaborative Real-Time Editing:** More and more software platforms, often cloud-based, permit multiple users to work on different parts of a single document simultaneously, displaying changes in real time. This permits each user to have up-to-date information as soon as it becomes available. This technology is becoming increasingly powerful and simpler to deploy at the organizational level.
- **Data Visualization:** Making sure that users can easily digest information is a critical aspect of reporting. Consider the impact and clarity of a pie chart or bar graph compared to a dense table of numbers. Whether the user is a CRO or a floor manager, being able to clearly visualize risk-management data can dramatically improve work processes. Many dashboard applications now have the ability to create graphs or presentations seamlessly with underlying data, making it far more impactful and actionable.
- **Data Lineage:** How many times have you asked yourself where a number came from? Or gotten into a debate with colleagues about who has the right data? Modern reporting systems tag data with important information about its origin and subsequent iterations. These dashboard systems can indicate from whom or where the data came, time it was last updated, and the origin of any changes at each stage of the data's lifecycle. Modern dashboard systems not only show a certain data element in its current form, but also allow users to drill into each previous incarnation. This history of change and evolution of the data allows users to understand the data's lineage, and audit it over time.
- **Data Governance:** With the implementation of the Dodd-Frank Act in the United States, The Federal Reserve, OCC, and FDIC have placed considerable emphasis on process integrity and data governance.[4] The ERM reporting system must provide a sustainable process for capturing and maintaining data as well as mechanisms to ensure proper data governance. Modern dashboard systems manage both elegantly. Simply put, these systems provide for centralized data governance and decentralized data ownership. In this environment, each piece of data has an owner who is responsible for its development and quality. But the governance of where or how that data is used, and who has authority to access, read, or edit, can be centrally managed.
- **Interactive Data Displays:** The best data presentation is dynamic, allowing users to see summaries but giving them the ability to drill down into the underlying details. The next step in interactivity, however, will allow users to have a "conversation" with the data by asking human-readable questions of the database and receiving answers pertinent to business objectives.

The first generation of ERM dashboards focused on integrating and displaying *content*, but most required the support of a data warehouse. Current cloud-based technologies enable the integration of both *content* and *analytics* based on the attributes discussed above. Today's systems can provide embedded or user-defined data analytics, as well as allow the user to ask "what-if" questions regarding risk drivers and management responses. With the advent of big data and artificial intelligence, I predict the next generation of ERM systems will go further and *deliver* real-time updated risk analytics, alerts, and reports based on continuous monitoring of the company's risk profile and external variables. In other words, risk intelligence will not only be *pulled* based on user demands but *pushed* based on new information.

GENERAL DASHBOARD REQUIREMENTS

Dashboard systems abound in today's market, but in order to achieve the objectives listed above, the best programs must offer several key capabilities. Many dashboard programs include these features out of the box, but if not, it is up to the company to implement them. Here is a list of what I feel are critical features for dashboard applications:

Role-Based Reporting

Earlier in the book we touched on the importance of defining the three lines of defense in any ERM program: board, management, and business operations. Now we will be taking those lines of defense and defining decision-support requirements in the dashboard. For example, a plant manager may need to track incident reports or absentee rates. But senior management and the board do not need to see these specific numbers. Rather, they look at summary metrics at the enterprise level, and may only note safety incidents if they exceed a specific company-wide threshold that indicates a systemic problem. Though multiple roles are possible, we'll consider three generalized ones for the sake of simplicity: board, management, and business operations. Each role will have access to certain metrics and reports according to their responsibilities.

Board members will engage with company-wide reports tied to key strategic goals. The board's dashboard will provide an overview of major threats and opportunities that may affect company value. This dashboard will let directors know at a glance where the company stands vis-à-vis its risk appetite, allowing them to satisfy their fiduciary oversight duties as well as track strategic performance. Board-level dashboards can supplement or replace the hefty board packages that are produced today.

At the management level, continuous reporting offers a consolidated view of the company's risks by risk category, by business line, and by functional or operational unit. The goal is to provide corporate and risk managers with the data necessary to monitor business functions and ensure that they comply with risk-management policies. At the same time, management can monitor the performance of risk and compliance programs, assessing effectiveness and improving or replacing them as necessary. Management's overall aim is to maintain a risk profile within the company's desired risk tolerance and appetite.

As the first line of defense, business operations have a critical role in managing risk at its source. The operations view of a risk dashboard would offer pertinent risk information to users at various levels and functions across the organization. Exactly what information each user sees would vary depending on department and role to provide a focused, actionable view free of extraneous information. For example, an energy company might have separate divisions for natural gas, oil, and renewable energy, each with its own strategic initiatives and business operations. The operations level is also where a majority of metrics will originate. For that reason, it may make sense to station a risk manager at this level to monitor the quality of data as it flows up the information chain—at least until reporting and monitoring systems are well established.

Intuitive Interface

A clear view of pertinent data will empower employees to manage risk within their area of responsibility and expertise. It has the added benefit of internalizing a strong risk culture company-wide. As those at the operational level get accustomed to recognizing and mitigating risk, the company will become more risk aware as a whole, bringing its collective intelligence to bear on uncovering previously unforeseen obstacles and opportunities. The key to success is making the ERM dashboard program so intuitive that it becomes a natural extension of the user's work habits.

Controlled Collaboration

When looking for an application to support their risk management processes, companies should consider which one would best facilitate collaboration. Today's work environment is team-based, and thus inherently collaborative. While the cloud was born out of the desire to gain efficiencies of scale, a by-product has been enabling much richer collaborative environments. Cloud-based software allows all parties to effectively and efficiently visualize, collaborate, and report on their data into a single repository, thereby eliminating duplication and its inherent errors as well as reducing the usual emailing back and forth that often characterizes information sharing efforts. Additionally, having a computational process set in place for data validation and lineage will increase accuracy while likely saving time and money, not to mention reducing risk.

Flexible Graph Database Technology

The complex interrelationship among various risks, business goals, risk drivers, and other components of risk management requires an underlying database structure capable of defining and storing these relationships and making them available for analysis. These three-dimensional webs can become mind-bogglingly complex. While traditional databases store information as tables of data, where each row or field is a discrete item and each column represents a property of that item, a graph or graph-oriented database stores information about relationships. A graph database can be thought of as a web made up of nodes and edges or spokes. Each node represents an item, and each edge is the relationship between one node and another. This focus on relationships makes graph-database technology ideal for its most prominent application: social media. But it is also ideal for ERM. In order to allow users to draw meaningful information from this manifold data, the system must be able to interpret deceptively simple human-readable queries, for example, "What effect would a 10% drop in oil price have on our overall risk profile?" Graph database technology's flexibility, combined with the ability to abstract the essence of a complex, network data model, makes it well suited for supporting ERM data and the what-if queries that drive analysis.

Scalable, Reliable, and Secure

As a mission-critical function, ERM generates data, insights, and decisions that help an organization successfully navigate potential pitfalls and capture unanticipated opportunities. The ERM dashboard must be robust enough to do this continuously, 24 hours per day, every day of the year. It must support operations around the globe while ensuring the data and information it houses is safe from hackers and other cybersecurity threats. In short, a system to manage risk must demonstrate risk mitigation in the strongest way possible. Just as cloud-based systems have proven scalability, reliability, and availability, they have also demonstrated excellent security. In fact, they are now recognized as being much more secure that existing corporate datacenters.[5]

IMPLEMENTING ERM DASHBOARDS

ERM dashboard implementation is part and parcel of implementing an ERM program as a whole. For this reason, the responsibility for dashboard development would best fall on an individual or group within the larger ERM implementation team. Additionally, at least one member of this team should have a working knowledge of the technology currently in use, as well as those available in the marketplace. The team might also incorporate a member of the company's IT function. The ideal candidate will be well versed in cloud applications, integrating that application into the company's current IT environment, and tuning the application to the needs of the ERM dashboard's users.

Stages of Implementation

The following are common stages of ERM implementation that can also be applied to deploying a company dashboard. We'll look at these steps in greater detail later in this chapter. Note that while I am outlining the typical stages of an implementation, I am not specifying a specific methodology or timeframe. This is because the one depends on the other. For example, the company may adopt an agile methodology, in which case implementation will progress through some or all of the stages in a cyclical, iterative fashion, focusing each time on just a small subset of dashboard elements.

Stage 1: Identification The main goal of this initial stage is to identify any major risks that might affect the company either positively or negatively. The project owner should start from the big strategic picture, restating the business objectives and then asking what risks could impede them. This stage is often comprised of interviews and questionnaires meant to gather information from the company's main risk players in order to find and clarify potential risks. It will result in a list of risks organized by business objectives that will ultimately inform the organization of the dashboard. During this stage, initial reporting requirements should be identified for the users in the three lines of defense.

Stage 2: KPIs and KRIs Developing KPIs and KRIs is an important step in the overall ERM process as well as the implementation of a company's dashboard. These metrics can serve as performance and forward-looking indicators to keep the organization on track by facilitating decisions to avert or mitigate potential future risk or take advantage of new opportunities.

Stage 3: Measurement The next stage in ERM deployment is to determining how to measure the risks that the team has identified. In addition to this defining metric, each risk should have an acceptable tolerance range to indicate safe or desirable levels per the company's risk appetite statement (RAS). The implementation team should also rank risks according to likelihood and severity (heat-mapping) in order to set priorities and visibility levels on the dashboard. The relationships between risk exposures and tolerance levels can determine the colors and flags in risk reporting.

Stage 4: Mapping At this stage the implementation team maps risks and their associated metrics back to those responsible for monitoring and responding to them (usually but not necessarily the risk owner). By the same token, risk mapping will determine who needs to see what metric on their specific dashboard view.

Stage 5: Monitoring Once the data is incorporated into the dashboard, the team can begin to monitor risks. Of course, merely monitoring isn't enough. Companies must determine how they'll respond to the data. In this stage, the company's risk policy will determine how to deal with the risks the team has identified, and additionally, what actions need to be taken by whom.

Risk Identification: Assessing Decision-Support Requirements

The first and most important step in ERM dashboard implementation is to understand the decision-making requirements of the intended audience. In an earlier chapter we reviewed the general risk-management decisions at the board, executive management, and business- and functional-unit levels. However, these decisions and the roles of specific committees, functions, and individuals are unique to each organization. As such, the implementation team should perform a broad review to assess decision-support requirements. These reviews include:

1. **Current corporate risk policies,** particularly those covering risk tolerance levels, appetite, escalation, and delegation of authority. The focus of each review should be the associated reporting requirements, including exception reporting. This review is also part of RAS development, so the team can leverage that work by drawing from the results.
2. **Risk committee charters** at the board and management levels, including reports and minutes that may document key decisions that these groups have made in the past.

3. **Existing reports, metrics, and risk assessments.** It would be useful to highlight the specific risk analyses that executives use to support key decisions. The implementation team should also review key performance goals and objectives of various risk committees and functions.
4. **Individual preferences and ideas.** Reviewing current requirements is just a start. The implementation team should also interview select board members and managers to uncover additional sources of data to support the decision-making process.

At this point, there should be enough information to create a high-fidelity prototype ERM dashboard, or at a minimum a series of sketches, that documents optimal structure and content. Prototype dashboard reports are a low-cost way to refine the final product as the team continues to identify critical gaps or superfluous information within the existing reporting processes. A key benefit of this process is the elimination of metrics and reports that may have accumulated over time but are no longer useful. The team should circulate this prototype across the organization for feedback.

Risk Measurement: Choosing Metrics

Metrics are the bread and butter of a good risk-reporting program. They can serve as a backbone for data-based decisions. They can provide early warning signs for risk exposure in different areas of the company. And they can serve as a gauge for assessing business performance against benchmarks. The type of metric defines how they may be displayed in a dashboard:

Standard metrics: This information is always on display. Think of speed, engine RPM, fuel level, and engine temperature on a car's dashboard. They are key data that need to be monitored at all times. They must remain within acceptable limits, yet can change quickly. For each risk type, standard metrics should be defined to support ongoing monitoring.

Optional metrics: This type of data is less time-sensitive than standard metrics, and only available when requested. In a car, relevant examples would be miles remaining on a tank of gas, fuel mileage, or a trip odometer. These metrics are informative, but are not critical to the vehicle's ongoing operation and safety. In ERM, these special metrics may include scenario analysis and stress-test results.

Elevated metrics: Certain metrics are displayed only when they surpass an acceptable tolerance level. Indicators for low oil, low fuel, or engine trouble tell a driver that she must resolve a specific issue soon.

In risk management, elevated risk metrics may include those that exceed risk limits or tolerance, or a metric or collection of metrics that may materially impact a key strategic objective.

It is important to keep in mind that every metric should have associated benchmarks in order to be most effective. With these benchmarks in place, dashboard users can properly measure risks; otherwise the metrics are just numbers. To set these limits, the dashboard implementer should meet with the risk owners and determine the minimum and maximum acceptable value for each performance and risk metric, as well as the appropriate corrective actions needed in order to bring these measures back into the acceptable tolerance. Much of this information may already be available in the company's risk appetite statement.

Risk Mapping: Building a Risk "Map"

The best way to know where you're going is to look at a map. As I mentioned, the ERM dashboard is really a navigation system. The business environment is the topography, and the company's strategic goals are the destination. One way to map a long-term route is to start from the destination and work backward. Each measurable outcome is a milestone the company passes on its way. Of course, external factors such as wind or weather will influence specific turns along the route, but with a clear direction, they are just bumps on the road.

Similarly, the implementation team should sketch a map of risks that may affect the business. Most dashboards are very flexible, so risk owners will be able to map their dashboard however they see fit. We've already discussed how risks should be mapped to strategic goals, and touched on how KRIs can map to the performance outcomes they help foretell. Similarly, the team should map specific risks to their owners. Some broad risks will map back to more granular risks, and may thus have multiple owners. For example, one aspect of reputational risk could be owned by an IT manager while another maps back to a manufacturing executive, since each area (data integrity, product quality) can affect reputation. Other techniques include mapping risks along the organizational structure of the company, or breaking them down by category (regulatory, operational, etc.) and assigning groups to monitor each one.

Successful mapping puts managers in touch with the operations and performance under their purview. This in turn informs decisions affecting the direction the company takes toward its goals. While the implementation team should tailor dashboard reports to the specific needs of the organization, certain functions help link users to the data they need. These include:

- **A warning system:** Warning indicators are useful for a quick-glance visual representation of the current risk trajectory. To create warning notifications, take the target minimum and maximum of each risk metric and pair it with a visual cue. I recommend the stoplight method. Pair the target maximum, or favorable conditions, with the green light and the target minimum, or unfavorable conditions, with the red light, with the measure leading up to minimum being yellow. One can determine these target areas based on how soon the risk needs to be acted on, for example, by drawing on the risk severity determined during the initial risk assessment. If a certain risk exceeds acceptable levels, the red light will appear on the dashboard to show action is required.
- **Basic and advanced statistical calculations:** Dashboard reports should provide basic statistical calculations, including mean, maximum, minimum, standard deviation, and confidence level. Beyond basic statistics, reports should also provide data on positive and negative correlations and regression as necessary. These statistical capabilities can also support data analytics, such as when key metrics exceed three standard deviations.
- **Linkage between qualitative and quantitative data:** Reports should provide decision-makers with the ability to combine qualitative and quantitative data in order to link business strategies, objectives, KPIs, risk assessments, and KRIs.
- **Risk accountability and ownership:** Dashboard reports play a large part in the risk-escalation processes. In this regard, they should track escalations from reporting through to resolution, explicitly assign monitoring, management, and oversight responsibilities, and also track risk-mitigation projects.
- **Customized reporting and analysis:** Reports should be flexible enough to present data in multiple formats to suit the audience. While the ERM dashboard provides centralized risk reporting, the reports themselves should be role-based. In other words, the reports made available to board members, senior executives, and business managers should be customized based on each audience's informational and decision-making requirements.

Risk Monitoring: ERM Functionality

In 2008, a group of software developers in Israel launched Waze, a mobile navigation app. Although it used GPS, Waze was unlike the navigation apps that came before it, because it used both passive and active information from each of its users to inform one another about current road conditions including traffic, accidents, police traps, and more. This new kind of "social network mapping" is similar to how ERM dashboards function. The trajectory is set at the top, by the driver, but inputs throughout the organization provide real-time information that allows the driver to steer clear of trouble areas.

The crowd-sourced data gathering approach used by Waze can also be adopted in the ERM system. For example, RCSAs can be updated by information from internal and external stakeholders such as front-line employees and customers. This process depends on an effective monitoring strategy. Exactly how each company monitors its risk activity is largely a function of the ERM framework, and will vary depending on the firm's size, complexity, and needs. One of the most common approaches is role-based. The risk function collects data across the organization and distributes it to those responsible for monitoring and acting upon it. Risk managers determine these roles, giving key players in each area of the company access to information pertinent to their jobs. Ideally, the scope of the data these individuals receive will match the scope of their responsibilities: A factory head will receive input pertinent to her operations, while the head of manufacturing will receive consolidated data from all facilities. These key players can then provide feedback that gives senior management the information it needs to set the company's course.

One important consideration for monitoring is frequency. With traditional risk reporting, companies were often limited to quarterly or at best monthly reports because of the effort involved in creating them. By the time reports were available, they were often already outdated. But modern dashboard reporting has lifted that restriction. Information, whether generated on a quarterly, monthly, weekly, or even continuous basis, all feeds into the same system and in standardized formats to allow for apples-to-apples comparison and greater analytical depth. As with other aspects of dashboard reporting, frequency depends largely on the user. A chief information security officer monitoring cyberrisks may need to monitor it on a continuous basis, but further up the corporate hierarchy, event-driven alerts or perhaps weekly or monthly reports derived from the same information showing trends over time would likely be more valuable.

As you can see, an ERM dashboard has a lot of moving parts: It's a new technology that requires new processes and even new roles. Each implementation plan must take into consideration change-management issues such as buy-in, training, and realignment of those involved. As the team plans deployment, it should address the question: Will this technology be easy enough to use for front-line employees and managers to integrate it into their daily routines? Is it intuitive enough for risk managers and the CRO to benefit from it without a steep learning curve? If not, the team should take some time to rethink the process to make certain the dashboard is as easy to use as possible for all involved. As many companies have learned when deploying technology, it's only useful if everyone uses it, and indeed benefits from it.

To make sure that users are getting the most out of the ERM reporting system, the implementation team should develop feedback loops within the monitoring process itself. Self-assessments can be invaluable in this regard, allowing each risk owner to report on process efficiency, response time, and the effectiveness of countermeasures. Managers should use this information for continuous process improvement by sharing examples of best practices across the organization.

Once the dashboard is up and running, it will likely become the most visible part of the ERM program. Not only will it help the company avoid or mitigate negative risk, but it will also expose favorable risk/reward scenarios that might otherwise go unnoticed. Implementing a dashboard throughout the company will also improve risk culture by allowing key players to take greater control of their areas of responsibility while keeping the company's strategic objectives top of mind.

AVOID COMMON MISTAKES

Despite the many advantages of dashboard reporting, there are several common pitfalls that can hinder a successful deployment. Consider these issues and how to avoid them:

Using Metrics Nobody Needs

Many companies will collect data without fully understanding the reasons behind it. They run the risk of considering any step forward a good one—even if it overcomplicates the process and floods the dashboard with unnecessary metrics. The result is a lot of data, but little of actual use. To combat this, companies should spend more time determining which metrics would be useful, and making sure the intended audience fully understands those chosen metrics and how to interpret them. The best data sources provide up-to-the-minute information that is accurate, reliable, and easy to maintain.

Too Much Complexity at the Start

Even if the team is providing what it believes is the right information, it's easy at the beginning of a new task to get overly ambitious and bite off more than one can chew. Given the wide scope of the dashboard implementation process, many companies are overwhelmed with their risk-identification, assessment, documentation, and reporting procedures. It's best to avoid providing too much right off the bat—highly-detailed dashboards that cover every business challenge and also allow users a high level of customization. The objective of dashboard reporting should not be to address all of the risks the company faces, but rather to support decisions by the board, management, and business and operational units around key risks and opportunities. An effective dashboard reporting system should prioritize risk information for the company's key decision makers. For that reason, it is best to work one's way through a series of simple iterations, testing and adjusting each before adding complexity.

Imbalance of Qualitative and Quantitative Data

Many risk-assessment processes produce large volumes of qualitative information that offers the board and management little help in their decision-making. In order to support policy and business decisions, the dashboard system should quantify critical risks and report them clearly and concisely. That is not to say quantitative data is more valuable than qualitative information, but rather that they should be in balance. For the company's most critical risks, quantitative analysis can be used to show trends, risk-adjusted metrics, compliance with policy limits, and performance against established standards. For the same risks, qualitative analysis can provide expert risk assessments, alternative strategies and actions, management recommendations, and other contextual information.

Lack of Efficiency in Data Collection

As we've seen, traditional methods of collecting data are slow and inefficient. A company can't build a successful dashboard system without also revamping its data collection processes. It will wind up spending too much time collecting data and not enough time making informed decisions. Rather than continue to waste time sending out individual surveys or emailing Excel files back and forth, companies should consider some of the more automated and integrated methods discussed earlier in this chapter. A successful dashboard program should lessen the administrative burden of managing and tracking incoming data. Let the technology do the heavy lifting.

BEST PRACTICES

Enough of what not to do. Here are some thoughts about the best ways to focus the company's energy and resources while building out a successful ERM dashboard.

Choose Metrics That Matter

Choosing which metrics to include in the dashboard is critical to its success. Those charged with development and implementation should be highly selective in determining which metrics to incorporate into the dashboard. Metrics that pass muster must not only be relevant to the job at hand, but also easy to measure. To help determine if a metric is necessary, teams should take care to address the following questions:

- How does this metric contribute to our key objectives?
- Is this metric truly necessary to support decision-making?
- Can we build an ongoing means of measuring it?

As with other aspects of ERM development, it is important to start with a clear understanding of the company's business objectives when choosing metrics to track. How can data acquisition best support those objectives? The implementation team should review all the KRIs that are currently in place, as well as other metrics that serve as leading indicators for strategic objectives. Once the team has compiled a comprehensive list, it should bring in key decision-makers to weed through it and keep only what is necessary.

Make It Visual

The point of a dashboard is to create a fast and easy way to read and analyze risk data. However, a lot of companies settle for bulky text-based reports and tables. It is considerably faster for the brain to process data when it is presented visually rather than with words and numbers. For that reason, data visualization should be a top priority when constructing a dashboard. Instead of trying to interpret complex data, users can decide how to use it. Remember, too, that presentation is important. Taking the time to design a clean, uncluttered dashboard will result in happier users and faster decisions.

Make It Interactive

Dashboards are made to bring everything and everyone together in one place, looking at the same data. But each user will have different questions to ask of that data. Even when a dashboard display has been designed for a specific user, there's no way to predict exactly how much detail they'll want at any particular moment. The best way to create this flexibility is with interactive data displays. A user should be able to click on a piece of information—say, a summary report—and drill deeper and deeper into the underlying data in order to uncover root causes. Dashboards can also foster a different kind of interactivity: collaboration. By permitting simultaneous collaborative editing and perhaps a built-in messaging system, a dashboard system can connect users to each other as well as to the shared data.

Make It User-Friendly

Even though (or perhaps because) they communicate complex data, dashboards should be easy to use. The usability standard should be that even the least tech-savvy person in the company can understand what's being presented and interact with it. Users should be able to customize the dashboard to their liking, so that information is arranged in a way they can best understand and utilize. What's more, with today's mobile technology, there's no reason that the dashboard can't be accessible just about anywhere: online, offline, and on various devices.

Real-Time Is the Right Time

The goal of a dashboard is to provide the right amount of information exactly when it is most needed. Companies should check their ERM dashboard regularly to ensure the clearest understanding of its current risks and opportunities. For the board, every month is sufficient unless there is a major risk event or policy exception. For management, every week, or even every day depending on the risk and area, will help stay on track. The data can be from this quarter, this year, or week, or this hour, whatever is the right timeline for the business. Real-time updating will allow the data to appear on the dashboard as soon as it is entered in a report. Out-of-date data can lead to bad decisions, so make sure the data is up-to-date.

Never Stop Improving

It is naïve to think that the first try will produce the perfect ERM dashboard. It is equally naïve to believe that whatever ERM dashboard the company settles on after the first implementation will be the version that endures for a long period. Rather, just as the business adapts to a changing environment, so will the ERM dashboard need to change over time. As we discussed earlier, even if the organization doesn't adopt the agile methodology wholesale, it should adopt one of the methodology's core principles—iteration. That is to say one should never stop working to improve the ERM dashboard. Just as continuous ERM is about monitoring and evaluating risk on an ongoing basis, agile implementation is about continuously iterating to improve and refine the ERM dashboard.

Ultimately, the value of risk information is not in its development, but in its application. As such, to realize the full potential of ERM, risk professionals must deliver the right information to the right decision makers at the right time. That is the purpose of a risk dashboard. This critical set of tools offers each user a tailored view of the risks he or she is responsible for identifying, monitoring, and responding to. It is the primary method by which risk managers—and the organization as whole—navigate the often treacherous waters of the business environment to chart the best route to achieving and advancing strategic objectives. In the following chapter, we'll discuss how feedback loops can facilitate continuous improvement in setting this course.

NOTES

1. *Global Risk Management Survey, Seventh Edition: Navigating in a Changed World*, Deloitte Touche Tohmatsu Limited, 2011.
2. Egan, Matt. "Bank of America's Big Math Error," *CNN Money*, 2014. Retrieved from http://money.cnn.com/2014/04/28/investing/bank-of-america-stress-test/index.html.
3. Hurtado, Patricia. "The London Whale," *Bloomberg View*, 2016. Retrieved from http://www.bloombergview.com/quicktake/the-london-whale.
4. Tracy, Ryan. "Regulators Reject 'Living Wills' of Five Big U.S. Banks," *Wall Street Journal*, April 13, 2016. Retrieved from http://www.wsj.com/articles/regulators-reject-living-wills-of-five-huge-u-s-banks-1460548801.
5. Linthicum, David. "The Public Cloud Is More Secure than Your Data Center," *InfoWorld*, December 1, 2015. Retrieved from http://www.infoworld.com/article/3010006/data-security/sorry-it-the-public-cloud-is-more-secure-than-your-data-center.html.

CHAPTER 19

Feedback Loops

INTRODUCTION

ERM is an organization-wide effort that requires significant time and resources in order to develop the requisite talent, policies, processes, and systems. The key question for board members, corporate executives, and regulators is this:

How do we know if the ERM program is working effectively?

The purpose of this chapter is to answer that question. The key lies in establishing an objective performance feedback loop for ERM. The feedback loop is essential for starting a new ERM program or enhancing an existing one. Based on my work in ERM, I strongly believe that this is a critical missing link to which many companies do not pay sufficient attention.

In the last few chapters, we have discussed ways in which companies can measure risk, evaluate performance, and track where they stand in relation to strategic objectives. While risk policies articulate processes and requirements for ERM, the board and management still need information and feedback in order to ensure that ERM programs not only remain on track, but continue to evolve and improve. The solution to these issues lies in the assurance processes established by the organization, which include monitoring and reporting to the board, independent assessments, and objective feedback loops.

This chapter will discuss how feedback loops permit effective evaluation of risk management performance,[1] provide critical risk information to boards and senior management, and offer actionable data to capture error and improve processes. We'll look at how feedback loops work in general and how they can be used to measure and improve performance in ERM.

WHAT IS A FEEDBACK LOOP?

At its most basic, a feedback loop is a system that uses the outputs from one action as inputs to the next, eventually creating a continuous loop of inputs and outputs. A performance feedback loop, therefore, is a critical concept that supports self-correction and continuous improvement by adjusting a process according to the variances between actual and desired performance. Such feedback loops can be used in the context of business for measuring effectiveness of certain efforts against goals, then refining processes based on the resulting feedback.

The goal of a feedback loop in a risk context is to determine if risk management is working effectively, and if not, to provide a route toward improvement. The feedback loop consists of three main steps: establishing business and risk objectives, carrying out the ERM program, and reviewing the program's results. First, an organization must determine its business and risk objectives, which will dictate the structure of its ERM program. When a predetermined feedback period ends, the organization assesses the results to determine which parts of the program were successful and which need improvement. This analysis in turn informs the objectives for a revised or augmented ERM program, and thus the cycle begins again. Figure 19.1 provides an illustration of an ERM performance feedback loop. If the business and risk results are not consistent with the objectives, something has to change: people, incentives, processes or systems—or all of them.

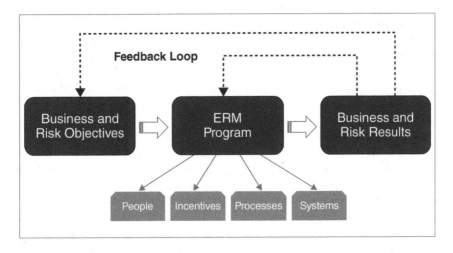

FIGURE 19.1 ERM Performance Feedback Loop

EXAMPLES OF FEEDBACK LOOPS

Feedback loops are not unique to business organizations. In fact, they form the core of the scientific method and empirical inquiry. Successful research requires the ability to gather and synthesize data to refine, reformulate, or reject a hypothesis in the development of general scientific theories.

Even the human body uses natural feedback loops to maintain homeostasis. After an increase in activity, the brain sends signals to the heart to help stabilize internal temperature. Another feedback loop incorporating the senses of sight and touch and muscle movement informs us of where we are in the physical world and how to maneuver our way through it. Feedback keeps us upright and allows us to manipulate objects.

Perhaps most relevant to our discussion are the feedback loops that guide monetary policy: The Federal Reserve uses them to identify policies intended to keep the economic measures of unemployment, inflation, and GDP growth within acceptable, sustainable parameters. The Fed's primary lever is setting interest rates, but it can take more dramatic forms such as the quantitative easing policies implemented in response to the 2008 financial crisis.

Feedback loops have also become common in computer programming, manufacturing, and other fields, particularly in the use of iterative development structures such as scrum and lean manufacturing. In these processes, large projects are broken down into smaller practical units that can be tested and corrected at each stage of the operation. More recently, the use of feedback loops has gained traction in hedge fund management, health-care interventions, and the effective altruism movement.

Bridgewater is one of the largest and most successful hedge funds in the world. The founder, Ray Dalio, argues for the use of a performance feedback loop to monitor and shape organizational effectiveness.[2] Akin to the basic feedback loop described in the previous section, Dalio's model has three main stages: goals, the "machine," and outcomes. Dalio likens the organization to a machine fueled by objectives, or goals, which in turn produces certain results, or outcomes. The machine has two major components: culture and people. If the outcomes do not match up with the goals, this indicates the machine is not functioning properly, and by that same logic the culture or the people are not working as they should. The last stage of the process is to determine which part of the organization is defective, and to suggest improvements. In order to ensure that a feedback loop is effective, it must cycle through numerous iterations. This establishes a large sample size and ensures that outcomes are accurate and not a result of human error. By conducting the performance feedback loop model this way, the "machine" will continue to develop and follow "a steep upward trajectory."

We often face far more difficult questions than whether our employees and culture comprise a well-oiled machine. How do you value life? And by extension, how do you compare life-saving interventions? One metric is the quality-adjusted life year, or QALY, which was developed to compare competing health programs. The QALY is calculated using two variables: time and quality. Time refers to the additional number of years a particular program could extend an individual's life. Quality is how an individual would rate the quality of his or her health, as a percentage of "full health." Multiplying time and quality returns a value for QALY. For example, if a program were to extend the life of a person at 70 percent health by 10 years, its QALY would be equal to 7. By testing different healthcare outcomes and comparing which programs maximize QALYs most cost-effectively, we can identify efficient interventions in a field plagued by finite resources and the constant need for triage.

William MacAskill, the cofounder of effective altruism, a new, evidence-based approach to charitable giving and social impact, expands this use of objective feedback loops to determine the effectiveness of altruistic pursuits in general. In his book, *Doing Good Better*, he provides an example of a program executed without a proper feedback loop.[3] In the 1990s, Trevor Field, a middle-aged South African man, came across a business opportunity he could not pass up: a water pump designed as a merry-go-round allowing water to be pumped out of a storage tank while children played. This invention seemed ingenious. Instead of requiring women to walk miles and miles to find a water source, they could have water available on demand nearby, and their children would be doing most of the work. In 1995, Field installed his first water pump, dubbed the PlayPump, and received sponsorships and donations from various organizations including a prestigious award from the World Bank.

However, what Field overlooked was the last stage in the feedback loop, analyzing the results of the program. Yes, his objectives had been fulfilled: He had built water pumps in the hopes of improving and increasing water access. But were these good intentions translating into the desired outcomes? Definitely not, as it turns out. Children were exhausting themselves pushing the merry-go-round, which required constant force. Some even vomited or suffered broken limbs. Thus, their mothers were forced to take on this tiring and demeaning task. Also, the old water pump system was easier to handle and provided five times the amount of water provided by the PlayPump.

MacAskill also describes a successfully implemented feedback loop. An MIT development economist, Michael Kremer, became involved with a Dutch charity program in Kenya that was trying to improve school attendance and test scores. The program provided schools with new text-books, more teachers, and free uniforms. Before expanding the program to several additional schools, Kremer suggested testing it using a randomized controlled trial: The researchers compared seven schools that had been given the additional resources to seven schools without them. In the end, the program had no discernible effect on student performance and attendance.

Kremer decided to test other programs one by one using the same method, thus creating a feedback loop: At the conclusion of each trial, he measured outcomes against the program's goals, and adjusting the program accordingly. He eventually came up with an idea that worked: deworming. By giving children a simple, inexpensive pill to remove parasites from their intestines, their health improved and thereby increased school attendance and performance. Following up with the students ten years later, Kremer found that on average they worked more hours, and their incomes were 20 percent higher than those of their peers who had not been dewormed.

The effective altruism movement has even leveraged this approach to evaluate and improve the charity industry at large. Its flagship organization, GiveWell, uses data from double-blind, randomized control trials and other metrics to rate and rank the cost-effectiveness of different charities. This completes a badly needed feedback loop in a sector that is rarely held accountable for concrete results. It should come as no surprise that the co-founders of GiveWell both came from Bridgewater!

As the above examples illustrate, a performance feedback loop is a highly worthwhile tool for evaluating and improving any process. They also underscore an important lesson that applies to most disciplines: Ex ante judgments and intuitions only go so far. In order to reach one's goals in a timely and efficient manner, it is essential to incorporate ex post information into the decision-making apparatus. Risk management is no exception!

ERM PERFORMANCE FEEDBACK LOOP

In order to establish a performance feedback loop for ERM, companies must first define its objective in measurable terms. As I've mentioned previously, a prime objective of ERM is minimizing unexpected earnings volatility. It is important to note that the goal is not to minimize *absolute* levels of risks or earnings volatility, but just that from unknown sources. Once we define the objective, we can create the feedback loop.

Based on this defined objective for ERM, Figure 19.2 provides an example of using earnings volatility analysis as the basis of a feedback loop. At the beginning of the reporting period, the company performs ex ante earnings-at-risk analysis and identifies five key earnings drivers—business plan execution, interest rates, oil price, key initiatives, and expense control—that may result in a $1 loss per share, compared to an expected $3 earnings per share.

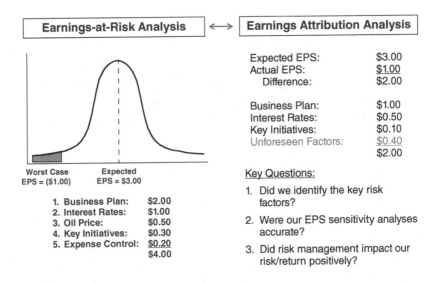

FIGURE 19.2 Earnings Volatility Analysis

At the end of the reporting period, the company performs ex post earnings attribution analysis and determines the actual earnings drivers. The combination of these analyses provides an objective feedback loop on risk management performance. In this example, three of the actual earnings drivers were identified in the beginning of the period. But $0.40 of the variance resulted from unforeseen factors (e.g., operational risk loss).

Over time, the organization strives to minimize the earnings impact of unforeseen factors. Consider two extremes: (1) with no risk management the entire $2.00 would come from unforeseen factors since the company is completely in the dark, and (2) with perfect risk management the contribution from unforeseen factors would be zero since the company would have perfect foresight. Of course, no ERM program is perfect but the feedback loop enables management to make continuous improvements to drive unexpected earnings variance to a minimum. Management can also address three key questions with respect to the ERM program:

1. **Did we identify the key risk factors?** If the RCSA process was effective, we would have identified the key risks that can impact business performance. If there is a material risk or loss that was unforeseen, we need to review and improve our RCSA process.
2. **Were our EPS sensitivity analyses accurate?** Even with effective risk identification and assessment, our risk analytics and quantification models need to accurately measure their earnings sensitivities. If actual

earnings variance (negative or positive) resulted from model risk, then we need to examine the data, assumptions, and formulas used in the risk models.

3. **Did risk management impact our risk/return positively?** Risk management is also about creating opportunities and adding value. Did the risk team work effectively with corporate and business management to enhance our risk profile, such as risk-based pricing or resource allocation?

Using feedback loops, a company can measure the efficiency of its ERM program both qualitatively and quantitatively. Qualitative methods include achievement of key milestones as well as records of policy violations, and root-cause analyses of material losses or other unexpected events. Quantitative methods might include tabulations of data such as ERM Scorecards (explained in greater detail below) that measure performance relative to expectations and calculate the gap between actual and expected results. These permit a more focused effort to improve underlying processes and minimize unexpected earnings variance. In addition to earnings, the same feedback loop can be created for other performance metrics, such as cash flows and enterprise value. Not only do these feedback loops measure responses to key risk issues, but when taken cumulatively, they can gauge the effectiveness of the ERM program as a whole.

MEASURING SUCCESS WITH THE ERM SCORECARD

We have already discussed the most important outcome of feedback loops: continuous improvement of ERM. Now we can delve into a secondary outcome: measuring success. Just as we rely on negative feedback (unexpected earnings variance) to recognize what needs improvement in the risk management process, we also need positive feedback to recognize what is going well. Both help to gauge the effectiveness of an ERM program.

ERM Scorecard: Performance-Based Feedback

Although board members do not involve themselves in the day-to-day activities of the business, they are still ultimately responsible for the effectiveness of a company's ERM program and should establish assurance processes and feedback loops in order to gauge its effectiveness. Using a scorecard—essentially an ERM dashboard snapshot—allows the board to achieve this goal by representing results at a specific moment in time and reporting virtually any feedback loop's quantitative output.

A scorecard measures the effectiveness of the ERM program in terms of the following:

- **Achievement of ERM development milestones:** Milestones could include developing an ERM policy, implementing a new risk system, establishing risk appetite and tolerance levels, etc.
- **Lack of regulatory/policy violations or other negative events:** Directors and executives would account for "no surprises"—such as regulatory violations and fines, risk limit breaches, customer or reputational events—as a key success factor in ERM.
- **Minimizing the total cost of risk:** The total cost of risk is defined as the sum of expected loss, unexpected loss (or economic capital charge), risk transfer costs, and risk management costs.
- **Performance-based feedback loops:** These include minimizing unexpected earnings variance, minimizing variances between ex-ante risk analytics (e.g., risk assessments, audit findings, and models) and ex-post risk results (actual losses and events), and contributions to shareholder value creation.

Optimizing the Feedback Loop System

An ERM feedback loop system is a powerful tool for obtaining actionable data and improving processes. Of course, even feedback loops require maintenance. As these loops help improve operational efficiency and reduce variance between expected and actual outcomes, the board and senior management can improve the efficiency of the loops themselves. The following principles, which emerge intuitively from improving individual performance, provide useful instruction for optimizing feedback loops over time:

- **Greater frequency:** Perhaps the most effective way of improving feedback efficiency is shortening the interval between loops. Long gone are the days when annual or semi-annual reviews could adequately gauge employee performance in time for effective management. Many companies are now catching on to the fact that frequent feedback available immediately after the relevant outcome can reinforce positive behavior and limit undesirable outcomes. A rapidly iterating loop can also better capture time-sensitive factors that drive risk, such as market and return opportunities (stock prices, customer demand, and competitive pricing actions).
- **More data points:** Just as quantifying the risk bell curve in each feedback loop yields more effective strategic decisions, so too does increasing

the number of relevant metrics during each iteration. Over time we have seen the traditional 360-review model of employee feedback morph into a more crowd-sourced framework. That is, the 360-model included evaluations by an employee's subordinates, colleagues, and superiors. Of course, whom you work with, whom you report to, and who reports to you are only subsets of those affected by your actions. Employee evaluations are now including these other parties, even if they do not bear a direct relationship to you. In the same way, a crowd-sourced ERM feedback loop will not only include information throughout the organization, but also incorporate customers, business partners, vendors, regulators, and other key stakeholders.

- **Nesting feedback loops:** Organization-wide feedback loops are effective at narrowing down the source of inefficiency or underperformance. The next step would be to create feedback loops within functional and business units to further refine this analysis. Understanding that the company's poor sales stem from a weak marketing division is a good first step, for instance, but the issue becomes far more tractable once it is clear that the problem can be traced to the marketing department's social-media group, and even to specific individuals within that group. Similarly, identifying unwanted variance due to some part of the business plan is productive, but having the specific loops for market analysis and general management nested within this general loop will allow for far more targeted interventions. As the board and senior management review their feedback system, they should continue to refine the level of detail available in accounting for key risk factors.

Summary

As risk management works to minimize unexpected earnings volatility, it should also be increasing efficiency with the goal of reducing the total cost of risk across the enterprise. Companies can accomplish this by deploying feedback loops a number of ways. A quantitative approach uses feedback to minimize costs such as expected loss (EL), unexpected loss (UL), risk-transfer costs (i.e., hedging and insurance), and risk-management costs (i.e., staffing, systems, etc.). On the qualitative side, companies can assess ERM development milestones (drafting an ERM policy, setting risk tolerance levels, establishing risk appetite, etc.) against the expected results of these implementations in order to make improvements as necessary.

Feedback loops can track and minimize the variances between ex-ante risk analytics (i.e., risk assessments, models) and ex-post risk results (i.e., actual losses and events), highlighting which parts of the ERM framework need improvement. The earnings-at-risk analysis I discussed earlier is one of the most effective ways to decrease unexpected earnings volatility.

When an organization has effective feedback loops, it provides reassurance to the board, management, regulators, and all other stakeholders that the ERM program is indeed working effectively.

NOTES

1. Lam, James. "The Role of the Board in Enterprise Risk Management," *RMA Journal,* 51–55, 2011.
2. Dalio, Ray. *Principles,* Bridgewater, 2011, p. 72. Retrieved from http://www.bwater.com/Uploads/FileManager/Principles/Bridgewater-Associates-Ray-Dalio-Principles.pdf.
3. MacAskill, William. *Doing Good Better*, Gotham Books, 2015.

Other ERM Resources

CHAPTER 20

Additional ERM Templates and Outlines

INTRODUCTION

The focus of this book is on implementing ERM programs. In my work with board members, CROs, and other business leaders, I have found the use of best-practice examples, templates, and outlines to be highly effective in accelerating ERM development and implementation. The purpose of this chapter is to provide the reader with such materials for the following policies and reports:

1. Strategic Risk Assessment
2. CRO Report to the Risk Committee
3. Cybersecurity Risk Appetite and Metrics
4. Model Risk Policy
5. Risk Escalation Policy

Each company should develop its own policies and reports based on its business model, size, and complexity. The purpose of these outlines is to provide examples and ideas to support those implementation efforts.

STRATEGIC RISK ASSESSMENT

The following outline provides a summary of the key sections of a strategic risk assessment report that is provided to executive management and the board:

Executive Summary

In this section, the CRO provides a recap of the overall strategy, strategic priorities, and key business objectives.

Strategic Plan Development and Monitoring

This section refers to the Strategic Risk Policy, the ERM framework, and the Risk Appetite Statement. It also summarizes the process of developing the Strategic Plan and ongoing governance, reporting, and monitoring processes at the board and management levels.

Financial Plan

Key financial projections—including business volumes, revenues, expenses, cost of risk, earnings, RAROC, and key performance ratios—make up this section.

Strategic Risk

This section summarizes the key analyses and insights of the strategic risk assessment, including:

- **Macroeconomic risk sensitivities**—such as interest rates, housing prices, unemployment rates, credit defaults, mortgage prepayments—and the impact of these macroeconomic risks to the strategic plan objectives.
- **Risk assessments for key risks,** including interest rate, credit, market, liquidity, legal and regulatory, operational, and reputational. [Note: Each risk section includes a commentary and 1 or 2 graphics].
- **Objective-based risk assessments** involving a risk assessment of each business objective or group of objectives. Relative to the company's strategic plan, this would include the KPIs and KRIs associated with key strategic objectives.

Earnings Sensitivity Analysis

The section provides a summary of the strategic risk assessment with respect to how key risks can impact earnings (and economic value). Combining this earnings-at-risk analysis with earnings attribution analysis establishes a useful strategic performance feedback loop.

CRO REPORT TO THE RISK COMMITTEE

The following provides a best-practice benchmark outline and content for a monthly or quarterly report from the CRO to the risk committee of the board:

Executive Summary

This section provides a review of the aggregate risk profile and the key risk exposures for the organization overall. The CRO would also discuss "what keeps him or her up at night," including concerns about the risk culture, business unit-level risks, or specific risk concentrations from one of the risk summaries below. The CRO may also include an updated enterprise-wide "heat map."

New Risk and Loss Events

This section provides a summary write-up and initial loss/impact estimates of material risk and loss events. These events may include business practices, regulatory issues, IT and cybersecurity events, financial and operational risk events, or any key risk policy exceptions.

Follow-up on Prior Risk and Loss Events

This section provides a summary of any conclusions or updates from previously reported risk and loss events.

Emerging Risks

This section provides emerging risks faced by the organization, or observed or forecasted risk trends for the industry.

Risk Reviews, Including KRIs vs. Risk Tolerances

In this section, the CRO, with input from the functional risk leaders, provides a summary of the major risk areas. Each summary includes expert commentary as well as a risk appetite dashboard for the key risk metrics against risk tolerance levels. It would also explain any deviations from risk tolerance levels (red or yellow indicators).

- Strategic Risk
- Market Risk
- Interest Rate Risk
- Credit/Counterparty Risk
- Liquidity Risk
- Operational Risk
- Cybersecurity Risk
- Reputational Risk
- Legal, Regulatory, and Compliance Risk
- Capital Adequacy and Ratios

Progress Against the ERM Roadmap

This section provides an update on the key accomplishments, progress to date, and major initiatives relative to the ERM Roadmap.

Terms and Definitions

This is a compilation of short definitions for technical terms, RAS metrics, and acronyms used.

CYBERSECURITY RISK APPETITE AND METRICS

Definition

Cybersecurity risk is the risk of loss of corporate or customer data and/or reduced systems availability due to compromise of the company's information security environment (e.g., computers, mobile devices, data centers, cloud storage, etc.). The most significant cybersecurity risks include:

- **Reduced availability** or loss of customer-facing systems due to a cyber-incident, such as a Distributed Denial of Service (DDoS) attack
- **System vulnerabilities** resulting in a loss of corporate or customer data, or data integrity
- **Software coding practices,** including the use of open source technologies that could expose the company's systems to known or unknown cyber-vulnerabilities
- **Cyberattacks** on IT systems that directly or indirectly impact the company's operations, customers, or reputation
- **Compromised systems** from inappropriate employee or customer user access

Risk Appetite Statement

The following is a sample cybersecurity risk appetite statement:

Our risk appetite for cybersecurity risk is low. While cybersecurity risk cannot be completely eliminated, we seek to minimize our exposures through the following activities:

- Continuously identify potential threats and areas of vulnerability by conducting periodic risk-control self-assessments, independent testing and reviews, and internal and external loss-event tracking.
- Proactively create strategies designed to prevent, detect, and respond to cybersecurity threats, including deploying cyberattack countermeasures and redundant systems to protect the confidentiality, availability, and integrity of customer and company information.

- Develop key risk indicators (KRIs) and risk tolerance levels to support ongoing monitoring and reporting at the management and board levels.
- Minimize vulnerabilities and cybersecurity threats associated with doing business with third parties.
- Allow only limited and appropriate access to systems and customer data in both our physical and electronic environment.
- Conduct table-top exercises and/or scenario analyses to ensure that risk mitigation strategies, including internal and external communications, are effective.
- Maintain written policies, procedures, and control standards in line with our cybersecurity program and strategies.

Risk Appetite KPIs/KRIs

General Information Security

- Number of systems and applications, including % deemed critical
- Number of outstanding information security issues from RCSAs, internal audits, and regulatory exams; aging of, and delays in, resolving such issues
- Number and % of critical systems without disaster recovery plans
- % of critical systems that have failed annual contingency testing
- Coverage and performance of application security testing
- Number and % of changes with security exceptions
- Performance of table-top exercises, scenario analyses, and third-party testing

Prevention

- Average time to patch
- Patch policy exceptions
- Number of known vulnerabilities; average time to mitigate vulnerabilities
- % of production systems/servers that have been classified to be patched

Detection

- Average time to detect a cybersecurity incident, or "attack dwell time"
- Number of security incidents; average time between incidents
- % of incidents detected by internal controls
- % of incidents covered by RCSAs and cybersecurity KRIs

Response

- Average time between detection and full remediation (response KRI)
- Downtime or poor systems performance due to DDoS attacks and other cyber-incidents

Risk Capacity

- Information security budget as a % of IT budgets
- Number of unfilled information security positions
- Insurance coverage for cybersecurity losses

MODEL RISK POLICY

The following provides a best-practice benchmark outline and illustrative content for a Model Risk Management Policy:

Purpose and Scope

This section defines the scope of the model risk management policy, including the legal entities, business processes, and models (e.g., vendor models, internal models) that are covered. It includes summaries of the key objectives and requirements of the policy, such as overall policy governance and ownership. Objectives may include:

- Establish a set of principles and guidelines to mitigate model risk
- Ensure models are well documented and independently validated with respect to applications, assumptions, and performance standards
- Provide a governance framework for model implementation, maintenance, change, and performance reviews
- Define roles and responsibilities for model risk oversight and management

This section may also include a set of guiding principles, such as:

1. Model owners are ultimately accountable for model risk management, including the appropriate usage.
2. A rigorous model development process should include effective challenge from model users and other key internal stakeholders.
3. All models should be documented, benchmarked, and/or back-tested.
4. Mission-critical and other important models should also be independently validated by Risk and/or Internal Audit.
5. Model owners should specify performance benchmarks for their models, and actual performance vs. benchmarks should be monitored regularly. Exception reporting and management processes should be established if a model fails to meet performance standards.
6. No "black box." The key formulas, methodologies, assumptions, and data sources of all models should be clearly documented and readily available.

7. A governance process should be in place to review, and approve as appropriate, key changes in the model, usage, formulas, methodologies, assumptions, and data sources.

Model Risk Management Framework

This section provides the key guidelines and requirements for model risk management, including:

- Model definitions
- Model inventory
- Model risk assessment and rating system (e.g., mission critical, important, other)
- Model governance and oversight: development (internal), selection (vendor), user testing and acceptance, approval, implementation, and change requirements, including documentation standards
- Model performance standards and risk appetite tolerances
- Independent validation and back-testing requirements
- Model review and resource planning
- Issue rating and remedial actions

Governance, Roles and Responsibilities

This section provides the governance structure and roles and responsibilities for model risk management. Key roles include risk governance and independent oversight for model risk management. Specific committees and individuals may include:

- Board of Directors
- Risk Committee
- CEO
- Risk Management Committee
- Model Risk Oversight Committee
- CRO
- Risk Analytics
- CFO
- Corporate Treasurer
- Internal Audit

Model Risk Reporting and Exception Approval

The section provides the reporting requirements for this policy. It also includes policy exception reporting and management processes.

RISK ESCALATION POLICY

As part of enterprise risk management, an effective risk escalation process is vital. The objective of this process is not to replace the primary responsibility held by businesses and operations in relation to risk mitigation, but to ensure that notification of risk events up and across the organization occurs in a timely manner. Effective escalation and communication of material risk events enhance risk transparency, ensure timely risk response, and minimize potential loss.

The following provides a best-practice benchmark outline and illustrative content for a Risk Escalation Policy:

Purpose and Scope

This section provides the scope and objectives for the Policy, including overall policy governance and ownership. Policy objectives may include:

- Specify the definition of "risk events"[1] with respect to potential business, financial, and reputational impact.
- Develop the escalation and reporting protocol for risk events, including severity levels, mandatory escalation requirements, and mandatory reporting requirements.
- Enhance timely communication and cross-functional coordination of risk response in order to minimize the impact of negative events.
- Define the roles and responsibilities for the first, second, and third line of defense given the occurrence of a material risk event.
- Meet the communication expectations and reporting requirements of key internal and external stakeholders, including the board and regulators.
- Support the collection, documentation, and reporting of risk events, including root-cause analyses and lessons learned.
- Promote a risk culture in which risk events are identified, communicated to the appropriate individuals, and responded to in a timely and constructive manner.

Governance, Roles and Responsibilities

This section provides the governance structure and roles and responsibilities for risk escalation. Specific committees and individuals may include:

- Board of Directors
- Risk and Audit Committees of the Board

- CEO
- Risk Management Committee
- CRO
- CFO
- General Counsel
- Internal Audit

Escalation and Reporting

This section provides the escalation and reporting protocol with respect to risk events. A risk escalation matrix may include the following components:

Event Severity	Loss Level	Mandatory Escalation[2] (including timing)	Mandatory Documentation[3]
Level 1 (most severe)	$x loss and/ $y EPS (or % of net income or EPS)	Immediately to CRO and Executive Committee (EC), CRO will report immediately to Risk Committee (RC) Chair; escalation to full Board at discretion of the RC Chair	Next EC and RC meetings
Level 2	$x loss and/ $y EPS	Immediately to CRO and EC, CRO will report to RC and/or Board at the next scheduled meeting	Next EC and RC meetings
Level 3	$x loss and/ $y EPS	Immediately to CRO and relevant EVP	Next Business Segment Risk Committee
Level 4	$x loss and/ $y EPS	Event reporting into SVP, Operational Risk Management	Next Business Segment meeting
Level 5 (least severe)	$x loss and/ $y EPS	Event reporting into business segment risk manager	Next Business Segment meeting

Material Risk Events

Certain risk events have specific business impacts and/or quantifiable financial losses (see the financial loss and customer/employee examples below) while others may require management judgement. The Risk Escalation Policy should include all material risk events, such as:

- Unexpected and/or unbudgeted financial loss exceeding (a) $x million operational loss, or (b) $xxx million market, credit, or counterparty loss
- Significant impact on more than 10% of the customer or employee base
- Material violations of policy, regulatory, and/or legal requirements (e.g., significant fraud, criminal, or unethical activities)
- Resignation of key personnel and/or mass attrition within the organization or a certain department
- Information security incidents, including unauthorized access or compromise of information technology assets, networks, or information
- Identification of a critical control deficiency, including financial controls that have led to a material financial misstatement
- Significant bodily harm to an employee or customer as a result of the company's business operations
- Outages or potential strategic issues related to a critical vendor
- Material public safety concerns
- Other significant business, operational, or reputational events based on judgment

Other Risk Policies

In addition to the risk escalation requirements discussed in this Policy, other risk-management policies may have embedded exception management and reporting requirements. The escalation policy should provide reference to these other policies, which may include:

- ERM Framework and/or Policy
- Risk Appetite Statement
- Code of Professional Conduct and Ethics
- Enterprise Compliance Policy
- Strategic Risk Policy
- Financial Risk Policy
- Reputational Risk Policy
- Operational Risk Policy
- Loss-Event Tracking Procedures
- Business Contingency Policy
- Whistleblower Policy
- Other risk policies, as appropriate

NOTES

1. For example, a risk event may be defined as a discrete, specific occurrence that may materially and negatively impact the organization's ability to achieve its business objectives, and/or its reputation with key stakeholders. A risk event may also be a recurring pattern of occurrences, which may lead to similar consequences.
2. Escalation requirements may include individuals and/or committees. Individual discretion may also apply (for example, Level 1 risk incidents are reported immediately to the CRO and Executive Committee. In turn, the CRO reports immediately to the Chair of the Board Risk Committee but escalation to the full Committee and/or the Board is at the discretion of the Risk Chair).
3. Documentation and reporting requirements may include mandatory reporting at the next scheduled board and/or executive committee meeting.

JAMES LAM is President of James Lam & Associates, a risk management consulting firm. He serves on the Board of Directors of E*TRADE Financial and chairs the Risk Oversight Committee. Lam is a Board Leadership Fellow at the National Association of Corporate Directors (NACD). He is a member of the COSO ERM Advisory Board that is commissioned to update and improve the COSO ERM Framework. Lam is widely recognized as the first-ever Chief Risk Officer and a pioneer in the field of enterprise risk management. In a Euromoney survey, he was nominated by clients and peers as one of the world's leading risk consultants. Previously, Lam held positions as Partner of Oliver Wyman, Founder and President of ERisk, Chief Risk Officer of Fidelity Investments, and Chief Risk Officer of GE Capital Markets Services. In 1997, Lam received the inaugural Financial Risk Manager of the Year Award from the Global Association of Risk Professionals. *Treasury & Risk* magazine named him one of the "100 Most Influential People in Finance" in 2005, 2006, and 2008.

Index